THE COMPLETE GUIDE
TO SERVICE LEARNING

"Service learning expert Cathryn Berger Kaye writes a powerful guide to invigorate students, teachers, and youth leaders. The practical service learning strategies and diverse themes will awaken and engage even the most reluctant learners."

—Denise Clark Pope, Lecturer, Stanford University School of Education and author of *"Doing School": How We Are Creating a Generation of Stressed Out, Materialistic, and Miseducated Students*

"Cathryn Berger Kaye's energy, commitment, knowledge, and compassion are an inspiration. *The Complete Guide to Service Learning* captures all of these qualities, along with her practical advice and years of experience in educating the hearts and minds of the young. She connects reading to reality, using literature as a springboard for change. Putting these ideas into action in your classroom will forever change the lives of your students and just might help change the world."

—James Howe, author of *Bunnicula* and *The Misfits*

"Through combining her love of service with her love of children's literature, Cathryn Berger Kaye has given a great gift to classroom teachers everywhere in the publication of this book. Through its innovative approach to service learning, this volume reflects the integrity and compassion we all need to bring alive our classrooms and the world outside."

—James C. Toole, Ph.D., Compass Institute and University of Minnesota

"This is the resource teachers need to make service learning a reality for every kind of learner. This is education at a deeper level."

—Susan Meyers, Ph.D., Dean of College of Education, San Jose State University

The Complete Guide to Service Learning

Proven, Practical Ways
to Engage Students in Civic Responsibility,
Academic Curriculum, & Social Action

Cathryn Berger Kaye, M.A.

free spirit
PUBLiSHiNG®

Meeting kids'
social & emotional
needs since 1983

Library of Congress Cataloging-in-Publication Data
Kaye, Cathryn Berger.
    The complete guide to service learning : proven, practical ways to engage students in civic responsibility, academic curriculum, and social action / Cathryn Berger Kaye.
        p. cm.
    ISBN 1-57542-133-X
1. Student service—United States—Handbooks, manuals, etc. 2. Civics—Study and teaching—United States—Handbooks, manuals, etc. I. Title.
    LC220.5.K39 2003
    373.119—dc21   2003004437

At the time of this book's publication, all facts and figures cited are the most current available. All telephone numbers, addresses, and Web site URLs are accurate and active; all publications, organizations, Web sites, and other resources exist as described in this book; and all have been verified as of August 2006. The author and Free Spirit Publishing make no warranty or guarantee concerning the information and materials given out by organizations or content found at Web sites, and we are not responsible for any changes that occur after this book's publication. If you find an error or believe that a resource listed here is not as described, please contact Free Spirit Publishing. Parents, teachers, and other adults: We strongly urge you to monitor children's use of the Internet.

Service learning occurs in each of the fifty United States and internationally. While project descriptions and scenarios are not attributed to specific schools or youth groups, some are identified by city, state, or region. All efforts have been made to ensure correct attribution.

Edited by Jennifer Brannen
Cover and interior design by Marieka Heinlen
Index by Ina Gravitz

15 14 13 12 11 10 9 8 7
Printed in the United States of America

Free Spirit Publishing Inc.
217 Fifth Avenue North, Suite 200
Minneapolis, MN 55401-1299
(612) 338-2068
help4kids@freespirit.com
www.freespirit.com

Dedication

With great admiration, to the students and teachers who bring service learning to life every day.

Acknowledgments

Just as it takes a village to raise a child, a community has contributed to this book. This has been a journey of commitment and passion influenced by many in the service learning world. The following people made exceptional contributions. Truly, I thank you with a full and grateful heart. Many thanks to:

- the authors for their inspiring interviews

- my colleagues for recommendations to the Bookshelf

- Deena Metzger for her encouragement

- Joe Follman, Florida Alliance for Student Service, for his valuable response to my early manuscript and our frequent conversations

- Jill Addison-Jacobson, Youth Service California, for suggestions regarding this book's title and our helpful talks

- Don Hill, Service Learning 2000 at Youth Service California, for book title advice, and the questions that guide reflection on page 27

- Dave Donahue, Mills College, for sharing thoughts about reciprocity

- Betty Berger, my sister, for information essential to the special needs and disabilities chapter

- Madeleine Yates and Luke Frasier, Maryland Student Service Alliance, for service examples and permission to model my curriculum webs on their interdisciplinary service learning webs

- Vicki Lee and Barbara Weiss for urging me to publish the original *Service Learning Bookshelf*

- Children's Book World in Los Angeles for book recommendations

- Judy Galbraith for her vision and the Free Spirit Publishing staff for wholeheartedly embracing this project, especially Nancy Robinson and my editor Jennifer Brannen

- and my wonderful family—husband Barry, and daughters Ariel and Devora—for challenging my thinking, critiquing Bookshelf books, reading these pages, and giving me daily support and love

And to colleagues from across the country:

California: Mike Brugh, CalServe; Daphne Dennis and Diane Kahn-Epstein, City of West Hollywood; John Duran, Galt School District; Carolina Goodman and Claire Money, P.S. #1 Elementary School; Kathryn Lee, Prospect Sierra School; Cathleen Micheaelson, East Bay Conservation Corps Charter Elementary School; Lisa Morehouse, Balboa High; Emmy Poling, Fairmeadow Elementary; Donna Ritter, Elementary Community Service Association; Valerie Sorgen, Youth Community Service; Kim Stokely, Adopt-A Watershed; Barbara Thomas, The Willows Community School. *Florida:* Cynthia McCauley, Bay High School; Ossie Hanauer, Miami-Dade College. *Maine:* Fran Rudoff and Barbara Kaufman, Kids Consortium; Glenn Nerbak, Lyman-Moore Middle School. *Maryland:* Judi Bard, The Howard County Office on Aging. *Massachusetts:* Lynn Barclay and Bob Kumin, Hampshire Educational Collaborative; Jenny Lisle, Zoom into Action, PBS Kids; Roberta Sullivan, Sullivan Elementary; Debbie Coyne, North Adams School District. *Minnesota:* Rich Cairn; Nan Peterson, The Blake School. *Oklahoma:* Jessie Craig, Briggs Schools; Donna Gourd, Cherokee Nation Learn and Serve Program; Rebecca Jim, L.E.A.D. Agency; Nancy Scott, Cherokee Nation. *Oregon:* Kate MacPherson, Project Service Leadership. *Texas:* Linda Robinson, Alvin Junior High. *Vermont:* Joe Brooks and Susan Bonthron, Vermont Community Works. *Washington:* John Traynor, Gonzaga Preparatory School. *Wisconsin:* Marcia Applen and Kirk Schneidawind, St. Peter Middle/High School; Janet Levy and Holly Ryan, Cedarburg High School

To students, educators, community groups, and colleagues too numerous to mention by name whose projects inspired the descriptions of service learning scenarios in this book—many thanks.

CONTENTS

LIST OF REPRODUCIBLES

FOREWORD

Service learning is emerging as a critical topic in K–12 schools, higher education, and community organizations that work with youth. Why? Studies show, for example, that:

- half of all high schools have service learning projects.

- several million students participate in service learning projects each year.

- students participating in service learning show improvements in academic achievement, career preparation, feelings of self-efficacy, behavior, attendance, and civic engagement.

- students participating in service learning are more likely to continue to volunteer later in life.

Federal, state, and local governments support and encourage service learning projects. Foundations invest millions of dollars each year to initiate, expand, improve, and institutionalize service learning. Service learning earns praise from all points along the political spectrum.

Numbers don't lie, but they also don't explain. They don't explain that service learning is growing in popularity worldwide because it has youth using, through helping others, the knowledge and skills they need to learn. Numbers also don't explain that students and teachers respond positively to learning when it is applied and used in their own communities. Statistical findings don't explain that service learning works and appeals because it brings head and heart together and develops both at the same time. Or that youth are yearning to do good things and service learning allows them to do so *and* have a voice in how and what they contribute.

It is important to state that service learning is not simply a fad or the latest "thing" to come along in education and youth development. I would argue that service learning is not a "thing" at all, or an end in itself that must be added to the countless other "things" educators have to deal with. Service learning is rather a marvelously flexible strategy or tool for educators to better teach students about themselves and the world, while meeting existing goals and objectives. It can be and has been used in every subject and grade level and is equally effective outside the school context.

Service learning, as explained in this invaluable guide, is a relatively new term but not a new idea. Countless teachers over the years have engaged students in experiential activities, many of which provide a real service to other students or to communities. In some cases, these educators have never heard the term, "service learning." In the last several years, however, research and an examination of service learning practice have brought about a consensus on what makes service learning an effective "win-win" proposition—that is, what makes it help both the server and those being served. Understanding these elements and how to apply them are keys to implementing successful service learning and the purpose of the guide.

Cathryn Berger Kaye has been deeply engaged in all aspects of service learning as a teacher; a local, state, and national service learning program developer and advisor; and as one of the nation's leading service learning trainers. She helped shape how service learning is defined and played leading roles in helping us recognize the essential roles that literature and demonstration play in effective projects. I am happy that Cathryn is sharing her knowledge and experience with all of us.

The Complete Guide to Service Learning puts all the pieces together in a readable and practical format to help you initiate, expand, improve, and/or sustain your service learning efforts. With its background, wealth of examples, reproducible documents, interdisciplinary approach, links with curricula, and common-sense suggestions, it can give you what you need to take that first, second, or twentieth step in combining service with learning to help improve youth, schools, communities, our nation, and our global society.

Joe Follman
Director, Florida Alliance for Student Service
Florida State University

INTRODUCTION

At a service learning workshop in the mid-1980s, I asked twelve teachers to think back to their earliest memories of service—of giving service, receiving service, or observing service. They willingly shared images of visiting retirement homes with a youth group, collecting money for UNICEF, working in a hospital as a high school student, and tutoring a young neighbor who was struggling with reading. One woman described living in a rural community with few financial resources. Still, her mother prepared food each week that her father loaded onto the back of their pickup to deliver to families whose needs were more urgent than their own. She described watching this and wondering, "Why are they giving away our food?" She paused, reflecting. Then she said, "Maybe that's why I take care of foster children. Maybe that's why I'm a teacher."

I have continued asking this question over the years and I continue to find a connection between people's early personal experiences and memories of service and their later choice to become teachers or otherwise work with youth. Teachers—along with others who work in service professions—clearly have a natural affinity with service learning. Part of what draws us into this career is the opportunity it offers us to reach children and make a lasting—even profound—difference in their lives. Service learning provides deep and wondrous ways for this to happen.

My own experience with service learning began long before the term was commonly used. I was teaching in a very small school in rural Maine. One morning, a seventh-grade student brought in a newspaper article.

"That's my street," she said, pointing at the photograph. "See that tree? It's two houses away."

"What's wrong with the tree?" another student asked her.

"Dutch Elm Disease."

None of us was familiar with the term, but by the end of the day, we had all learned quite a bit about this disease that threatened the magnificent elms in our neighborhoods. The students wanted to get involved. Before long, they were making phone calls to the state and local departments of agriculture and were directed to a science department at the local university. Within a week, they were trained in assessing elm trees. Clipboards in hand, they traveled from street to street diagnosing and reporting on the condition of each tree.

Suddenly, subjects came alive for our middle and high school students. The study of plant cells took on new meaning. In math classes, record-keeping methods and statistics gained an importance they had not had before. Students described their excitement and frustrations in journals and stories with feedback from other students and teachers. As a culmination of their work, students submitted their findings to state agencies and made a summary presentation to a college class.

The students couldn't save every tree, of course, but they did help to protect some of the majestic elms. Along the way, they learned and practiced scientific reporting methods, became aware of the roles of state officials, and developed partnerships with college students. Motivated by a sense of purpose, our students identified themselves as community activists and came to speak with ease about civic responsibility.

> You should know that the education of the heart
> is very important. This will distinguish you
> from others. Educating oneself is easy,
> but educating ourselves to help
> other human beings to help the community
> is much more difficult.
>
> CÉSAR E. CHÁVEZ, SOCIAL ACTIVIST

Since my first experience with service learning, I have worked as a classroom teacher, in program development locally and nationally, and as a leader of educational workshops. *The Complete Guide to Service Learning* reflects my experiences both as an educator, who presents about service learning and develops and refines its concepts and practices, and as a student, who acquires new ideas from the people I meet.

Why Is Service Learning Important?

You may be coming to service learning for many different reasons—and all of them are valid. Perhaps you're drawn to service learning because of your own experiences as a student or because of personal or community values. You may want to introduce service learning to your classroom or school after hearing about the many ways students become motivated and engaged by this hands-on teaching method. You may approach service learning to respond to specific community needs or concerns or to promote involvement with social justice issues. (Many educators see the direct link between service learning and civic responsibility and character development.) Or perhaps you're responding to school or district requirements on incorporating service learning into curriculum and teaching methods, and you want to maximize the benefits for all involved. Regardless of which scenario seems most familiar to you, you're probably going to find yourself asking—or answering—the question, "Why is service learning important?"

- Service learning provides meaningful ways for students, teachers, administrators, and community agencies and members to move together with deliberate thought and action toward a common purpose that has mutual benefits.

- Students benefit academically, socially, and emotionally; develop skills; explore numerous career options; and may come to appreciate the value of civic responsibility and actively participating in their community.

- Teachers make school and education more relevant for their students, often seeing their students blossom and develop previously untapped strengths in the process; collaborate with their colleagues and community partners to develop exciting curriculum; and may find themselves professionally re-energized.

- School administrators may observe a boost in the morale of staff and students as they achieve desired academic outcomes while seeing the profile of the school raised in a positive way in the community.

- Community partners receive much needed help and may find themselves learning from the students as they teach or interact with them.

By encouraging and supporting thoughtful civic involvement and participation by young people, the entire community benefits. Young people are acknowledged—and see themselves—as resourceful, knowledgeable, and agents of change who can harness their ideas, energy, and enthusiasm to benefit us all.

The beauty of service learning is that something real and concrete is occurring. Learning takes on a new dimension. When students are engaged intellectually and emotionally with a topic, they can light up with a revelation or make a connection between two previously separate ideas. What they've learned in school suddenly matters and engages their minds and their hearts. Teachers also frequently respond to service learning, finding their students' eagerness and curiosity invigorating. Education is relevant in the classroom and in the larger community. Math, science, social studies, languages, literature, the arts—all are applied, used, and placed in contexts where they really matter.

In addition to the educational benefits, our society depends on active participation of its members to thrive. Our acts of service can shape the society we live in. Even young children marvel at how their thinking and planning and doing makes a difference. While it may seem cliché, the truth is, service learning enables a wealth of "differences" to happen. Relationships develop between people, with an attendant understanding and appreciation for similarities and differences. Eyes become accustomed to looking for needs in the community and are followed by the recognition of possibilities to, yes, make a difference.

Even though service learning can be exciting for teachers as well as students, you may feel daunted by the idea of integrating service learning into an increasingly complicated curricular mix. If so, you're not alone. Often teachers arrive at one of my service learning workshops tired and frustrated by the newest set of mandates to arrive on their desks. Then something happens, as they hear of their colleagues in schools across the country who try service learning and use it again and again. They see that it's really possible to meet the standards, improve literacy, increase test scores, and enjoy their profession while they enhance and strengthen their ability as educators.

About This Book

This book is designed to help you successfully use service learning in your classroom or youth group. It can also help you sow the seeds for a culture of service learning in your school or community. You will find ideas and strategies to build a strong service learning foundation as well as practical ways to implement service learning with children of all ages. There are thematic chapters that cover a wide variety of issues that are jumping-off points for service learning. Some of the ideas in the themes are probably very familiar, others less so. But all of the issues are important and the concepts and suggestions have all been used in schools around the United States and around the world.

How to Use This Book

This guide has two main parts, and it's designed to be used in a specific order. Part 1 addresses the various elements of service learning, how to get started, and the different ways to use the theme chapters; Part 2 is a series of thematic chapters. By reading Part 1 before moving on to the theme chapters, you will be prepared to apply the principles of service learning.

- **Part 1, The Service Learning Handbook,** includes three chapters that provide definitions and background information on service learning and describe the necessary components for successful service learning in your school, organization, or community. In addition, it includes many reproducible documents and forms to adapt and use as you carry out service learning projects or share ideas with peers. Chapter 1 discusses the nature of service learning in detail. Chapter 2 gives you a blueprint for how to begin using service learning in your classroom and includes reproducible forms to help you. Chapter 3 explains how to use the theme chapters and the service learning bookshelf which appears in each theme chapter.

- **Part 2, Service Learning Themes,** is made up of eleven thematic chapters that give you ideas for specific areas for action, including such themes as "Animals in Danger," "Community Safety," "Hunger and Homelessness," and "Special Needs and Disabilities." Each thematic chapter includes activities, a curriculum web to help you make cross-curricular connections, theme-specific resources, examples of actual service learning projects, and an extensive bookshelf of nonfiction and fiction, including picture books and novels. Each thematic bookshelf is annotated and arranged by topic as well as by theme and identified by level. The books are also cross-referenced where they are applicable to more than one thematic chapter, as noted on an easy-to-reference chart. To help you select books more effectively, each thematic service learning bookshelf is divided into sub-themes. For example, the sub-themes in the Environment chapter bookshelf are "Natural Resources," "Recycling," and "Appreciating Nature."

- **The book concludes with "An Author's Reflection"** and a general resource list to help you explore service learning further.

About the Bookshelf: The Important Link Between Service Learning and Literature

Books and reading are the basis of all literacy and learning, so it isn't a surprise that they can also be the foundation of service learning. Books and reading can and should be an integral part of the service learning process. Over the years, I have read and gathered many outstanding and memorable books—fiction and nonfiction—that have an authentic connection with service learning themes. A well-chosen book can become the linchpin for an entire service learning project or unit, introducing students to relevant issues as they start working on a project. Compelling books can keep them thinking about the implications of their endeavors during the project and provoke them to reflection throughout. Both teachers and students gravitate toward a well-told story.

When I travel to lead service learning workshops, books pour out of my suitcases. These traveling companions enliven service learning presentations as educators see the relevance and connections between the books, their students, and service that meets genuine community needs. I have included hundreds of my favorite books in the service learning bookshelf sections in the theme chapters of this book.

Is Service Learning for You?

If you're a teacher, youth worker or group leader, counselor, principal, or administrator who wants to help kids be more engaged and effective learners and take responsibility in their communities, *The Complete Guide to Service Learning* is for you. While this book primarily addresses service learning within a K–12th grade school setting, service learning is also thriving in many colleges and universities. Community organizations, youth groups, and after-school programs also use service learning because it enriches their programs and helps to increase academic achievement and personal growth and development of young people.

Above all, the purpose of this book is to encourage the practice of service learning—to offer a variety of ways you can integrate service learning projects into different curricula so that more young people will reap the benefits. Instilling the concept of civic responsibility and enriching educational opportunities for young people of all ages as they become engaged in social action is a gift to your students, your community, and yourself.

In reading this book, you will find that my commitment to service learning is deep. I am part of a dynamic group of countless educators, community members, writers, social activists, artists, and young people of every age who believe we can repair, improve, and save this world—I stand with those who believe this is perhaps the finest work to be done. Welcome to the group!

Cathryn Berger Kaye

Part One:
The Service Learning Handbook

CHAPTER 1

WHAT IS SERVICE LEARNING?

Simply put, service learning connects school-based curriculum with the inherent caring and concern young people have for their world—whether on their school campus, at a local food bank, or in a distant rainforest. The results are memorable, lifelong lessons for students and foster a stronger society for us all.

This is what service learning can look like:

• A teacher reads *A Day at Wood Green Animal Shelter* aloud to her first graders to prepare for a field trip to the local animal humane society. The trip is a central part of their studies about "our community." After discussing the need to care for pets responsibly, the first graders decide to write and illustrate a booklet called "Taking Care of Your Pet" to hand out to students at their school and a nearby preschool.

• On a visit to a local elementary school, high school students demonstrate garden tool safety and soil preparation as they act out *Jack's Garden* for second graders. During the next visit, the older and younger students work together to plant vegetables in a community garden, using math skills to measure and place the seeds appropriately. Follow-up visits include tending the garden and reading *Down to Earth: Garden Secrets! Garden Stories! Garden Projects You Can Do!* The students collaboratively design and paint a garden mural to keep the plants "blooming" year-round. The harvested food is gratefully received by a local food pantry.

• Before students from a middle school English class tutor first through third graders in literacy skills, they read *Thank You, Mr. Falker*. Using the book as a springboard, the class discusses the feelings young children may have when they don't read as well as their peers. The students write personal stories in their journals before and following tutoring sessions.

• A social studies teacher reads *Pink and Say* to her tenth-grade students as part of their study of the Civil War. They discuss social injustice and prejudice and how stories can be lost if they are not handed down to the next generation. Students decide to interview veterans of recent wars to record their stories.

• As part of a school-wide program to eliminate bullying and name-calling, all elementary classes read *Toestomper and the Caterpillars*, *The Hundred Dresses*, or *The Misfits*. After various learning activities, students develop peacemaking strategies to create a safe school environment for everyone.

• A teen youth group decides to learn ballroom dancing and recruits several experienced dancers, men and women who attend a nearby senior activity center. After mastering the basics of the fox trot, waltz, and east coast swing, the young dancers meet with the senior center staff and discuss ways to show their appreciation and gratitude for the lessons. The youth plan and host a "Senior Senior Prom" attended by over 60 dancing seniors.

[**Note:** Annotated descriptions of all books listed can be found in the subsequent theme chapters.]

This chapter is designed to give you an overview of service learning from common terms to the criteria that ensure success. An FAQ section will answer key questions to help you get started. You'll be introduced to the process that constitutes the foundation of all service learning activities and how you can maximize the success of your projects and your students. You may find that the questions in this chapter and their answers help you reflect on what service learning means to you and what forms it can take for the young people you work with. For example, you may find yourself considering the meaning of community and how it will need to be defined to best serve your project ideas. Or you might think about what forms of service will be most appealing or effective in your classroom. Of all of these questions, perhaps the most fundamental is: "What exactly is service learning?"

A Definition of Service Learning

Service learning can be defined in part by what it does for your students. When service learning is used in a structured way that connects classroom content, literature, and skills to community needs, students will:

- apply academic, social, and personal skills to improve the community.

- make decisions that have real, not hypothetical, results.

- grow as individuals, gain respect for peers, and increase civic participation.

- experience success no matter what their ability level.

- gain a deeper understanding of themselves, their community, and society.

- develop as leaders who take initiative, solve problems, work as a team, and demonstrate their abilities while and through helping others.

These important and documented academic and social results have helped validate service learning as a valuable, respected, and widely recognized teaching method. They may be why you're using service learning already or looking for ways to introduce it into your classroom, program, or youth group.

Wherever you plan on using service learning, you'll need a solid definition to guide you in your specific situation. You don't have to start from scratch to create your own definition, though you may need to tailor a general definition of service learning so that it reflects the specific needs of your students, community, and curriculum. While the essential structure and process of service learning stays the same, the resulting activities can take a great variety of forms. In a school context and in other learning situations,

service learning **can be defined as a teaching method where guided or classroom learning is deepened through service to others in a process that provides structured time for reflection on the service experience and demonstration of the skills and knowledge acquired.** This definition also works in nontraditional, less formal educational environments such as after-school programs and youth groups. In these settings, staff find meaningful opportunities to infuse the experience of helping in the community with an acknowledgment of what is also being learned.

Before You Start: Frequently Asked Questions

Defining service learning is only the beginning and it often leads to other important questions that need to be answered before you can start using or refining service learning. These are some common questions that come up in my workshops.

Q: *How is service learning different from community service or volunteer work?*

A: Service learning differs from other forms of community service or volunteer work because the education of students and young people is always at its core. Students are actively participating in the process of understanding, integrating, and applying knowledge from various subject areas as they work to improve their communities. The question "Why am I learning this?" disappears as students help older people or register voters or work to restore a fragile ecosystem and see what they've learned in action.

Q: *Can service learning be used with everyone? Or is it only for older kids? Or gifted kids?*

A: Service learning works with kindergartners and college students as well as every grade in between. Students of all ages and most ability levels can participate successfully, and almost every subject or skill can be enhanced through the practice of service learning. Because it can be applied to almost every subject area, this naturally encourages cross-curricular integration, which can help students grow and improve in several areas simultaneously.

> Real learning gets to the heart of what it means to be human. Through learning we re-create ourselves. Through learning we become able to do something we never were able to do. Through learning we re-perceive the world and our relationship to it. Through learning we extend our capacity to create, to be part of the generative process of life. There is within each of us a deep hunger for this type of learning.
>
> PETER M. SENGE, EDUCATOR AND AUTHOR

Q: How can I get my students interested in service learning?

A: An important aspect of service learning is student participation, not only in the actual activity, but in the planning and suggestion phase. When students have a voice in choosing and designing a service project, they are intrinsically more vested emotionally and intellectually. Since projects often utilize student strengths and talents that aren't always apparent in day-to-day lessons, service learning can motivate students to impressive accomplishments both in and out of the classroom. From the primary grades through high school, teachers use this method to do more than meet educational needs and fulfill academic standards but also as a way to excite students and build on their skills and talents.

Q: Won't service learning just mean more work for me?

A: Initially, as you're learning to use service learning as a teaching method and finding ways to integrate it into your curriculum, you may find that it takes a little more time than regular lesson or activity planning. However, as you become more adept and comfortable with the practice, you'll start to see curricular connections and the possibilities for projects and community partnerships much more easily. More than likely, you'll also find that your own levels of engagement and enthusiasm reflect that of the young people you work with and guide through service learning. The academic results and accomplishments in the community reward the effort for everyone involved.

Q: Service learning means reaching out to the community. What is community? How do I define it?

A: Any discussion of service learning is going to include many references to community. Service learning helps students to build and improve community, yet sometimes the who or what of community is unclear. *Community* can mean many different things geographically and socially in service learning, so its definition often depends on the nature of the service learning activity or who's doing the defining.

For some schools, service learning activities may be working toward improving interpersonal relationships or safety on the school campus, establishing cross-age tutoring programs, or beautifying the grounds. *Community* in this case may be defined as the school campus and population, which includes the immediate surrounding area, parents, and any outside agencies assisting with the issues being addressed.

Other schools extend their communities geographically and socially to include the surrounding neighborhood, city, or region. Some communities are international in nature, even if students never leave the school grounds. Examples of off-site locations for projects include: a local watershed to help with plant restoration, a refugee center where students assist with child care during adult English-language classes, and a radio station where students record public service announcements. In these situations, *community* usually includes agency partners.

Whatever is included in your definition of *community*, students engaging in service learning will come to know that community develops and builds through interaction, reciprocal relationships, and knowledge of people, places, organizations, governments, and systems. Through service learning, the often elusive idea of "community" takes shape and has a more tangible meaning for all involved. Recognizing and becoming active in a community builds a true foundation for civic responsibility that lasts well beyond the school years.

Q: I understand what service learning means, but what does service mean?

A: In the context of service learning, "service" is the implementation of a plan, designed or influenced by students, that combines classroom learning with meeting an authentic community need. In some cases, the need is apparent and even urgent—for example, when elementary students rescue duck eggs from a rice field just prior to harvest. In other cases, the students may be supplementing or supporting a larger community effort—for example, by taking dictation of letters for elders in a residential facility. In all cases, service is meant to evoke the spirit of caring in those involved as well as to provide a constructive context for their knowledge.

Q: *Are there different kinds or categories of service?*

A: Service can take many forms. Usually, though, the "service" in service learning can be classified as direct service, indirect service, advocacy, or research.

- *Direct Service.* Students' service directly affects and involves the recipients. The interactions are person-to-person and face-to-face, such as tutoring younger children or working with elders. Students engaged in direct service learn about caring for others who are different in age or experience, developing problem-solving skills, following a sequence from beginning to end, and seeing the "big picture" of a social justice issue. Interacting with animals is also included in direct service.

- *Indirect Service.* Indirect activities do not provide service to individuals but benefit the community or environment as a whole. Examples include restoring a wetland area, constructing park benches, stocking a food pantry, donating picture books to a Head Start program, and collecting clothing for families living in a shelter. Students engaging in indirect service learn about cooperation, working as a team, taking on different roles, organizing, and prioritizing. They will also gain project-specific skills and knowledge that relate to academic content.

- *Advocacy.* The intent of advocacy is to create awareness of or promote action on an issue of public interest. Related activities include writing letters, sponsoring a town meeting, performing a play, and public speaking. Student advocates learn about perseverance; understanding rules, systems, and processes; civic engagement; and working with adults.

- *Research.* Research activities involve students in finding, gathering, and reporting on information in the public interest. For example, students may develop surveys or conduct formal studies, evaluations, experiments, or interviews. They may also test water or soil, or conduct environmental surveys. The students in the Introduction who surveyed local elms for Dutch Elm Disease are a good example of this kind of service. By participating in research-based service learning, students may learn how to gather information, make discriminating judgments, and work systematically. They enhance their skills in organization, assessment, and evaluation as well.

> As you go through life, act in such a way
> as not to deprive others of happiness.
> Avoid giving sorrow to your fellow man,
> but to the contrary, see that you give him joy
> as often as you can.
> SIOUX PROVERB

Q: *Is one type of service learning better than another?*

A: Each of the service categories offers its own benefits to the community and to the students. And all types of service raise questions that continue to engage students in study and learning. Students involved in service continually apply and develop their knowledge in ways that meet and enrich the academic curriculum.

Q: *What do I do if I've been assigned to coordinate service learning for my grade/school/organization?*

A: Many of the previous questions and issues are useful jumping-off points for faculty or group discussion. The more people work together to discuss and understand service learning to meet the specific needs of their organization, the more likely they are to believe in the actual process of service learning. Included in this book are forms and information that can guide you and your colleagues and community partners into a quality service learning experience. (See Chapter 2 for more information on this topic.)

The Process of Service Learning: The Big Picture

At this point, you've thought about what service learning means, how you may choose to define community, and what forms of service might work best for your students. Now it's time to look at the actual process you'll be using. It is the basis of every service learning activity. When the process of service learning is broken down, four essential and interdependent stages emerge:

- Preparation
- Action
- Reflection
- Demonstration

Together these constitute a process that is key to student effectiveness and success. Even though each stage is examined separately, keep in mind that they're linked together and often used simultaneously. It may help to visualize how overlays are used in an anatomy book to reveal what is occurring in the human body system by system. Each stage of service learning in action is like one of these overlays, revealing one part of an interdependent whole.

Preparation

> I cannot predict the wind
> but I can have my sail ready.
> E. F. SCHUMACHER, AUTHOR

All service learning begins with preparation. This covers a wide variety of activities and includes identifying a need, investigating and analyzing it, and making a plan for action. In the preparation phase, the teacher and students work together to set the stage for learning and social action. With guidance from their

teacher, students identify a real community need, perhaps with the input of community partners or by conducting their own investigation using surveys, media reports, or other information sources. They go on to research and discuss the subject using books, interviews, the Internet, and field trips. They may examine it through role plays or more complex simulations (such as turning the classroom into an Ellis Island waiting room). In this process of active learning and critical thinking, students grow to understand the underlying problem as well as related subject matter. Investigation, discussion, and analysis lead to plans for action. The class draws on the skills, talents, and interests of individual students as it plans and shapes the service to come. Students may also find and establish partnerships with other teachers and classrooms, local agencies, colleges or universities, or national groups that offer resources.

Action

> If you need a helping hand,
> you will find one at the end of your arm.
> YIDDISH PROVERB

Action is the direct result of preparation. Solid preparation enables students to confidently carry out their plan of action, applying what they have learned to benefit the community. Perhaps they plant flowers to beautify the school grounds, collect school supplies to be sent for use by students in Africa, or create a recycling campaign—the possibilities are almost limitless. The plan may be carried out over the course of an academic year, a semester, two weeks, or a single day. As the students put their plan in motion, they come to recognize vividly how classroom lessons fit into their daily lives and shape the lives of others.

During the action stage, they continue to develop knowledge and resources as they meet new people and interact with their environment in meaningful ways. Over the course of the project, students raise questions that lead to a deeper understanding of the societal context of their efforts. They experience the real results of their actions and observe their strengths and attributes in relation to those of others, which can give them a new appreciation of their classmates and people in the community. By taking action, they identify themselves as community members and stakeholders and, over time, learn how to work within social institutions. Transforming plans into action enables young people to use what is inherently theirs: ideas, energy, talents, skills, knowledge, enthusiasm, and concern for others and their natural surroundings.

Reflection

To look backward for a while is to refresh the eye, to restore it, and to render it more fit for its prime function of looking forward.
MARGARET FAIRLESS BARBER, AUTHOR

Reflection is a vital and ongoing process in service learning that integrates learning and experience with personal growth and awareness. Using reflection, students consider how the experience, knowledge, and skills they are acquiring relate to their own lives and their communities. The academic program is often so jam-packed that it's all too easy to miss the meaning behind the details or within the experience. Reflection is a pause button that gives students the time to explore the impact of what they are learning and its effect on their thoughts and future actions.

In the course of reflecting, students put cognitive, social, and emotional aspects of experience into the larger context of self, the community, and the world. This helps them to assess their skills, develop empathy for others, and understand the impact of their actions on others and on themselves. To really work, reflection must go beyond students simply reporting or describing what they are doing or have done. When students can compare their initial assumptions with what they have seen and experienced in the real world, reflection can be a transforming experience. They can ask questions and probe deeper into an issue, leading the class to further levels of investigation and understanding. They can use poetry or music to express a change in feelings that occurred or their appreciation of a classmate. They can also consider what they would change or improve about a particular activity.

While reflection in service learning is structured, with the times and activities usually established by the teacher, reflection also occurs spontaneously, stimulated by a student comment or class discussion of a passage in a novel. Reflection may occur before, during, and after implementation through the use of different approaches and strategies. In all cases, feedback from adults helps students use reflection to elevate their ability to observe, question, and apply their accumulated knowledge to other situations. To be effective, adults who interact with the students must model reflective behaviors. You'll find that soon, students can devise their own strategies for reflection and lead each other through the reflective process.

Demonstration

The job of an educator is to teach students to see the vitality in themselves.
JOSEPH CAMPBELL, AUTHOR

The fourth stage of service learning is demonstration, which provides evidence of what students have gained and accomplished through their community involvement. They exhibit their expertise through public presentations—displays, performances, letters to the editor, class lessons—that draw on the preparation, action, and reflection stages of their experience. Presenting what they have learned allows students not only to teach others but also to identify and acknowledge to themselves what they have learned and how they learned it. Students take charge of their own learning as they synthesize and integrate the process through demonstration.

What about celebration and recognition? Descriptions of service learning often list celebration as a key part of the service learning process. Celebrating accomplishments and good work is definitely valuable, but demonstration is more in keeping with the intentions of service learning because students confirm what they have learned and continue the process. It is a significant achievement for students to demonstrate what they've learned clearly and publicly, and celebration can be interwoven with the demonstration. For example, students can invite community members to see their new hiking trail at a nature preserve and also plan a picnic and songfest. Celebration, when planned with thought, can benefit service learning.

While the emphasis should remain on the intrinsic benefits of learning and the satisfaction of helping to meet community needs, recognizing student accomplishment in a public way may show students that the school and community members understand and appreciate their contribution. For many students, this may be the only time their school success is acknowledged.

What Makes Service Learning Successful?

In order to maximize the value and benefits of each stage in the service learning process, certain elements need to be present. Each one helps students to learn and improves the quality of the service provided. These elements can even be used as criteria for creating successful activities and projects. Is each element always a part of a service learning? Ideally, yes. Experience has shown that when all of the elements are present—the criteria are all met—there is a much greater impact on the students and the community. Service learning is a process, though, and every activity or project is unique. So depending on the project and what approach you take, some of these elements may be more evident than others. However, the more familiar you, your students, and your community partners become with service learning strategies, the more likely it is that all of these elements will be seamlessly integrated into the process.

These are the elements that should be present to ensure a successful service learning project:

Integrated Learning. Students learn skills and content in a variety of ways. Academics come alive and knowledge is applied through interaction, research, practice, literature, discussion, and planning for action. Ideally, the learning and the service weave together and reinforce each other, with the service informing the content and the content informing the service.

Genuine Needs. Students identify, learn about, and articulate a genuine, recognized community need. This is often verified through the media, surveys, observation, or discussion with informed community partners. By addressing an important community need, student actions take on a greater value and importance. They can see their actions making a noticeable difference even as they learn and apply academic skills and knowledge.

Youth Voice and Choice. Young people need ample opportunities to express their ideas and opinions and to make decisions. Service learning gives students the opportunity to take initiative, make decisions, interact with community representatives, learn about the role of government in social issues, develop critical-thinking skills, and put their ideas into action. Students meet significant age-appropriate challenges with tasks that require thinking, initiative, problem solving, and responsibility in an environment safe enough to make mistakes and to succeed.

> No one is born a good citizen; no nation is born a democracy. Rather, both are processes that continue to evolve over a lifetime. Young people must be included from birth. A society that cuts itself off from its youth severs its lifeline.
>
> KOFI ANNAN,
> SECRETARY-GENERAL, UNITED NATIONS

Collaborative Efforts. Students participate in the development of partnerships and share responsibility with community members, parents, organizations, and other students. These relationships give the students opportunities to interact with people of diverse backgrounds in diverse settings. Through these dynamics, students and community members learn about each other, gaining mutual respect, understanding, and appreciation.

Reciprocity. Reciprocity is the mutual exchange of information, ideas, and skills among all participants in the learning and service experience. Reciprocity exists when each person sees the other as having something to share. Everyone is teaching and has the opportunity to learn. This process occurs in personal relationships and also between institutions, as, for example, when the members of a school and a service organization come together to work on a project.

Civic Responsibility. Being "response-able," being "able to respond"—to local and global issues that matter is what develops an active populace. When young people recognize their vital role in improving society, working for social justice, and caring for the environment, then they truly understand the concept of democracy. Students recognize how participation and the ability to respond to authentic needs improves the quality of life in the community, which may lead to a lifelong ethic of service and civic participation.

An Example of Putting It All Together: Service Learning Meets the Canned Food Drive

So what happens when you put all of the pieces together? A good illustration is to take an activity that you've probably done at some point: a canned food drive. The average canned food drive may be community service, but it isn't actually service learning.

Typically, the way a canned food drive is run ranges from general public-address announcements, such as "Bring in cans of food and put them in the box by the school office," to a contest in which the class contributing the most cans wins a pizza party. Regardless of the form it takes, the motivation to participate is weak and student learning is negligible. In the end, students are no more informed about the issues of hunger in the community than when they began, and the cans collected often don't meet the needs of the receiving agency or the community members who depend on the food bank.

An elementary teacher, "Mr. Baker," describes how a student made a huge difference in one school canned food drive by accidentally introducing the concept of service learning to his school:

For years, the same procedure had been followed. An announcement on the loud speaker asked students to bring in their cans and place them in the box by the office. Being new to the school, I was placed in charge of delivering the boxes to a local food bank. Jamal, a student known as a "troublemaker," was asked to cart the boxes to my car. Jamal looked inside at the assorted foods: lima beans, pesto sauce, water chestnuts, tomato sauce. Jamal had one comment, "This food stinks." I agreed, adding, "What should we do about it?" Jamal broke into a huge smile and told me his idea. The result? Rather than delivering the boxes, we hosted a luncheon to thank the teachers for helping with the canned food drive. The menu? You guessed it!

After seeing the poor selection from the food drive offered as a meal, the faculty revamped the canned food drive and considered real learning connections in every classroom. Kids began reading books on hunger, doing research about our community, talking with a representative from the local food bank, and creating all sorts of persuasive written materials that got everybody eager to participate. With ideas and leadership from Jamal and other students, we established our most productive and meaningful canned food drive ever. Communication between students and teachers improved as we talked about what we accomplished and shared our experiences and future plans with parents and community partners. Unexpectedly, we found additional ways to collaborate with the food bank throughout the school year.

The new kind of food drive at "Mr. Baker's" school provided opportunities for learning and applying skills that resulted in a significant benefit to the community. During a follow-up discussion, teachers noted that a new group of students had emerged as leaders and that a partnership had been established with a community organization. Student interest in community matters generated classroom conversations about additional local needs and ways in which students could plan and participate. The process of service learning became clear through experience.

What follow are more examples of real-life activities used in effective and meaningful canned food drives. While grade levels are noted, much of the material studied, the resources used, and the actual methods employed are relevant or can be easily adapted for many grade levels.

First Graders and Uncle Willie

While studying "community," first graders read *Uncle Willie and the Soup Kitchen* to identify the many ways people participate in meaningful service. The class takes a field trip and assembles sack lunches for a local agency which delivers meals to people in need. Back at school, the students plan a drive to collect food that that will help this agency prepare balanced, healthy meals. With assistance from their fourth-grade buddies, they make posters and flyers, which are given to each class; sort collected food into categories, keeping track of quantities on a large graph; and check cans for expired dates and damage. Together, they write reflective stories with illustrations of their experiences and compile the stories into a book. A copy is sent to the partner agency, and one is presented to the school library at an assembly.

Fourth Graders and The Long March

A fourth-grade teacher reads *Feed the Children First: Irish Memories of the Great Hunger*, a book describing the potato famine, and *The Long March: The Choctaw's Gift to Irish Famine Relief* aloud. The class learns that in 1847, the Choctaw tribe sent $170 (the equivalent of more than $5,000 today) to help the starving Irish. For homework, students ask an adult to describe how people in need of food were helped in times past. As the students continue their study of American Indians, they examine the parallel of Native Americans' loss of lands and displacement onto reservations with the experience of people who lose their homes today because of poverty. When the school's annual canned food drive occurs, students make a presentation to every class about the Irish and their distant Choctaw friends, including information about the meaningful canned food drive. Students keep journals that become part of their portfolios.

Sixth Grade Initiative

A sixth grader selects *Generation Fix* as a nonfiction book to read to fulfill a language arts assignment. The book tells the story of a student who collected thousands of boxes of cereal for food pantries. The sixth grader asks if the class can design a food drive in the spring to help fill local food banks for the months to come. The teacher revises an essay assignment to mirror the learning, planning, and implementation that follow. At the end of the project, the teacher remarks that student involvement and the writing for this unit are the best of the entire school year.

Seventh Graders Learn About Social Services

A middle school social studies teacher reads a newspaper article aloud that describes the increased unemployment in the region and the growing strain on local social service agencies, including food banks. Most students are unfamiliar with social service agencies, and this realization begins their research. Students generate questions regarding what social services are available, what circumstances can lead to the need for assistance, and what organizations help in their community. They want to know: Who receives this food? What foods are the staples of this population? Does this population have supplies to open cans and cook the food, or are prepared foods preferred? What nutritional foods or food groups are in short supply? Teams of students take on specific research tasks, including contacting food banks for lists of foods that are needed to meet current demands. They collaborate with the student council to inform the student body about hunger in their community and what they can do to help. At Back-to-School Night, students create a display and serve as docents showing parents and other guests their full program, from research to deliveries to the food bank. The students sign up the families of students to volunteer directly with the food bank during the summer months.

High School Health

During a ninth-grade health class, students review the foundations of a nutritious diet. They follow up with a guest speaker from the local food bank to learn more about issues of malnutrition, especially how childhood hunger can affect physical growth, learning, and the ability to function. Students then develop a school-wide marketing plan to promote participation in the canned food drive and emphasize foods that are healthy for kids. They culminate their activities by creating an original coloring book about fruits and vegetables to give to children through the food bank.

American History Gets Nickel and Dimed

An American History class reads *Nickel and Dimed: On (Not) Getting By in America* and draws quotes from the book for discussion. The students are inspired to continue their investigation of poverty in the community through student-designed projects. To learn more, student committees contact local social service agencies to determine their needs and find out about policies that affect low-income and poor people in their community. At the end of three weeks, building on their interests and talents, students present an original video at a chamber of commerce meeting. The video presents their analysis of local, state, and national policies toward homelessness and outlines agency needs and possible community responses. A newspaper runs a student editorial on the class's research and findings. Many letters are printed in response thanking the students for educating the community.

High School Electives Participate

- A drama class responds to an agency request to write a theatrical adaptation of the book *The Can-Do Thanksgiving* for elementary school assemblies to launch a citywide canned food drive.

- Photography students capture images related to the need for food donations. They create a photo display with personal comments that is displayed both at school and at the local public library.

- In a computer class, students create a pamphlet entitled, "Easy Steps to Improve Your Canned Food Drive," post it on a Web site, and send it to all local schools and many agencies.

What Next?

While you sort through the terms, definitions, and ideas presented here and throughout this book, remember that every teacher has a first service learning activity or project. Most begin with practical, manageable efforts that allow them to become familiar with the process. The following chapter offers guidance and a detailed blueprint for launching your efforts. Over time, as teachers, students, and agency partners gain experience with the value and impact of service learning, the efforts and collaborations may expand. If you've used service learning as a teaching method before, then this book will give you new resources and ideas to work with and may help you refine the practice in your classroom or organization. Advanced service learning teachers continually look for creative ideas and resources and seek out new partnerships, collaborations, and ways to encourage student leadership and initiative. The possibilities and promise of service learning grow with each activity no matter where you are in your service learning career.

CHAPTER 2

A BLUEPRINT FOR SERVICE LEARNING

Service learning offers a tremendous array of exciting opportunities, choices, and challenges. If you're considering your first service learning activity, you may ask, "Where do I start?" And even if you're a seasoned veteran, you may wonder how to improve your service learning strategies and methods. This chapter will take you through each step of the service learning process, providing a blueprint to follow as you get started. It will also address issues common to service learning and ways to troubleshoot problems or unexpected situations that may arise both when you're getting started and when you're developing your practice.

> In doing we learn.
> GEORGE HERBERT, POET

Getting Started: A Blueprint

Getting started with service learning can seem overwhelming because there are many different concerns that you need to address and balance. However, with planning you can establish a solid foundation for your students to build on in their service learning activities. To help you successfully plan out your activity and curricular ties and prepare for different issues you may encounter, use the step-by-step blueprint of the service learning process featured below. This blueprint maps out the service learning process in an easy to follow sequence that you can refer to as you and your students plan and carry out service learning projects. It begins with finding entry points to service learning in your curriculum and closes with the important final step of assessing the overall experience. Each step lists the forms provided in this book that can help you get organized and maximize your resources. You'll also find suggestions in these steps for ways to continue developing your service learning practice as you become more experienced.

> **Note:** The forms referred to in the blueprint and throughout the text appear at the end of this chapter, starting on page 31.

An Overview of the Service Learning Blueprint

The following steps will guide you through the service learning process. Each step includes a reference to useful forms, with page numbers noted in parentheses. Students can assist with and participate in these steps as is appropriate for their age and ability, taking on more responsibility as they gain experience.

Step One: Points of Entry. Think about what you're teaching. What are the underlying skills and content you want your students to come away with? All of these are entry points into service learning and can help you make curricular connections. Ongoing school projects, student-identified needs, and community-identified needs are also good ways to find your entry point into service learning activities.

Form: Establishing Curricular Connections: Points of Entry (page 31)

Step Two: Map Out Your Plans. Next get more detailed and start mapping a plan. Identify and write down your service idea. Include in detail the content and skills that will be taught, the cross-curricular connections you can make, the books the students will read, and the community contacts that would be

continued ⟶

helpful to find and cultivate. Think about where your students will have their voice in the project. Be specific about your plans for preparation, action, reflection, and demonstration.

Forms: The Four Stages of Service Learning (page 36), Planning for Service Learning (page 38)

Step Three: *Clarify Partnerships.* Here is where you seek out partnerships that will support and enhance the service learning. Establish contact with collaborators—teachers, parents, community members, agency representatives, or others—who you want to participate. Discuss and clarify specific roles and responsibilities for all involved to avoid any confusion once the project is underway.

Form: Community Contact Information (page 43)

Step Four: *Review Plans and Gather Resources.* Review your plans. Determine the kinds of resources you'll need, and start gathering and organizing them. These may include books, newspaper articles, and reference materials from partner agencies. Also, schedule any visits, guest speakers, or field trips. Many of these are good tasks for your students to take on as they gain skills and experience.

Form: Planning for Service Learning (page 38)

Step Five: *Begin the Process of Service Learning in Action.* Now you can begin the process of service learning in your classroom or group. Initiate the four stages of the service learning cycle: preparation, action, reflection, and demonstration. Encourage youth voice and choice as you move through the service learning process. It's important to be flexible for two reasons: Unexpected things can happen and service learning works best when students are able to see their own ideas in action. Continue to look for opportunities for ongoing reflection.

Forms: The Essential Elements of Service Learning (page 37), Planning for Service Learning (page 38), Four Square Reflection Tool (page 48)

Step Six: *Assess the Service Learning Experience.* Once demonstration and closing reflection have been completed, review and assess the learning accomplished, the impact of the service, the planning process, the reciprocal benefits for all involved, and ways to improve for next time. Debrief with all partners, and of course include the students.

Forms: Community Response Form (page 44), Assessment for Service Learning Form, Parts One and Two (pages 49 and 50), Student Self-Evaluation (page 51)

As you start following the blueprint, questions often arise. Common ones include:

- How do I come up with ideas for service learning projects that have strong curricular connections?

- How do I ensure that service learning advances student learning?

- How can I plan ahead while leaving room for "youth voice and choice"?

- How can I encourage students to develop a sense of civic responsibility?

- How do I establish partnerships in school *and* in the community?

What follows are the answers to these questions, instructions on how and where to use the forms in this book, and more detailed exploration of the issues common to embarking on service learning. These will all help you to plan your first service activity.

> Even if you are on the right track, you'll get run over if you just sit there.
> WILL ROGERS, HUMORIST

How do I come up with ideas for service learning projects that have strong curricular connections?

Where can you get ideas for projects with genuine curricular connections— projects that will truly combine community service with academics? First, think about what skills, content, and themes you're already teaching. Using the Establishing Curricular Connections: Points of Entry form on pages 31–32 may be very helpful to you because it identifies five strategies you can use to generate service learning project ideas complete with sample project ideas and literature resources. Following, each entry point is examined in more detail.

As you think about various ideas for projects, keep in mind that service learning ideas are best developed as a "team sport." Draw others into your planning sessions. Brainstorming possible activities with students, colleagues, and others is a method guaranteed to produce a wealth of options (and excitement). This often leads to collaborative service learning activities: a teacher who has contributed a suggestion is more likely to participate, students whose ideas are taken seriously make a stronger commitment, and agencies become more involved partners.

Point of Entry #1: Identify an existing program or activity to transform into authentic service learning. The familiar canned food drive, mentioned in Chapter 1, can easily become a service learning project. It's a simple matter for teachers, students, and community partners to find related learning opportunities, such as studying nutrition, interviewing the receiving agency to identify what foods are needed, visiting a food bank, and investigating underlying issues of poverty and local housing costs. The learning process can include such books as *The Other America* and *Asphalt Angels*.

Point of Entry #2: Begin with standard curriculum, content, and skills and find the natural extension into service. What are the specific content and skill areas you need to address in the classroom? Fill in those spaces on the Planning for Service Learning form (page 38) first, and consider a service emphasis that extends this classroom learning into a hands-on experience. When students are learning about times of war in American history, for example, and you want them to improve their verbal communication skills, consider having them interview elders about their wartime experiences. This project works as well for elementary students as it does for high school students. Books such as *Growing Older: What Young People Should Know About Aging, Hurry Granny Annie,* and *Too Young for Yiddish* can elicit a related discussion about the aging process; and *We Were There, Too! Young People in U.S. History* and *Charlie Wilcox* can add depth to the historical aspects while addressing specific academic standards.

Point of Entry #3: From a theme or unit of study, identify content and skill connections. Most broad themes or topics, such as "interdependence" or "the rainforest," have service implications. Identify the specific content and skill areas to be addressed, and then select a service application that is developmentally appropriate for your students. For example, with the theme "the individual's role in society," students may read nonfiction stories of exemplary acts such as *Rabble Rousers: 20 Women Who Made a Difference* and *Sisters in Strength: American Women Who Made a Difference.* Younger children can dramatize the lives of people they admire, highlighting their civic contributions and sharing the knowledge through performances for other classes, senior citizen groups, or at a community celebration. Older students can research agencies that meet community needs and find ways to provide assistance while studying underlying social issues. After conducting the research, they can produce a series of informative pamphlets on these agencies for young people.

Point of Entry #4: Start with a student-identified need. There are several ways to use student-identified needs as departure points. As a class, identify students' skills, talents, and interests using the Personal Inventory form on page 33. Then have students think about local problems that may be extensions of their interests or talents, identify the causes of the problems, list who is already helping (it might already be a student in your classroom), brainstorm ways in which young people can help, conduct research to learn more, and create an action plan. The Taking

Action in Our Community form on page 34 provides a tool for this process. Next, students can prepare a formal proposal using the Service Learning Proposal form on page 35. Alternatively, students may volunteer ideas and concerns with no prompting. For example, a student may come into class and proclaim that "something has to be done about the empty lot next to the school," and suggest a clean-up or a community garden. Another student might burst into class upset that "the skateboard park is about to be closed" and want to let people know how unfair that is. Or a student could describe how a fire destroyed a neighbor's home and wonder what could be done to help the family. These unpredicted "teachable moments" can initiate the process of clarifying immediate community needs and determining ways to become involved.

Point of Entry #5: Start with a community-identified need. Good news travels fast, and once a school has a reputation for providing service or has established community partnerships, agencies or organizations may ask your students for assistance. Stories in the local media are another common way of identifying community needs. A newspaper article or an evening news report can also make a need apparent to the students. For example, either method could lead to your students providing a day-care center with one-on-one literacy preparation, perhaps with children who do not speak English. Students can create lessons to introduce basic language skills or lead activities in which the younger children make letter shapes with their bodies. Older and younger pairs can enjoy writing and illustrating bilingual books on themes chosen by the younger children. Children can take copies of the books home, and copies can also be donated to the library, a day-care facility, and other places that need books such as health clinics and family shelters. Again, literature (such as *A Movie in My Pillow—Una película en mi almohada* or *La Mariposa*) can be excellent to use in preparation.

> **Note:** All of the books mentioned in this chapter can be found in the service learning bookshelves of Part 2.

How do I ensure that service learning advances student learning?

Planning is the answer. Service learning advances and enhances student learning when teachers plan ahead to establish authentic curricular connections.

The Planning for Service Learning form on page 38 helps you map out a service learning project and identify opportunities for learning. On this form, you can write down each step, including specific content, skills to be developed, opportunities for youth voice, literature to be used, and community contacts to be made, as well as curricular connections—all on one page. Many teachers have found that this tool serves as a continuing reference and a reminder of the steps to be followed and the elements to be considered and integrated. As new learning opportunities arise during the service learning process or at the conclusion, you can update this form for documentation and record keeping purposes and to share with others.

To use the form, insert whatever information you have and then use that information to generate ideas, ideally in collaboration with peers, community partners, and students. If you're a single-subject teacher, you may find opportunities for interdisciplinary collaboration as you identify related areas of study.

To give you an idea of the various ways the form can be used, four examples of filled-in forms are provided. The elementary project on page 39 began in one classroom and evolved over four years to include many students and teachers. The environmental theme and activities developed as several teachers exchanged ideas. Each teacher made adjustments for grade level, class needs, and personal teaching style. When implementing the plan, each teacher also made changes as students added or modified ideas and community partnerships were identified. The middle school project on page 40 was a natural extension of a classroom study of immigration. Students' enthusiasm and interest compelled the teacher to engage in community outreach, greatly benefiting the academic achievements of his class while meeting an authentic community need. The high school literacy project on page 41 began as a one-time interaction in which older students were going to read books to younger children. With student leadership, the project evolved into a comprehensive bookmaking activity over three weeks that included extensive preparation and several class visits. Through the fourth project on page 42, children with autism in elementary through middle school grades learned about plants while also being helpful neighbors.

How can I plan ahead while leaving room for "youth voice and choice"?

It's important to create a service learning framework that provides ample opportunities for student learning to occur. Often this planning occurs well in advance of any service projects. Standards, textbooks, and mandates from many directions usually require you to have a well-thought-out plan for the upcoming year even before the first day of school. The initial framework for service learning projects may be part of this plan. So how can you leave room for genuine decision making by students, for their "voice and choice"—one of the essential elements of service learning? The key is to remain flexible, so that plans can be revised as students and partners introduce new ideas.

Even when the original plan remains intact, there are many opportunities for students to make choices:

- A first-grade teacher decides that having her class paint a mural depicting the local community fits well into her language arts and social studies curriculum. After she leads discussions about what a community is, the class makes field trips to fire stations and food markets, and many books are read aloud, she lets the students determine the content and design of the mural.

- Middle school students interviewing seniors at a retirement community for a social studies project find that many of the older people have extensive experience gardening. Although gardening was not an original focus of the project, students see the need for a change. The students and their senior friends suggest potting plants and writing an intergenerational gardening guide together.

- High school biology students conduct research on water quality using a real-world set of water quality testing methods. They must analyze land use, set their sampling sites to take account of a feedlot or construction project,

and collect and analyze the data. They must figure out the best way to apply these methods locally, which offers many opportunities for student input and direction.

- A youth group agrees to learn how to be docents at a children's museum and are given program materials and a script to learn for greeting and guiding the participants. They are asked to review all the documents and make suggestions for improvement. Students recommend both new written text for the museum brochures and ways to make the tours and activity centers more kid-friendly and engaging.

Encouraging youth voice and skill development also involves having students take on clearly defined roles and responsibilities that add to project productivity and efficiency and may, over time, reduce your workload. Students can form teams that have assigned tasks such as:

- Communication Specialists make and keep a project log of phone calls and write correspondence.

- Photographers take pictures that create the visual timeline of memorable moments.

- Publicists learn how to write captivating press releases to send to school board members and media outlets.

- Historians assemble a scrapbook of artifacts—program materials, photographs, news articles—that tell the complete service learning project story.

The teams' success depends upon being prepared for the tasks, which will require lessons and practice activities to hone the skills they require. However, once accomplished, the students build on this foundation through practice, ongoing support, and constructive feedback. Students have been known to compose a guidebook to teach other students about their roles and even lead peer workshops to establish teams in other classes. Students can also help determine what the teams are and rotate jobs so they learn and develop multiple skills. When can you start using this approach? The answer is: Any age when you can match age-appropriate skills that fit the project and plan accordingly. First graders at a rural school formed teams called "The Greeters," "The Appreciators" (they write thank-you notes), and "The Scrapbook Keepers" as part of their school's nature trail project.

The more familiar you become with the service learning process and the unique talents of your students, the earlier you can draw students into the planning process. (For more suggestions on this and other ways to refine this area of your service learning practice, see "Developing Youth Initiative" on pages 24–25.)

> Why not go out on a limb?
> Isn't that where the fruit is?
> FRANK SCULLY, AUTHOR

How can I encourage students to develop a sense of civic responsibility?

Participation in service learning creates the potential to develop civic knowledge, community awareness, and literacy. Enliven the idea of civic responsibility through activities that promote understanding and knowledge about the different roles that individuals, collaborative efforts, and government all play in a thriving democracy. Consider the following activities as strategies you can use to build a foundation of civic responsibility into your service learning programs.

Personal Impact. Include stories of individuals who have made contributions to the well-being and advancement of society through their initiative and collaborative efforts. Books provide stories such as *The Adventurous Chef: Alex Soyer*, who applied his culinary knowledge to help create soup kitchens in Dublin during the potato blight and famine of the 1840s. Use the book *You Forgot Your Skirt, Amelia Bloomer!* to teach about a suffragette who made a fashion statement with long-term impact. At every age, students also benefit from meeting people within their communities who participate as volunteers, service providers, civic leaders, and elected officials. Students can meet and conduct interviews with people they know or read about in local newspapers who make ongoing contributions through their work,

such as police officers, council members, and even teachers. Questions may include, "What do 'service' and 'civic responsibility' mean to you?" "How does your work contribute to our community?" This can lead students to discuss the importance of what an individual can contribute and what each of them hopes to accomplish through service learning.

Collaborative Experience. Introduce anthropologist Margaret Mead's quote, "Never doubt that a small group of citizens can change the world. Indeed it is the only thing that ever has." Have students discuss what this means in small groups, and look for evidence that supports or contradicts this statement. Students can draw from the period of history they are studying or from literature (fiction or nonfiction) to substantiate their perspective.

The Role of Government. Have students identify and contact the government agency associated with their service learning efforts. For younger students, the teacher or a parent may help with this task. For example, there are state agencies that govern the rules and regulations for convalescent facilities. Many states offer free education packets about recycling or toxic waste. City council members or their staff can provide information about services offered for people who are homeless. The role of government becomes more vivid as students gain familiarity with its range of offices, services, and policy. They can make contact through phone calls, the Internet, letters, or visits with city officials. Students can also make presentations at school board meetings, city council meetings, or to the state legislature or just attend simply to learn how the meetings work.

A Thriving Democracy. Have students discuss the foundations and principles of a democratic society. Service learning activities can be developed based on student generated ideas that will support these principles. For example, a fourth-grade class initiated a local campaign to "Vote for America," a nonpartisan effort to increase voter registration and turnout. A middle school social studies class planned and led a town meeting on usage of a town park. A high school Spanish class partnered with an adult education citizenship class to improve their Spanish conversation skills and tutor the adult students about the Constitution.

How do I establish partnerships in school and in the community?

Collaboration can be the lifeblood of service learning. Partners add a variety of perspectives to the process, which can fuel debate and reflection as well as help students gain a better understanding of social issues and generate ideas for civic improvement. Collaboration can provide additional opportunities to acquire knowledge and expertise. Teachers often ask how to set up constructive partnerships with other teachers, community members, and parents.

Partnerships with Teachers. Communicating peer to peer effectively establishes a network of teachers who bring service learning to life within a school. By telling colleagues about the value of service learning, how the basic process works, and any personal experience, you may ignite someone's curiosity or uncover willing partners. Sharing an article from an education journal or an example found on the Internet is another way to stimulate conversation and ideas. Administrative support can also give service learning vital credibility as a teaching method, which can lead to staff development sessions that foster knowledge and faculty interest.

Consider these ideas to bring other teachers on board:

• Even casual discussions often reveal that colleagues are curious about service learning and may be willing to participate. During a lunchtime conversation, for example, one teacher mentions that her second graders want to donate an original picture book to a day-care center. Another teacher suggests that her class could make a companion counting coloring book. A third teacher recommends contacting a friend who teaches Spanish at the local high school. As the result of a simple conversation, the day care receives a bilingual picture book, along with a coloring book and, as a bonus, a relationship between three classrooms in two schools is established.

• More formal meetings can also be used to initiate collaborations. During a small group planning session among fourth-grade teachers, a middle school teaching team, or high school English department, request time to develop an idea for a service learning unit for your class. The Planning for Service Learning form on page 38 can provide a road map that the group can help fill in, and it also helps novices understand the different aspects. Some teachers may be willing to participate, others may want to observe and join in later. Be certain to let your colleagues know how their input impacted the project, and make a point of sharing this information with your students, because they may choose to express appreciation to these teachers verbally or with a written note.

• Are you in search of ideas for cross-curricular collaborations in the middle and high school grades? Brainstorm with students for original ideas. Students can often approach teachers in other subject areas and ask them to help meet specific project needs. Here are some examples: A computer teacher agreed to have her students help a social studies class design a brochure for a local meals on wheels organization; a photography class documents high school science students leading chemistry experiments with fifth graders; and several music students compose background melodies for a family consumer education class' public service announcements on nutrition and exercise.

• Showcase student success! Have students demonstrate their learning and service at a faculty meeting. A creative display of the knowledge acquired, skills developed, and community involvement achieved may encourage other teachers to learn more or to get involved.

> If opportunity doesn't knock, build a door.
> MILTON BERLE, COMEDIAN

Establishing Partnerships in the Community. Service Learning offers wonderful opportunities to involve partners from outside the traditional school setting. Everyone concerned benefits in ways that they wouldn't have otherwise. The degree of need and commitment usually dictates the involvement of the partners. A community partner may simply provide written materials to help a class learn about setting up a recycling program at school. Another partner may be more involved; for example, a convalescent facility sends a staff person to lead a simulation about the aging process with a class preparing for a site visit. Sometimes, community partners actually identify learning opportunities within their organizations that match classroom objectives for content or skill development. Always, partnerships are best developed with an explicit purpose and clearly defined roles, responsibilities, and benefits for all involved.

Who can be a partner? Nonprofit organizations, service clubs, businesses, and government offices and agencies are all potential partners in the service learning world. Interacting with youth frequently appeals to members of these groups, especially as they find out about how they enrich student learning and the meaningful contributions made by young people.

Community colleges and universities also make excellent service learning partners. Across the country, colleges and universities are integrating service learning in various curricular areas, and with this trend comes abundant opportunities for collaboration. These might include joint service learning projects; elementary, middle, or high school students demonstrating their expertise to a college class; programs in which classroom teachers provide mentoring in the service learning process to education students (or vice-versa); and cross-age tutoring projects that include service learning as one aspect of the relationship. Many institutions of higher learning have service learning coordinators for general education and are integrating service learning into teacher preparation classes.

Find partners for your project by first identifying the purpose of the relationship: How do the interests of the partners intersect? How will this partnership support and strengthen the learning or service aspect of your project? What are the reciprocal benefits? Teachers and students can come up with lists of potential partners with students getting additional ideas from their families or by interviewing the school principal.

Teachers or parents frequently initiate contact with potential partners. This is a skill that students should learn, too. They will become proficient at finding and interacting with potential community partners when they have ample practice in making phone calls, writing correspondence, and even using telephone or online directories. These skills are valuable in general and are especially helpful as students take more initiative in planning and preparing for service learning. Even very young students can begin developing such skills, though an adult usually calls ahead to provide a general introduction and lay the groundwork for the child.

As contacts are made, the Community Contact Information form on page 43 helps the class or school maintain an ongoing record of interaction that can be used from project to project and year to year. In some schools, students conduct interviews with numerous agencies to create a notebook, directory, or database of willing partners. The directory serves as a useful reference during a given project and in the future.

Once you've identified and established relationships with your partners, keep them informed and appropriately involved at all stages of your service learning efforts. You can include them in reflection as well—the Community Response Form page 44 is designed for just this purpose. The form provides a structure for students to collect feedback and learn more about the impact of their contribution. Often, the community partner also appreciates participating in any public demonstration of the service learning process. Students have made presentations to board of directors of community groups, to local chambers of commerce, at city council meetings, and in other venues with partners in attendance and sometimes participating. When the time comes to express gratitude for the partnership, students can design their own special way of saying, "thank you!" through cards, presentations, skits, songs, or other creative methods.

Parents as Partners. Schools want parents to be involved in the education of their children. In fact, active school-family relationships provide the best educational atmosphere for all children. In terms of service learning, parents can contribute valuable resources, information, and ideas. They can help in the planning and implementation of service learning, identify community partners, assist with group work, join in field trips, collect and prepare supplies, document activities, and help write grants for funding. Even parents who work during the school day may be able to help make phone calls or cut fabric squares for a quilting project.

To find a role for every parent, begin by identifying your parent resources and your program needs. Students in grades 3–12 can survey parents and other family members to develop a database of information: when parents are available to help, their personal hobbies and talents, and their connections and involvement in the community. Some schools even have parent liaisons for service learning. Once parent leaders emerge, they can coordinate parent involvement school-wide, facilitate workshops giving information on service learning and ways to get involved, and even identify opportunities for families to join together outside of school hours to perform service together.

Beyond the Basics: Advancing Your Service Learning Practice

Perhaps you're so familiar with the basic issues of service learning that addressing them has practically become second nature. If you're looking for ways to enhance your approach to service learning, here are some important areas to focus on:

- developing youth initiative in planning service learning activities
- infusing reflection in preparation, action, and demonstration stages
- assessing student learning and service
- publicizing student activities

Developing Youth Initiative

Why should you work on developing youth initiative in planning service learning activities? Youth initiative means youth involvement. When students play a key role in choosing and defining their service activities, their commitment and satisfaction are intensified. They become more confident in their actions and better able to recognize their impact on the community. If students are truly to grow as individuals and leaders through the service learning experience, they must take this step.

Launching a project that has evolved through student brainstorming and planning may seem risky. Certainly, it can involve a greater sense of the unknown. Your role is still the same—you remain a steadfast guide and mentor. Sometimes you are

providing an overall framework, often setting boundaries, giving encouragement, and making sure that the project includes clear academic connections.

Taking an Inventory of Student Skills and Knowledge

Every student brings skills, talents, and interests to the class. Finding out what they are is one of your first tasks. Create a class database or chart of this useful information to help you get to know your students and to facilitate them getting to know each other. (Older students can help create this database.) They will frequently discover unexpected commonalities and sometimes fascinating differences.

This information can help the class in a variety of ways. A student who enjoys talking on the phone, for example, with a bit of skill development and practice, can become a group asset by contacting and making arrangements for a service outing. Do you have an "expert shopper" in your midst? Harness that talent for getting items donated or finding the best price on a "must purchase" item. Uncovering a "green thumb" will come in handy, too. What about interests? Knowing that some students have an interest in stopping vandalism or helping animals may set your service learning activity in a particular direction.

Using the Personal Inventory form on page 33, have students interview each other in pairs to reveal abilities and interests that will ultimately be helpful to the group. (For language development, it's enlightening to clarify the terms *skill*, *talent*, and *interest*.) Before the interview process, guide students through steps of active listening, note taking, and asking probing questions so that interviews will yield more detail and useful skills are developed. A student may say he is interested in music. The interviewer could then ask, "Do you play an instrument or listen to music? What kinds of music do you like?" The interviewers record their partners' responses on the form.

The activity should also include having students describe a time when they helped

continued ⟶

someone and a time when someone helped them. This develops the recognition of personal reciprocity in the big picture of service learning. By honing their interviewing skills and becoming better acquainted, students are not only preparing for the service learning experience but for other activities outside of school (such as job interviews) as well.

With young children, especially those who aren't writing yet, you can adapt this activity using art. Have the children draw pictures showing their favorite activities and their talents. Alternatively, you can explore skills, talents, and interests through class discussion. In either case, you can develop a list of skills, talents, and interests for the class.

For all age groups, post the list and invite students to add new skills and interests as the year progresses. Refer to this list as you continue to shape your service learning projects.

Developing a Plan for Action and a Project Proposal

Students can use the Taking Action in Our Community form on page 34 to develop a plan, beginning with defining a need and extending through specific ideas for implementation. Using the Taking Action form, students identify, among other things, a problem in the community and an action they can take to help solve it. When possible, community partners should be involved in the process so that students can learn how respectful collaborations are built and maintained.

The Taking Action form provides a guide in the initial planning process; the final description can be recorded on a Service Learning Proposal form found on page 35. When writing a proposal, students clearly articulate their ideas in terms of the need for the action they propose, the purpose of the action, the roles of various partners, the anticipated results, the budget for supplies or transportation, the ways in which the effects of their effort will be measured, and even a timeline for the project. Students may work in committees to perform their designated tasks. While the plans described in the proposal may—and usually

do—change during implementation, the document provides an overview and direction as students move forward. The complete document can also be submitted to the school administration for approval, to partners to confirm their participation, and to funding sources if monies or supplies are needed. Students can make changes as required and at the end can use the document as part of their reflection and assessment.

How old do students need to be to participate in making an action plan and writing a proposal? With guidance from their teacher, students in third grade have worked with the Taking Action form and a modified proposal form—Our Service Project, on page 45. Even in the early grades, much can be accomplished through class discussion and by working in small groups. In first and second grades, for example, you can make a chart of ideas for action generated in class discussion. The ideas can lead to concrete plans, to action, and to the rewarding conclusion: We did it!

Seeking Funds for Service Learning?

The Service Learning Proposal form on page 35 is based on a standard grant application form. After writing a few proposals, many students have successfully applied their proposal writing skills to apply for service learning project funds, even in the primary grades! Curious about service learning grant opportunities? Several are included in the Resources section (pages 216–217). Also, investigate your own community—older students can do the detective work, too—for financial support through service organizations, businesses, local foundations, city council offices, and even your school district. You may find that funders respond most favorably when they know that students have been part of the grant writing process.

Identifying Community Resources. With your guidance, middle and high school students can become involved in identifying community resources and related tasks. Using the Project Promotion—Turning Ideas into Action form on page 46, students start with an agreed-upon service idea and work in small groups to identify possible new alliances, sources for fundraising (if needed), presentation opportunities, media options, and so forth. Existing community partners may join in the activity, giving students practice in collaboration that leads to community networking.

Reflecting on Reflection

Reflection is indispensable to the entire service learning process and is what weaves it all together intellectually and emotionally for everyone involved. Through reflection, students can integrate both the learning and the service achieved into their frameworks of experience. Since reflection is so central, how you design and conduct it is important. It is a vital area for you to develop and refine. Understanding what you're trying to achieve with reflection can guide what methods and activities you choose. Do you want students to:

- connect their experience with classroom content and studies?

- integrate their experience with other areas of their life?

- develop a sense of community among the class or with partners?

- clarify misunderstandings, perceptions, or biases?

- improve observation and analytical skills?

- develop an appreciation of others in the group and the community?

- deepen their knowledge and understanding of community and social issues?

Reflection is just as integral for educators as it is for students. You reflect on the process to design meaningful and appropriate reflection activities for your students. Keep these thoughts in mind as you read about weaving reflection into the service learning process, ways to vary your reflection strategies, ideas for using journals, overcoming discussion hazards, the importance of feedback, and opportunities for student leadership. The Sequence for Reflection form on page 47 can help guide your reflection with students or you can use it as a checklist. Maintaining your own reflection over the course of a project can be helpful, too.

Opportunities for Reflection

As emphasized earlier, reflection occurs both through activities structured by the teacher and spontaneously during all stages of the service learning process. As you plan your service learning strategy, include opportunities for reflection during the preparation, action, and demonstration stages in addition to the actual reflection stage.

Reflection during preparation. Before the service learning process begins, find out what students know. What beliefs, assumptions, and attitudes are already in place? Where and how were they learned? What do students expect will happen? Students can role play situations they imagine will occur to practice and prepare and also to uncover anxieties or misconceptions. Students can consider such questions as, "What will you do if the child you're tutoring won't listen to the story?" "How do you think the convalescent home will look, sound, or smell?" Depending on the situation, you may give students a thought or question to take with them into the service experience. This may encourage them to be more observant or heighten their awareness of a particular need or action being taken.

Reflection during action. As students perform their service, be observant. What do you notice the students paying attention to? What comments do you overhear? What behaviors do you see? Make notes and refer to them later during the reflection that follows the service. As service is actually going on, you may have time to draw students together for on-the-scene reflection and response. Conversation can draw upon your observations. Students can also take the initiative by raising concerns, sharing their excitement, or posing questions. Or you might pose a question such as, "Is there a better way to sort the recycling?" During this on-the-spot reflection, students sometimes have insights or make recommendations that improve their experience and the impact of their contributions right then and there.

Reflection following service. Following the service, use a variety of different methods for reflection: art, poetry, music, role playing, journals, mime, sculpture, drama, movement, photographs. Since people naturally reflect in different ways, you are more likely to elicit a range of responses and involve more students by varying the methods you use. Students can write a recipe for developing youth leadership skills or create a skit that shows a dilemma faced and ask others to step in and respond. Each student can write a haiku to contemplate and describe the experience of a morning spent in a garden. Experiment with less traditional reflection methods as well. For example, have students enter class after a service experience to find their work space covered with butcher paper. In silence, students represent their thoughts and feelings of the experience through art. After drawing for ten minutes, each student finds a private place to sit and write silently for five minutes about the experience. Afterward, discuss both the process and the product. (This method of reflection has been used successfully with groups of all ages.)

Reflection during demonstration. As students prepare their public demonstration—perhaps a presentation to another class or an article for a school newspaper—have them draw upon their reflections, and even use the actual word *reflection,* to concretely explain this essential dynamic to others.

Journal Writing

Consider having students write their reflections in a journal. Keeping a journal encourages writing and personal expression that's often more unbridled than the formal structure of an essay-writing lesson. Once young people are introduced to keeping a journal, many continue to do so on their own. As one of the strategies for journal entries, consider using The Four Square Reflection Tool on page 48. This approach pushes students to write their responses in four categories:

- *What happened?* This is the cognitive realm, where students can describe what they thought and what they observed.

- *How did you feel?* Students' emotional responses may differ in tone from their cognitive responses. Separating the social and emotional from the cognitive helps students create a more complete picture.

- *What are your ideas?* They may suggest new ways to plan or collaborate with an agency or come up with new service activities that would meet other community needs.

- *What questions do you have?* What do students want to know about as a result of this experience?

This question can help guide their own investigation or assist the class in planning the next steps for learning.

Students can refer to these filled-out Four Square forms for discussions, presentations, and other writing assignments based on their service learning experience.

Reflection Prompts

Whether reflection involves writing poetry or prose, taking photographs, or having a discussion, reflection prompts such as the questions that follow may assist in the process. Questions can be simplified for younger children and adapted to fit the activity. They can be used during preparation and action stages.

- What was special about this activity today?

- What did the experience remind you of?

- What did you learn that you didn't know before? (What you learned might relate to yourself, a peer, the people/place we are helping, or an idea you want to investigate further.)

- How did you feel being at the service site? How did your feelings change from when you first arrived to when you left?

- How did you make a difference today?

- Five years from now, what do you think you will remember about this project?

- Consider the books you read in preparing for this activity. Do you understand the characters better after your personal involvement with service?

A person's mind stretched to a new idea never goes back to its original dimensions.
OLIVER WENDELL HOLMES, JURIST AND WRITER

Beware the "Smelly Elephants." Have you ever taken a group of young children to the zoo? After the trip, imagine the students reflecting on their trip through a class discussion. The teacher asks, "What was special about today's activity?" The first child answers, "The smelly elephants," and everyone laughs. Before you know what has happened, every child is describing the smelly elephants, and then the smelly monkeys, and so on until the conversation seems to go in a circle. As in general class discussions, this can be a hazard when students reflect on their service learning experience in a discussion format. The remedy? Have students write down responses to prompts in brief notes before the class starts its discussion, so that they can refer to their written thoughts in conversation. (Young children can draw, instead of writing notes.) This simple act preserves the integrity of each student's experience before it can be influenced by others' impressions and assures that everyone has something to contribute. Many teachers have found this "smelly elephant" remedy so effective, they use it frequently in all sorts of classroom discussions.

Closing the Loop: Giving Feedback. The cycle of student reflection is completed with feedback from you. Your nonjudgmental feedback and response to the students' reflections is important to them individually and to the service learning process as a whole. If journals are kept and you may read them, ask if you can write a response in the journal or on an attached piece of paper. In discussions, listen carefully and ask questions. Either way, it's important that you appreciate what's being revealed and discovered, and that you respond honestly with your own thoughts or with a reflective quote, poem, or passage from a book.

Student Leadership of Reflection. Students can become skilled at creating reflection prompts for their classmates. In some classrooms, pairs of students eagerly accept the assignment of leading reflection. Often, this leads to including music, making links to historical figures the class is studying, creating a game-show interaction, or some other innovative twist. Even second grade students delight in composing questions for their classmates to think about regarding the value and experience of service. Teachers can always review the plans and give students feedback prior to use.

Assessing Student Learning and Service

For students, the conclusion to the service learning process is demonstration. For you, it will most likely involve assessing the success of the actual activity, what your students learned, and the effectiveness of your planning and partnerships. This is a perpetual process and may be a little different for every project. Teachers continually look for ways to assess the service

learning process to ensure that it has produced appropriate learning for the students and real value for the community. Traditional assessment methods—essays, quizzes, research papers—can be used, along with other forms of inquiry and analysis, including review of documents from student portfolios or of products made, pre- and post-service questionnaires for students and others involved, student presentations or reflective writings, discussions with community partners, and comments from any recipients of the service provided. A conversation with colleagues not directly involved also can help teachers to review and improve the service learning process and find ways to strengthen the teaching methods used.

Whatever the method used, the assessment can focus on the following questions:

- *Student learning.* Were the defined content and skill objectives met? Were there any unforeseen outcomes? Did students show initiative or develop leadership skills? Were students able to reflect and place their experience in the larger context of community or society in general? Could students identify both their cognitive and affective growth?

- *Impact of the service.* Were students able to clearly state the need for and purpose of their service efforts? What contribution was made? Did the service help or hinder community efforts? What did the students accomplish? Is the partner agency or service recipient satisfied with the interaction? Have new relationships been formed? Were planned service programs, activities, or products completed?

- *The process.* How effective was project planning? Do you have ideas for specific areas you'd like to improve? For overall improvement? In future activities, how can students participate more and take greater ownership? How can you continue to develop community partnerships?

The two-part Assessment for Service Learning form on pages 49–50 provides a basic method for reviewing these issues. Part one covers student learning, the impact of the service, and the service learning process. Part two asks you to identify the methods used in each of the four stages and to assess whether each of the essential elements was present. You can select questions from the form to present to students so that they can participate in assessing their service learning experience. The Student Self-Evaluation form on page 51 lets students analyze their learning and contribution. Several service learning organizations have developed more sophisticated instruments for assessment. For more information on these, see the Resources listing (pages 216–217).

> "One can't believe impossible things."
>
> "I daresay you haven't had much practice," said the Queen. "When I was your age, I always did it for half-an-hour a day. Why, sometimes I've believed as many as six impossible things before breakfast."
>
> LEWIS CARROLL,
> *ALICE'S ADVENTURES IN WONDERLAND*

Telling Your Service Learning Story

Service learning has produced media-worthy stories all across the country. The act of publicizing service learning activities contains valuable learning opportunities. Publicizing service learning doesn't just take place at its conclusion—many moments throughout the process provide great stories. Post an attractive student-made flyer about an upcoming field trip to a watershed and other teachers may become inspired to get involved. A student article in a school paper while the project is in process may get other kids wanting to take part in similar "cool" activities and interact with the "real world." A summary news story in a local paper informs the public about what's happening within the school walls and about the positive impact students are having in the community.

Where can you tell your service learning story? Everywhere! Post the story on the Internet through state and national service learning organizations and newsletters (see Resources, pages 216–217). Find opportunities for students to give presentations to other students, to community groups, on cable or local access television, in organization newsletters, or on the radio. Local newspapers often seek good news, and sometimes students actually write the article. *The Kid's Guide to Social Action* (see page 196) includes a section called "Power Media Coverage and Advertising" with tips for getting attention and ways students can promote and publicize their projects both before and after they occur. Your service learning story can be a source of youth and community pride.

It's Time to Play—Know Your Audience

This activity can help upper elementary, middle, and high school students consider the best way to promote a project to a particular audience. For example, a tutoring project would be presented very differently to second graders than to a parent group. This activity makes that distinction extremely vivid.

For this role play, select a service project idea, preferably one that the students are enthusiastic about. Create small groups, with each one presenting information about the project to a different audience. Students can get started by brainstorming the reasons for addressing each audience. Here are some suggestions for potential audiences:

- elementary children (specify grade)
- middle school students
- high school parents
- faculty meeting
- community agency
- prospective funding source
- chamber of commerce
- news reporters

As students consider why they're addressing their particular audience, they should start thinking about what methods will present their message most effectively. Encourage students to be creative and dynamic in their presentations, and even to involve their audiences. Students may also use visual aids (posters), skits, or songs to enhance their presentations. After each group makes its presentation, allow time for constructive feedback from the class. The ideas that emerge can be put into practice to inform the broader community about service learning in action.

Curve Balls and Stumbling Blocks in Service Learning

It happens. After all the planning and collaboration and a phone confirmation just two days ago, your well-prepared fourth-grade students arrive at the senior center to begin their oral history project. A stop at the information desk reveals that your contact person has suddenly resigned and no replacement has been hired. The oral history project? "Sorry, we have nothing in place for you." This situation may seem extreme, but service efforts occasionally go awry. What do you do?

In the case of the "failed" visit to the senior center, the group convened in the parking lot for an emergency discussion. Students asked questions and looked for holes in their thinking and planning. After reviewing their contingency plans, this situation was determined to fall into the category of "truly out of our control." Deterred? No, only delayed. A team of students headed back to the senior center to ask for a brief meeting with the person responsible for scheduling special activities. After describing their plans and exercising their communication skills by using just a little persuasion, they established a new contact and made an agreement to reschedule.

Challenges found in service learning are, not surprisingly, very much like real-life challenges. When students work through these situations, they learn to create options, as well as to develop resiliency, problem-solving skills, persistence, and the concept of having a "plan B"—an important and practical concept. Students of all ages can contribute ideas and strategies that help to repair the moment and often improve the original plan. What better time than while in school to learn about meeting a stumbling block with thoughtfulness and resolve?

> We all want to live in the moment
> but there isn't enough time.
> DAVID ZASLOFF, MUSICIAN

A completely different kind of challenge you may face is aligning other school or organization programs and practices with service learning. For example, in an elementary school with a strong parent-run community service program, several parents resisted a classroom-based service learning program. The remedy was to educate everyone involved about the benefits of service learning and explain how to collaborate in the best interest of the students. In another school, children received stickers and prizes when they were "caught being good." Although the intention was to promote an ethic of service, children were actually refraining from engaging in kind acts unless they were certain an adult was watching and ready to dole out a reward. When administrators came to realize that the appropriate focus of service learning is the intrinsic reward that comes from cooperation and civic responsibility, the program was eliminated and not one child objected.

Some school administrators and teachers claim there is "no time for service learning" because of other priorities, such as improving math scores or creating a safer school climate. Service learning, however, can be an effective strategy to support many, if not most, important school priorities, including improved attendance, higher test scores, academic improvement, parent involvement, character education, and safety at school (reducing bullying, teasing, and name-calling). More information about these proven service learning results can be found throughout this book and in many of the resources on pages 216–217.

Other challenges you may encounter are more systemic. Is the school schedule flexible enough for service learning experiences? Are any funds available for supplies and transportation? Will the district apply for grants to support staff development and other professional opportunities? If the district or school policy requires that students stay on campus, will there be exceptions for classroom-related service learning outings? Many schools and districts with strong commitments to service learning establish advisory groups to unravel these and other issues. Models and prototypes can be found through state and national education agencies, other service learning organizations, and the Internet. Experienced service learning practitioners are usually more than willing to share ideas and resources.

> If you can't make a mistake,
> you can't make anything.
> MARVA N. COLLINS, EDUCATOR

1. Identify an existing program or activity to transform into authentic service learning.

- Identify an activity or project already existing on campus.

- Examine it for learning opportunities.

- Exchange resources and ideas with teachers, students, and community partners.

Example: Canned Food Drive

Before students began bringing in cans of food, teachers integrated meaningful academic activities related to the food drive in their class curriculum. Activities included studying nutrition, contacting the receiving agency to identify what foods were needed, visiting a food bank, encouraging student leadership in identifying the quality and kinds of foods to be provided (in partnership with the agency), having math students graph the food collected, reading books related to hunger and homelessness, and demonstrating to other schools how to connect the canned food drive to academics.

Bookshelf suggestions: *The Can-Do Thanksgiving, Soul Moon Soup*, and *The Other America*

2. Begin with standard curriculum, content, and skills, and find the natural extension into service.

- Identify the specific content and skill areas to be addressed.

- Select an area of emphasis that supports or adds to classroom learning and addresses learning objectives or state standards.

- Look for additional learning opportunities in other subject areas.

Example: Learning History through Discussion with Elder Partners

Teachers wanted students to be better informed about current events and to improve their listening and communication skills. This led to a partnership with a senior center and weekly interactions between students and older adults. Activities included studying recent historical events; learning about aging; practicing interviewing skills; interviewing older people to learn about their knowledge and experiences; collaborating on articles, stories, and photo essays; and displaying the results in the school and public library.

Bookshelf suggestions: *Stranger in the Mirror, Growing Older*, and *We Were There, Too! Young People in U.S. History*

3. From a theme or unit of study, identify content and skill connections.

- Begin with a broad theme or topic, often with obvious service implications.

- Identify specific content and skill areas.

- Select a service application.

Example: The Individual's Role in Society

As teachers identified ways for students to learn about the individual's role in society, they encouraged students to consider how they could participate in social action. Curriculum included reading nonfiction stories of contributions made by adults and young people to their communities, researching the needs of local agencies, providing regular assistance to one of the agencies, and publishing an informative pamphlet on the agency for young people.

Bookshelf suggestions: *Sisters in Strength: American Women Who Make a Difference, Generation Fix*, and *Free the Children: A Young Man's Personal Crusade Against Child Labor*

continued ⟶

Establishing Curricular Connections *continued*

4. Start with a student-identified need.

- Identify student skills, talents, and interests.

- Students define a problem, a need, and solutions.

- Students lead implementation as teacher facilitates, adding learning opportunities.

Example: Transform an Empty Lot into a Community Garden
At the beginning of a class, a student initiated a conversation about starting a community garden in an empty lot near the school. The teacher guided the students in identifying a local government agency to contact about the property, conducting Internet research to find funding sources, partnering with special needs youth at the school to plant and maintain the garden, and donating the harvest to a local shelter.

Bookshelf suggestions: *Seedfolks, Just Kids: Visiting a Class for Children with Special Needs,*
            and A Kid's Guide to Social Action

5. Start with a community-identified need.

- Community requests assistance, perhaps through an agency that has worked with the school before.

- Teacher, students, and community partners identify learning opportunities.

Example: Tutoring/literacy
A school received a flyer inviting the students to participate in a city-wide book collection to benefit local youth service agencies and organizations. Teachers in several grades collaborated on cross-age projects in which older students helped younger children to write and illustrate bilingual books on mutually agreed-on themes. The books were donated to libraries, hospitals, and day-care facilities; and student representatives served on a city committee regarding literacy.

Bookshelf suggestions: *La Mariposa, Just Juice,* and *Thank You, Mr. Falker*

Personal Inventory

Interests, skills, and talents—we all have them. What are they?

Interests are what you think about and what you would like to know more about—for example, outer space, popular music, or a historical event like the Civil War. Are you interested in animals, the movies, mysteries, or visiting faraway places? Do you collect anything?

Skills and talents have to do with things that you like to do or that you do easily or well. Is there an activity you especially like? Do you have a favorite subject in school? Do you sing, play the saxophone, or study ballet? Do you know more than one language? Can you cook? Do you have a garden? Do you prefer to paint pictures or play soccer? Do you have any special computer abilities?

Work with a partner and take turns interviewing each other to identify your interests, skills, and talents and to find out how you have helped and been helped by others.

Interests: I like to learn and think about . . .

_____

_____

Skills and talents: I can . . .

_____

_____

Being helpful: Describe a time when you helped someone.

_____

_____

Receiving help: Describe a time when someone helped you.

_____

_____

_____

Taking Action in Our Community

Step 1: Think about the needs in our community. Make a list.

Step 2: Identify what you know.

- Select one community need:
- What is the cause?
- Who is helping?
- What are some ways we can help?

Step 3: Find out more.

- What do we need to know about this community need and who is helping?

- How can we find out?

Step 4: Plan for action.

- To help our community, we will:

- To make this happen, we will take on these responsibilities:

Who	will do **what**	by **when**	Resources needed

Service Learning Proposal

Student names: _____

Teacher: _____

School: _____

Address: _____

Phone: _____ Fax: _____ Email: _____

Project name: _____

Need—Why this plan is needed:

Purpose—How this plan will help:

Participation—Who will help, and what they will do:

    Students: _____

    Teachers: _____

    Other adults: _____

    Organizations or groups: _____

Outcomes—What we expect to happen as the result of our work:

How we will check outcomes—What evidence we will collect and how we will use it:

Resources—What we need to get the job done, such as supplies (itemize on back):

Signatures:

The Four Stages of Service Learning

Preparation

With guidance from their teacher, students:

- identify a need.

- draw upon previously acquired skills and knowledge.

- acquire new information through a variety of means and methods.

- analyze the underlying problem.

- collaborate with community partners.

- develop a plan that encourages responsibility.

- recognize the integration of service and learning.

- become ready to provide meaningful service.

- define realistic parameters for implementation.

Action

Through direct service, indirect service, research, or advocacy, students take action that:

- has value, purpose, and meaning.

- uses previously learned and newly acquired academic skills and knowledge.

- offers unique learning experiences.

- has real consequences.

- offers a safe environment to learn, to make mistakes, and to succeed.

Reflection

During systematic reflection, the teacher or students guide the process using various modalities, such as role play, discussion, and journal writing. Participating students:

- describe what happened.

- examine the difference it made.

- discuss thoughts and feelings.

- place experience in a larger context.

- consider project improvements.

- generate ideas.

- identify questions.

- receive feedback.

Demonstration

Students demonstrate skills, insights, and outcomes to an outside group. Methods used might include:

- reporting to peers, faculty, parents, and/or community members.

- writing articles or letters to local newspapers regarding issues of public concern.

- creating a publication or Web site that helps others to learn from the students' experiences.

- making presentations and performances.

- creating visual art forms, such as murals.

The Essential Elements of Service Learning

Integrated Learning

Students **learn** skills and content through varied modalities; the service informs the content, and the content informs the service.

Meeting Genuine Needs

Students **identify** and **learn about a recognized community need.** Student actions are **valued** by the community and have **real consequences** while offering opportunities to **apply** newly acquired academic skills and knowledge.

Youth Voice and Choice

Students experience **significant age-appropriate challenges** involving tasks that require thinking, initiative, and problem solving as they demonstrate **responsibility** and **decision making** in an environment safe enough to allow them to make mistakes and to succeed.

Collaborative Efforts

Students participate in the development of **partnerships** and **share responsibility** with community members, parents, organizations, and other students. These relationships afford **opportunities to interact** with people of diverse backgrounds and experience, resulting in mutual respect, understanding, and appreciation.

Reciprocity

Student benefits evolve through **mutual teaching and learning, action, or influence** between all participants in the learning and service experience; this reciprocity extends to relationships between institutions as well as relationships between people.

Civic Responsibility

When young people have a role in improving society, working for social justice, and caring for the environment, then they truly understand the **concept of democracy.** Students recognize how participation and the ability to respond to authentic needs improves the quality of life in the community, which may lead to a lifelong **ethic of service and civic engagement.**

Planning for Service Learning

Grade level: _____

CONTENT—LEARNING ABOUT:

SERVICE NEED:

SERVICE IDEA:

PREPARATION:

ACTION:

REFLECTION:

DEMONSTRATION:

YOUTH VOICE and CHOICE:

NOTES:

CURRICULAR CONNECTIONS:

❑ *English/Language Arts:*

❑ *Social Studies/History:*

❑ *Mathematics:*

❑ *Science:*

❑ *Languages:*

❑ *Art and Music:*

❑ *Other:*

SKILL DEVELOPMENT:

BOOKS:

COMMUNITY CONTACTS:

Planning for Service Learning: *Example (Elementary)*

Grade level: __3__

CONTENT—LEARNING ABOUT:

- Ecology
- Composting
- Waste reduction
- Recycling

SERVICE NEED: There is too much waste in our community that could be recycled; if the students and community are informed on options about composting, they can choose to participate.

SERVICE IDEA: Give It to the Worms
Promote composting at school and in the community.

PREPARATION: Study ecosystems, hear guest speaker from Integrative Waste Management Board, create school map and chart to record waste quantities and reduction, prepare video presentation and talk on ecology and school waste management.

ACTION: Install compost and worm bins, monitor school food waste, donate soil from compost to school garden and nearby senior living community (gardening by elder residents), host parent information night with site tour and composting lesson.

REFLECTION: Make journals out of recycled paper at school with regular entries, weekly meetings to discuss and review project success, annual discussion and review of progress with partners at IWM (Integrative Waste Management Board).

DEMONSTRATION: Distribute monthly copies of newsletter "Warm Ways" to school community, participate in Chinese New Year parade as a giant worm while handing out informational pamphlets on worm bins and composting called "Give It to the Worms!"

YOUTH VOICE and CHOICE: Since the project is ongoing, each year students add a new component based on their ideas (for example, making journals, being worm in parade).

NOTES: This activity began small with one teacher and grew to involve more; this plan shows what evolved over four years.

CURRICULAR CONNECTIONS:

☒ *English/Language Arts:* Design a campaign to promote use of school composting and reduce waste at school, write video script, write letter to parents describing project, write "Warm Ways" newsletter, plan and write "Give It to the Worms" brochure

☒ *Social Studies/History:* Study Rachel Carson

☒ *Mathematics:* Graph waste quantities

☒ *Science:* Study life cycles; review ecosystems, waste reduction, and composting; maintain compost and worm bin with signage written by children

☒ *Languages:* Spanish-language signs by compost and worm bin

☒ *Art and Music:* Design poster campaign

☒ *Other:* Video and computer technology

SKILL DEVELOPMENT:

- Paragraph construction
- Graphing
- Time management

BOOKS:

Compost Critters

I Want to Be an Environmentalist

Compost! Growing Gardens from Your Garbage

You Are the Earth: Know the Planet So You Can Make It Better

Rachel Carson

COMMUNITY CONTACTS:

Integrative Waste Management Board

Chinese New Year Planning Committee

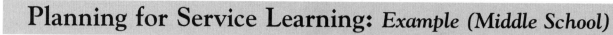

Grade level: __6–7 Social Studies__

CONTENT—LEARNING ABOUT:

- Immigration to the United States
- Process of becoming a citizen
- Resettlement of refugees
- Civic involvement

SERVICE NEED: Becoming citizens requires dedication and hard work that deserves to be honored by the community; to increase tolerance and understanding between cultures.

SERVICE IDEA: In Honor of New Citizens
Sponsoring a citizenship swearing-in ceremony at school.

PREPARATION: Meet with Immigration and Naturalization Services (INS), read about countries of origin of people being sworn in, plan the event, get food donations, decorate the auditorium and library, arrange for coverage by educational television channel.

ACTION: Set up rooms, greet guests, interview the new citizens, take photographs.

REFLECTION: Journal writing, student-led discussion groups, identification of need for written materials and resources for children of these families, letter to INS to share what has been learned and ideas for next time, forms sent to partner agencies for feedback, unsolicited letters received from new citizen families thanking students for meaningful and special event.

DEMONSTRATION: Compilation of interviews and photographs for each family; making "welcome kits" for the children of the immigrant families that include: cartoon-style map of the area, places to go for entertainment and sports, lists of after-school and weekend youth activities, translation guide for youth expressions, small journal, and pen.

YOUTH VOICE and CHOICE: Develop the idea, establish partnerships, organize into committees, plan interviews, design and make transition kits for children of the families.

NOTES: The project evolved from student interest and initiative resulting from an Ellis Island simulation and learning more about their community as a resettlement area for people from all over the world. Partnerships with INS and city offices were essential components.

CURRICULAR CONNECTIONS:

- ☒ *English/Language Arts:* Writing letters for donations and thank-you letters, keeping journals, reading literature about the immigrant experience, writing press releases, vocabulary

- ☒ *Social Studies/History:* Participate in Ellis Island simulation, hear guest speaker from INS, research countries of origin of 32 people being sworn in at the ceremony—history, current events, culture (foods, music, traditions), interview immigrants about their transition to citizenship (permission received)

- ❏ *Mathematics:*

- ❏ *Science:*

- ☒ *Languages:* Identify greetings in languages of countries studied, including the correct pronunciations; use greeting on banners

- ☒ *Art and Music:* Collect music from many cultures, school choral group participates by singing a medley with cultural references

- ❏ *Other:*

SKILL DEVELOPMENT:

- Organization and planning
- Interviewing
- Teamwork
- Letter writing
- Problem solving

BOOKS:

The Skirt

The Middle of Everywhere: The World's Refugees Come to Our Town (excerpts)

Stella: On the Edge of Popularity

Behind the Mountains

The Whispering Cloth: A Refugee's Story

The Kid's Guide to Social Action

Immigration: How Should It Be Controlled?

A Very Important Day

COMMUNITY CONTACTS:

Immigration and Naturalization Services

City multicultural program

Educational TV channel

Portland Press (newspapers)

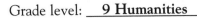

Planning for Service Learning: *Example (High School)*

Grade level: __9 Humanities__

CONTENT—LEARNING ABOUT:

- Interpersonal relationships
- Civic participation
- Child Psychology
- Bookmaking
- Being role models

SERVICE NEED: There is a reciprocal learning that occurs in mentoring relationships between older and younger children with mutual benefits; young children need encouragement to read and write.

SERVICE IDEA: Book Buddies
Instruct young children in bookmaking and collaborate on making books for the community.

PREPARATION: Write reflections on childhood and favorite books; interactive workshop with child psychologist about learning styles and Howard Gardner's eight types of intelligence; read children's books; in small groups, discuss methods of working with young children; design lessons reflecting different types of intelligence; reach consensus on theme for books ("friendship" chosen to combat bullying); get resources for bookmaking; learn bookbinding techniques; arrange logistics and transportation.

ACTION: Visit kindergarten class three times: (1) get acquainted with children and read books, (2) discuss book ideas on theme of friendship and begin story development, (3) write and illustrate story. Copies of books given to children and to school and public libraries.

REFLECTION: Students have peer "journal partners" who read entries and respond; teacher reads and gives feedback weekly. Class discussion follows each visit, with role plays and problem solving.

DEMONSTRATION: Present project with the elementary children at the school district service learning advisory committee meeting.

YOUTH VOICE and CHOICE: Revise project, find partner classroom, write proposal, make phone calls, get donations, design activities.

NOTES: This project began as a service requirement of the department. The initial plan to read books to elementary children one time changed, through student initiative and planning, into a three-week comprehensive program. An ongoing relationship was established between the classrooms and the schools.

CURRICULAR CONNECTIONS:

☒ *English/Language Arts:* Proposal writing; reading and analyzing children's books for content, format, and style; book writing; letter writing for donations or reduced cost for supplies

☒ *Social Studies/History:* Child psychology

☒ *Mathematics:* Budget management for funds received from school, literacy grant

☐ *Science:*

☒ *Languages:* Prepare for working with bilingual children with assistance from a Spanish language teacher; several books are bilingual

☒ *Art and Music:* Advanced art students at school make presentations on illustration to make students aware of various styles; create illustrations with children; bookbinding

☒ *Other:* Computer skills to create a design and template for the book-making process

SKILL DEVELOPMENT:

- Organization
- Leadership
- Planning
- Writing in different styles—proposals, thank-you letters, stories
- Communication—phone calls for supplies, interaction with elementary teachers, interaction in small planning groups, partnerships with children

BOOKS:

The Sissy Duckling

Toestomper and the Caterpillars

Margarite y Margarita (bilingual)

La Mariposa

Hey, Little Ant!

COMMUNITY CONTACTS:

Will Rogers Elementary School

Kelly Paper Supplies

Service Learning Advisory Committee

Planning for Service Learning: *Example (Special Needs)*

Grade level: __Preschool–8 Special Needs**__

CONTENT—LEARNING ABOUT:

- Our neighborhood
- Elders
- Acts of kindness and generosity
- Life cycle of plants

SERVICE NEED: Two populations are in close proximity with no interaction; this could be mutually beneficial.

SERVICE IDEA: Being Good Neighbors
Giving flowering plant pots to older people at a senior residential center

PREPARATION: Study about plants, grow plants from seeds to seedlings, paint and decorate pots with glitter and ribbons, work with mainstream teens in high school environmental science class to plant pots.

ACTION: Deliver plants, interact with older people at senior residence, give copies of stories to the senior center.

REFLECTION: Staff reflect on the activity and discuss each child's level of participation and development. Students write about or give dictation to teachers about their experiences.

DEMONSTRATION: The project's success leads to a follow-up activity the next weekend in which the children and their families help plant an outdoor garden in a courtyard at the senior residence. Many seniors and staff help or watch and interact with the children. Most parents noted this was the first time their children had participated in community service.

YOUTH VOICE and CHOICE: Making choices is a significant skill for autistic children; this project affords many opportunities: selecting colors, choosing plants to grow, asking to plant pots for their families.

NOTES: The program is individualized to student ability. The school is on a high school campus. All of the students with autism visited the environmental science class and the high school students came to their classrooms. Some students requested extra pots to plant for their parents and gave them a book of stories written about their service and learning experience.

CURRICULAR CONNECTIONS:

- ☒ *English/Language Arts:* Learn about life cycle of plants through story books and flannel board activities, make sequence books about life cycles of plants, practice what to say with the older people

- ☒ *Social Studies/History:* Learn about the community (the high school and the senior residential facility); discuss community involvement, service, and generosity

- ☒ *Mathematics:* Measure plant growth and chart data

- ☒ *Science:* Plant seedlings in plastic bags to watch seeds sprout, transfer seedlings to soil, draw diagrams of plants

- ❑ *Languages:*

- ☒ *Art and Music:* Draw and label pictures, write picture stories

- ☒ *Other:* Computer skills—typing stories

SKILL DEVELOPMENT:

- Art—cutting, pasting, tracing
- Handwriting
- Drawing
- Making choices
- Staying on task
- Transitioning from one setting to another
- Social communication and interaction

BOOKS:

Jack's Garden

Bud

A Harvest of Color: Growing a Vegetable Garden

COMMUNITY CONTACTS:

High school environmental science teacher

Elder care facility

**Children with autism, assisted in part by high school students grades 10 and 11.

Community Contact Information

Name of agency: _____

Key individual: _____

Address: _____

Phone: _____ Fax: _____ Email: _____

Location (note proximity to school):

_____

Service needs (note ongoing versus short-term):

_____

_____

Learning opportunities:

_____

_____

_____

Date contact made: _____

Contact made by: _____

Follow-up information (record all calls, visits, etc.; continue on back or new sheet as necessary):

_____

_____

_____

_____

_____

Community Response Form

Name of agency: _____

Address: _____

Phone: _____ Fax: _____ Email: _____

Contact person: _____

Teacher/class: _____

Date of visit: _____

Purpose of visit: _____

Please respond to the following questions to help us learn from today's service experience and better meet your agency's needs in the future.

What were the benefits of today's experience for your agency?

What suggestions do you have for future visits or interactions?

What service needs do you have that our school could assist with in the future?

What did you and others at your agency learn about children and our school that you did not know before?

Additional comments are most appreciated.

Thank you! Please return this form to the teacher listed above at the following address:

Our Service Project

Our names: _____

Teacher: _____

School: _____

Address: _____

Phone: _____ Fax: _____ Email: _____

Project name: _____

Our idea: _____

This helps others by: _____

Student names and jobs:

My name _____ My job _____

My name _____ My job _____

My name _____ My job _____

Others who will help:

  Students: _____

  Teachers: _____

  Other adults: _____

  Organizations: _____

Supplies needed: _____

Our expectations: _____

Signatures:

Project Promotion—Turning Ideas into Action

What We Already Know

Service idea:

Need—the community issue:

Community partners:

New Ideas and Possibilities

New community alliances: Think outside the box

Evidence: Keeping track of our activities, accomplishments, and outcomes

Donations: What is needed (e.g., flyers, T-shirts, balloons)? Who might donate items?

Media madness: Press releases, radio spots, cable access, news stories

Fund-raising ideas and resources

Presentation opportunities: School and community events, organizations

Follow-up

Roles and responsibilities: Who will do what?

Sequence for Reflection

Use this document as a checklist and to record your own reflections.

In Preparation

As the service learning process begins, find out what students know: What beliefs and assumptions are already in place? Where and how were they learned? What do students expect to happen? What do they expect to learn, and how do they expect to feel? Depending on the situation, you may give students a thought or question to take with them into the service experience. This may encourage them to be more observant or heighten their awareness of a particular need or action being taken.

What happened:

During Action

Be observant. What are the students paying attention to? What comments do you overhear? What behaviors do you see? You may make notes and refer to them later, during the reflection that follows the service. During on-the-spot reflection, students sometimes have insights or make recommendations that improve their experience and the impact of their contributions.

What happened:

Following Service

Vary the reflection methods. As students become more adept, ask them to design a reflection process for themselves and their classmates. Before discussing the service, ask students to first write their responses to discussion prompts. This can protect the integrity of each student's experience and assure that everyone has something to contribute. Have students draw upon their reflections during demonstration of their service learning.

What happened:

Feedback

Provide *nonjudgmental* feedback. If you may read journals, ask if you can write a response in the journal or on an attached piece of paper. Listen well. Ask questions. Appreciate what is being revealed and discovered.

What happened:

Four Square Reflection Tool

WHAT HAPPENED?	**HOW DO I FEEL?**
IDEAS?	**QUESTIONS?**

Assessment for Service Learning: *Part One*

Service Learning Project: _____

Respond to the questions that are relevant to your service learning activities.

Student Learning

- Were the defined content and skill objectives met?

- Were there any unforeseen outcomes?

- Did students show initiative or develop leadership skills?

- Were students able to reflect and place their experience in the larger context of community or society in general?

- Could students identify both their cognitive and affective growth?

Impact of the Service

- Were students able to explicitly state the need and purpose for their service efforts?

- What contribution was made?

- How did the service help or hinder community improvement efforts?

- Is the partner agency satisfied with the interaction?

- Have new relationships been formed?

- Were planned service programs, activities, or products completed?

Process

- How did this project affect or change how teachers teach and how children learn?

- How effective was project planning?

- What are your ideas for overall improvement?

- In future activities, how can students take greater ownership?

- How can community partnerships be improved or strengthened?

Assessment for Service Learning: *Part Two*

Service Learning Project: _____

Identify what methods were used for each stage and whether each element was present.

Stages of Service Learning

Preparation

- Research

- Literature

- Field trips

- Interviews

- Other:

Action

- Direct service

- Indirect service

- Research

- Advocacy

Reflection

- Discussion

- Journals

- Role play

- Other:

Demonstration

- Presentation

- Performance

- Article

- Other:

Elements of Service Learning

- **Integrated learning**
  Example of curricular connections:

- **Meeting genuine needs**
  Example of students verifying need:

- **Youth voice and choice**
  Example of student responsibility and decision making:

- **Collaborative efforts**
  Example of partnership/shared responsibility:

- **Reciprocity**
  Example of reciprocity in relationships between persons and between institutions:

- **Civic responsibility**
  Example of students' increased awareness of their role in community improvement and/or students' knowledge of civic institutions:

Student Self-Evaluation

Name: _____ Date: _____

Service Learning Project: _____

Learning

- What information did you learn in preparing to do service?

- What skills did you develop through the activities?

- How did this project help you to better understand ideas or subjects we have been studying?

- Through this service learning project, what did you learn about:

  - yourself?

  - working with others, including people in your class?

  - your community?

- How will you use what you learned in this experience?

Service

- What was the need for your service effort?

- What contribution did you make?

- What overall contribution was made by your class?

- How did your service affect the community?

Process

- How did you and other students help with project planning?

- In what ways did you make decisions and solve problems?

- Were there any differences between the initial project plans and what you actually did?

- What ideas do you have for improving any part of the project?

CHAPTER 3

THE THEME CHAPTERS AND THE SERVICE LEARNING BOOKSHELF

Now that you've learned what service learning is and how you can use it, it's time to get started. You're ready to explore common themes for service and literary resources you can use with your students. Part 2 of this guide consists of chapters on eleven different themes that are commonly selected for service learning activities and were identified through interactions with teachers and students from across the United States. In these theme chapters, you'll find several tools, activities, ideas, and resources that will help you create and tailor service learning projects around a given theme. A primary part of each theme chapter is the Service Learning Bookshelf, which contains a cross-section of books for different ages you can use with your students. This chapter will explain the structure and resources of the theme chapters and how you can use their content and ideas to enhance your service learning activities.

Getting Oriented:
About the Thematic Chapters

As you consider designing a service learning project, you may be wondering:

- What social concerns are most often addressed through service learning?

- What activities can help prepare my students for service?

- What are some tried-and-true service learning ideas?

- What books can be used to teach young people, motivate them to read, and inspire them to action?

The thematic chapters answer these questions with a wealth of ideas and resources for service learning in action. The theme chapters address: AIDS awareness and education, animals in danger,

community safety, elders, environment, gardening, hunger and homelessness, immigrants, literacy, social change, and special needs and disabilities. For convenience, the topics are arranged alphabetically.

Each thematic chapter includes:

- **Introductory comments** regarding the theme and service learning. This will provide you with basic information about the theme and give you an idea of why it's important.

- **Quotes for inspiration.** These quotes may inspire you or you may find ways to use them with your students.

- **Activities** to help you prepare your students for service learning on the theme. Some provoke preliminary thought and discussion on the theme, while other activities promote learning and skills development related to the theme. The activities usually address all age ranges and many of the activities can be adapted to different grade levels and settings.

- **Organizations and online resources** specific to the content of the theme rather than being general to service learning. They will direct you to reputable organizations or information-rich Web sites that can help you and your students get started on research and planning.

- **A curriculum web** that provides you with a wide sampling of cross-curricular connections you can make specific to the theme.

- **Examples of service learning** that have been successfully carried out by elementary, middle, and high school students. You may find one idea or resource that is just what you've been looking for, or an example might spark another idea that better suits the needs of your students and community. Note that grade levels are given as a reference, but most project ideas transcend age groups and can be adapted to suit younger or older students.

- **A Service Learning Bookshelf** for each theme. Here, you will find a comprehensive listing of literature that helps to connect classroom learning and literacy with service to the community. These Bookshelves contain more than three hundred book titles that are annotated and categorized for easy identification, reference, and use.

As you use the activities in the theme chapters of Part 2, continue to use Part 1 as a reference, especially if the practice of service learning is relatively new, if you are developing teacher training programs to provide others with service learning knowledge, or simply as a reminder of the four stages and the essential elements of service learning. The reproducible pages at the end of Chapter 2 can give you a jumpstart in planning and organizing as you continue to apply the key concepts.

About the Service Learning Bookshelf

Clear off a shelf and start collecting! The Service Learning Bookshelf in each thematic chapter is filled with nonfiction books, picture books, and novels selected to enhance your service learning activities. Included on each bookshelf are titles that:

- describe the service experiences of others
- introduce important social themes
- tell stories from history
- increase student interest in reading
- promote critical thinking and discussion
- prepare students to interact with diverse populations
- enhance the experiences students have in the community
- inspire students to serve

Whether read aloud or silently, the books included in each bookshelf are guaranteed to make you and your students smile, laugh, cry, think, wonder, dream, plan, hope, and act.

Well-written books such as those in the bookshelf lists provide many benefits. They tap into students' curiosity and desire to know. They can give students the information they need to move to the next level of competency or inspire them to consider important topics. Authors model how to write, how to think creatively, and how to tell one's own story. When the story has at its heart a concern shared by the students, it can give them a range of possibilities for their own actions.

> Reading is to the mind what exercise is to the body.
> JOSEPH ADDISON, POET

Reading is clearly the foundation of learning, but books can only go so far. In our classrooms, we want books that inspire students to action—that provide not just knowledge but *motivation* for service. Each book on the Service Learning Bookshelf has been selected with this in mind. The bookshelves hold a myriad of titles that belong in the hands of students and that are resources for teachers, program staff, or family members who want to introduce a topic, expand knowledge, or develop an inquiring mind.

Books as Catalysts for Action

Books can lead students to consider many questions:

- What do I have in common with these characters?

- How are the characters' actions changing how the characters think about themselves?

- What actions are making a difference in the lives of others?

- Are any of the problems or conflicts in the story occurring in my life or the lives of people I know or see?

- What questions do I have after reading this book?

continued ——▶

- What can we do to address problems in our community that are similar to the ones described in the book?

  Use these questions with your students to deepen their relationship with the text, as well as to stimulate their thinking and concern for community needs and issues. You can adapt the questions for writing assignments, discussion groups, or journal entries during reflection. The books listed in the theme bookshelves are ideal for activities that promote critical thinking.

What's on the Shelf? Features of the Service Learning Bookshelf

Each bookshelf includes the following:

- An annotated bibliography of works related to the chapter theme. The list is arranged under the general categories of nonfiction books, picture books, and fiction. Nonfiction and fiction selections include the book's length and recommended grade levels.

- A quick reference chart that classifies the books according to topics within the theme so you can find the books you want more easily.

- Recommendations made by service learning practitioners, with ideas for service learning activities.

- Author interviews to provide the "story behind the story" and more service connections.

This section will describe these features in more detail and start suggesting ways you can use them. Two other important aspects of titles in the Bookshelves are also discussed: the artwork and illustrations featured in many books and special selections written by young authors.

A note about bookshelf titles: Books do go out of print—even our favorites. Almost all of the bookshelf titles listed were in print at the time of publication. A few out-of-print exceptions were included because of their outstanding content and presentation; these books are identified as out of print in the bookshelves. Libraries and used books stores—including those accessible via the Internet—are good sources for these out-of-print gems.

Nonfiction Books

Nonfiction books can cover a wide range of topics, coming in a variety of forms from straightforward narrative prose to songs—with everything in between. They can be collections of plays, songs, and poems such as *Cootie Shots: Theatrical Inoculations Against Bigotry for Kids, Parents and Teachers* (Community Safety Bookshelf), a collection that promotes tolerance. They can be photo essays such as *Rosie, A Visiting Dog's Story* (Special Needs and Disabilities Bookshelf), which is a series of photo essays of a pet bringing joy to infirm children and elders. They can even take the form of a coloring book such as *Conversation Starters As Easy As ABC 123: How to Start Conversations with People Who Have Memory Loss* (Elders Bookshelf).

History is frequently a topic for nonfiction books, and a number of nonfiction books link the study of history with events in the present day. *Orphan Train Rider: One Boy's True Story* (Hunger and Homelessness Bookshelf) describes how orphaned or abandoned children from the eastern states were sent westward on trains to be placed in homes between 1854 and 1929. *Linda Brown, You Are Not Alone: The Brown v. Board of Education Decision* (Social Change Bookshelf) presents different perspectives and insights about a historical event that impacts students' lives in school every day. *When Plague Strikes: The Black Death, Smallpox, AIDS* (AIDS Education and Awareness Bookshelf) shows the parallels linking three epidemics.

Other books describe acts of service, as in *Nights of the Pufflings* (Animals in Danger Bookshelf), which tells how young children rescue small birds from the perils of the city and release them over the ocean waves. Youth activists are profiled in *Generation Fix* (Social Change Bookshelf). And students will be amazed to read how a young activist took on international child labor in *Free the Children: A Young Man's Personal Crusade Against Child Labor* (Social Change Bookshelf).

> Read books. They are good for us.
> NATALIE GOLDBERG, AUTHOR

Picture Books

Picture books can be read and enjoyed by people of all ages. The language and artwork convey messages that transcend age. As a result, picture books can be effective tools for teaching sophisticated concepts and issues at all grade levels. Older students may be surprised to learn that complex social issues and ideas—such as memory loss or the struggles of refugee children forced into manual labor—can be presented to and understood by young children through the medium of picture books.

Most people like to be read to, yet we usually stop reading aloud to students once they reach middle school. Hearing a story read aloud is different from reading to one's self. In a class environment, reading a picture book aloud creates a common experience for discussion and stimulates interest or curiosity regarding an important subject. High school students have been known to sit on the edge of their seats listening to *Too Far Away to Touch* (AIDS Education and Awareness Bookshelf) and *Stranger in the Mirror* (Elders Bookshelf) and laugh out loud when they hear *The Wartville Wizard* (Environment Bookshelf), a hilarious tale of litter flying back to stick to the litterer.

Needless to say, younger children devour picture books, enjoying the pranks of *Stella Louella's Runaway Book* (Literacy Bookshelf) and the thoughtful revelations in *My Diary from Here to There/Mi diario de aquí hasta allá* (Immigrants Bookshelf). These titles also model for students how to write and construct their own stories of service to the community.

Books can also have a direct connection to the service activity. Meeting a young child with spina bifida in *All Kinds of Friends, Even Green!* (Special Needs and Disabilities Bookshelf) is an ideal way to prepare students of any age to interact with special needs youth.

Many picture books provide excellent resources for finding subject matter that engages and motivates children. The importance of preserving our natural habitat, for example, is conveyed in a folktale from India, *The People Who Hugged the Trees* (Environment Bookshelf). There is wonderful storytelling, weaving imagination and reality, in *La Mariposa* (Literacy Bookshelf). These and other titles are useful for tutoring and language development as well as encouraging young people to learn more about their themes.

Fiction

Fiction runs the gamut from easy-to-read beginning chapter books to young adult novels. These selections are well-written stories that challenge and compel the reader. In *Hope Was Here* (Social Change Bookshelf), for example, a teen moves to a new city and finds herself embroiled in a hot political campaign that may rip apart her community. In *Seedfolks* (Gardening Bookshelf), each chapter represents the voice of a different community member bringing his or her seeds and story to a neighborhood garden, acknowledging real struggles and personal dreams. *A Corner of the Universe* (Special Needs and Disabilities Bookshelf) tells the story of a young girl stunned to meet her uncle when he returns after years in a residential program. *Dream Freedom* (Social Change) is a sophisticated interweaving of many lives affected by the slave trade in the Sudan and a classroom of students in the United States working to reach across an ocean to help. Some novels are ideal to read aloud. For example, *Judy Moody Saves the World* (Environment Bookshelf) reinforces the benefits of teamwork. When *Butterflies and Lizards, Beryl and Me* (Gardening Bookshelf) is read to a group of students, it provokes conversations about loneliness, teasing and ridicule, and the needs of elders in the community, all within the metaphor of plants growing. Many of the suggested books integrate English and language arts with other academic subjects and develop awareness, sensitivity, and understanding about the human condition and our society.

While high school reading assignments often neglect the riches to be found in young adult literature, hopefully this list will encourage you to look for—or remind you of—the jewels that can be found in this category of books. "Young adult" literature is so named for a good reason. The stories reflect the challenges, dilemmas, and relationships particularly faced by this age group. They offer the complexity and conflicts that often mirror the situations students observe and experience. Whether you choose *Big Mouth and Ugly Girl* by Joyce Carol Oates (Community Safety Bookshelf) or *Before We Were Free* by Julia Alvarez (Social Change Bookshelf), or one of the many other selections, treat yourself and read a young adult novel. You may be surprised at how compelling you find the story and that the power of the words convinces you to include the book and others like it in your service learning curriculum.

Looking It Up:
The Bookshelf Charts

The chart in each bookshelf is arranged by topics commonly associated with the theme and can help you quickly find books that are appropriate for your particular service learning activities. For example, the chart in the Community Safety chapter groups books under the topics of personal safety, bullying, conflict resolution, local violence, hate crimes, the world stage, and community building. The books under the topics generally include a cross-section of nonfiction, picture books, and fiction and encompass a broad range of reading levels. Books that feature young people in service-providing roles are flagged in the chart. Books that can be used for more than one theme are cross-referenced to where they appear in other themes. Out-of-print—but still worthy—titles are also indicated.

Recommendations from the Field:
The Classics and Beyond

"I would like to involve my students in service learning, but we are reading *Romeo and Juliet* this semester. What could I do?"

Substitute any title you like—*Walk Two Moons, Tuck Everlasting, Fahrenheit 451*—and you have identified a quandary for many teachers: how to connect the required classroom literature with service learning. To address this issue, I asked many service learning colleagues—both adults and youth—from around the country to choose and read a curriculum classic and make recommendations for how it could be used

in service learning. Reviewers came from across the service learning spectrum and include a fourth-grade student, a college freshman, parent/child teams, K–12 teachers, university professors, program directors, and policy makers. One high school contributor is autistic.

Most of the books they reviewed are familiar titles, like the kindergarten favorite *Make Way for Ducklings* (Animals in Danger Bookshelf) and the high school classic *Siddhartha* (Community Safety Bookshelf). Other books stretch the idea of "classics" to include more modern literature that tells a significant story in writing of high quality. Book selection occurred in a variety of ways. Based on research, I provided a list of recommended titles. Many reviewers suggested their own favorite books. Several people said this project gave them a chance to pick up a book they had always meant to read. One contributor was relieved to finally finish reading a lengthy novel that had escaped her during high school; she followed up with a letter to her high school teacher saying, "I finally read the book!"

Each of the recommendations provides a summary of the story and offers ideas for service learning connections. Many include questions to initiate discussion regarding service-related themes. Look for these books in most of the thematic chapters, labeled as a "Recommendation from the Field." All of these titles are gathered together for your easy reference in the chart on the next page.

Is one of your favorite books missing? If so, you have a perfect opportunity to create your own service learning classic connection.

Recommendations from the Field

Elementary

Animals in Danger	*Make Way for Ducklings*	(page 85)
Community Safety	*Harry Potter and the Sorcerer's Stone*	(page 100)
Elders	*The Hundred Penny Box*	(page 117)
Environment	*Island of the Blue Dolphins*	(page 133)
Immigrants	*The Skirt*	(page 170)
Literacy	*A Series of Unfortunate Events*	(page 184)
	The Library Card	(page 183)
Social Change	*The Little Engine That Could*	(page 198)
	Walk Two Moons	(page 200)

Middle School

Community Safety	*Holes*	(page 101)
Elders	*Tuck Everlasting*	(page 118)
Immigrants	*Dragonwings*	(page 169)

High School

Community Safety	*Romeo and Juliet*	(page 102)
	Siddhartha	(page 102)
Elders	*The Bonesetter's Daughter*	(page 117)
Hunger and Homelessness	*Grapes of Wrath*	(page 155)
	Nickel and Dimed: On (Not) Getting By in America	(page 154)
Literacy	*Fahrenheit 451*	(page 182)
Social Change	*In the Time of the Butterflies*	(page 199)
Special Needs and Disabilities	*Of Mice and Men*	(page 212)

Author Interviews

Have you ever been curious about the story behind the story? Would you sometimes like to pick up the phone, call an author, and ask, "So why did you have the *Wartville Wizard* get the power over trash?" Perhaps you would ask the author to discuss the evolution of the character Nissa in *The Strength of Saints* (Literacy Bookshelf) as she considers consolidating two libraries in a racially divided city. Or perhaps you would ask what caused Richard Michelson to tell the story of sustaining language and tradition in *Too Young for Yiddish* (Elders Bookshelf).

These questions and more are what led to me doing just that—getting in touch with the authors of books I liked and interviewing them. Each interview gives a window into the process that goes into creating a story. Each demonstrates the writer's intelligence and desire to reach others, and their passion for the written word. All of the writers offer thought-provoking insights into the writing process and the subject matter, and some even describe service learning ideas they've heard about from readers.

As the interviews illustrate, there are as many different approaches to writing and reasons for telling a story as there are writers themselves. Francisco Jiménez's memoirs of a young migrant farmworker in *The Circuit* and *Breaking Through* (Immigrants Bookshelf) share the travails faced by his family as they struggled to survive financially. *Hey, Little Ant!* (Community Safety Bookshelf) began as a song written by a father and daughter team, Phillip and Hannah Hoose. In *Wanda's Roses* (Gardening Bookshelf), Pat Brisson wanted to tell of a girl willing to work hard to make her dream come true. The loss of a dear friend inspired Lesléa Newman to write *Too Far Away to Touch* (AIDS Education and Awareness Bookshelf). Through *The Misfits* (Community Safety Bookshelf), James Howe wanted to demonstrate how young people can collaborate to improve peer relationships for an entire school community.

Through the author interviews, teachers and students can enter the writers' worlds. Hopefully, as a result of the interviews, your students will experience added depth when reading the books. Ideally, the interviews will also inspire many young people, and older ones as well, to craft their own experiences, ideas, and feelings into poems, plays, short stories, novels, picture books, memoirs, and nonfiction.

Contact Your Favorite Bookshelf Author or Illustrator

The Internet offers an easy way to contact many authors and illustrators. Some have their own Web sites and welcome notes and letters from readers. For those who do not have personal Web sites, you can write to the book's publisher, who will then forward letters to the author. Many publishers' Web sites also offer guides and supplementary materials for their books on the bookshelf lists.

What to write about? One idea for students is to write about their responses to the book and describe the service learning connection. In their interviews, several authors discussed receiving this kind of correspondence and how appreciative they were and described some wonderful service learning projects!

Using Author Interviews in the Classroom

You can use an interview for ideas on how to teach and use a book. An interview can provide you with ideas for reflections and questions for class discussions. You start a discussion by asking your students what they think the author wanted to get across in the book, what they think the author's inspiration could have been, or what they think the author was thinking when she wrote a particular plot twist. Interesting discussions can result from these questions and others like them, and the discussions only get better when you read to them what the writer really *was* thinking. Your students may be surprised, amused, touched, or even motivated to write. No matter what their reactions, the class discussion can be enriched by exploring them.

The Importance of Illustrations and Artwork

Visual images communicate the message of a story as much as text. The bookshelf titles employ innumerable illustration techniques and styles that educate as well as inspire. Illustrations and other artwork show us what happened and where it happened. They also sometimes give information not provided in any other way. For example, in Patricia Polacco's *Chicken Sunday* (Community Safety Bookshelf), one image shows an aged shopkeeper with a number tattooed on his forearm, indicating that he was in a concentration camp during World War II; this fact is never mentioned in the story text. The last picture in *Click, Clack, Moo: Cows That Type* (Social Change Bookshelf), illustrated by Betsy Lewin, reveals the resolution of the ducks' quest for a diving board; no words at all appear on the page.

The bookshelves offer an array of options to students exploring ideas and methods for illustrating original stories or helping younger children create a book. Here is a sampling:

- *Can You Hear a Rainbow? The Story of a Deaf Boy Named Chris* (Special Needs and Disabilities Bookshelf), illustrated by Nicola Simmonds, and *One Day at Wood Green Animal Shelter* (Animals in Danger Bookshelf), by Patricia Casey, mix photographs and art.

- Artist Paul Yalowitz begins the story *Somebody Loves You, Mr. Hatch* (Elders Bookshelf) with dreary colors to match Mr. Hatch's mood. The colors brighten as Mr. Hatch thinks, "Somebody loves me."

- Gerardo Suzán's colorful images in *Butterfly Boy* (Elders Bookshelf) are a mix of representational and modern art.

- In *One Good Apple: Growing Our Food for the Sake of the Earth* (Environment Bookshelf), author-photographer Catherine Paladino presents beautifully composed images to enrich the nonfiction text.

- Tomek Bogacki recreates the colors and the details of his home, the town, and the garden he planted in *My First Garden* (Gardening Bookshelf), which resembles a photo album of art in pastels.

- Ann Arnold uses pen and watercolor illustrations in the information-filled book *The Adventurous Chef: Alexis Soyer* (Hunger and Homelessness Bookshelf) to show the dramatic innovations and inventions made to benefit Irish famine victims and soldiers in the Crimean War; she also shows the actual floor plan of his kitchen.

- Artist and author Susan L. Roth makes collages with photos, fabrics, and other found objects to tell the story *It's Still a Dog's New York: A Book of Healing* (Community Safety Bookshelf).

- In *Jack's Garden* (Gardening Bookshelf), Henry Cole uses sparse, repetitive text in combination with artwork that is dense with information about soil, weather, worms, and seeds.

- Elizabeth Goméz's brilliant use of color and fantastical imagery in *A Movie in My Pillow/Una película en mi almohada* (Immigrants Bookshelf) could inspire murals.

- Lauren Child's *What Planet Are You From, Clarice Bean?* (Environment Bookshelf) integrates text into drawings that form every shape and move in every direction imaginable.

- Two books by Michael J. Rosen, *The Greatest Table: A Banquet to Fight Against Hunger* (Hunger and Homelessness Bookshelf) and *Down to Earth: Garden Secrets! Garden Stories! Garden Projects You Can Do!* (Gardening Bookshelf) include collections of donated artwork by highly regarded children's book illustrators; these are veritable visual feasts.

> Some painters transform the sun into a yellow spot, others transform a yellow spot into the sun.
> PABLO PICASSO, ARTIST

Young Authors at Work

Several of the bookshelf titles were written by authors under the age of twenty. These young authors are models that the young people you work with can draw on for inspiration both for their own creative endeavors and what they can achieve. If you'd like to highlight the achievements and writing of young authors for your students, here are titles on the bookshelves that are written or co-authored by young people:

- *Hey, Little Ant!* (Community Safety Bookshelf), a song-turned-book that ends with the question, "What would you do?"

- *Conversation Starters* (Elders Bookshelf) and *Increase the Peace: The ABCs of Tolerance* (Community Safety Bookshelf), both in ABC formats.

- *Potato: A Tale from the Great Depression* (Hunger and Homelessness Bookshelf), by an eight-year-old, telling a story passed down through her family.

- *We Need to Go to School: Voices of the Rugmark Children* and *Free the Children* (Social Change Bookshelf) about international child labor.

Using the Service Learning Bookshelf

You can use the Service Learning Bookshelf contents in a remarkable variety of ways throughout your service learning projects. This section will show you how you can use books in every stage of the service learning process, with different partners on a project, and as a source of inspiration for your students. Several charts will help you make quick and easy curricular connections and serve as useful cross-references when you're brainstorming ideas and planning projects. The chart "Connecting the Bookshelf to the Four Stages of Service Learning" suggests ideas for linking reading to each service learning stage. The "Bilingual Books" chart identifies titles you can use in English and Spanish, while the "Historical Content and the Bookshelf" chart lists a selection of bookshelf titles by historical period.

Connecting the Bookshelf to the Four Stages of Service Learning

During Preparation, use books:

- to introduce topics.

- for research.

- to enhance understanding of a historical time period through parallel reading of a novel or picture book. (See "Historical Content and the Bookshelf" at the end of this chapter.)

- to show different approaches to or writing styles on a similar theme.

During Action, use books:

- to begin the service activity with a common experience for all involved.

- to help children learn to read.

- to teach concepts or ideas.

- to dramatize an educational program.

continued ———→

During Reflection, *use books:*

- to introduce inspiring thoughts related to the service experience.
- to share the reflective comments of others.
- to show the results of similar service experiences by others.
- in response to a student's expression of thought or feelings.

During Demonstration, *use books:*

- in a display to show what books were used as resources for student learning.
- to read aloud and share the impact of a story, similar to what the students experienced in class or in other situations.
- in a choral reading format or selected excerpts to read in presentations to tell the scope of the learning and service experience, and emphasize specific information.
- in a list of recommended reading to help others learn more about the subject.

Publish, Publish, Publish

The titles in the Service Learning Bookshelf can inspire students to write about their own service experience and serve as templates for good story-telling about significant social issues. Students' stories and books can be donated to hospitals, libraries, family shelters, and other classrooms. With donated time and materials from community partners, students may even be able to publish their book and use it as a fund-raiser. Consider having the students record audiotapes especially for children or elders who are more able to listen than read. Consider, too, translating the stories for multilingual publications.

Act It Out: The Play's the Thing

Students can also transform favorite stories into plays—or even musicals—that will help the audience learn about social issues. The performance may become an essential part of a service learning activity. The following books are easily adapted into plays and skits:

- *Toestomper and the Caterpillars* (Community Safety Bookshelf) shows how a "rowdy ruffian" is transformed into a kinder fellow by caring for squiggly blue caterpillars.

- *Hey, Little Ant!* (Community Safety Bookshelf) has been staged as an opera and a musical.

- *Pinky and Rex and the Bully* (Community Safety Bookshelf) is about a boy who has to make hard choices about friendships and his identity.

- *Cootie Shots: Theatrical Inoculations Against Bigotry for Kids, Parents and Teachers* (Community Safety Bookshelf) is a ready-to-use collection of plays.

- Even a novel, like *The Misfits* (Community Safety Bookshelf) about middle school kids trying to stop name-calling at school, has been transformed into a play.

- *Somebody Loves You, Mr. Hatch* (Elders Bookshelf) is a heartfelt story perfect for a Valentine's Day theme of valuing all community members, particularly those who are isolated and lonely.

- *The Wartville Wizard* (Environment Bookshelf) is a comical depiction of trash sticking to the people who litter in a small town.

- *The Can-Do Thanksgiving* (Hunger and Homelessness Bookshelf) demonstrates how knowing where the can of food is going can make all the difference.

- Any of the biographical collections can be adapted for "Living History" productions, where students become the people and tell their stories.

Library Partnerships

Books, too, can be a source of community partnerships. Consider all the possible ways you could collaborate with school and public libraries to promote books with service-learning-related themes. Students can set up displays, provide book reviews, or design bookmarks with recommendations. A first-grade class created an attractive calendar for four local libraries featuring books they enjoyed about gardening. Every month, they promoted a new favorite book. Ask your students what they'd like to do—they will have plenty of ideas.

> The future belongs to those who can give the
> next generation reasons to hope.
> PIERRE TEILHARD DECHARDIN, PHILOSOPHER

Tutoring Programs

Many bookshelf titles, particularly ones in the Literacy, Community Safety, and Immigrants Bookshelves, are helpful in various ways during preparation for or implementation of tutoring programs in which elementary, middle, or high school students tutor younger children or peers.

- Nonfiction books such as *Illiteracy* and *Learning Disabilities* (Literacy Bookshelf) provide background information.

- Several books describe the frustrations and embarrassment experienced by challenged readers, like *Just Call Me Stupid* and *Thank You, Mr. Falker* (Literacy Bookshelf). Such books help students learn about how peers may differ by skill, how they are affected by life experience, and how peer teasing and ridicule can present a hurdle.

- Learning English as a second language is hard work and is described in *The Circuit* and *Breaking Through* (Immigrants Bookshelf).

- In *Prairie School* (Literacy Bookshelf), a young boy doesn't see any reason to learn to read, until his persistent aunt comes to visit. A tutor with a particularly reluctant student may find this book

inspiring and may even find it helpful to read it to the resistant tutee.

- *My Name Is María Isabel* (Social Change Bookshelf) reminds students and adults of the importance of treating all children with respect, including in classroom settings.

- Skills such as counting can be reinforced by *Ducks Disappearing* and *Cat Up a Tree* (Animals in Danger Bookshelf). These books also tell the stories of individuals teaching adults about our responsibility to care for living creatures.

- Students may find that the love of words can be contagious when they read the humorous *The Bookstore Mouse* (Literacy Bookshelf), a witty fantasy of a mouse with a colorful vocabulary helping a young medieval scribe to rescue storytellers from a dragon.

- In *Dear Whiskers* (Literacy Bookshelf), a young girl expresses frustration with a partner in a cross-age tutoring project, and comes to recognize appreciation for diversity and learning.

- A classroom with a place for every child, including one who is deaf, can be found in *The Year of Miss Agnes* (Literacy Bookshelf).

- *Sahara Special* (Literacy Bookshelf) tells of a girl who resists participating in school yet has a secret talent as a writer. This can inspire tutors to look for and encourage the secret (or not so secret) talents of their tutees (and recognize their own "secret" talents as well).

- If your tutoring program involves students with special needs, *Just Kids: Visiting a Class for Children with Special Needs* (Special Needs and Disabilities Bookshelf) provides an informative and engaging story.

- High school students with low reading skills can develop their own ability while preparing to read quality picture books to younger children.

- Tutors can read books aloud to younger readers to communicate the joy of reading.

- Use the bookshelf to find books of interest to particular tutees. The titles reflect diverse cultures and experiences and should provide something for everyone.

Bilingual Books

Community Safety Bookshelf
It Doesn't Have to Be This Way: A Barrio Story/No tiene que ser así: Una historia del barrio

Elders Bookshelf
Remember Me? Alzheimer's Through the Eyes of a Child/¿Te acuerdas de mí? Pensamientos de la enfermedad, Alzheimers a través de los ojos de un niño

Environment Bookshelf
Fernando's Gift/El Regalo de Fernando
This House Is Made of Mud/Esta casa está hecha de lodo

Gardening Bookshelf
Gathering the Sun: An Alphabet in Spanish and English
Carlos and the Cornfield/Carlos y la milpa de maíz

Immigrants Bookshelf
A Movie in My Pillow/Una película en mi almohada
My Diary from Here to There/Mi diario de aquí hasta allá

Social Change Bookshelf
¡Sí, Se Puede!/Yes, We Can! Janitor Strike in L.A.

Special Needs and Disabilities Bookshelf
The Treasure on Gold Street/El tesoro en la calle Oro

School, City, and State Reading Programs

Programs that promote literacy and community building through reading are growing in popularity. The bookshelf lists are good sources of material for large-scale reading programs. All middle school students in a district, for example, might read *Any Small Goodness* (Immigrants Bookshelf), a chronicle of an adolescent's experience relocating in East Los Angeles. An entire city might be invited to read *Fahrenheit 451* (Literacy Bookshelf) or *To Kill a Mockingbird* (Social Change Bookshelf) and participate in related discussions. A statewide reading program might include *The Grapes of Wrath* (Hunger and Homelessness Bookshelf) among the selections. Community events associated with such programs might include art exhibits on related themes, staged productions of the book, readings, and speakers.

If a citywide or statewide reading program takes place in your community, get involved. If the selection is geared toward adults, recommend an additional book selection appropriate for youth, with follow-up activities at school or the library. Young people can select the book and design worthwhile and exciting learning opportunities. What may begin as a class or school activity could ultimately have citywide reach.

Community Agencies and Organizations

Although the discussion of the Service Learning Bookshelf focuses on school settings, community agencies and organizations can also make use of the lists. Organizations promoting racial diversity and tolerance can refer to the Social Change Bookshelf when looking for recommended readings for a middle or high school class. A staff member at a retirement home may read a book such as *Sunshine Home* (Elders Bookshelf) aloud to elementary children coming for a service activity as part of an orientation to the facility. Students can compile a list of books to read about special needs (or another theme) for an agency, complete with their original annotations or reviews, and develop analytical and writing skills in the process. Share the booklists with your community partners to find additional ways the resources can be helpful.

Historical Content and the Bookshelf

Refer to this listing when seeking books depicting a particular period or issue. Dates are approximate. Please note that titles identified as recommendations in the bookshelves are not included in this historical chart.

The Middle Ages

When Plague Strikes: The Black Death, Smallpox, AIDS (AIDS Education and Awareness)

Across a Dark and Wild Sea (Literacy)

The Bookstore Mouse (Literacy)

General United States History

Rabble Rousers: 20 Women Who Made a Difference (Social Change)

Sisters in Strength: American Women Who Made a Difference (Social Change)

We Are the Many: A Picture Book of American Indians (Social Change)

We Were There, Too! Young People in U.S. History (Social Change)

1845–1852

The Adventurous Chef: Alexis Soyer (Hunger and Homelessness)

Black Potatoes: The Story of the Great Irish Famine, 1845–1850 (Hunger and Homelessness)

The Long March: The Choctaw's Gift to Irish Famine Relief (Hunger and Homelessness)

Feed the Children First: Irish Memories of the Great Hunger (Hunger and Homelessness)

Civil War and Slavery

A School for Pompey Walker (Literacy)

Pink and Say (Social Change)

1870–1910

A Different Kind of Hero (Immigrants)

Indian School: Teaching the White Man's Way (Literacy)

Oranges on Golden Mountain (Immigrants)

Prairie School (Literacy)

Rodzina (Hunger and Homelessness)

They Came from the Bronx: How the Buffalo Were Saved from Extinction (Animals in Danger)

A Train to Somewhere (Hunger and Homelessness)

World War I

After the Dancing Days (Community Safety)

Charlie Wilcox (Community Safety)

When Christmas Comes Again: The World War I Diary of Simone Spencer (Community Safety)

1920s

Orphan Train Rider: One Boy's True Story (Hunger and Homelessness)

Jemma's Journey (Social Change)

White Lilacs (Social Change)

The Depression—1930s

The Gardener (Gardening)

Butterflies and Lizards, Beryl and Me (Gardening)

Potato: A Tale from the Great Depression (Hunger and Homelessness)

Esperanza Rising (Immigrants)

The Strength of Saints (Literacy)

World War II

The Victory Garden (Gardening)

The Yellow Star: The Legend of King Christian X of Denmark (Community Safety)

Passage to Freedom: The Sugihara Story (Social Change)

Slap Your Sides (Social Change)

Boxes for Katje (Community Safety)

Bat 6 (Social Change)

Civil Rights

Richard Wright and the Library Card (Literacy)

Tomás and the Library Lady (Literacy)

Goin' Someplace Special (Literacy)

A Bus of Our Own (Literacy)

Through My Eyes (Social Change)

Linda Brown, You Are Not Alone: The Brown v. Board of Education Decision (Social Change)

Part Two:
Service Learning Themes

CHAPTER 4

AIDS EDUCATION AND AWARENESS

> I said education was our "basic weapon."
> Actually, it's our only weapon. We've got
> to educate everyone about the disease
> so that each person can take responsibility
> for seeing that it is spread no further.
>
> C. EVERETT KOOP, FORMER U.S. SURGEON GENERAL

Education is the primary prescription for preventing the spread of HIV and AIDS. With education, we can equip youth for the challenges that confront not only them and their society but our global population. In this continually shrinking world, our neighbors are no longer just the folks down the block; they now include the peoples of Africa, Asia, and South America, where the numbers of people who are HIV positive or living with AIDS are increasing at a staggering rate. Even with medical advances in more affluent countries, the problem is far from being under control. Consider these facts:

- More than 2,000 children are infected with HIV each day worldwide.[1]

- In the United States, it is estimated that two adolescents are infected with HIV each hour.[2]

- More than 6,000 young people between the ages of 15 and 24 become infected with HIV every day. *That is about four young people every minute.*[3]

- There are approximately 11 million children in Africa who have been orphaned by AIDS.[4]

- More than 95 percent of people with HIV live in the developing world.[5]

In our uncertain world, we can help young people deal with facts like these by providing information, resources, and prevention strategies. We can equip them to make healthy personal choices, be advocates for a healthy society, and promote well-being in all parts of the world. We must be involved, continue to create educational opportunities based on current information and resources, help young people separate fact from fiction, and act for prevention.

Preparation: Getting Ready for Service Learning Involving AIDS Education and Awareness

The following activities can be used in the preparation stage to promote learning and skill development related to HIV and AIDS education and awareness. These activities can be used with different age ranges during preparation to help your students examine key issues through research, analyze community needs, and gain the knowledge they need to effectively contribute to the design of their service plan. Since literature is often an important part of preparation, you can find recommended titles on this theme in the AIDS Education and Awareness Bookshelf later in this chapter.

Activity: Understanding Leads to Action. Providing age-appropriate information helps students gain knowledge that can lead to action. For young children up to third grade, AIDS education is often included with information concerning other health problems. The emphasis is on staying healthy—eating well and getting adequate exercise and sleep.

---

[1]*Report on the Global HIV/AIDS Epidemic: December 2002, UNAIDS Joint United Nations Programme on HIV/AIDS*
[2]*Youth Report 2000—White House Office of National AIDS Policy*
[3]*Young People and HIV/AIDS: Opportunity in Crisis—A Joint Report by UNICEF, UNAIDS and WHO*
[4]*UNAIDS Fact Sheet 2002, Sub-Saharan Africa, UNAIDS Joint United Nations Programme on HIV/AIDS*
[5]*AIDS Epidemic Update: December 2002, UNAIDS Joint United Nations Programme on HIV/AIDS*

Children are also often taught to differentiate between communicable and noncommunicable diseases. While most children know they can "catch" a cold, young children can be assured that being friends and playing with a child who is HIV positive or living with AIDS is safe.

Young people can also have great empathy for people who are in the hospital or who are taken to emergency rooms or clinics. By revisiting their own experiences with being sick or going to the doctor's office, students can come up with ideas to reach out to others who are affected by HIV or AIDS. Guide your students' empathy with readings from the bookshelf, research, and class discussions. Start looking for organizations in your community that work with people living with HIV or AIDS or who are working to stop the spread of AIDS. Early collaborations with these kinds of agencies can help students develop project ideas that meet real local, or even global, needs. Project ideas that could result include:

- younger students writing "Have a Good Day" greeting cards to be inserted in lunches to be delivered to people living with HIV or AIDS

- making blankets for babies living with HIV or AIDS

- collecting materials for, assembling, and decorating holiday gift baskets for people living with AIDS

- developing programs to replace myths about HIV and AIDS with accurate information

- older students helping to assemble and deliver meals, providing pet care, or participating in other forms of outreach to people living with HIV or AIDS.

Activity: Discussion and Research. Through reading, students can continue to learn about the ever-changing world of education, research, and prevention of AIDS. What is the most current information regarding the spread of HIV and AIDS, strategies for prevention, and the search for a cure? Students can begin by reading one of the nonfiction books listed in this chapter, such as *When Plague Strikes: The Black Death, Smallpox, AIDS,* discussing it in small groups, and generating questions. If needed, you can add any of the following to their list:

- How much funding is allocated to research?

- Do socioeconomic factors affect who is getting treatment for AIDS and what treatments are available?

- How do developing countries cope with the spread of HIV and AIDS?

- What populations are most susceptible to contracting HIV and AIDS?

- What are the resources for children, particularly in developing countries where many have the disease or have been orphaned by it?

In groups, students can use the Internet, newspapers and journals, and local organizations to find answers to these questions and can then share their findings. This research can help students determine what would be a worthwhile and meaningful activity to assist people in the community or in other parts of the world who are affected by HIV or how to educate others to stop the spread of AIDS.

Find Out More About
AIDS Education and Awareness

To learn more about these issues and to get ideas for service and action, visit these Web sites and organizations online:

www.nylc.org At the National Youth Leadership Council Web site, click on their HIV/AIDS and Service Learning Initiative to promote youth involvement in organizations at home and abroad in finding solutions to this global pandemic.

www.unicef.org/programme/hiv/overview.htm UNICEF works closely with national governments, nongovernmental organizations, and other United Nations agencies to improve the lives of children, youth, and women.

www.kff.org/worldaidsday The Kaiser Family Foundation serves as a resource for information about HIV/AIDS policy, public opinion and knowledge about the disease, and media-based partnerships, plus the annual Worlds AIDS Day.

www.cdc.gov/hiv/dhap.htm The Centers for Disease Control is a good source for current information and statistics on HIV and AIDS. They have a Frequently

continued ⟶

Asked Questions section that answers general questions about what causes AIDS, how it's transmitted, and how it can be prevented. It also has a page devoted to debunking common hoaxes and rumors about HIV and AIDS.

Making Connections Across the Curriculum

Some service learning activities naturally lend themselves to interdisciplinary work and making connections across the curriculum. These connections strengthen and broaden student learning, helping them meet academic standards. More than likely, you'll be looking for these connections and ways to encourage them well before the students ever start working on service learning activities. As with the entire service learning process, it helps to remain flexible, because some connections can be spontaneously generated by the questions raised throughout and by the needs of the project. To help you think about cross-curricular connections and where you can look for them, the Curricular Web for this chapter (page 69) gives examples of many different ways this theme can be used in different academic areas. (The service learning scenarios in the next section of the chapter also demonstrate various ways this theme can be used across the curriculum.)

Service Learning Scenarios: Ideas for Action

Ready to take action? What follows are projects that have been successfully carried out by elementary, middle, or high school students. Most of these scenarios and examples explicitly include some aspects of preparation, action, reflection, and demonstration. These scenarios can be a rich source of project, resource, and curriculum ideas for you to draw upon. While the grade levels are given as a reference, most project ideas can be adapted to suit younger or older students, and many are suitable for cross-age partnerships.

International Support and Learning: Grades 1–12. Through classroom studies, students in Maryland learned about the history, geography, and population of Malawi, a country in southeastern Africa, where approximately 500,000 children under the age of 15 have lost their parents to AIDS. A partnership with the American Red Cross enabled the students to help these children attend school. Attending school in Malawi is free but only possible if you bring your own supplies. The Red Cross provided a list of items needed and an "International School Chest" to fill with paper, pens, markers, jump ropes, and other essentials. Three hundred chests were filled in one state. Students at an alternative high school made jump ropes; they tooled the wood with designs and measured the ropes. At another school, students made a mural about Africa. The result: international awareness and more children in Malawi were able to attend school.

Blankets for Babies: Grade 4. Fourth-grade students took turns bringing in news articles for class discussion. One student brought an article about babies born with AIDS. The class agreed they wanted to help in some way and decided to make baby blankets. They looked at pictures of quilts made by pioneer women and decided to use similar patterns for decoration. Using soft fabric and fabric markers, they worked with geometric patterns in soothing colors. A parent volunteer sewed the edges, and the completed blankets went on "tour" in the school to teach others about this important subject. Students created mini-lessons to make their classroom presentations interactive. They received a letter of thanks from the organization that received the blankets.

Teaching Respect: Grade 5. After learning about people being mistreated because of illnesses such as AIDS, fifth-grade students considered various ways to get across a message of respect for all people. They decided to create a comic book character who would teach younger children to be thoughtful toward people living with HIV or AIDS. After consulting with a local health organization, students developed several story lines, combined them into one magazine, and made copies for younger children. These were distributed in school and at a community health fair.

Using the AIDS Memorial Quilt: Grade 7. While studying ways to prevent HIV infection and AIDS, two middle school classes in Pennsylvania decided to bring information to the community. After learning about the AIDS Memorial Quilt—an ongoing community art project that includes more than 44,000

AIDS Education and Awareness Across the Curriculum

English/Language Arts

- Discuss the importance of friendship with children who are living with HIV or AIDS
- Read written material from a clinic offering HIV/AIDS prevention information and adapt to a teen or younger child's version
- Study the impact of media coverage, entertainment, and/or mass marketing campaigns to eliminate misconceptions about people living with HIV or AIDS

Social Studies/History

- Create an AIDS historical timeline
- Study medieval history and the pattern of scapegoating (irrational intolerance toward certain people or groups) during plagues
- Compare approaches to AIDS prevention by different governments

Languages

- Find out how HIV/AIDS impacts countries internationally
- Read HIV/AIDS information in the language being studied as prepared by different countries
- Translate HIV/AIDS prevention information for community organizations and outreach

Theater, Music, & Visual Arts

- Research how theater and storytelling have been used to teach about social issues, including AIDS awareness in the United States and abroad
- Find out how music has influenced HIV/AIDS prevention both through fund-raisers and messages in songs
- Examine how the AIDS Memorial Quilt has grown as an international art project

AIDS Education and Awareness

Math

- Research the cost of hospital stays for various ailments
- Graph the funds allocated by governments to research and prevent HIV/AIDS
- Review the statistics of HIV and AIDS by age and sex

Physical Education

- Research the role of exercise in healthy living
- Have a physical therapist demonstrate adaptive exercise programs
- Create a simplified exercise protocol for children or teens who have health limitations

Computer

- Design pocket-size information cards with community health resource information
- Create a multimedia presentation on an HIV/AIDS related subject
- Use the Internet to learn how African nations are responding to the AIDS crises

Science

- Learn about the body's regulatory and immune systems and healthy life habits
- Interview doctors at local health clinic about epidemics
- Research the transmission factors that put youth at risk

three-by-six-foot memorial panels, each commemorating a person who has died from AIDS—they wanted to participate. After receiving names and biographies from eleven individuals who died from AIDS and were not yet represented in the quilt, the students made and contributed eleven panels. They mastered sewing, silk screening, and the art of gathering and recycling assorted fabrics and materials. Students proudly displayed their artwork to the community.

Informational Brochures: Grade 8. An English teacher read *Too Far Away to Touch* to his middle school students to stimulate a conversation about HIV and AIDS in our society. This sparked a lengthy discussion of personal experiences involving both losses and new research. Students were allowed to choose a project that would involve developing and using persuasive writing skills, and they decided to help break down some of the myths surrounding AIDS. They found an HIV/AIDS quiz on the Internet and got permission to use it as a teaching tool. Working in small groups, they created brochures, which included the quiz, and informational packets that were used in several schools in their area.

> Once every generation, history brings us to an important crossroad. Sometimes in life there is that moment when it's possible to make a change for the better. This is one of those moments.
>
> ELIZABETH GLASER,
> FOUNDER OF THE PEDIATRIC AIDS FOUNDATION

Building Awareness: Grade 9. Using *AIDS: Can This Epidemic Be Stopped?* plus Internet research, high school students in Oakland, California, worked in small groups to plan a series of activities concerning issues affecting people with HIV/AIDS. They conducted an Awareness Day with speakers, in-class workshops, and presentations; prepared a short unit to teach in a ninth-grade health class; and wrote an editorial to the local paper advocating greater respect for persons living with HIV/AIDS.

Tolerance Campaign: Grade 10. Reading *When Plague Strikes: The Black Death, Smallpox, AIDS* as a class text, students in Minnesota learned how people have been blamed for the spread of diseases throughout history. A parallel study emerged of ways in which some teens were scapegoats in their school. Students formed strategy groups to plan campaigns to help eliminate the ridicule and harassment that undermines confidence and isolates their peers. Strategies included public service announcements, meetings with administrators to discuss policy issues, a proposal for "safe school guidelines," and a "teach-in" devoted to music and poetry about building tolerance among teens. The students conducted a survey to find out how the school population was responding to their efforts. The survey indicated that a substantial number of students had become more thoughtful about their actions and were also more likely to interrupt disrespectful actions by their friends.

Get Cookin': Grade 10. A local organization relied on volunteers to prepare and deliver food six days per week to people living with HIV and AIDS. A group of students helped over a holiday break and then decided to recruit their peers to help more often. Eight classes signed up to help on a rotating basis to cook and package the food. They learned about careers in nutrition and food services while discovering there are many people in their community willing to help their neighbors.

Taking a Stand for Youth Voice: High School. Students have a vested interest in participating in developing ideas and strategies to help teens avoid HIV and AIDS. This was the position of high school students in upstate New York as they requested positions on a school district AIDS advisory committee. After making a strong case to the local school board, with a concerted expression of ideas and ways they truly "represent the voice of youth," several students (identified by the youth) were appointed to the advisory group.

Teams for Understanding: High School. High school students who were HIV positive or who were living with AIDS collaborated with uninfected peers to form speaking teams to teach middle and high school youth about the disease. With guidance from professionals, students developed basic scripts and practiced public speaking skills. They rehearsed with their classes how to respond to questions and developed a handout with facts, figures, myths, truths, and Web sites to provide more information.

Theater Works: High School. After research and study, and with guidance from local AIDS activists, high school students in northern Missouri prepared and presented skits depicting youth in situations requiring that choices be made. Because the skits called for audience participation, debate and discussion followed. Through performance, the students hoped to reinforce healthy behavior, give strategies for dealing with peer pressure, and promote community awareness. Ongoing role playing and reflection helped the actors to refine their skills and deal with challenging teaching situations and audience reactions.

Learning About Policy and Speaking Out: High School. Youth activists attended an international AIDS conference to make their voices heard, since 50 percent of new HIV infections worldwide occur among youth ages 15–24*. Through workshops, students learned about policy and current strategies. They returned to their communities to write articles for the school paper, form study groups, and help design an informational brochure about confidential testing for a local AIDS prevention organization.

> A pitcher cries for water to carry
> And a person for work that is real.
>
> FROM *TO BE OF USE* BY MARGE PIERCY, POET

A Mural to Remember: High School. Fifteen participants in a New York City youth program whose lives had been touched by AIDS designed a mural to face a busy city street. The entire teen group then helped to paint and create this 150-foot long, 10-foot tall masterpiece, unveiled to the community on World

AIDS Day. Elected officials, community members, parents, and friends gathered to see the art and hear the poetry written by these young people.

The AIDS Education and Awareness Bookshelf

The AIDS Education and Awareness Bookshelf contains a modest number of selections compared with other themes. Still, these selections represent a range of opportunities to learn and develop meaningful service connections. To help you find books relevant to your particular projects, the book chart classifies the titles into several topic areas: historical overview, our stories, and relationships.

In general, the bookshelf features:

- An annotated bibliography arranged and alphabetized by title according to the general categories of nonfiction (N), picture books (P), and fiction (F). For nonfiction and fiction, length and recommended grade levels are included. The entries in the picture book category do not include suggested grade levels, since they can be successfully used with all ages.

- A chart organized by topic and category to help you find books relevant to particular projects.

- Recommendations from service learning colleagues and experts that include a book summary and ideas for service learning connections. (The number of recommended books varies in each bookshelf.)

> From what we get, we can make a living; what we give, however, makes a life.
>
> ARTHUR ASHE, ATHLETE

Listen, Learn, Live! World AIDS Campaign with Children and Young People: Facts and Figures, UNAIDS Joint United Nations Programme on HIV/AIDS

AIDS Education and Awareness Bookshelf Topics

Topics	Books	Category
Historical Overview What do we already know about this disease that continues to spread at an alarming rate?	AIDS	N
	AIDS: Can This Epidemic Be Stopped?	N
	A Life Like Mine: How Children Live Around the World * (see page 196)	N
	People with AIDS	N
	When Plague Strikes: The Black Death, Smallpox, AIDS	N
Our Stories The voices of the people living with HIV or AIDS or those close to people who are infected add personal experience to the facts and statistics.	*Be a Friend: Children Who Live with HIV Speak* *	N
	A Small, Good Thing: Stories of Children with HIV and Those Who Care for Them ‡	N
	You Can Call Me Willy: A Story for Children About AIDS	P
Relationships Meaningful relationships demonstrate the caring response of family and community to the AIDS crisis. Learning of these interactions reminds us to reach out and create similar relationships.	*Alex, the Kid with AIDS*	P
	Earthshine	F
	Far and Beyon'	F
	Too Far Away to Touch	P

Page references are given for books that do not appear in the AIDS Education and Awareness Bookshelf but that can be found in the bookshelf lists of other chapters.

* These books include examples of young people in service-providing roles.

‡ These books are out of print but still worth finding.

Nonfiction: *AIDS Education and Awareness*

AIDS by Lori Shein (Lucent Books, 1998). This overview of AIDS from the late 1970s to the late 1990s includes information about its discovery, methods of prevention, testing for HIV infection, the global epidemic, and what the future holds. Includes a glossary and resources. 112pp., young adult

AIDS: Can This Epidemic Be Stopped? by Karen Manning (Henry Holt, 1995). This book provides a history and medical overview of the epidemic. While many advances have been made since publication, the information remains useful for a solid background. Includes resource information and a glossary. 64pp., grades 5–7

Be a Friend: Children Who Live with HIV Speak by Dr. Lori S. Wiener, Aprille Best, and Dr. Phillip A. Pizzo (Albert Whitman, 1994). A moving collection of art and writings by children who are HIV positive or have siblings with AIDS. Each letter uncovers the emotion and courage of young people who just want to be normal and have friends who will stay friends. *All proceeds are donated to the Pediatric AIDS Foundation.* 40pp., all ages

People with AIDS by Gail B. Stewart (Lucent Books, 1996). Following an introduction with facts and a brief overview are four profiles, three of adults and one of an eight-year-old. The candid stories remind us of the people who often get lost with the label. Darrel collects masks and is a popular speaker about AIDS. Cindy unknowingly passed the AIDS virus to her son, who died. Jessica has outlived her mother. Stephen lives "day by day" with support from friends. 96pp., grades 6–12

A Small, Good Thing: Stories of Children with HIV and Those Who Care for Them by Anne Hunsacker Hawkins (W.W. Norton, 2000). Children born with HIV are often an overlooked group. These six portraits, developed through extensive interviews and observations, present both the overwhelming obstacles and the community support provided for these young people. The book is a vivid, life-affirming depiction of the caretakers and the effects of this disease. Out of print, but still worth finding. 286pp., grades 10–12

Maria and several other children in our clinic have experienced a reversal of fortune, surviving well beyond expectation. But the future for these children—one, three, or seven years hence—is unpredictable and uncertain. . . . The best hope of breaking what seems a cycle of predestined tragedy is that they will come to accept, even embrace, an ethic founded on loving responsibility to others.

FROM *A SMALL, GOOD THING: STORIES OF CHILDREN WITH HIV AND THOSE WHO CARE FOR THEM*

When Plague Strikes: The Black Death, Smallpox, AIDS by James Cross Giblin (HarperCollins, 1995). This compelling study of three deadly epidemics, separated by centuries, shows the similarity of social, political, and cultural reactions. Each disease brought medical advances. At the same time, in each case, blame was placed on people where none was deserved. The insights into the human condition are as provocative as the studies of history and medical advances. 212pp., grades 6–12

Picture Books:

AIDS Education and Awareness

Alex, the Kid with AIDS by Linda Walvoord Girard (Albert Whitman, 1991). Michael tells of his growing friendship with Alex, a new kid in fourth grade with AIDS. Alex turns out to be a funny, friendly guy, who learns pretty quickly that their teacher requires proper behavior from everyone in the class.

Too Far Away to Touch by Lesléa Newman (Clarion, 1995). Little Zoe and her Uncle Leonard enjoy adventures together. While at the Planetarium, Zoe asks, "How far away are the stars?" "Too far away to touch, close enough to see," her uncle answers. When Leonard becomes weaker due to AIDS, the message from the Planetarium has special meaning.

You Can Call Me Willy: A Story for Children About AIDS by Joan C. Verniero (Magination Press, 1995). Willy tells about her life with AIDS. She describes the care she receives from her grandmother, her best friend, and other adults. Most of all, she wants to have friends and play baseball.

Fiction: *AIDS Education and Awareness*

Earthshine by Theresa Nelson (Orchard, 1994). Twelve-year-old "Slim" has to attend a support group for kids whose parents are living with AIDS. Her adoration for her father, a charismatic actor, is well-deserved. Even as he is dying from AIDS, his charm, humor, and love keep her spirits high at the most fragile of times. Now, Isaiah, a kid in this group, has an idea to head to the mountains for a "cure." Everyone goes for an adventure of a lifetime, and finds "magic." 192pp., young adult

Far and Beyon' by Unity Dow (Aunt Lute Books, 2002). Set in Botswana, this novel draws from the author's experience in the women's rights struggle while sharing a contemporary family's loss due to AIDS. This is a family in conflict, both between and within individuals. At the center is Mora, age 17, who watched her two brothers die, and is torn between her ancestral traditions and the influence of western medicine and culture. After a pregnancy and an abortion, Mora returns to school, only to face the abuse of female students in the corrupt school system. But Mora takes a risk, and joined by other female students, makes a dramatic stand to stop the violence and obtain dignity. 199pp., Grades 9–12

Interviews with Authors: The Story Behind the Story

In the following interviews, we find out the "story behind the story" from James Cross Giblin (*When Plague Strikes: The Black Death, Smallpox, AIDS*) and Lesléa Newman (*Too Far Away to Touch*). James Giblin's book captivated me because of its description of the scapegoating that occurred during three terrible plagues, as well as its depth of information. I was drawn to interview Lesléa Newman after reading *Too Far Away to Touch* aloud to high school students as they began planning an AIDS education project. The students were spellbound by the story and began to talk about their own experiences of loss.

James Cross Giblin, author of When Plague Strikes: The Black Death, Smallpox, AIDS

I'm probably best known as a writer of nonfiction books for young people, but *When Plague Strikes* came from my work as an editor of children's books. In the mid-1980s, as editor-in-chief of Clarion Books, I knew and worked with two young, talented men, Gary Bargar and Ron

Wegen. Neither man knew the other; they lived in different parts of the country. Both died from AIDS in the summer of 1985. I had published two of Gary's novels and two picture books by Ron and was looking forward to working with both of them again. When they died within two weeks of one another, it struck me as so unfair. I began to think about AIDS in the context of two other plagues that had hit humankind through the centuries. How were they similar, and how did they differ? I realized the book I had in mind would be a major commitment, and I didn't feel ready to start writing it until almost a decade later, in the early 1990s. When it was finally finished I decided to dedicate the book to the two men who had inspired it: Gary and Ron.

Research reveals much that is provocative and surprising. For example, before I researched *When Plague Strikes* I didn't realize how religion had thwarted the development of medicine for centuries. Because the Catholic Church forbade the dissection of human bodies, doctors were stuck with what the Greeks, and to some extent the Arabs, had discovered hundreds of years earlier. Medical advancement was frozen, and this contributed to the spread of awful plagues like the Black Death and smallpox. People were not permitted to study medicine—everything was colored by religious interpretations and prohibitions.

Also, I didn't realize how scapegoating keeps rearing its ugly head when people are confronted with a plague like smallpox or AIDS. Whatever the crisis, people invariably feel the need to blame someone else—a scapegoat. This pattern struck me when I delved into the history of all three diseases.

On the other hand, I met remarkable people in the course of the research—women like Lady Mary Wortley Montague, who took the lead with her own son in testing the effects of inoculation as a protection against smallpox. She was far ahead of her time. Some of the people who surfaced during the AIDS epidemic were outstanding, too—men like Dr. C. Everett Koop, U.S. Surgeon General in the Reagan administration, who surprised his conservative backers when he urged that all kids be educated about AIDS.

Even if I feel emotional about the content, I try in my writing to simply lay out the facts. I would rather have the reader feel the shock and horror of people boarding up their neighbors in their own homes to prevent the spread of a disease than spend a lot of words editorializing about it. I believe a factual approach is far more effective in the long run.

My hope is that *When Plague Strikes* will provoke discussion. We need more thoughtful interchange, especially where social issues are concerned. I would hope a teacher, a parent, a librarian could get a conversation going about these plagues. A dialogue might start with a question: "What stood out for you in the section about smallpox?" for example. Other questions might be as simple as, "What did you find interesting?" or "What did you discover from reading about AIDS that you didn't know before?" Building on the participants' comments, the person leading the discussion could draw them out further.

I have heard of several splendid ideas for using *When Plague Strikes* with students. One imaginative teacher had her kids write poems about grief and examples of prejudice that they had observed in their community. I read one poem by a middle school girl whose favorite teacher had died of AIDS. The poem movingly conveyed her reactions. Another idea was to set up a mock town meeting where students as "townspeople' considered ways to halt the spread of the Black Death. Imagine a student arguing, "We should board up the victims' doors and windows so they won't be able to leave their houses." How would the other students at the gathering respond?

While the book was published in 1995, the foundations of each section are still valid today. But if I were writing about AIDS now, I'd add information about the drug "cocktails" that lessen the assault on the immune system and help to bolster the patient's white blood cell count. I'd expand the section about the tragic spread of AIDS in third world countries, especially in Africa. In the original edition, I refer to thousands of African children orphaned by AIDS, and unfortunately this is even more true now than it was then. Also, I would go further into the spread of AIDS in Eastern Europe, Russia, and Asia—regions of the world where there has been much social and political change. I would also weave in more about today's terrorist threat, including the possibility that disease could be used as a weapon in the wake of September 11. (A good exercise for students after reading the book would be to have them research and write new sections that they would like to see added in a revised edition.)

Above all, I hope the young people who pick up *When Plague Strikes* will find it a compelling read. Every good book, both fiction and nonfiction, contains a story line that unfolds in the natural progression of events. This is what makes a nonfiction book entertaining as well as informative.

I also hope the book's readers will gain a better understanding of how to deal with new threats concerning AIDS and acts of terrorism that employ deadly viruses. In the years to come, they're likely to confront many such threats. Books they've read like *When Plague Strikes* should help them to decide on the best and most intelligent ways to respond.

Lesléa Newman, *author of*
Too Far Away to Touch

Too Far Away to Touch was written after my friend Gerard died of AIDS. I was inconsolable. We'd been roommates at Naropa Institute in Boulder, Colorado, where we had studied poetics with writer Allen Ginsberg. Gerard was 32 years old.

When I feel such enormous grief, I am moved to a childlike state—a state of being utterly inconsolable and having a huge howl of grief inside. All I could do to console myself was to write a children's story. Something happens to me in the process of writing: I feel better. It also felt very satisfying to put that book into the world, because many children have lost a loved one to AIDS. My friend Gerard had nephews, and this book was read to these children who were so important to him. That was most satisfying for me.

The message of the book? Love never dies. People you love may die, but they will always be inside of you, and as you remember them, you keep them alive in your heart. There is also a message of hope, because Uncle Leonard is still alive at the end of the book. More often than not, characters living with AIDS in children's books die at the end of the story. This book was written in 1992 and published before many of the new drugs and drug combinations were developed. Today, because of these advancements, I am more hopeful. And while in the story Uncle Leonard says there is no cure for AIDS, there is still hope for him and his niece, Zoe.

Another more subtle message in the book concerns Uncle Leonard and his companion, Nathan. I purposely did not make a big deal about this relationship. There is a message here about how Uncle Leonard and Nathan love each other and take care of each other. Clearly, Uncle Leonard and Nathan are part of Zoe's family. Her mom sends her off with them to have an adventure. Inclusion and respect for each other are present in the lives of Zoe's family members; it is not questioned.

I see this book as being particularly meaningful for children who have relatives who are sick or have died from AIDS or any other disease. For children who have no experience with people with AIDS or another serious illness, the story puts a human face on illness: Uncle Leonard is a person with a full life, he loves his niece, and he happens to be sick.

Children can get involved in helping people living with AIDS in many ways. With adult support, children can volunteer with people who need company and who want to be read to. Children can help walk dogs, deliver meals, and provide companionship. For children, this would be a wonderful opportunity to get to know a person who they might not meet otherwise and to do something that is helpful.

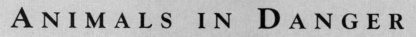

CHAPTER 5

ANIMALS IN DANGER

> Every individual matters. Every individual
> has a role to play. Every individual
> makes a difference. And we have a choice:
> What sort of difference do we want to make?
>
> JANE GOODALL, FROM *THE CHIMPANZEES I LOVE:*
> *SAVING THEIR WORLD AND OURS*

Nature is all about balance, and maintaining a desirable balance in nature depends on the survival of a web of species. Yet animals are threatened everywhere by human development that encroaches on natural habitats and disrupts migratory patterns. Honoring the symbiotic relationship among the species requires awareness, education, and action. If we are to prevent extinction and preserve biological diversity, it is important to understand our options while they still exist.

Children seem to be naturally drawn to animals, eager to learn about the Asian elephant, blue whale, and giant armadillo. It often surprises students that animals in their own region may be rare, threatened, vulnerable, or endangered. When they find out about such situations, they are usually eager to get involved. As they observe, compare and contrast, categorize, analyze, and report findings about animals in their own backyards or regions, young people develop scientific inquiry practices and apply their knowledge. The controversies that students may come across in their research can enliven social studies, civics, and government classes and familiarize them with local and national advocacy groups.

Preparation: Getting Ready for Service Learning Involving Animals in Danger

The following activities can be used in the preparation stage to promote learning and skill development related to endangered animals. These activities can be used with different age ranges during preparation to help your students examine key issues through research, analyze community needs, and gain the knowledge they need to effectively contribute to the design of their service plan. Since literature is often an important part of preparation, you can find recommended titles on this theme in the Animals in Danger Bookshelf later in this chapter.

Activity: Beginning with the Buffalo. Most students are familiar with the majestic buffalo that roamed the plains of the Old West. What students may not know is how these animals were saved from extinction through human intervention. Have students read (or read aloud to students) *They Came from the Bronx: How the Buffalo Were Saved from Extinction* to learn about the American Bison Society, which was established in 1905 at the Bronx Zoo to return a "mother herd" to the wild. Then have students conduct research to find out about the endangered animals in their own region. They can contact government agencies or animal protection groups (such as the ones listed on page 77) and use the Internet to begin their investigation about what animals are at risk and why. In groups, students can then select an animal to study in more detail. They might ask: Why are these animals important? What do they need to survive? What is happening that is harmful to them? How can people protect them? Students can also find out what other young people are doing to help save endangered species. They can share their knowledge with peers, put on displays in public venues such as libraries and community centers, and write articles and editorials for school and local newspapers to tell the public about what they can do to protect the endangered animals.

Activity: Assisting in Wildlife Rehabilitation. Wildlife rehabilitators rescue and care for animals and then release them back to the wild. Young people have been of great assistance to the local nonprofit organizations doing this important work. Students can conduct research in their region to find any such agencies and establish an ongoing relationship with them.

How can youth be involved with wildlife rehabilitation? Author Shannon K. Jacobs, in the book *Healers of the Wild,* offers these suggestions for ways to get started helping rehabilitation centers and protecting animals in the wild:

- Ask for a "wish list" from local rehabilitators. A variety of activities can result when students find out needs and start looking for ways to meet them. They could collect supplies by gathering donated produce daily from grocery stores, picking up fallen fruit under fruit trees and unwanted produce from community gardens, or organizing donations from the community of other supplies the rehabilitation center may need.

- Ask what kinds of help the rehabilitation center needs. They may need help cleaning cages at a rehabilitation center. Or perhaps they might welcome assistance with fundraising and publicity efforts, which could lead to students writing articles, letters to the editor, and press releases, or painting native animals for display or sale. Or perhaps their needs fall into a technical area and they would welcome students setting up and maintaining computer programs that assist with tracking volunteer hours, data about admission/discharge of animals, donations, and the budget.

- Do research and consult with rehabilitation experts, so that students can learn how to design and build birdhouses, bat houses, or cages for mammals.

- Research and consultation could also result in: school presentations and community programs about fascinating native wildlife and how to protect them; the creation of materials to help younger students develop compassion for wildlife; inviting wildlife rehabilitators to speak at school; or the design and organization of a cleanup campaign to pick up litter from schoolyards, parks, and shorelines.

Find Out More About Animals in Danger

To learn more about these issues and to get ideas for service and action, visit these Web sites and organizations online:

www.animaland.org This youth-oriented Web site of the American Society for the Prevention of Cruelty to Animals (ASPCA) offers a range of educational information and resources from domestic pet care to lists of endangered animals to "real issues" and ideas for student action.

www.americanhumane.org/ev-public The special events section of the American Humane Society Web site offers resources and opportunities for involvement for both kids and adults.

www.kidsplanet.org Kids' Planet is the youth Web site of Defenders of Wildlife, an organization dedicated to the protection of all native wild animals and plants in their natural communities. At this Web site you will find extensive information about endangered species all over the world.

www.rootsandshoots.org Roots & Shoots is the Jane Goodall Institute's international environmental and humanitarian program for young people. One strand of the program is addressing care and concern for animals locally and globally.

Making Connections Across the Curriculum

Some service learning activities naturally lend themselves to interdisciplinary work and making connections across the curriculum. These connections strengthen and broaden student learning, helping them meet academic standards. More than likely, you'll be looking for these connections and ways to encourage them well before the students ever start working on service learning activities. As with the entire service learning process, it helps to remain flexible, because some connections can be spontaneously generated by the questions raised throughout and by the needs of the project. To help you think about cross-curricular connections and where you can look for them, the Curricular Web for this chapter (page 78) gives examples of many different ways this theme can be used in different academic areas. (The service learning scenarios in the next section of the chapter also demonstrate ways this theme can be used across the curriculum.)

Animals in Danger Across the Curriculum

English/Language Arts

- Find books to read to younger children that teach respect for animals
- Create an ABC book of endangered animals and ways to help
- Write essays from the perspective of endangered animals seeking human assistance

Social Studies/History

- Visit an animal shelter or zoo to learn about its role in the community
- Research the government agencies that oversee endangered animals
- Learn about the Progressive Era (1890–1913) and the inception of organizations to protect animals

Languages

- Find out about animal rescue projects run by kids in different countries and correspond by email
- Create multilingual informational brochures about a local endangered animal
- Make presentations to other classes in the language being learned on a topic related to protecting animals

Theater, Music, & Visual Arts

- Write and perform plays with animals as characters teaching about their care or how to protect them
- Learn and perform songs that show respect for animals and nature
- Using drawing, painting, photography, or any visual art medium, create an art show of animals in both dangerous and protected environments

Animals in Danger

Math

- Develop a budget for the weekly cost of pet care
- Study the math concepts used to build small animal shelters or create a bird habitat
- Compare statistics on changes in the status of an endangered animal

Physical Education

- Do exercises that you've developed or drawn from yoga or other movement systems, that mimic the ways animals naturally move
- Learn how domesticated animals are affected when they don't get exercise
- Conduct research locally to find community needs for animal walkers or runners

Computer

- Find out how computers are used to track migratory patterns
- Create a Web site to help advertise and promote pet adoption
- Research and inform classes about Web sites with information about endangered animals

Science

- Research pet care, including nutrition, physiology, and psychology; also learn about and compare to their relations in the wild
- Learn about endangered animals in your region and groups that work to rescue and restore
- Visit a natural wildlife habitat to make observations, learn about the ecosystems, and ways to protect the animals living there

Service Learning Scenarios:
Ideas for Action

Ready to take action? What follows are projects that have been successfully carried out by elementary, middle, or high school students. Most of these scenarios and examples explicitly include some aspects of preparation, action, reflection, and demonstration. These scenarios can be a rich source of project, resource, and curriculum ideas for you to draw upon. While the grade levels are given as a reference, most project ideas can be adapted to suit younger or older students, and many are suitable for cross-age partnerships.

Animal Care: Kindergarten. Most children love animals and enjoy learning about how to provide them with the best possible care. Kindergarten children in Los Angeles listened to many books on animals, including *Nights of the Pufflings* and *One Day at Wood Green Animal Shelter*. An animal specialist and the owner of a hospital companion dog visited their classroom, and the children also took a field trip to visit an animal rescue organization. The children helped to plan and promote a school-wide project to collect old bedding for donation to the rescue group and made dog bandanas to be sold by the local Society for the Prevention of Cruelty to Animals.

Ducks and Organic Rice: Grade 1 (with High School Partners). Wildlife-friendly agriculture in the Central Valley of California led to community partnerships on a river preserve where nearly a thousand acres of organic rice are farmed each year. After the rice is harvested in the fall, the fields are flooded, providing a superb habitat for migrating ducks, swans, geese, and cranes. In spring, ducks nest in the fields before they are plowed and planted. Five first-grade classes integrated a duck egg rescue project into their study of animal life cycles. Students visited the preserve wetlands in the fall, observing shorebirds and waterfowl. Over the next few months, the students learned about the life cycles of many types of animals. In April, just before plowing, the students returned to the preserve. Led by the farmer, with help from preserve staff, volunteers, and a high school biology class, first-grade students walked through the fields, rescuing several nests from the tractor. Eggs were taken back to school and hatched in incubators. Students

kept incubation logs, plotted duckling growth and development, and read many duck- and bird-related stories and poems, including *Ducks Disappearing* and *Nights of the Pufflings*, a true story of very young children rescuing baby birds in Iceland. Office and administrative staff volunteered to help with weekend feeding duties. Volunteers working with the state waterfowl association raised the ducks during the summer. The ducks were then banded and released into the wild on the preserve. Not only did students have the opportunity to watch duck eggs hatch in their classrooms, they also participated in an environmental action project.

> If you think you're too small to have an impact, try going to sleep in a room with a mosquito.
>
> ANITA RODDICK, ACTIVIST
> AND FOUNDER OF THE BODY SHOP

Zoo Story: Grade 2. A second-grade teacher in Santa Monica, California, connected community studies with her science theme of "living things" through a zoo project: students made "brain challenges" for primates. Research shows that animals are healthier when mentally active rather than bored. With student help, animals would be challenged to get food out of containers. The children eagerly agreed to assemble papier-mâché tubes and pine cones stuffed with food for primates. On their first zoo visit, the students learned about primates and zoo life. Back at school, they determined ways to collect supplies: paper tubes, sugar-free cereal, dried fruits, and pine cones. They distributed flyers about their project to school families and neighbors and decorated bins to collect donations at two local

supermarkets. The students researched and wrote reports on primates, made graphs to chart items received and needed, solved mathematical equations about what they could assemble, mimicked body movements of gorillas and lemurs, and determined methods for storing vast quantities of paper tubes. They discussed why they had more donations of recycled goods (tubes and pine cones) than of more costly items (sugar-free cereal and dried fruits). Then, on the second trip to the zoo, they worked with zoo educators to stuff food into paper tubes and cover them with papier-mâché and to put peanut butter and dried fruit into pine cones. Both sets of primates—those at the zoo and the children—mastered brain challenges through this project.

Turtle Experts: Grade 3. Sometimes a teacher shares her passion with her students, and for one teacher in Los Angeles, the passion is turtles. Third-grade students read *Interrupted Journey: Saving Endangered Sea Turtles* and saw turtle videos. A box turtle was their class mascot. On the field trip to, yes, a local turtle museum, the docent admired the students' knowledge and asked them to make a museum kit that could be loaned to other classes before they come to visit. The third graders took the challenge and prepared a variety of teaching tools to help their peers learn about and appreciate turtles. The box containing the tools looked just like a turtle!

Wildlife Habitat at School: Grade 5. As part of their fifth-grade science program, students in Mount Vernon, Washington, learned about the migratory patterns of birds in their region. They constructed bird nesting boxes and feeders to attract and support the birds. Parents joined students on weekends to construct the feeders just outside the classroom. As birds arrived, the students moved quietly to the windows to watch and logged their observations in notebooks. Art projects showed a greater awareness of colors and detail of these feathered guests, as well as a greater appreciation and knowledge of nature.

Don't Mess with the Lizards: Grade 5. When it came time for fifth-grade students in San Angelo, Texas, to select an endangered animal to study, they wanted to learn about something close to their home. They chose the Texas long-horned lizard. After extensive research, students became experts on

the subject and were invited to speak to a community college class and appear on local access cable television. To demonstrate their knowledge, they prepared "Don't Mess with the Texas Long-horned Lizard" kits, complete with a lizard constitution (linked to studying government) and ways to protect their green friends. The kits were distributed to every fifth-grade class in their school district.

Interactive Learning Stations: Grades 6 and 7. Middle school students enjoyed a week-long educational experience learning about animal habitats. In small cooperative groups, the students then developed an educational program with interactive learning stations for elementary children. Using puppets, skits, and other attention-getting methods, the middle school "teachers" enjoyed enacting the different situations, such as "I am a salmon and this is what is happening to me!"

Land and Water Appreciation: Grades 6–8. Taking advantage of its rural setting in Middleburg, Florida, a middle school developed environmental service learning projects to teach students personal responsibility and how to take care of natural resources. For example, students worked with the local water management district to maintain and develop a 900-acre nature preserve for public use. The students built an eagle observation site at the preserve so visitors could view an active nest from a safe distance and learn about eagle needs and habits. The experience helped students recognize the necessity for preserving precious land and water resources.

International Exchange: Grade 7. Students visiting the Cosumnes River Preserve in central California in the fall and winter observed magnificent sandhill cranes that travel thousands of miles to winter in these wetlands. As the students learned about cranes and their amazing life story, wetland restoration efforts become even more significant. In class, students read about cranes from around the world, studied crane anatomy and physiology, and wrote stories and poems about the bird, which is a symbol of peace and beauty in many cultures. In collaboration with the International Crane Foundation, the students created over 200 pieces of artwork and poems to be displayed at the Sandhill Crane Festival in Ciego de Avila, Cuba. At the same time, they had the opportunity to contribute much-needed school supplies to Cuban children. Four local biologists and educators visited Cuba to collaborate with Cuban teachers on crane curriculum and to teach lessons on cranes and wetland conservation. Cuban elementary students got involved in service learning, joining biologists in the search for the rare and endangered Cuban sandhill cranes as part of the annual crane census. Students recorded sightings, crane behavior, and calls. (See *When Agnes Caws* on page 85 for a book connection.)

Animal Enrichment Activities: Grades 7–9. Students in Trinidad and Tobago got together with experts from the local zoo to develop enrichment projects for the animals at the zoo. The students worked in teams and selected a variety of animals, from ocelots to otters. The group who chose otters created a feeding ring for a river otter and also purchased a ball for the otter to play with in the water. Students documented the animals' behavior before and after the enrichment activity was introduced. Stories from the book *A Pelican Swallowed My Head— and Other Zoo Stories* provide examples of how zoos help with animal preservation.

Save Our Species: Grade 8. A middle school group focused its efforts on a local species with a declining population—the Channel Island fox, a small canine found on six of the eight California islands. They developed an Island fox sponsorship form, presented educational assemblies, and established an annual Fox Festival at the Santa Barbara Zoo. This dedicated group made a presentation to the school board, received numerous awards, and gained recognition from the city and the National Park Service.

Lost Animals: Grade 9. A ninth-grade English class for remedial readers wrote a book called *What Happens When an Animal Gets Lost?* Working with the county animal shelter and the Society for the Prevention of Cruelty to Animals, the students developed educational materials stressing the importance of licensing and identification tags. They also taught kindergarten and second-grade classes and spoke on local television.

Writing Children's Books: Grades 9–11. For an end-of-term high school biology class project, students have a choice of activities. The most popular was writing a story for children about an endangered or extinct species. The assignment was twofold: research what makes an engaging children's book, and learn enough about the chosen animal to make the book informative. The teacher used *Pipaluk and the Whales* and *Intimate Nature: The Bond Between Women and Animals* to show a variety of storytelling approaches. Students agreed to produce three copies—one to keep and two to donate to local schools or organizations of their choice. In their journals, students described this as a favorite activity.

Pet Population Control: Grades 9–12. High school students described as "at risk" were working on strategies to improve reading and writing. Their teacher introduced them to the world of nonfiction through articles on local community problems related to pet overpopulation. They analyzed the articles to develop questions to help them write a report on the subject without plagiarizing. Questions generated included: Why is there a problem? What can be done? What are the consequences of too many cats and dogs? After practicing social skills, especially how to talk with adults, the students invited two speakers, an animal control officer and a veterinarian, to address the class. The students decided to develop lessons for kindergarten children, with each group focusing on a different problem: dog care, cat care, avoiding dog bites, and being respectful to wildlife. Students wrote and taught five lessons for each theme. To demonstrate what they had learned, students made a presentation with recommendations on pet overpopulation to the city council. Students also assisted at rabies clinics in the area, used Spanish language skills to teach people why they needed to spay or neuter pets, and made public service announcements in Spanish.

> Never doubt that a small group of thoughtful, committed citizens can change the world; indeed, it's the only thing that ever has.
>
> MARGARET MEAD, ANTHROPOLOGIST

Pet Adoption Program: Grades 9–12. As part of a work experience program, developmentally disabled students in Massachusetts walked dogs and cleaned cages at an animal shelter. One student described the work to a high school teacher, who expressed interest in adopting a pet. This initiated a media campaign led by the developmentally disabled students to promote pet adoption within the school. To prepare, they received instruction in photography and videography from a class of students with behavioral and emotional problems. Using these technologies every week to photograph and videotape animals for posters and school cable television enhanced student learning both in skills and vocabulary. Many pets were adopted, and the students expanded the project to inform the broader community about the animal shelter adoption program.

Science and Government Connections: Grades 10–12. What recreational activities threaten our endangered species or disturb sensitive habitats? High school students began to investigate this question in science classes, which led them to approach their government teacher for assistance. Through phone calls and email, students found state officials willing to provide information about state policy. They also partnered with local parks and recreation staff to prepare brochures on safe use of local recreation areas. Students made coloring books about the endangered animals in the area to be given to any young visitors coming to the park.

Young Scientists: Grades 11 and 12. Science students in Crystal River, Florida, conducted surveys and collected data from government agencies regarding animal populations in a wetland area near the school to track the patterns of migratory wildlife. The students analyzed the information and distributed it in a brochure during an open house at school and at community environmental events. Extended activities also included helping with adoption and release of redfish, water protection programs, and demonstration lessons at primary schools. Ongoing partners included state parks, an animal hospital, a mariculture center, and government fish and wildlife agencies.

The Animals in Danger Bookshelf

The Animals in Danger Bookshelf adds much to the process of finding out about threatened species. Through books such as *ChaseR* and *There's an Owl in the Shower*, students can read about other young people facing dilemmas and choices related to the balance of animals and humans. Other books, such as *Nights of the Pufflings*, make a case for young people's help in restoring that balance. To help you find books relevant to your particular projects, the book chart classifies the titles into several topic areas: for the future, rescue and restore, and caring relationships.

In general, the bookshelf features:

- An annotated bibliography arranged and alphabetized by title according to the general categories of nonfiction (N), picture books (P), and fiction (F). For nonfiction and fiction, length and recommended grade levels are included. The entries in the picture book category do not include suggested grade levels, since they can be successfully used with all ages.

- A chart organized by topic and category to help you find books relevant to particular projects.

- Recommendations from service learning colleagues and experts that include a book summary and ideas for service learning connections. (The number of recommended books varies in each bookshelf.)

Nonfiction: Animals in Danger

Can We Save Them? by David Dobson (Charlesbridge, 1997). Twelve species of endangered animals are featured, from the Florida panther to the Puerto Rican parrot to the ciu-ui fish of Truckee River, Nevada. Learn about present dangers and ways to restore natural environments. Filled with ideas for action. 30pp., grades K–6

The Chimpanzees I Love: Saving Their World and Ours by Jane Goodall (Scholastic, 2001). Jane Goodall's personal narrative describes her many years of coming to know chimpanzees. Photographs show the chimpanzees living within their communities, relationships between mothers and babies, and a glimpse at how chimpanzees think. Strategies presented for taking action include learning about conservation and "showing care and concern: (1) for animals…; (2) for the human community; (3) for the environment we all share." 80pp., all ages

Animals in Danger Bookshelf Topics

Topics	Books	Category
For the Future Books in this category discuss issues that we must think about as we consider how to protect animals from extinction.	Can We Save Them?	N
	Issues in the Environment (see page 131)	N
	There's an Owl in the Shower (see page 134)	F
Rescue and Restore Many organizations and individuals actively work to protect, rescue, and save animals from extinction, giving us models for our own work. Notice that young people are included among the activists.	The Animal Rescue Club *	F
	Backyard Rescue *	F
	Cat Up a Tree	P
	Come Back, Salmon: How a Group of Dedicated Kids Adopted Pigeon Creek and Brought It Back to Life *	N
	Healers of the Wild *	N
	Hoot *	F
	In Good Hands: Behind the Scenes at a Center for Orphaned and Injured Birds *	N
	Interrupted Journey: Saving Endangered Sea Turtles *	N
	Nights of the Pufflings *	N
	Once a Wolf: How Wildlife Biologists Fought to Bring Back the Gray Wolf	N
	One Day at Wood Green Animal Shelter *	N
	On the Brink of Extinction: The California Condor	N
	A Pelican Swallowed My Head—and Other Zoo Stories	N
	Pipaluk and the Whales *	P
	Saving Lilly *	F
	They Came from the Bronx: How the Buffalo Were Saved from Extinction	P
	Washing the Willow Tree Loon *	P
	The Wheel on the School	F
Caring Relationships This category includes stories, fiction and nonfiction, about people whose lives are touched by their animal neighbors.	ChaseR: a novel in e-mails	F
	The Chimpanzees I Love: Saving Their World and Ours	N
	The Deliverance of the Dancing Bears	P
	Ducks Disappearing	P
	The Four Ugly Cats in Apartment 3D *	F
	Hey! Get Off Our Train	P
	Intimate Nature: The Bond Between Women and Animals	N
	Make Way for Ducklings	P
	Mr. Lincoln's Way * (see page 99)	P
	When Agnes Caws	P

Page references are given for books that do not appear in the Animals in Danger Bookshelf but that can be found in the bookshelf lists of other chapters.
* These books include examples of young people in service-providing roles.

Come Back, Salmon: How a Group of Dedicated Kids Adopted Pigeon Creek and Brought It Back to Life by Molly Cone (Sierra Club Books, 1992). With teacher guidance, elementary students clean a stream, stock it with salmon, and preserve it as an unpolluted place where salmon can return to spawn. 48pp., grades 4–8

Healers of the Wild by Shannon K. Jacobs (Johnson Books, 2003). In this comprehensive guide for young people and their families, schools, and communities, we learn about the valuable work of wildlife rehabilitators. As legal caregivers for wild animals, they heal hundreds of sick, orphaned, and injured animals every year and release them back to the wild. Learn more about rascally raccoons, Buddy the bald eagle, and the endangered ridley sea turtle. Find out what young people are doing across the country to assist in rehabilitation. A glossary and reproducible pages are included. 212pp., all ages

In Good Hands: Behind the Scenes at a Center for Orphaned and Injured Birds by Stephen R. Swinburne (Sierra Club, 1998). Hannah, a sixteen-year-old volunteer, cares for injured owls, hawks, eagles, and other birds of prey, as they are nursed back to health and eventually released. 32pp., grades 3–8

Interrupted Journey: Saving Endangered Sea Turtles by Kathryn Lasky (Candlewick Press, 2001). Comprehensive text and photographs depict the dedicated work of volunteers and professionals protecting endangered sea turtles, particularly Kemp's ridley turtles. From ten-year-old Max and his mother, who patrol Cape Cod's beaches, to veterinarians, to a hotel owner who turns his pool into an aquarium, we see people who make a difference in a variety of ways. 48pp., all ages

Intimate Nature: The Bond Between Women and Animals edited by Linda Hogan, Deena Metzger, and Brenda Peterson (Fawcett Columbine, 1998). In this collection of stories, poetry, and essays, women scientists and writers speak out about their kinship with animals. The readings are simultaneously a wake-up call and celebration of this "ancient . . . dialogue between species." The seventy contributors include Barbara Kingsolver, Jane Goodall, Diane Fossey, and Marge Piercy. 455pp., young adult

> She communicated in sign language, using a vocabulary of over 1,000 words. She also understands spoken English, and often carries on "bilingual" conversations, responding in sign to questions asked in English. She is learning the letters of the alphabet, and can read some printed words, including her own name. . . . She laughs at her own jokes and the jokes of others. . . . The person I have described—and she is nothing less than a person to those who are acquainted with her—is Koko, a twenty-year-old lowland gorilla.
>
> FROM "THE CASE FOR THE PERSONHOOD OF GORILLAS" IN *INTIMATE NATURE: THE BOND BETWEEN WOMEN AND ANIMALS*

Nights of the Pufflings by Bruce McMillan (Houghton Mifflin, 1995). Travel to Heimaey Island, Iceland, where children stay up all night when the pufflings are ready to take flight for the first time. Many birds, confused by the village lights, head toward town instead of the open sea. The children rescue the birds from the dangers of cats and cars and set them on their proper course. 32pp., grades K–4

Once a Wolf: How Wildlife Biologists Fought to Bring Back the Gray Wolf by Stephen R. Swinburne (Houghton Mifflin, 1999). With rare and powerful photographs, the reader follows a study that led to heightened appreciation of the magnificent gray wolf and its reintroduction into Yellowstone National Park. 48pp., grades K–3

One Day at Wood Green Animal Shelter by Patricia Casey (Candlewick Press, 2001). The author describes a busy day at this shelter, where volunteers of all ages care for dogs, cats, a curious fox, a gecko, a horse, and a baby pigeon named Roast Potato. The visuals are a mix of art and photo collage—a unique blend to inspire the creative author/illustrator in us all. 29pp., grades K–6

On the Brink of Extinction: The California Condor by Caroline Arnold (Harcourt, 1993). Follow the California Condor Recovery Team as they attempt to restore the North American condor population by breeding these birds in captivity. An easy-to-read story of survival; includes photographs. 48pp., grades 4–8

A Pelican Swallowed My Head—and Other Zoo Stories by Edward Ricciuti (Simon & Schuster, 2002). The Wildlife Conservation Society runs the Bronx Zoo in New York City and has programs to save endangered species in more than fifty countries. These amazing stories explain the work of dedicated individuals at the zoo who create safe sanctuaries and natural habitats for lovable gorillas, Andean condors (the world's largest flying birds), rare and shy okapis, reticulated pythons, mole-rats, and many other animals. This book is filled with photographs and remarkable facts, including how a pelican swallowed a person's head—completely by accident! 222pp., grades 3–8

Picture Books: *Animals in Danger*

Cat Up a Tree by John and Ann Hassett (Houghton Mifflin, 1998). Nana cries, "Help!" when she sees a cat up a tree, but no help arrives from the firefighters or city hall or anyone else in town. In this counting book with a cause, more and more cats keep coming. Nana cleverly rescues these strays and, in the process, teaches the city about lending a hand.

The Deliverance of the Dancing Bears by Elizabeth Stanley (Kane/Miller, 2003). In this contemporary fable, a dancing bear terribly mistreated by her keeper dreams of freedom—wandering in the forests, drinking from mountain streams, catching fish among the rocks. To the keeper's surprise, an old man offers to buy the bear, and with this event comes the bear's taste of freedom.

Ducks Disappearing by Phyllis Reynolds Naylor (Atheneum, 1997). Young Willie solves the mystery of disappearing ducks. Most importantly, he explains to the adults how ducks "belong to everyone." A lovely story of a child who pays attention and cares to make a difference.

Hey! Get Off Our Train by John Birmingham (Crown, 1989). At bedtime, a young boy takes a trip on his toy train and rescues endangered animals, returning just in time for school. Did the trip really happen? If this was a dream, then why is there a seal in the bathtub?

Recommendation from the Field
by Nan Peterson, The Blake School

Make Way for Ducklings by Robert McCloskey (Viking, 1941). Beautiful brown and white drawings illustrate this lovely story of Mr. and Mrs. Mallard looking for a safe place to raise their ducklings. They are met with appreciation, respect, and delight by the citizens of Boston in the Public Garden.

Children can explore service learning themes of respect for nature, park appreciation, animal rights or animal protection, and environmental issues. Students can investigate the needs of the community and the wildlife that lives or migrates through the area. Activities may include:

- Visiting a wildlife center or park, where the need might be to pick up trash, plant annual flowers, dig out invasive plants such as buckthorn or loosestrife, or write a walking guide to the park or center or animals that live in the area.

- Forming a partnership with an animal humane society and collecting needed items like newspapers, leashes, collars, towels, and small rugs.

- Making simple bird feeders or bird baths to give to a senior center or your school.

Pipaluk and the Whales by John Himmelman (National Geographic Society, 2002). Never before had Pipaluk and her father seen thousands of whales trapped in a narrow opening of ice. "The whales have helped keep our people alive for many centuries. We owe them too much to slaughter them while they are helpless," he explains. The villagers keep the whales alive, even using their own food supplies. But when the icebreaker ship makes a passage for the whales, they do not move. Pipaluk follows the song in her heart to set the whales free. Based on an event that took place off Russia's Chukchi Peninsula in 1984.

They Came from the Bronx: How the Buffalo Were Saved from Extinction by Neil Waldman (Boyds Mills Press, 2001). On an October morning in 1907, a Comanche grandmother and her grandson await a train that carries a herd of buffalo for reintroduction to Oklahoma. Two stories interweave: one that shows the near destruction of this mighty animal, and one that shows the rescue efforts led by concerned conservationists. In the historical note, other efforts to restore the buffalo to their native lands in Canada and the United States are described.

Washing the Willow Tree Loon by Jacqueline B. Martin (Simon & Schuster, 1995). When a barge hits a bridge and a thick rush of oil coats the birds of Turtle Bay, people from all walks of life stop their work as bakers, doctors, house painters, and artists to help.

When Agnes Caws by Candace Fleming (Aladdin, 2002). Eight-year-old Agnes, who has an extraordinary talent for bird-calling, is sent to locate the elusive pink-headed duck. Little did she suspect that a dastardly bird collector would attempt to use her skill to capture and stuff this precious rare bird. Can Agnes save the duck and herself?

Fiction: *Animals in Danger*

The Animal Rescue Club by John Himmelman (HarperCollins, 1998). Who can help a squirrel trapped in mud or a baby opossum caught in a drain? The Animal Rescue Club: dedicated kids who work with a wildlife rehabilitator to help the wild animals in their neighborhood. An author's note provides thoughtful advice and safety information. 48pp., grades 2–5

Backyard Rescue by Hope Ryden (Tambourine, 1994). Two ten-year-old friends, Lindsey and Greta, set up a back-yard wildlife hospital for wounded animals. They hatch snapping turtle eggs and find a safe home for an injured raccoon. When faced with closure due to Fish and Game laws, they find local resources to protect the animals in their care. 128pp., grades 3–6

ChaseR: a novel in e-mails by Michael J. Rosen (Candlewick Press, 2002). Chase's family has moved from an urban to a rural community, a monumental shift for a teenager. Fortunately, he has his computer and uses email to stay connected with his city friends. Unfortunately, he is caught in a complex dilemma regarding local hunters and their prey. Will Chase come to terms with hunters and hunting? 152pp., young adult

The Four Ugly Cats in Apartment 3D by Marilyn Sachs (Atheneum, 2002). Lily, a ten-year-old latchkey kid, lives near grouchy Mr. Freeman and his four yowling cats. A single gesture of kindness from this crotchety man changes Lily's disposition toward him. When he dies, Lily steps in, determined to "do the right thing" and accomplish the impossible: find the perfect home for the cats that nobody wants. 67pp., grades 3–5

Hoot by Carl Hiaasen (Knopf, 2002). Roy Eberhardt never could have guessed that being bullied by his nemesis Dana Matherson would lead to rescuing small endangered burrowing owls. In fact, every surprising event—seeing potty-trained alligators, meeting a renegade eco-avenger, and making several unexpected friends—leads Roy to think he may enjoy his middle school years after all.

Saving Lilly by Peg Kehret (Simon & Schuster, 2001). After learning about animal abuse, Erin and her friend

David create an uproar by refusing to go on the class field trip to the Glitter Tent Circus. Their next challenge is saving Lilly, a mistreated elephant, from being sold to a hunting park. Will sixth graders succeed in standing up to the circus owner's greed and make a difference? 149pp., grades 3–6

> "What are you kids going to do with an elephant?" Mr. Hinkley asked. "They aren't cheap to feed, you know. Lilly weighs two tons and eats a lot of hat every day."
>
> "We're going to send her to an elephant sanctuary in Tennessee," I said.
>
> "Of all the fool ideas I have ever heard," Mr. Hinkley said, "that one takes the cake. Have you thought what you could buy for eight thousand dollars?"
>
> Yes, I thought. *I can buy freedom for Lilly.*
>
> FROM *SAVING LILLY*

The Wheel on the School by Meindert Dejong (Harper, 1954). Why did storks stop coming to our town? Lina wonders. Guided by her teacher's words, "sometimes when we wonder, we can make things begin to happen," Lina and her classes infuse the villagers with the challenge and excitement to bring back the storks, renew the environment, and build an inclusive community. 298pp., grades 4–7

Interviews with Authors:
The Story Behind the Story

These interviews with Shannon K. Jacobs (*Healers of the Wild: People Who Care for Injured and Orphaned Wildlife*) and Deena Metzger (*Intimate Nature: The Bond Between Women and Animals*) tell the "story behind the story." For many years, I have attended writing classes taught by Deena Metzger, who actually lives with wolves and consistently demonstrates the interconnection between the animal and human worlds by her teaching and actions. In contrast, I learned of Shannon Jacobs's book by accident—a fabulous find that resulted from an Internet search. After

speaking with her on the phone for a few minutes, I decided she had a unique story to tell and a definite passion for the well-being of animals.

Shannon K. Jacobs, author of
Healers of the Wild: People Who Care for Injured and Orphaned Wildlife

About eight years ago I found a couple of injured birds. One probably had been poisoned by pesticides. I asked everyone I knew, "Who takes care of hurt birds?" No one had an answer. I discovered that most veterinarians and zoos don't treat wildlife because of concern about diseases and because they don't have the expertise to care for native wildlife. Fortunately, someone suggested I take the birds to a wildlife rehabilitator outside of Denver who cares for small mammals and birds. The rehabilitator works full time as a teacher during the school year and cares for wildlife in the summer. She pays for everything herself. I found her work absolutely fascinating. Later, I asked friends what they knew about wildlife rehabilitation. Like me, they knew almost nothing. Quickly my interest turned into a passion to write a book that would provide needed information and a national overview.

Through research I met people from all parts of the country who are committed to taking care of animals that most people don't know about, care about, or even think about. Most have worked intimately with wildlife for many years. These wildlife experts know more about wild animals than many vets and government wildlife people.

Even with good intentions, I would have done everything wrong if I had cared for the sick and injured birds I found. I knew nothing about their natural history. Now I know that all wildlife cannot be treated the same. Each species needs specific care. Some birds eat mainly fruits, others insects, and others eat both. Some have to be taught how to fish or hunt. If the animals don't get proper care, they won't be able to survive in the wild when released. The goal of wildlife rehabilitation, always, is to release healthy animals back to the wild.

Wildlife rehabilitators take care of our neglected native wildlife. No one else does this. Most kids probably know more know about elephants and hippos than about the fascinating crows in their backyards or the raccoon family living in a dead tree. How many students know about opossums, the only marsupials in North America, or about prairie dogs? Prairie dogs are a "keystone" species, meaning that several other species depend on them for survival; we are losing them to development every day.

Healers of the Wild integrates two of my favorite interests: native wildlife and helping kids learn about the natural world. I began the book by interviewing wildlife rehabilitators in Colorado, where I live, and branched out to other places in the country. I contacted wildlife rehabilitators in each state to be sure I had information about most regions of the country. I feature a cross-section of wildlife: birds, marine animals, mammals, land mammals, and reptiles.

Since beginning my research, I have volunteered with several wildlife rehabilitators. I fell madly in love with baby birds while feeding and caring for them over a few summers. One day I was in an outside enclosure, putting food and water out for birds soon to be released. In the same enclosure were a pine siskin, a goldfinch, and a meadowlark, and it struck me what an honor it was to be so close to such magnificent wild creatures. Wildlife rehabilitation is the only way to experience truly wild creatures up close.

Find out who your local wildlife rehabilitators are, and then contact the rehabilitators and ask what they need. Most have a "wish list." Usually they need volunteers, supplies, donations, and experts in a variety of areas. Although young people under eighteen typically are not allowed to work directly with animals, they can help in other important ways. For example, they prepare formulas for the babies or chop up fruits and vegetables for the older critters. Kids also build cages.

There is a picture in my book of a Birds of Prey Foundation volunteer holding a Swainson's hawk in a classroom. This is an education bird, kept with a special license because of extensive injuries that would not allow it to survive in the wild. The volunteer and hawk visited a seventh-grade class that had studied raptors and knew about their natural history. The students had raised money to "adopt" the bird. They donate money to the rehabilitation center and receive photos and information about their "adopted" animal. Through the process of helping the center and seeing the bird up close, the students enhance their knowledge and appreciation of these majestic birds.

I hope *Healers of the Wild* conveys the value of our native wildlife. By being better informed, we can learn how to protect our wild neighbors. Since humans cause at least 90 percent of wildlife injuries, we also can learn how to prevent injuries and what to do (and not do) should we find an injured or orphaned animal.

Wildlife rehabilitation has been called "the last frontier of medicine." Interested in becoming a wildlife veterinarian, veterinarian technician, or volunteer? Our native wild creatures need all the help they can get.

Deena Metzger, *coeditor of*
Intimate Nature: The Bond Between Women and Animals

The book *Intimate Nature: The Bond Between Women and Animals* was inspired by the relationship that I have had with animals—I have lived with wolves for seventeen years—and the bond I have felt with women who honor animals as intelligent and sensitive beings. Indigenous peoples have always recognized animals, but most of us no longer remember who animals are. Women have unique relationships with animals because we value the knowledge that comes from intimacy as much as the knowledge that comes from scientific observation. I wanted to be able to document these relationships and their profundity, so that they would be visible to the world.

Animals carry different and varied intelligences. It is possible to have relationships with animals in which we understand and learn about and from each other. The great tragedy is that animals and other species are becoming extinct at a horrendous rate because of diminishing habitats, hunting, poaching, human use, enslavement, and environmental degeneration. Their fate and the fate of the earth are intimately tied. We may not only lose them but ourselves; we may lose the whole world.

Intimate Nature reaches out through essays, interviews, stories, and poetry. Some can be read to or told to children who are not yet ready to read themselves. The stories recapitulate real events; they are stories that move and inspire anyone who is ready to learn. The stories open a world that has been closed for a long time in our culture but is a world that children remember. These stories tell of the many faces of animals and the possibility of living in friendship with them. In "The Chimpanzee at Stanford," a short, nonfiction story by Fran Peavey, a chimpanzee recognizes the humans who will be her allies. In "I Acknowledge Mine," Jane Goodall describes visiting a research laboratory where experiments on chimpanzees are being conducted. One chimpanzee recognizes that she is crying for him. This confirms his intelligence, ethical awareness, and spiritual development.

Through *Intimate Nature*, I want to support young people's instinctive love for and camaraderie with animals. I want them to hold on to this basic knowledge without thinking they must outgrow it. There are a thousand ways to support animals, from political activity on behalf of endangered whales, elephants, and wolves, to fighting against cruelty to animals, to stopping use of pesticides that destroy the environment. We can help work with any number of nature preserves for endangered, abandoned, or abused animals. And we can be sure there is enough food and homes for all animals by feeding the birds or rescuing animals from shelters. Let us not injure animals for our entertainment. We can discern which circuses or zoos are inhumane and cruel and insist that the animals be well treated and happy and content in the places they are required to work.

We can all find our own way to honor those animals that are important to us or come to us. And we can find ways—imaginatively and actively—to enter into dialogue with them. Regard your friendships and relationships with animals as being as complex and important as your relationships with human beings.

COMMUNITY SAFETY

In today's world, everybody is bombarded with issues related to community safety, and unfortunately young people are no exception. On school playgrounds, children wonder how to react to a bully, with teasing and taunting being important issues both for the children who are struggling to stand up for themselves and those who know their behaviors are hurtful. Youth wrestle with peer pressure and worry about exclusion. Gang activity and other acts of violence create fear and feelings of helplessness. Acts of terrorism and war know no national boundaries. Service learning provides an educational strategy for sorting through these challenging and complex issues. Through literature and research, students can learn about the issues at the same time they are discovering new questions to examine. This can help them determine ways to participate in constructive actions.

Whether the concern is safety on a playground, in a neighborhood, or in a war zone, community safety issues offer the opportunity to examine the concept of community. What is community? Is it local or is it global? Although the term is a common one, the actual meaning can be difficult to grasp and define. Each person brings a different understanding based on his or her own experience. One perspective comes from looking at the history of the term itself. The word *community* has roots reaching back to the Indo-European bases *mei*, meaning "change" or "exchange," and *kom*, meaning "with," which combined to produce the word *kommein*: "shared by all."* We might define *community*,

then, as a shared change or exchange. This definition shows community in a dynamic state that can be influenced—in this case, by service learning.

Preparation: Getting Ready for Service Learning Involving Community Safety

The following activities can be used in the preparation stage to promote learning and skill development related to a variety of community safety issues. These activities can be used with different age ranges during preparation to help students examine key issues through research, analyze community needs, and gain the knowledge they need to effectively contribute to the design of their service plan. Since literature is often an important part of preparation, you can find recommended titles on this theme in the Community Safety Bookshelf later in this chapter.

Activity: Draw Your Community. To make the idea of community more concrete, have students present the idea visually. Provide lengths of butcher paper and plenty of markers. Invite students to be absolutely silent as they draw "community." This silence can help maintain the integrity of each student's concept of community, but it also encourages them to collaborate differently and strengthens the reflection that comes after this exercise. Students may work on the same paper or in small groups around smaller sheets as they draw whatever community looks like to them. Following five to ten minutes of art, have students discuss their drawings and their observations. Did the students work individually? Were they aware of what others drew, and did that influence them? What is most apparent in their drawings—people, buildings, animals? Is something missing? Does the art reflect the best of the community or the challenges? What

*This definition was offered by Peter M. Senge, Art Kleiner, Charlotte Roberts, Richard B. Ross, and Bryan J. Smith in *The Fifth Discipline Fieldbook* (Doubleday, 1994).

would they add to improve their community, and how could this be done?

Activity: A Look at Conflict and Community Building. Exploring the nature of conflict can be valuable in examining issues of community safety. Ask a group of people whether conflict is positive or negative, and the majority will probably respond "negative." However, the Latin root of conflict—*confligere*—means "to strike together." This implied friction is an absolute necessity for moving forward and motivating change. Perhaps the personal and collective skills that are key to resolving the conflicts that inevitably occur are more important than the conflicts themselves. Use these ideas to help you explore the nature and importance of conflict with your students.

In class, read aloud any book from the Community Safety Bookshelf, and examine the story line for conflict. Where is it? What is the dilemma facing the characters? Stop the story at any point, and ask, "What would you do?" Have students write the next part of the book. Delve into conflict as the compelling element in all forms of storytelling, including literature, television, film, and song lyrics. Next, have your students identify what the characters in the books do to build community. What ideas do your students have about safety needs, for repairing conflict, and for promoting positive social interaction? How could older students be role models for younger children in promoting healthy, thoughtful behaviors? What shared experiences do they think bring community members together? All of these questions can help you and your students lay the groundwork for a range of different kinds of community safety-based service projects.

Find Out More About Community Safety

To learn more about these issues and to get ideas for service and action, visit these Web sites and organizations online:

nationaltcc.org Teens, Crime, and the Community is a national program of the National Crime Prevention Council enabling teens to "get involved in crime prevention to make themselves safer and their communities stronger."

www.esrnational.org/home.htm Educators for Social Responsibility (ESR) helps educators create safe, caring, respectful, and productive learning environments.

---

www.nationalsave.org/index.php The National Association of S.A.V.E. (Students Against Violence Everywhere) is a student-driven organization encouraging young people to learn about alternatives to violence and practice what they learn through school and community service projects.

Making Connections Across the Curriculum

Some service learning activities naturally lend themselves to interdisciplinary work and making connections across the curriculum. These connections strengthen and broaden student learning, helping them meet academic standards. More than likely, you'll be looking for these connections and ways to encourage them well before the students ever start working on service learning activities. As with the entire service learning process, it helps to remain flexible, because some connections can be spontaneously generated by the questions raised throughout and by the needs of the project. To help you think about cross-curricular connections and where you can look for them, the Curricular Web for this chapter (page 91) gives examples of many different ways this theme can be used in different academic areas. (The examples in the next section also demonstrate various ways this theme can be used across the curriculum.)

> It is better to be part of a great whole than to be the whole of a small part.
>
> FREDERICK DOUGLASS, ABOLITIONIST

Service Learning Scenarios: Ideas for Action

Ready to take action? What follows are projects that have been successfully carried out by elementary, middle, or high school students. Most of these scenarios and examples explicitly include some aspects of preparation, action, reflection, and demonstration. These scenarios can be a rich source of project, resource, and

Community Safety Across the Curriculum

English/Language Arts

- Write stories or skits that feature characters being bullied or teased and the ways they deal with it
- Make a library display of books that teach about friendship
- Compare coverage of a story on a local act of violence with one about community building

Social Studies/History

- Role-play scenarios that focus on various social skills including how to make friends and stop name-calling
- Research hate crimes and the organizations that intervene
- Follow current events that demonstrate efforts by governments and grassroots organizations to resolve international turmoil; compare strategies and the results

Languages

- Research the symbols used for public safety in different countries
- Learn how to say words related to peace in many languages
- Make multilingual posters that promote peace and peer conflict resolution

Theater, Music, & Visual Arts

- Create and perform skits that illustrate peer mediation skills and problem solving in settings where conflicts often occur, such as in the lunchroom, on the school bus, or on the playground
- Research the origin of and perform songs from different countries about peace
- Find political cartoons that use images to comment about issues related to crime, violence, bullying, or conflict on the world stage

Community Safety

Math

- Research and create a report on local crime statistics
- Monitor the rate of discipline referrals before and after peer mediation or conflict resolution programs are instituted
- Survey students to find out how often they're teased, bullied, and pressured to conform with peers; tabulate and report statistics

Computer

- Using the Internet, read about global events as reported by newspapers in different countries or by different participants; compare findings
- Research student-created Web sites that discuss safety issues such as gun safety, peace forums, and anti-bullying campaigns
- Brainstorm ways that computers can be used for community building, i.e., setting up Listservs and sharing information about community events

Science

- Discuss with family and friends the risks associated with smoking or drinking
- Study about human physiological reactions when experiencing strong emotions such as anger, love, hurt, fear, and joy
- Research stories of how community building has occurred through environmental activities such as beach clean-ups, community gardens, and student-led recycling campaigns

Physical Education

- Play noncompetitive games and invent new ones
- Learn strategies for what to do in risky situations; be certain to make these age-appropriate
- Mentor younger children in sports as a means of community building

curriculum ideas for you to draw upon. While the grade levels are given as a reference, most project ideas can be adapted to suit younger or older students, and many are suitable for cross-age partnerships.

Peace Keepers Everywhere: Grades K–5. An elementary school administration decided to educate youth in ways to reduce bullying and teasing. With faculty and student council agreement, educators from a local nonprofit organization led workshops and trainings on conflict resolution and peer mediation for teachers. Parent information sessions were held and an article was published in the back-to-school newsletter about the new campaign. Education on conflict resolution was carried out in all classrooms. To augment student skills and involvement, eighty children in the third through fifth grades attended workshops to become "peace keepers" and peer mediators on the playground and school buses.

Reaching Out Across the Globe: Grades K–12. Students in schools across the United States have found ways to reach across the globe to war-torn countries and places that have been devastated by natural disasters. They have:

- Made health kits for people who have had to leave their homes because of war. The kits, which can be distributed by relief agencies such as the Red Cross, contain a towel, a toothbrush, and soap.

- Made T-shirts to sell at community fairs to raise money for the Heifer Project. The Heifer Project (*www.heifer.org*) buys cows, sheep, and chickens for families around the world.

- Collected canned goods for earthquake victims.

- Participated in a bike-a-thon to raise money for Bikes not Bombs (*www.bikesnotbombs.org*), which is a group that collects old bikes, fixes them, and gives them to people in other countries who cannot afford them.

- Collected used eyeglasses for "The Gift of Sight," a Lions Clubs (*www.lionsclubs.org*) program that repairs and gives eyeglasses to people in other countries. On Halloween, this program sponsors Sight Night. Children leave signs on their neighbors' doors in late October to let them know that they will be collecting eyeglasses. Then, on Halloween night, they pick up the glasses as they trick-or-treat. Collected eyeglasses are cleaned, repaired, and hand-delivered during optical and medical missions to developing countries.

A Community Finds Heroes: Grades 1–5. As a response to events of September 11, 2001, elementary school children in West Hollywood, California, were invited by their city council to contribute art and poetry based on several themes: "Wishes for the World," "We Give Thanks," and "Our Heroes." Age-appropriate discussion allowed students to share thoughts and feelings and to ask questions of adults. The students' artwork and words were displayed in City Hall. After reviewing the heroes identified by students, teachers and after-school-program specialists scheduled visits to bring these people face-to-face with the kids through field visits. In pairs (a male and female in each set), students interviewed doctors and sheriffs. Firefighters received first-grade visitors at the fire station, and a third-grade class met farmers at the local farmers' market. Students conducted thorough interviews with their heroes and published a series of books, with words and art: *Our Heroes.*

Slow Down—You Move Too Fast! Grade 3. Third-grade students in Wisconsin observed that the speed limit in front of their school was too high and decided to do something about it. They partnered with local police to record the speeds of the cars going by and created a graph showing how fast cars were going. Next, they held a car wash and surveyed adults regarding the speed in front of the school. Finally, they prepared a presentation for the city council requesting that the council immediately lower the speed limit in front of the school. When the students delivered the presentation, the council members were so impressed that they suspended the rules and voted to lower the speed limit that night. The result? A lower speed limit in front of the school and a safer place for the children.

Spreading the Ideas of Conflict Resolution: Grades 4 and 5. In an annual event sponsored by a city government in California, elementary students at two schools meet to celebrate their peer mediation programs. The Conflict Wizards and Peace Patrol groups began with getting-acquainted activities and then role-played common situations they encounter on the playgrounds, such as disagreements over game rules. The groups then created a spiral-bound book together. Previous titles written by the students include *The ABCs of Peer Mediation*, *Poems for Peace* and *Creating Safe Schools for Kids*. These books are distributed to every local school and library and made available to community agencies. As a "thank you" to the students for their dedication, the city awards certificates of merit and presents each young person with a copy of Barbara Lewis's *Kids with Courage: True Stories About Young People Making a Difference*.

> You must be the change
> you wish to see in the world.
> MAHATMA GANDHI, STATESMAN

Documenting Stories of War and Peace: Grades 4–12. Social studies and government teachers have used the parable *Feathers and Fools* to examine issues of combat and coexistence, when teaching about war and conflict. The students drew parallels between the book and the specific dilemmas faced in historical or current events. From this launch pad, students have interviewed war veterans, as well as people who did not serve in the military but felt the impact of war at home. They have asked, for example, questions about how living through times of war has affected how these people have lived in times of peace. Stories have been compiled into books, presented at community gatherings, posted on the Web, used to create a "living museum," and used as the basis for dramatic presentations.

Building Friendships: Grade 6. A sixth-grade English/social studies teacher asked students to write about their earliest experiences of friendship or bullying. Through discussion, the class concluded that elementary children often struggle with both—how to maintain and build strong friendships and how to

stand up to bullying behaviors. They identified third grade as a place where they could have an impact and wrote letters to the third-grade classes in a nearby elementary school to verify the need. The project: to lead interactive lessons that model friendship. Using the book *How Humans Make Friends*, the middle school students developed skits and scenarios, which they presented to the younger kids, and made posters, which they left in the classrooms. The students visited three classes weekly for three weeks. Feedback from the third-grade teachers in between visits made the reflection sessions instructive and improved the project and experience for everyone involved.

A Symposium for Peace: Grades 6–12. Bringing students and community together offers an opportunity for learning, community building, and collaborative action. Following the attacks on September 11, 2001, adults and students in St. Cloud, Minnesota, designed a symposium that allowed them to spend time together examining issues of mutual concern. Topics included religious tolerance, dispute resolution, teen suicide, and local refugee programs. Students invited agency representatives to visit classes, and agencies asked youth to participate in community forums and planning meetings.

Teen Violence: Grades 7 and 10. Seventh-grade students read *Making Up Megaboy* as part of their English studies. As the students discussed the multiple points of view represented in the story, they asked questions about real instances of youth violence in their region. With their teacher, they designed a course of study to learn about the issue. Their studies included collecting articles on teen violence from the Internet and inviting a local reporter to their classroom for a discussion of responsible journalism. Based on what they had learned, they developed an educational evening for parents and other students. They read selections from *Megaboy* and discussed ways to maintain ongoing mutually respectful parent-child communication. Later, they documented the resulting recommendations in an article for their school newspaper, which included "Tips on Talking with Your Teen."

A high school teacher who learned of the seventh graders' project replicated it in her tenth-grade class using the book *Give a Boy a Gun*. The high school students discussed the challenges of breaking down cliques and reaching out to students known as "loners" or just "different." They initiated a "Mix-It-Up Day" in which some students agreed to have lunch with randomly assigned people and then to meet with their lunch partners once a week for three weeks. During the second semester, the project was repeated with twice as many students. Later, students even encouraged a similar project for improved teacher-to-teacher interaction. Comments during reflection showed an increase in tolerance and appreciation that extended even to students and faculty who had not taken part.

> Every month, seven percent of eighth graders stay home from school because they are afraid of being bullied by another child.
>
> ELIZABETH RUSCH, *GENERATION FIX: YOUNG IDEAS FOR A BETTER WORLD*

Oral Histories on Violence: Grade 9. After conducting a community needs survey in their study skills class, students in San Francisco chose to study violence. They conducted research on one of the four types of violence—hate crimes, relationship violence, gang violence, and police brutality. Students read biographies, fiction, a play, newspaper articles, and expository text. They formed a coalition with local organizations and planned a community conference to raise issues and have discussions about violence. Also, after conducting a practice interview with a former teacher who had been the victim of police brutality, students conducted interviews with people who had perpetrated or been the target of violence. Their compilation of these people's stories, *I Have Been Strong: Oral Histories on Violence*, has been given to many local agencies and schools.

Transforming the "Bully": Grades 9 and 10. High school students in the Youth Explorers Program in central California worked with local law enforcement to reach out to younger children. They selected *Toestomper and the Caterpillars* as the ideal book for their Friendship Campaign. Students created posters highlighting the key points of the story. At after-school programs, the Explorers held the kids' attention with the humorous story and dramatic effects and led small group discussions about friendship and transforming the "bully" in all of us.

Lessons from the Middle Ages: Grades 9–12. High school teachers in Berkeley used *When Plagues Strike: The Black Death, Smallpox, AIDS* to address issues of tolerance on their campus. The book discusses the issues of intolerance, blame, and scapegoating as they relate to the diseases in the title. Students have used their studies to plan a tolerance campaign at their high school, educating their peers about the perils of scapegoating and the possibilities of creating a more tolerant and inclusive campus.

The Campaign for "Truth": Grades 9–12. Creativity hit a peak when Florida high school students were given a voice in developing "Truth," an antismoking social marketing campaign using tobacco settlement funds. Their candid approach and youthful appeal has reduced smoking by teens in Florida, and now their public service announcements have hit the national airwaves. On the other side of the United States in Hawaii, students used theater to discourage smoking. They conducted pre- and post-tests with their young audiences to find out the impact of their original performances. The results: Similar to their Florida peers, the teens' dramatic efforts have been more effective in making an impact than adult-initiated forms of prevention.

Rock Out on Tolerance: Grades 11 and 12. High school students in Florida used popular culture to send an important message to their peers about tolerance. Tapping their collective creative talents, students wrote an original song addressing three relevant issues of prejudice: race, physical differences, and sexism. Through their campus media center, the students learned the skills necessary to create a rock video that would illustrate the drama of discrimination and cause viewers to think about their personal behavior.

The Community Safety Bookshelf

The Community Safety Bookshelf covers a broad spectrum of topics, from personal safety and bullying to community building and the world stage. To help you find books relevant to your particular projects, the book chart classifies the titles into several topic areas: personal safety, bullying, conflict resolution, local violence, hate crimes, the world stage, and community building.

In general, the bookshelf features:

- An annotated bibliography arranged and alphabetized by title according to the general categories of nonfiction (N), picture books (P), and fiction (F). For nonfiction and fiction, length and recommended grade levels are included. The entries in the picture book category do not include suggested grade levels, since they can be successfully used with all ages.

- A chart organized by topic and category to help you find books relevant to particular projects.

- Recommendations from service learning colleagues and experts that include a book summary and ideas for service learning connections. (The number of recommended books varies in each bookshelf.)

Community Safety Bookshelf Topics

Topics	Books	Category
Personal Safety Personal safety involves knowing how to take care of ourselves in a wide variety of situations at home, at school, and in the community.	50 Ways to a Safer World	N
	Geography Club	F
	Handbook for Boys (see page 117)	F
	Hands Are Not for Hitting	P
	Holes	F
	How Humans Make Friends	P
	The Safe Zone: A Kid's Guide to Personal Safety ‡	N
	Smoking: A Risky Business	N
	Stargirl	F
	A Step from Heaven (see page 170)	F
Bullying Inside every child who exhibits bullying behavior on the playground is a child who needs to be reached. These selections look at peer pressure, isolation, and being "different," as well as how to make friends.	Buddha Boy	F
	Cowboy Boy	F
	Don't Laugh at Me	P
	Harry Potter and the Sorcerer's Stone	F
	Hey, Little Ant!	P
	Hoot (see page 86)	F
	The Hundred Dresses (see page 156)	F
	I Miss Franklin P. Shuckles	P
	King of the Kooties	F
	The Misfits	F
	Mr. Lincoln's Way *	P
	Nobody Knew What to Do: A Story About Bullying	P
	On the Fringe	F
	Pinky and Rex and the Bully	F
	The Revealers	F
	Summer Wheels *	P
	Thank You, Mr. Falker (see page 182)	P
	Toestomper and the Caterpillars	P
	Wings	P
	Wringer	F

continued ⟶

Topics	Books	Category
Conflict Resolution The best defense has nothing to do with hitting, kicking, or punching. Finding the tools of tolerance and peaceful resolution helps to make communities safer.	*Cootie Shots: Theatrical Inoculations Against Bigotry* *Define "Normal"* *Feathers and Fools* *Increase the Peace: The ABCs of Tolerance* *Mole Music* *Siddhartha* *The Sissy Duckling* *The Skirt* (see page 170) *The Summer My Father Was Ten* (see page 143) *We Can Work It Out: Conflict Resolution for Children*	N F P N P F P F P N
Local Violence Making sense of violence is always a challenge. Books offer a safe haven to investigate what happens in our communities and help us to think about our choices.	*Any Small Goodness* (see page 169) *Bat 6* (see page 198) *Big Mouth and Ugly Girl* *Drive-By* *Give a Boy a Gun* *If You Come Softly* (see page 199) *It Doesn't Have to Be This Way: A Barrio Story/* *No tiene que ser así: Una historia del barrio* *Making Up Megaboy* ‡ *Romeo and Juliet* *Shadow of the Dragon* *Smoky Nights* *Stars in the Darkness* * *Your Move*	F F F F F F P F F F P P P

Hate Crimes
Breaking the cycle of hate requires taking a firm stand. When we read about an individual willing to risk personal safety to protect others or about a community that bands together, we are encouraged to stand stronger.
	Chicken Sunday
	The Christmas Menorahs: How a Town Fought Hate
	A Different Kind of Hero (see page 169)
	Passage to Freedom: The Sugihara Story (see page 198)
	When Plagues Strike: The Black Death, Smallpox, AIDS
	    (see page 73)
	The Yellow Star: The Legend of King Christian X
	    of Denmark
		P
		P
		F
		P
		N
		
		P

The World Stage Being informed about the challenges faced in other parts of the world develops knowledge and empathy. From Tibet to Ireland to Sudan to New York City, we can learn about others and become citizens of the world.	*After the Dancing Days* *Alloy Peace Book* * *Behind the Mountains* (see page 169) *Boxes for Katje* * *Charlie Wilcox* *The Clay Marble* (see page 169) *Dream Freedom* * (see page 199) *Girl of Kosovo* *Gleam and Glow*	F N F P F F F F P

continued ⟶

Topics	Books	Category
The World Stage continued	It's Still a Dog's New York: A Book of Healing	P
	A Life Like Mine: How Children Live Around the World * (see page 196)	N
	The Middle of Everywhere: The World's Refugees Come to Our Town (see page 167)	N
	Stand Up for Your Rights * (see page 197)	N
	When Christmas Comes Again: The World War I Diary of Simone Spencer	F
Community Building Coming together to build a diverse and thriving community is a memorable experience. Books in this category offer models to examine and stories to emulate.	DeShawn Days *	P
	The Green Truck Garden Giveaway *‡ (see page 142)	P
	Seedfolks * (see page 143)	F
	Somebody Loves You, Mr. Hatch (see page 116)	P
	Something Beautiful * (see page 198)	P
	Wartville Wizard (see page 133)	P

Page references are given for books that do not appear in the Community Safety Bookshelf but that can be found in the bookshelf lists of other chapters.
* These books include examples of young people in service-providing roles.
‡ These books are out of print but still worth finding.

Nonfiction: Community Safety

Alloy Peace Book by Tucker Shaw (HarperTrophy, 2002). Written in the aftermath of September 11, 2001, this book examines peace and what it means to young people around the world. A timeline of peace in the twentieth century is outlined; Nobel Peace Prize winners are featured; and young people speak, describing where they were when the September 11 attacks occurred, telling how they responded through social action, and sharing their fears and dreams. 144pp., young adult

Cootie Shots: Theatrical Inoculations Against Bigotry for Kids, Parents, and Teachers by Norma Bowles with Mark E. Rosenthal (Fringe Benefits, 2001). This unique collection of plays, songs, and poems designed for young audiences promotes tolerance and celebrates diversity. 144pp., grades 3–12

50 Ways to a Safer World by Patricia Occhiuzzo Giggans and Barrie Levy (Seal Press, 1997). This compilation of facts, ideas, and resources includes ideas to prevent violence and create a safer community. Among the ideas are tips on raising safety-smart and media-savvy kids, conducting school safety audits, and keeping guns away from children. 144pp., grades 7–12

Increase the Peace: The ABCs of Tolerance by Devora Kaye (ABCD Books, 2002). Written by a high school sophomore, this alphabetical exploration of tolerance includes practical ideas for social activism. The book will inspire students to action and may also inspire them to create their own books. A percentage of all sales is contributed to a nonprofit organization that supports educational programs for nonviolence. 29pp., all grades

The Safe Zone: A Kid's Guide to Personal Safety by Donna Chaiet and Francine Russell (Morrow, 1998). This book helps children consider ways to protect themselves without fighting by developing personal awareness, using body language, developing self-esteem, and communicating effectively. The book is filled with activities and ideas and offers plenty of scenarios for classroom discussion and problem solving, including situations that occur in public, at home, and even on the Internet. This book is out of print but still worth finding. 160pp., grades 3–8

Smoking: A Risky Business by Laurence Pringle (Morrow Junior, 1996). Tobacco is a legal product that, when used as directed, causes death. Despite educational and media campaigns to alert the public to the dangers of smoking, people of all ages continue to inhale. This book reviews science, political, media, and health issues related to smoking. Since tobacco companies spend vast amounts to promote smoking, it is vitally important for young people to be informed about the reasons to avoid addiction to tobacco. 124pp., young adult

> In 1604, King James of England wrote that smoking was a "custom lothsome to the eye, hatefull to the Nose, harmefull to the braine, dangerous to the Lungs."
>
> FROM *SMOKING: A RISKY BUSINESS*

We Can Work It Out: Conflict Resolution for Children by Barbara K. Polland (Tricycle Press, 2000). This book includes photographs and questions about conflicts that arise frequently in the lives of young children, along with an introduction for parents and teachers. The book provides a vehicle for discussing a range of topics that can help children become more successful in resolving conflicts. 64pp., grades K–2

Picture Books: Community Safety

Boxes for Katje by Candace Fleming (Farrar, Straus and Giroux, 2003). After World War II, Europe stood in ruins. In the United States, through the Children's Aid Society, many people made charitable contributions of soap, sugar, coats, and other necessary and valued items and sent them overseas. In May of 1945, Katje's family in Holland received such a box and began corresponding with the young girl and family who sent it. As Katje's letters described her family's needs, the American family and their community collected and shipped the goods. One day a box arrived in return—tulips from Holland! Based on a true story of a box sent to Holland by the author's mother.

Chicken Sunday by Patricia Polacco (Philomel, 1992). Three friends plan to surprise Gramma Eula with a special holiday hat. As they approach old Mr. Kodinski at the hat shop, they are mistaken for teens who have vandalized his store. They prove their innocence and make a new friend in the process.

The Christmas Menorahs: How a Town Fought Hate by Janice Cohn (Albert Whitman, 1995). Young Isaac saw a rock shatter his bedroom window and hit his Hanukkah menorah. When this hate crime occurred in Billings, Montana, during the holiday season of 1993, town residents of many races, religions, and backgrounds stood together.

DeShawn Days by Tony Medina (Lee & Low, 2001). Welcome to DeShawn's world. Age ten, DeShawn uses poetry to introduce us to "who I live with—who I love." Mother, uncle, cousin, grandmother, and friends matter to DeShawn. Life in the hood is a mixture of spray paint, magicians, and rap. DeShawn's community extends to people fighting across the globe and "mothers and kids crying," so he asks his teacher if the class can write to children in war-torn countries. The book's afterword shares the author's passion for imagination, reading, and writing and his hope that DeShawn's experiences "will inspire you to write poems, paint pictures, sing songs, and help others, too!"

Don't Laugh at Me by Steve Seskin and Allen Shamblin (Tricycle Press, 2002). The lyrics of the song "Don't Laugh at Me" are told in story form as characters express their dislike for being teased, left out, or chosen last in sports. Especially useful with discussion.

Feathers and Fools by Mem Fox (Voyager Books, 1989). Can peacocks and swans settle their perceived differences peacefully? Or will it take a new generation to learn peaceful coexistence and friendship? A parable for all ages.

Gleam and Glow by Eve Bunting (Harcourt, 2001). As war moves closer to their village, Victor, his little sister, and their mother must escape. Along with the other refugees, they carry their belongings, hoping to find a safe haven. Victor's treasures—his home, books, and two fish—are left behind. And what is much worse, his father is off fighting with the liberation army. How will Papa find them now? This story is inspired by real events.

Hands Are Not for Hitting by Martine Agassi (Free Spirit Publishing, 2000). Hands are for waving hello, playing with friends, helping each other, and definitely not for hitting. The book includes a teaching guide and references to promote nonviolence.

Hey, Little Ant! by Phillip and Hannah Hoose (Tricycle Press, 1998). In this song-turned-book, a boy is about to stomp on an ant when the ant speaks up: "Please, oh please, do not squish me." In the dialogue between boy and ant that follows, the boy wrestles with his conscience, peer pressure, and the logic of this teeny creature. The verdict? Read the book! Sheet music for the song is included.

How Humans Make Friends by Loreen Leedy (Holiday House, 1996). When Dr. Zork Tripork returns to his planet from his expedition to planet Earth, he explains to his fellow aliens just how humans make friends and work out their problems so they can stay friends.

I Miss Franklin P. Shuckles by Ulana Snihura (Annick Press, 1998). To stay popular at school, Molly decides to end her friendship with Franklin because "he has skinny legs and wears funny glasses." She soon misses this genuine friendship and learns the importance of kindness.

It Doesn't Have to Be This Way: A Barrio Story/No tiene que ser así: Una historia del barrio by Luis J. Rodríguez (Children's Book Press/Libros Para Niños, 1999). Reluctantly, a young boy becomes involved in neighborhood gang activity. Then a tragic event forces him to make a choice about the course of his life. In English and Spanish.

It's Still a Dog's New York: A Book of Healing by Susan L. Roth (National Geographic, 2001). In this poignant sequel to *It's a Dog's New York*, Pepper and Rover roam through New York City in the wake of the events of September 11. As they visit each landmark, they consider the tragedy that has occurred and express their sadness and confusion. By sharing their thoughts and feelings, helping others, appreciating the bravery of the rescue workers, and caring for each other, they can begin to heal.

Mole Music by David McPhail (Henry Holt, 1999). Though Mole digs tunnels by day, he has begun to feel that there is something missing in his life. After hearing beautiful music on television, he "wants to make beautiful music, too." With much practice, he learns to play, and his violin echoes through the night. He imagines his music reaching into people's hearts, dissolving anger, and "changing the world." Without knowing it, he does change the world.

Mr. Lincoln's Way by Patricia Polacco (Philomel, 2001). Eugene, a tough kid, always seems angry and picks on his classmates. School principal Mr. Lincoln sees him as a boy in trouble and is determined to reach him. Soon, Mr. Lincoln notices Eugene's interest in birds and a bird sanctuary project. But the trouble is still there. With insightfulness and caring, Mr. Lincoln guides Eugene to be more tolerant of others.

Nobody Knew What to Do: A Story About Bullying by Becky Ray McCain (Albert Whitman, 2001). When Ray is mistreated by his peers, the other children are confused about how to make the bullying behaviors stop. Finally, one child steps forward to enlist the help of a teacher. With adult support, the children learn that they can stand up for fair play and kindness toward all students.

The Sissy Duckling by Harvey Fierstein (Simon & Schuster, 2002). Elmer the duck is teased because he is "different." Bolstered by his mama's belief in his abilities, along with a wealth of creativity and ingenuity, Elmer demonstrates his courage by saving papa duck. What does Elmer ultimately learn? That he's not so different but will always be special!

Smoky Nights by Eve Bunting (Harcourt, 1994). Daniel, his mother, and their neighbors experience civil unrest in Los Angeles—violence, fires, and the loss of homes and businesses. When acts of kindness replace racial prejudice with friendship, new lessons are learned by people both young and old, and by cats, too.

Stars in the Darkness by Barbara Joose (Chronicle, 2002). A boy imagines street sirens to be howling wolves and shots fired by gangs to be stars cracking the darkness. When the brother he loves becomes a "banger," he comes up with a plan to save his brother, unite the neighborhood, and stand for peace. Based on a true story; includes resources for gang prevention.

Summer Wheels by Eve Bunting (Harcourt, 1992). The Bicycle Man offers friendship and the use of fixed-up bikes to neighborhood kids, even to a boy who intentionally does not return the bike. Two other boys set out to get the bike back and resolve this problem.

Toestomper and the Caterpillars by Sharleen Collicott (Houghton Mifflin, 1999). Toestomper and his group of Rowdy Ruffians are mean, and they like it that way. However, once Toestomper begins to care for a family of fuzzy caterpillars, he becomes caring and kind. A humorous story with a message about bullying and friendship.

Wings by Christopher Myers (Scholastic, 2000). Ikarus Jackson is different: He has wings and he can fly. But at school, his wings attract too much attention, and kids think he is "showing off." One girl realizes he must be lonely and resolves to step in and stop the hurtful words coming his way. A challenge to embrace differences and celebrate individuality.

The Yellow Star: The Legend of King Christian X of Denmark by Carmen Agra Deedy (Peachtree, 2000). A compassionate king is determined to protect all of his people during the Nazi occupation of Denmark. The author poses a question to the reader: "What if we could follow that example today against violators of human rights?"

Your Move by Eve Bunting (Harcourt, 1998). When James wants to prove he can be part of a gang, he places himself and his younger brother at risk. But being strong can mean having the courage to say "no."

Fiction: Community Safety

After the Dancing Days by Margaret I. Rostkowski (HarperTrophy, 1988). It's the end of World War I and Annie feels great relief at her father's return to their home in Kansas City after months away treating wounded soldiers in New York City. But life cannot return to normal. Uncle Paul died during the war in France and now father is a doctor at a local hospital, again treating the wounded. Against her mother's wishes, Annie visits the veterans, befriending an angry, young, disfigured soldier, and helping them all to value the power of friendship and courage. 217pp., young adult

Big Mouth and Ugly Girl by Joyce Carol Oates (HarperCollins, 2002). Matt Donahue sometimes says more than he should, but who would have suspected his words would be taken out of context and cause detectives to question him at school? Never would he have imagined that his friends and the community would turn against him or that high school loner Ursula Riggs would be the only one to stand up for him. This inside look at media frenzy and rumors shows how the temptation of "belonging" can distort reality and destroy relationships. 266pp., young adult

Buddha Boy by Kathe Koja (Farrar, Straus and Giroux, 2003). At Rucher High, the new kid, Jinsen, is called "Buddha Boy" and considered a freak. He dresses in tie-dye shirts, shaves his head, and begs for lunch money in the cafeteria. So when Justin, the book's narrator, has to work with Jinsen on a class project, he hopes to get this over fast. But the discovery of Jinsen's artistic talents leads to a friendship that changes both boys forever. 117pp., young adult

Charlie Wilcox by Sharon E. McKay (Stoddart Kids, 2000). Despite being born with a club foot, Charlie Wilcox, almost fourteen, is determined to work at sea like his father. Following a corrective surgery operation, he defies his parents' plan for his education and future at a university and stows away on a ship, but the wrong ship at that: This ship is headed to World War I! Charlie finds a medical team also from Newfoundland and learns a special courage as he volunteers tending the wounded and dying. 221pp., grades 5–9

Cowboy Boy by James Proimos (Scholastic, 2003). Ricky Smootz is terrified of sixth grade, especially since his friend has warned him of Keanu Dungston's gang of bullies and the wedgies sure to greet him on his first day of school. After two days of wedgies and being framed for throwing spitballs, Ricky feigns sickness to avoid the whole mess and find solace with his grandmother. Her stories of a distant cowboy cousin, courageous Crazy Enzio, gives Ricky a new perspective. Soon he dons a hat, vest, fuzzy pants, and his alter ego—Cowboy Boy—and brings a halt to the bullying varmints at school. 87pp., grades 4–6

Define "Normal" by Julie Anne Peters (Little, Brown and Company, 2000). When she agrees to meet with Jasmine as a peer counselor at their middle school, Antonia, an over-achiever, never dreams this "punker" girl with the black lipstick and pierced eyebrow will help her with a serious family problem and become a valued friend. 196pp., grades 6–8

Drive-By by Lynne Ewing (HarperTrophy, 1996). When his family is torn apart by a drive-by shooting, Tito wonders if his dead brother Jimmy was in a gang. Will Tito be forced into a gang to save his mother and sister? 85pp., grades 5–7

Geography Club by Brent Hartinger (HarperCollins, 2003). Russell Middlebrook is convinced he is the only gay student at his high school until he stumbles across a small group of other gay students. United by their secret, they form a club intended to appear so boring that nobody in their right mind would ever join: the Geography Club. The treacherous terrain of high school dynamics and the pull to be popular undermine even their best intentions and threaten every relationship. 226pp., young adult

Girl of Kosovo by Alice Mead (Farrar, Straus and Giroux, 2001). Eleven-year-old Zana appreciates village life in Kosovo with her close-knit Albanian family. She is aware of the growing strife between the Croatians, Bosnians, and Serbs and realizes that danger is coming closer daily. When a resistance leader is murdered, Zana's village is attacked. Zana experiences not only a brutal injury but the loss of

loved ones. To survive, she remembers her father's words: "Zana, don't let them fill your heart with hate. Whatever happens." This story is based on the experience of a boy from the Kosovo region. 115pp., grades 5–8

Give a Boy a Gun by Todd Strasser (Simon & Schuster, 2000). After two years of constant harassment and beatings from school jocks, two boys storm a school dance equipped with guns to take their revenge. This book gives voice to the many sides of the school violence issue—school counselors, parents, teens, teachers, and the troubled youth. Along with providing numerous facts about violence in America, the book insists that we consider whether this tragedy could have been prevented and what we can do now. 208pp., grades 7–12

Recommendation from the Field
by Terry Pickeral, Executive Director,
National Center for Learning and Citizenship

Harry Potter and the Sorcerer's Stone by J. K. Rowling (Scholastic, 1998). Harry Potter was born a wizard but isn't aware of his birthright until he is sent an invitation to attend Hogwarts School of Wizardry. Harry experiences the wonder of friendship, the joy of discovery, the pain of disappointment, and the courage to face challenges and the unknown. Over the course of the series, Harry learns the skills of wizardry, comes to understand how history shapes his life, and builds a sense of confidence in his own skills.

Students can explore the many feelings and relationships Harry experiences (fear of his extended family, honor from the wizards, jealousy on the part of some of his classmates, and trust from his friends) and identify similarities in their lives. Harry is aided by mentors, people who "show him the way" and help him to understand the complexities of school and life. Similarly, students can become mentors and guides to new students, using the story of Harry to find various themes facing "the new kid." 309pp., grades 4–12

King of the Kooties by Debbie Dadey (Walker &
Company, 1999). Fourth grader Nate is amazed that his
new friend Donald has never heard of "kooties." At first
Donald doesn't realize he is being insulted when called the
"King of the Kooties" by the class bully, Louisa. Nate
decides to teach Donald to defend himself—not with his
fists but with his wits. 84pp., grades 3–6

Making Up Megaboy by Virginia Walter (Delacorte Press,
1998). What provoked thirteen-year-old Robbie Jones to
shoot an old man in the neighborhood store? He isn't talking, but through the voices of people who know Robbie, we

may gain insight into this tragic event. Out of print but
worth finding. 63pp., grades 5–12

The Misfits by James Howe (Antheneum, 2002). Four students who do not "fit in" at their middle school create a third
party for student council elections: the No-Name Party.
These good friends laugh together, openly discuss their
upsets, and talk about important issues. This "Gang of Five"
(they say "five" to keep others off guard) enter the challenging world of adolescent popularity, politics, love, and loss and,
on the way, change their school forever. 274pp., grades 4–7

> Sticks and stones may break my bones,
> but names will never hurt me.
>
> Anybody who believes that has never been called
> a name.... I think that names are a very small
> way of looking at a person....
>
> Another thing I think about names is that they
> *do* hurt. They hurt because we believe them.
> We think they are telling us something
> true about ourselves, something other people
> can see even if we don't.
>
> FROM *THE MISFITS*

On the Fringe edited by Donald R. Gallo (Penguin
Putnam, 2001). Jeannie is called a boy by her peers because
of her short cropped hair and masculine clothes. Lacey
knows that standing up for the school "freak" threatens her
popularity. Gene brings a loaded rifle to school, fed up with
the persistent harassment. These eleven short stories place
the outsiders at the center, revealing struggles concerning
popularity, nonconformity, hate, and self-acceptance.
221pp., young adult

Pinky and Rex and the Bully by James Howe (Aladdin,
1996). Pinky has a dilemma: his favorite color is pink, his
best friend is a girl, and Kevin calls him a sissy. Will he
have to give up all his favorite things and his best friend to
stop the bullying? 40pp., grades 1–3

The Revealers by Doug Wilhelm (Farrar, Straus and
Giroux, 2003). At Parkland Middle School, three middle
school students—Elliot, Russell, and Catalina—have had
enough of the bullying that plagues their daily lives. By
starting an unofficial email forum at school, their collective
statements inspire words from other kids who are equally
fed up with these harmful acts. Just when the tide seems to
be turning for the better, an act of revenge by a few students still bent on bullying others threatens the underground rebellion that has the whole school talking. 207pp.,
grades 5–8

Recommendation from the Field
*by Denise Clark Pope, Lecturer,
Stanford University, School of Education*

Romeo and Juliet by William Shakespeare (Cambridge University Press, 1999/1595). Romeo and Juliet, two teens whose families are sworn enemies, fall in love. Juliet is supposed to marry Paris but weds Romeo in secret, aided by the Friar. Soon after, while attempting to stop a street fight, Romeo kills Juliet's cousin, which causes his banishment from Verona. The Friar devises a plan to bring the lovers together, but the plan fails. Romeo, believing Juliet is dead, kills himself. Juliet, seeing her dead lover, puts a dagger to her heart. The play ends in tragedy.

To generate ideas for meaningful service, ask students, "What issues from the play are relevant to teens today?" The topic of "families as enemies" can lead to a discussion of friendships, gangs, ethnic strife, or global relations. Another theme is that of teen suicide and love and how tragedy can lead a person to commit suicide. The Friar takes the side of the young people and helps them in deception. Who advocates for teens today, and how far should their role go?

Student service can take several forms. Ideally, students will come up with ideas and strategies. Teens might modernize scenes from *Romeo and Juliet* showing gang problems and perform and discuss the scenes with middle school youth. A high school class could organize a community education night for parents and teens about common causes of suicide. Students, in partnership with local agencies, could also create public service announcements or brochures to distribute on related and relevant themes. 224pp., young adult

Recommendation from the Field
by Ariel Kaye, university student

Siddhartha by Hermann Hesse (Bantam, 1982/1922). Siddhartha leaves his father and a life of privilege to live on his own and determine who he is. During his journey, he meets people who test his virtues and compassion. He gains wealth and experiences passion yet ultimately seeks a life of helping others. He also comes to respect what is found in nature—the beauty of the world. Siddhartha demonstrates the ability to learn from one's experiences and inner struggles as well as from others.

After reading *Siddhartha*, high school students can prepare a guide to help middle school students find their "true selves" in this confusing world, including suggestions for resisting peer pressure and resolving peer conflicts. This guide can include original stories with open-ended questions that stimulate thought and discussion to help younger students approach challenging situations in their lives within a broader context. For the high school authors, this project requires the application of many skills. They will create meaningful text and demonstrate an understanding of philosophy, and they might also lead mutually beneficial discussions with younger students. 152pp., young adult

Shadow of the Dragon by Sherry Garland (Harcourt, 1993). At sixteen, Danny Vo feels trapped between his American friends and his family's traditions. When Danny's cousin, a recent emigrant, falls in with a Vietnamese gang, hate crimes and violence threaten multiple families, and their lives change forever. 314pp., young adult

Stargirl by Jerry Spinelli (Knopf, 2000). Who would guess that Stargirl's arrival at Mica High would make such dramatic changes. With her nonconformist flair, Stargirl sings and strums her ukulele into the minds and hearts of students. Then the unexpected happens: students shun her for all that makes her different. Despite her attempts to be "normal," her individuality shines through. 186pp., grades 6–10

When Christmas Comes Again: The World War I Diary of Simone Spencer by Beth Seidel Levine (Scholastic, 2002). Simone grew up in New York City high society and never expected that World War I would completely alter her life. After her brother volunteers for military service, Simone searches for a meaningful way to join and becomes a "Hello girl," a volunteer switchboard operator for the Army Signal Corps in France. In addition to revealing class issues during this time period, the story describes ways women participated in the war effort. Includes historical notes and photographs. 172pp., grades 5–7

Wringer by Jerry Spinelli (HarperCollins, 1997). In Palmer's hometown, turning ten marks the biggest event of a boy's life: he can be a "wringer" at the annual Pigeon Day, a family festival. But Palmer dreads this day and his new role, which involves actually killing pigeons with his bare hands. An unexpected winged visitor on his windowsill further confirms his opposition to this violent activity and leads him to take a stand for his beliefs. 299pp., grades 4–7

Interviews with Authors:
The Story Behind the Story

In the following interviews, we find out the "story behind the story" from Sharleen Collicott (*Toestomper and the Caterpillars*), Phillip Hoose (*Hey, Little Ant!*, *We Were There, Too! Young People in U.S. History*, and *It's Our World, Too! Young People Who Are Making a Difference: How They Do It—How You Can Too*), and James Howe (*The Misfits*, *Pinky and Rex and the Bully*, and *The Drop Dead Inn*).

I have had the pleasure of meeting two of these authors. I attended a concert in Los Angeles where Phillip Hoose and his daughter sang their song "Hey, Little Ant!" for the first time in public. I met James Howe at a bookstore and immediately found we shared an interest in stopping bullying and intolerance in schools (and elsewhere). We have now co-led workshops for teachers and students on the theme "Words That Hurt, Words That Heal, Words That Lead to Social Action." While I have not yet met Sharleen Collicott, her captivating and amusing characters caused me to contact her and say, "Tell me more!"

Sharleen Collicott, author of
Toestomper and the Caterpillars

I have a wild imagination. I have many ideas, but putting them down and organizing them is difficult. For me, an idea is more important than being able to draw or write. Develop your idea, that's the main step. If you have one little tiny idea, you can go the next step and think of another. Now, if a child says, "I don't have an idea," I don't believe it! Even a stiff, corny idea is a fine beginning. I would ask, "What's your first idea?" If the child answered, "A butterfly walking across the room," I would ask for the next idea. "The butterfly sits in a chair." I would say, "Fine, and what's next?" And the child would say, "The butterfly flies to the moon!" One idea just leads to the next.

My desire to put my ideas on paper led to my being an author, and I worked hard at my art to accomplish my dream. The first books I wrote were crude; still, my editors liked my art so much they helped. Then I taught myself to write. I draw the pictures first, though not to the point where they are finished. I go over and over the words. I try to let the pictures tell everything, since I do not think of myself as a "writer." I like to write, but I am always learning. I keep in mind that the secret to a good book is the plot.

I create stories, including *Toestomper and the Caterpillars*, for my own pleasure and hope others enjoy the books as well. How did *Toestomper and the Caterpillars* develop? I had about eight different story lines I could follow with my initial drawings of Toestomper and the little caterpillars. He is a bit of a tough guy. I tried to think of a name that was mean but not too mean. In this story, Toestomper changes. First he is mean and hanging with the wrong guys. He changes because of the caterpillars. He becomes a "daddy" or a helper. He gets a little bit better. He also makes the caterpillars a little like him as you can see in the last drawing.

The story will continue with *Toestomper and the Bad Butterflies*. Naturally, the caterpillars turn into butterflies, and of course they are not really that bad. They just overstep their bounds.

I am surprised and pleased that *Toestomper and the Caterpillars* can be used as a teaching tool. I like the fact that this book can help someone learn about bullying and friendship and be used for elementary through high school students. It shows that Toestomper truly has a good side underneath his rough exterior.

Phillip Hoose, *coauthor of*
Hey, Little Ant!

Hey, Little Ant! began as a children's song that I cowrote with my daughter Hannah, who was then nine years old. When it occurred to us that the song would make a worthwhile children's book, I thought we would easily find a publisher. Wrong! Even with my track record as an author, finding a publisher for *Hey, Little Ant!* took five years. When editors bothered to respond about why they rejected the book, they usually informed us that children could not accept a book that ended with a question. They said, "Children need resolution." I said, "What about *The Cat in the Hat?*" "Well," they said, "Dr. Seuss is always an exception!"

How did I find a publisher? I asked teachers and performers who use this song to write letters explaining how the story and dialogue worked in their classrooms and onstage. Many people wrote me wonderful, helpful descriptions, so I began sending out large packages to publishing houses and included these letters with the manuscript. I finally received a letter from Tricycle Press saying that our submission had raised quite a debate around their office. But, alas, they still weren't going to buy it. I wrote right back saying they should do themselves and children everywhere a favor and take a chance on this book. To my astonishment it worked! I received a call saying that a consultant had agreed that the open ending was actually a strength. We negotiated a contract, and the publisher found a superb illustrator in Debbie Tilley. Since then, *Hey, Little Ant!* has sold over 35,000 copies and will soon be available in eight different languages: Hebrew, Dutch, Korean, Italian, French, German, Spanish, and English.

How did the story evolve? Basically, one summer day, my daughter Ruby, then two or three, was out in the driveway tromping ants. Hannah, then nine, and I were watching from the porch. Ruby didn't look angry, just bored. I went to her and said, "How would you like to be one of those ants?" "Wouldn't bother me any," she replied. Then I walked away. But Ruby quit stomping. My question and the idea it contained seemed to get to her, and she quit.

Hannah and I were writing songs pretty furiously that summer. Thinking about what had just happened in the driveway, Hannah and I began to script this negotiating session between a child and an ant. As we were wrapping up the song, we said, "How do you want to end it?" We agreed quickly that we did not want to resolve the story at all. The end question was too big for the author to say one way or the other. It's up to the reader. To say how it turns out would weaken the story. The power is in the reader's ability to decide for herself or himself. The story offers a chance for very young people to focus on alternatives to violence at a moment when they have their first opportunity to figure this out: when they're killing bugs. I remember deciding as a very young person my lifelong policy—I won't squish a bug deliberately, but if I do it accidentally I won't let myself feel bad. I believe there is real power in the dialogue between the child and the ant.

In performance, I would crouch down on stage as the ant and Hannah would loom over me with her foot up. Often kids in the audience would ask questions: "What if the bug was a mosquito?" "What if a hundred ants were on your kitchen counter, what would you do?" We would reflect the questions back: "What would *you* do?"

Hey, Little Ant! has achieved a reputation as a tool for exploring various things—tolerance, nonviolence, seeing the common worth of all living things. The song/book has been turned into plays, operas, and videos around the world to encourage children to reflect on these very serious questions in ways that are easy for them to think about.

In this story I see two creatures who appear to be very different but who, despite their obvious differences in size and physical power, have a lot in common. I think it is important to look for the common in all of us while we respect and appreciate the differences.

James Howe, *author of* The Misfits

Writing *The Misfits* had several starting points, with two at the forefront. My daughter had a hard time socially in seventh grade with all the name-calling and ostracism. It brought back my experience during those years and how hard it was for me feeling different from my peers.

The other compelling motivation was that I had recently come out as a gay man after many years in the closet. I wanted to write something that would help young people today not have to go through the experiences of my past. I wanted to write a young gay character who was okay with who he was and could start life on a different foot. While I do think things are changing, we have a long way to go. When I was growing up, being gay was considered an illness or something you did not want to be. Now I realize how much I had lived in fear of what people would think or say to me. "Coming out" made me see what a waste of energy it had been my whole life to not tell the truth. I have developed an impatience with the ways in which we all waste energy and our lives by living in fear, so often of such small things. I wanted to tell this story like it is, as best as I could, to convey the message that we can be part of change. It's possible.

The actual writing of *The Misfits* started with an unfinished short story on the theme of chocolate. I had a setting of a small town and a department store with Bobby selling ties. When I began writing this novel, I thought of Bobby's character and his strong voice that I loved and connected with. From the short story evolved this group of friends. They wrote the book.

Part of my intent in writing, especially for children, is to empower them, to open their minds to think about things in a different way. With *The Misfits*, I was writing a story with characters who, deep in their bones, understand about courage, taking a stand, and telling it like it is. Accepting differences and embracing difference in one's self as a good thing has been central to many of my books. The idea of difference as something we shy away from is a notion that boggles my mind.

That *The Misfits* is told with humor is only natural; humor is part of who I am and also where I come from. My father, a minister and social activist, frequently would wind humor into his sermons, even on serious topics, just as I do in my writing. I want the reader to care! Certainly I do not want readers to feel they are being told what to think. As a reader or audience member, I treasure the times I am laughing one minute and crying the next. Humor and sadness are so connected in life.

The characters in this book grow in their ability to see a larger world. Often, when one is the subject of injustice, it is easier to see there is a larger world. I imagine this book being used to open the reader, the class, the school—whoever is using the book as a community—to build a bridge to the bigger world. This book can open dialogue and suggest creative ways to deal with whatever problems exist. By being direct, and putting yourself out there, you are helping others to do the same.

While I have received very positive responses from kids regarding the book, some say they had a hard time accepting the ending: that two gay characters, Joe and Colin, could express their feelings to each other at the age of twelve and also that a really popular "in" kid would date a less popular kid. Some kids like this sort of "fairy-tale ending." I want the reader to ask, "Why do you think this is unrealistic? Why should it be otherwise?"

One school in California did create a "No Name Day" modeled on *The Misfits* that will be an annual event. Nothing would make me happier than this book being a catalyst to start political action in schools. I didn't start out knowing that this would be so political. But the seed was planted in the book with Addie when she refuses to say the pledge of allegiance. I realized that something larger than the book can come from the book, and that is thrilling.

I hope *The Misfits* opens the minds and hearts of readers. I would like young people to be able to think for themselves—to really consider what it would be like to be in someone else's shoes, how they would feel if they were the object of name-calling. That's a lot right there. I don't think you arbitrarily stop name-calling. I think you develop compassion and an understanding that the other person is a human being.

E L D E R S

> Imagine what a harmonious world it could be
> if every single person, both young and old,
> shared a little of what he is good at doing.
>
> QUINCY JONES, MUSICIAN

The intergenerational connection has a long and vibrant history in service learning—young people and older people naturally fit together. Their interactions are often based on shared interests and result in personal growth for everyone involved. Service and learning flow easily in both directions as an older person tutors a child or an adolescent teaches computer skills to a retiree. These partnerships evoke caring and provide an exchange that matters. The two groups often discover similarities more profound than their differences: a love of baseball or gardening, appreciation of music, caring for families, or pleasure in traditions.

Young people benefit from getting to know active elders in their communities as well as those who are infirm or suffering from memory loss. Each of these populations offers unique ways to interact and create meaningful relationships. It is often said that our mobile society separates the generations within families. While the relationships created through service learning are not substitutes, they are rich with their own rewards and exchanges and offer opportunities for contact between generations that might otherwise be missing.

Through intergenerational experiences, young people can explore:

- the learning of life's lessons.

- how different cultures treat older populations.

- how to stay healthy in body and mind.

- the joy of living.

- history related through personal experience and knowledge, which is hard to find in textbooks.

- the mutually beneficial relationships that can be achieved between people of different ages.

When preparing for intergenerational situations and activities, make sure that both your students and the elders are willing participants or recipients. A key purpose of service learning is creating mutually respectful relationships. When combining generations, be particularly attentive to the potential for imbalance or even condescension. It's important to explore and state the value of both the young people and the elders involved in the project and to be sure that the service is directed toward an actual need rather than an assumed one.

Preparation: Getting Ready for Service Learning Involving Elders

The following activities can be used in the preparation stage to promote learning and skill development related to elders. These activities can be used with different age ranges during preparation to help your students examine key issues through research, analyze community needs, and gain the knowledge they need to effectively contribute to the design of their service plan. Since literature is often an important part of preparation, you can find recommended titles on this theme in the Elders Bookshelf later in this chapter.

Activity: Coming to Know the Elder Population.
Who makes up the elder population in your community? How do they spend their time? Answering these questions and others can help generate possibilities for service learning. Sometimes the best way to get the information you need is to go straight to the source. Invite several elder community activists to class—business people, volunteers, educators,

historians—and aim for a ratio of one for every five to seven students. To find potential visitors, ask the students or other teachers for referrals, or check with the local volunteer or senior center. Before the visit, ask each of the older community members to submit a brief personal biography or résumé. In small groups, have students read the biographies to prepare questions for an interview session. Each guest may also be asked to prepare a topic for an interactive conversation. You might plan for multiple visits to provide time for both interviews and topic discussions. As a result of these meetings, students and their elder guests may decide to collaborate on social action projects. For younger children, one or two classroom visitors is ample to create a discussion. Have students develop their questions prior to the visit, and be certain every child has a turn to participate.

Activity: *Preparing for Oral History Projects.* Bringing people together from different generations can be most gratifying, especially when everyone is prepared. For oral history projects, if possible try to colead the activities with an agency partner who has experience with elders. Many books in this chapter's bookshelf also can be helpful, particularly *Growing Older* by George Ancona, which gives samples of oral histories collected from a diverse population. To get your oral history project off to a good start, try the following process.

Begin by meeting separately with the student group and the elders. With the students, ask, "What do you think of older people?" Most students think that elders have a disability. Present information—or have students conduct research—to demonstrate that this is not true. Many seniors are healthy, and even those with infirmities may lead active lives.

Similarly, members of the older group can be asked, "What do you expect from the students?" Often, they expect students to be rude or impolite; they may also express concern about safety issues when visiting a high school. Take this opportunity to present accurate information.

To prepare for the first interaction, students can work in small groups to develop questions to "break the ice." Students can also role-play the initial meetings to practice their personal introductions. Inform the older group that the students will be asking questions to help everyone become acquainted.

Consider this list of questions developed and used by high school students in various projects:

- What should I call you?
- Why did you decide to come today?
- How old are you?
- How many children do you have?
- As a child, what did you want to be when you grew up?
- What was the time of your life that you most enjoyed?
- What are some of your hobbies?
- How did you meet your significant other or others?
- What would you like to change about your life?
- What has changed in the world since you were a teenager?
- What are some major historical events that you lived through/participated in?

Allow time for the interaction and for feedback about the process at the conclusion. Reflection for this initial meeting can be held separately so each group can express any concerns as well as happiness about their new relationships.

Even very young children have successfully created oral histories in collaboration with elder partners. Younger children who cannot yet write may need to dictate their stories for older students or others to transcribe. Sometimes the books take the form of shared histories—for example, "We both like . . ." or "Our favorite animals are . . ." Preparation for these projects also includes getting acquainted with their older student helpers.

Find Out More About Elders

To learn more about these issues and to get ideas for service and action, visit these Web sites and organizations online:

www.gu.org Elderly United is a national organization promoting intergenerational strategies, programs, and policies.

continued ⟶

www.seniorcorps.org Senior Corps, a part of the Corporation of National and Community Service, is a network of programs that tap the experience, skills, and talents of older citizens to meet community challenges, including young and old people serving their communities together.

www.cps.unt.edu/natla/ The National Academy for Teaching and Learning About Aging promotes education about aging-related issues and has curriculum and project oriented resources.

 # Making Connections Across the Curriculum

Some service learning activities naturally lend themselves to interdisciplinary work and making connections across the curriculum. These connections strengthen and broaden student learning, helping them meet academic standards. More than likely, you'll be looking for these connections and ways to encourage them well before the students ever start working on service learning activities. As with the entire service learning process, it helps to remain flexible, because some connections can be spontaneously generated by the questions raised throughout and by the needs of the project. To help you think about cross-curricular connections and where you can look for them, the Curricular Web for this chapter (page 109) gives examples of many different ways this theme can be used in different academic areas. (The service learning scenarios in the next section of the chapter also demonstrate various ways this theme can be used across the curriculum.)

> The human contribution is the essential ingredient. It is only in the giving of oneself to others that we truly live.
>
> ETHEL PERCY ANDRUS, FOUNDER OF AARP (FORMERLY THE AMERICAN ASSOCIATION OF RETIRED PERSONS)

Service Learning Scenarios: Ideas for Action

Ready to take action? What follows are projects that have been successfully carried out by elementary, middle, or high school students. Most of these scenarios and examples explicitly include some aspects of preparation, action, reflection, and demonstration. These scenarios can be a rich source of project, resource, and curriculum ideas for you to draw upon. While the grade levels are given as a reference, most project ideas can be adapted to suit younger or older students, and many are suitable for cross-age partnerships.

Shared Moments: Grades 1–3. Elder volunteers in Iowa attended a three-part workshop on reading with young children hosted by a local agency (a school district can also sponsor the workshop). The volunteers were then placed in classrooms as Reading Buddies to help students at all levels to advance in their skills and literature appreciation. The students wanted to give back to their buddies, so they wrote special stories, which they read aloud and then gave to their partners. Each story was accompanied by a piece of art showing the buddy and the student together. The elder participants described this experience as a "true exchange between the generations."

Oral History Projects—Variations on a Worthwhile Theme: Grades 1–12. This tried-and-true service learning activity enables young people and other community members to learn from the collective experience of elders. Careful preparation will produce meaningful long-term partnerships. Literature connections can be made through many of the bookshelf titles. The epilogue of *Pink and Say*, for example, attests to the importance of keeping stories alive from generation to generation. *Too Young for Yiddish* illustrates what can be easily lost—or preserved. *Growing Older* presents anecdotal remembrances of older adults with very different backgrounds. Many books explore memory and the beauty of tapping into the stories of our elders.

First-Grade Historians: Grade 1. An elementary teacher in Tennessee described how, for more than twenty years, her first-grade students have documented the lives of local senior citizens and placed the collected stories in the public library. The teacher

Elders Across the Curriculum

English/Language Arts

- Discuss: Why should younger people care about elders?
- Take dictation and compose letters and other correspondence for elders
- Read and discuss a classic text with an elder partner

Social Studies/History

- Learn about Medicare, social security, and Medicaid
- Establish a current events discussion group with elders at a senior center
- Conduct interviews with older people about community history or significant historical events

Languages

- Contact senior centers to find elders who are fluent in the language being studied to visit and speak with the class
- Compare how elders are regarded by different cultures and countries
- Learn about colloquial expressions or proverbs used by elders in the language

Theater, Music, & Visual Arts

- Create a dramatic reading of passages written by people of all ages
- Learn and perform music enjoyed by a previous generation
- Study and learn to do folk or traditional arts from your community or region

Elders

Math

- Find out and graph statistics on the population of your region by age
- Learn about tax forms and help prepare tax returns for elders
- Create a "true or false" survey about elders and find out peer group opinions; create a statistical report and use this to teach others

Physical Education

- Learn and teach armchair exercises
- Research athletic programs and competitions for elders; observe and cheer participants
- Arrange for an intergenerational athletic or exercise experience

Computer

- Document elders' memories, pictures, and stories on a Web page
- Conduct Internet research on careers in gerontology and geriatrics
- Survey seniors about their attitudes toward and their uses of technology

Science

- Educate elder people about nutrition
- Study health care and dietary needs of elders; compare with those of youth
- Plan ahead and grow corsage flowers for a "senior senior" prom

and students identified candidates to interview through newspaper stories about contributions made by older community members (read aloud to the class by the teacher) and by publicizing the project on a flyer at the local senior center. The class developed a list of questions and conducted about ten interviews, adding drawings of the older persons and illustrations of their activities. Parents took photographs of the interviews, and a display was mounted in the library when the book was donated. The stories and art are enjoyed and appreciated every year.

Getting Physical: Grade 3. Third graders in West Hollywood, California, got into all sorts of positions while studying yoga, but the ones they enjoyed the most were collaborating with senior citizens. In weekly visits to the local senior center, students shared their yoga skills with the older people, and together, the two groups learned how to modify the yoga positions for people who are less agile. Students used their writing and communication skills to produce "We Love Yoga" brochures for community distribution. To reach more elders, students created a series of public service announcements (PSAs) on exercise for daily broadcast on local cable television. These PSAs were also played occasionally at the senior center.

> No matter what accomplishments you make, somebody helps you.
>
> WILMA RUDOLPH, ATHLETE

A Poetic Journey: Grade 4. Fourth-grade students in Maryland had a long-term, year-round collaboration with older people in the community. At the beginning of the school year, the students gave a "welcoming tea" party. Poetry sessions followed; seniors and students wrote poetry, produced a poetry book, and made poetry posters that were displayed in storefronts. The students and their senior partners had a holiday party, made collages, participated in science experiments with the support of college students, made scrapbooks, and had a storytelling event. The year concluded with a potluck dinner in honor of the senior partners.

A Gift of Tradition: Grades 4–8. More than a hundred students in northeast Oklahoma participated in a cultural event sponsored by the Cherokee Nation. Community volunteers worked with the students as they learned how to craft objects once used in daily life and now viewed as art forms, including stickball sticks and baskets. Students also made corn-husk dolls, traditional Cherokee dolls mothers and grandmothers make as playthings for children. Students met with representatives from the Cherokee Nation to determine appropriate places to donate the corn-husk dolls. Student representatives from every grade level went on field visits to personally give the gifts; one group went to local preschools, and the other went to a local nursing home. At each site, the students demonstrated how the dolls were made. Among the elder recipients were many Cherokee men and women who shared their own recollections of making these and other items.

Knitting Past and Present Together: Grade 5. As part of a unit of study, "Schools of the Past," students in Vermont learned how children helped during World War II by sewing blankets and knitting socks to be sent to soldiers overseas. They decided to learn to knit, which was described as extremely difficult by many children. They also found out that residents of a nearby nursing home had themselves made sweaters and blankets during the war. The class agreed this would be the ideal place to donate their creation, a handmade knitted blanket. The students sent a letter describing their project and asking if the facility would like to receive the blanket and if residents would be willing to meet and discuss their World War II experiences with the class. During a visit to the nursing home, the students listened as the older people described their experiences in the 1940s. Another benefit: The small-motor skills used in knitting improved the students' cursive handwriting.

Bingo Buttons: Grade 5. Fifth graders in New York City who visited a convalescent home each week noticed that while their older friends enjoyed playing bingo, they had difficulty picking up the bingo markers. They brainstormed ways to make the game easier to play. After conferring with the center's staff, they began to collect buttons to replace the traditional bingo chips. When the class initiated a school-wide button collection, the entire school learned about the visits and how much the students enjoyed the time spent in intergenerational activities. The button gathering culminated in an original rap song, a ceremony in which the song was presented to the seniors, and the best bingo game ever.

A Dance for All Ages: Grade 5. Two populations joined together to create a multimedia performance that combined the written word and movement. Elders and fifth graders in Maryland who were interested in movement, writing, and collaboration were recruited for the project. A series of workshops led by a high school dance teacher brought the two groups together. The older people wrote about "what it is like to be old," and the elementary students wrote about "what it might be like to be old." Dances were then created to accompany the written words and the multimedia performance was presented at a school PTA event, the senior center, and a state intergenerational conference.

Time Online: Grade 6. Sixth-grade students read and discussed *Doing Time Online* and reflected on many aspects of the novel: a student required to correspond online with a nursing home resident as the result of a joke that caused harm, the student's original skepticism, and the surprising benefits and relationship that developed. Students talked about finding their own "senior email pals" and began to research possible community sources of such partnerships. They found eight older people who had computers at home and four who regularly went online at the senior center and began to correspond with these elders via email. Sometimes the students or the seniors were slow in responding, and a few of the seniors had to leave the program. Still, there were benefits: companionship, an exchange of experiences, and face-to-face conversations in three gatherings during the school year.

Holidays of Old: Grade 7. A math teacher in Alvin, Texas, brought an idea to a faculty meeting with teachers from the various disciplines that made up the school's seventh-grade teaching team. Having recently visited her elder aunt in a nursing home, she thought that a visit to a similar local facility would make a good addition to the students' learning about "Holidays of Old." Through collaboration, all disciplines participated. Students eagerly contributed ideas and showed leadership. Even a young student with a history of discipline problems "shaped up" so he could go along. English teachers used literature to examine how older people are perceived; in history class, students planned and practiced interviewing so that they could interview residents and learn how holidays were celebrated in the past; health classes found out about residents' dietary restrictions and distributed appropriate recipes to volunteer bakers; math students constructed geometric holiday ornaments for tree decorations; science classes studied the aging process; and art students made papier-mâché picture frames to leave as gifts. Before the visit, residence staff members provided orientations for the students and the elders who chose to participate. The visit far exceeded the expectations of all involved, and the teachers became staunch advocates of service learning.

A Senior Register: Grade 7. Students collected oral histories from older African Americans who attended a church that was being closed. In preparation, students studied the era when the church was built. Interviews were transcribed into stories, and photos were taken of all contributors. Students wrote letters to help get the church placed on the historic register and preserved. At a final celebration, each elder was given a copy of the book. Copies were given to organizations, historical societies, and libraries as well.

Project Cook 'n' Serve: Grade 7. Middle school teachers in Massachusetts were concerned that many of their students lacked the social skills and manners to have appropriate conversations with peers and adults. They decided to build on an existing partnership with a senior center, and Project Cook 'n' Serve was born. Through collaboration between senior center staff and teachers, seventh graders and senior citizens studied nutrition together (this met an academic standard) and took a cooking class together. The students then interviewed their older partners about rules of etiquette, reported their findings in class, and practiced what they had learned. For a finale, the students prepared lunch at the senior center, served the food with proper manners, and had lovely conversations. But the program did not end— the students and seniors decided to collaborate on a community cookbook. After the projects had ended, students maintained communication with their senior friends through frequent emails and occasional visits. Teachers observed an increase in polite and appropriate verbal exchanges student-to-student and student-to-teacher. In their reflection journals, students noted that two of the books they used, *Growing Older: What Young People Should Know About Aging* and *Handbook for Boys* added to their understanding and appreciation for older people and what can be learned through friendships.

Poetry Partners: Grade 7. As the culmination of a poetry unit, middle school students in Wisconsin invited their grandparents and other elders from a local senior center to participate in a poetry event. The students performed poetry, shared music as poetry, and engaged in poetry activities, such as creating the longest alliterative sentence. Then intergenerational "poetry partners" composed collaborative poems: teens wrote on the theme "when I'm old, I'll . . . " and grandparents wrote "looking back on my life." After lunch, some read their poems aloud, and each student presented a previously written poem "Ode to my Grandparent/Grandfriend" to his or her guest.

Stimulating Conversations: Grade 8. Time spent with elders in convalescent centers or day-care facilities for people with memory loss can be designed to provide stimulation and interaction opportunities. After reading *Stranger in the Mirror* and *Conversation Starters: How to Start Conversations with People Who Have Memory Loss*, middle school students raised questions and concerns about working with this population. They learned more about Alzheimer's disease by viewing a video and attending three informational sessions led by staff from the partner day-care facility for people with memory loss. Students had time to develop and try out ideas for helpful activities, including crafts, musical programming for sing-a-longs, and current events discussions. From their journals, the students made a display and booklet for the agency with original poetry and art. They also presented their program to other classes in their school to familiarize students with service learning and to teach about Alzheimer's disease.

Where Were You When? Grade 8. The strategy for a "Where Were You When?" oral history project begins with finding out what subjects interest the senior

citizens who will be interviewed. A simple survey of participants at the senior center in Maryland revealed a range of intriguing subjects: a woman who knew Rosa Parks wanted to discuss civil rights, a woman whose brother repaired Charles Lindbergh's airplane had photographs to share, a man wanted to discuss how the Kennedy assassination had affected his life, and a woman was ripe with stories of her experience as a riveter during World War II. Eighth-grade students reviewed the list, and each selected a topic of interest. The students researched their topics to prepare for the first visit, a combination interview and lunch. The preparation created a level of comfort and facilitated exchange for all. During the next visit, the seniors heard the reports written by the students. A compilation of these conversations was given to each participant and the library.

Intergenerational Technology: Grades 9 and 10. What to do with your unwanted computers? A nonprofit organization in Maryland came up with an idea: bring high school students and senior citizens together and provide them with training in repairing and rebuilding computers. A technology center was created at a high school. With skilled volunteer trainers, equipment to repair, and needy recipient agencies and individuals, the center went into operation. Students completing the training program also earned credits toward graduation.

Intergenerational Learning: Grades 9 and 10. Thirty high school students and thirty senior citizens in Maryland formed a mini-university to learn about each other and about topics of mutual interest. Before the groups came together, each had workshops to express concerns about soon-to-be partners, as described in the "Coming to Know the Elder Population" activity on pages 106–107. A committee with representatives from each group selected the topics and planned the workshops, which were usually led by group members. At each monthly class, two topics were presented. For example, in the "Let's Cook" program, participants (1) prepared and brought their favorite recipes to share and (2) watched a cooking demonstration by a local chef. For ESL students and seniors with limited English-speaking skills, the program provided a safe environment for improving conversational abilities. In addition, high school students learned about careers in fields that involve elders.

They also learned grant-writing skills as they sought the funding needed to support the program. The seniors favorably commented on their relationships with their new teen friends. As a result of this project, students developed other service activities, such as a "senior prom," that were greatly appreciated.

Tennis, Anyone? Grades 9–12. Senior citizen tennis players were looking for a good game in preparation for a local tournament, and they found one—at the high school. They became regulars at the school, working out once a week with the tennis team during practice. The high school players became the cheering section at the tournament, and the seniors surprised the young athletes with a donation that helped them get team sweatshirts.

Tell Me Your Story: Grade 10. A tenth-grade "American Experience" class began an oral history project in partnership with a local neighborhood association to record histories of people who had lived in the school's community in Spokane, Washington. To help students prepare, a local news reporter taught them interviewing skills. Through a community meeting, the students identified people who had lived in the neighborhood in the 1930s and 1940s. The students then collected oral histories that reflected community life in those decades. Students recorded the histories, transcribed them, and gave copies of the written histories and recordings to participants. Copies were also kept in the archives of the partnering community organization. Letters from several of the participating older people described their appreciation for the opportunity to share their stories and for having copies of the interview audiotapes to give to their children.

At the Internet Café: Grades 10–12. At the senior citizen center "Internet café," high school students acted as Internet coaches. As the students refined their skills, they helped the elders feel more comfortable going online. The assistance helped many older people stay connected with family members who lived in different regions. The seniors said they especially enjoyed writing to and hearing from their grandchildren.

A Matter of Health: Grades 10–12. High school students who were learning about health sciences took their knowledge and skills directly to the senior citizens in their community of Sarasota, Florida. During six visits, relationships formed between students and their elders as tenth through twelfth graders practiced skills by measuring blood pressure and demonstrating CPR and choking relief measures. Students were well prepared through aging sensitivity training, and extensive research and discussion of aging, the illnesses affecting older people, and death and dying. Time was always made for socializing, which included the young people learning line dancing from their older friends. Students kept journals throughout the year and demonstrated academic competencies beyond the course requirements.

Remember the Women and Children! Grade 12. For an oral history project focusing on World War II, students in a government class divided into groups to interview veterans. Then a student asked, "What about the women?" Responding to this inquiry expanded the activity to include collecting stories from women who were at home during the war as well as adults who were children in the early 1940s. Questions included: "What different roles did you assume?" "What were some unexpected effects of the war?" One result of the project was a unique publication illustrating multiple perspectives on and memories of living through times of war.

> We have to reinvent the wheel every once in a while, not because we need a lot of wheels; but because we need a lot of inventors.
>
> BRUCE JOYCE, EDUCATOR

 # The Elders Bookshelf

Our elder generations offer wisdom and insights gained from years of experience. The titles found in the Elders Bookshelf can provide knowledge and support to inspire and sustain intergenerational interactions. To help you find books relevant to your particular projects, the book chart classifies the books into several topic areas: an overview of elders, active elders, intergenerational relationships, and memory loss and/or nursing homes.

In general, the bookshelf features:

- An annotated bibliography arranged and alphabetized by title according to the general categories of nonfiction (N), picture books (P), and fiction (F). For nonfiction and fiction, length and recommended grade levels are included. The entries in the picture book category do not include suggested grade levels, since they can be successfully used with all ages.

- A chart organized by topic and category to help you find books relevant to particular projects.

- Recommendations from service learning colleagues and experts that include a book summary and ideas for service learning connections. (The number of recommended books varies in each bookshelf.)

Elders Bookshelf Topics

Topics	Books	Category
An Overview of Elders Aging happens, actually, day by day. The "big picture" shows the complexity of aging and includes health concerns, family life, and cultural and societal changes.	*Grandparents Around the World* *Growing Older* ‡ *Growing Older: What Young People Should Know About Aging* ‡	N N N
Active Elders Recognizing the many roles played by elders enriches our lives and corrects misconceptions.	*Butterflies and Lizards, Beryl and Me* (see page 143) *The Cay* *A Day's Work* (see page 168) *Edwina Victorious* * (see page 199) *Hurry Granny Annie* *Rainbow Joe and Me* (see page 211) *Tuck Everlasting*	F F P F P P F
Intergenerational Relationships These books continue the theme of active elders but also emphasize the relationships between generations, capturing something special that occurs between young and old.	*Butterfly Boy* *Chicken Sunday* (see page 98) *City Green* * (see page 142) *Dancing with Dziadziu* *Doing Time Online* * *Grandma's Records* *Handbook for Boys* *Happy Birthday Mr. Kang* (see page 168) *The Hundred Penny Box* *Joe's Wish* *Mrs. Katz and Tush* *Petey* * *Somebody Loves You, Mr. Hatch* *The Summer My Father Was Ten* (see page 143) *Too Young for Yiddish* *The War with Grandpa*	P P P P F P F P F P P F P P P F

continued ⟶

Topics	Books	Category
Memory Loss and/or Nursing Homes With aging can come loss of memory or other conditions leading to a need for assistance. These stories share a range of experience and memories with respect and dignity.	*The Bonesetter's Daughter*	F
	Conversation Starters as Easy as ABC 123: How to Start Conversations with People Who Have Memory Loss	N
	The Graduation of Jake Moon	F
	The Memory Box	P
	Mosaic Moon: Caregiving Through Poetry	N
	Remember Me? Alzheimer's Through the Eyes of a Child/ ¿Te acuerdas de mí? Pensamientos de la enfermedad, Alzheimers a travez de los ojos de un niño	P
	Sachiko Means Happiness	P
	Singing with Momma Lou	P
	Stranger in the Mirror	P
	Sunshine Home	P
	Tiger, Tiger Burning Bright	F
	Wilfred Gordon McDonald Partridge	P
	A Window of Time	P

Page references are given for books that do not appear in the Elders Bookshelf but that can be found in the bookshelf lists of other chapters.
* These books include examples of young people in service-providing roles.
‡ These books are out of print but still worth finding.

Nonfiction: *Elders*

Conversation Starters As Easy As ABC 123: How to Start Conversations with People Who Have Memory Loss by Devora Kaye and Gabi Roussos (ABCD Books, 2000). Written by eighth-grade students, this ABC coloring book is a friendly guide for young people who are interacting with people who have memory loss. 29pp., all ages

Grandparents Around the World by Patricia Lakin (Blackbirch Press, 1999). Text and photographs provide a snapshot of the role that older people, especially grandparents, play in families in various countries, including Canada, Italy, Swaziland, Ecuador, Iraq, and Israel, as well as Native Americans in the United States. 32pp., grades 2–5

Growing Older by George Ancona (Duttons, 1978). In this collection of oral histories, you will meet, among others, an antique dealer from Texas, a woman who travels and gardens, a grandmother from the Yucatán, a Sauk and Fox Indian from Oklahoma, an immigrant from Lithuania, and residents of Nicodemus, Kansas, which began as a settlement of freed slaves. The author recommends, "Ask your grandparents for their stories. If you don't have grandparents nearby, borrow or adopt some, as certain Indian tribes do." Out of print but well worth finding. 48pp., grades 5–12

Growing Older: What Young People Should Know About Aging by John Langone (Little, Brown and Company, 1991). By 2025, American teenagers will be outnumbered two to one by people 65 and older. This book clears up myths and misconceptions about aging and provides information about cultural differences and physical ailments. It also asks, "What kind of old person will you be?" Out of print but worth finding. 162pp., grades 6–12

Mosaic Moon: Caregiving Through Poetry by Frances H. Kakugawa (Watermark Publishing, 2002). For one year, caregivers of people with Alzheimer's disease met each month. This book chronicles their work together and the resulting personal stories and poetry. Suggestions for "how-to" make this a worthwhile resource. 218pp., young adult

Picture Books: *Elders*

Butterfly Boy by Virginia Kroll (Boyds Mills Press, 1997). Emilio wheels his *abuelo*—his grandfather—outside each sunny afternoon to watch butterflies flutter around the white garage wall. With limited mobility and no speech, Abuelo brightens up watching the red admirals, a species of butterflies attracted to the color white. As the seasons change, Emilio and his grandfather await the return of the butterflies. But will they return when Papa paints the garage blue?

Dancing with Dziadziu by Susan Campbell Bartoletti (Harcourt, 1997). A young girl shares her ballet dancing and an early Easter celebration with her ill grandmother while the grandmother reminisces about her husband and her immigration from Poland.

Grandma's Records by Eric Velasquez (Walker, 2001). Eric loves summer with Grandma in Spanish Harlem. During the hot days, Grandma fills the apartment with the salsa and merengue music that she grew up with in Puerto Rico. When her nephew Sammy Ayala, a percussionist for Rafael Cortijo's band, "the best band in Puerto Rico," comes to town, Grandma and Eric are special guests at their first New York concert. The performance strengthens the bond between the generations.

> Grandma liked all types of music. But one record was very special to her. Whenever she played it, she would put her hand over her heart and close her eyes as she sang along. When it was over, Grandma would sometimes sit quietly, thinking about Grandpa and the old days in Santurce, her hometown.
>
> "Sometimes," Grandma said, "a song can say everything that is in your heart as if it was written just for you."
>
> FROM *GRANDMA'S RECORDS*

Hurry Granny Annie by Arlene Alda (Tricycle Press, 1999). Granny Annie runs so fast the children have to run their hardest to keep up. But they all want to find out what the "something great" is that Annie is determined to catch. Is it a fish, a butterfly, or a baseball? Annie's joy for what is most beautiful is ultimately contagious.

Joe's Wish by James Proimos (Harcourt, 1998). Joe Capri wishes on a star: "Please, I want to be young again." The Something or Other arrives, promising that "tomorrow I will grant your wish." But after a day of play with his grandson, Joe finds that the idea of being young again pales in comparison to the joy of his relationship with his grandson just the way it is.

The Memory Box by Mary Bahr (Albert Whitman, 1992). When Gramps realizes he has the beginnings of Alzheimer's disease, he starts a "memory box" with his young grandson, Zach, to keep memories of all the times they have shared.

Mrs. Katz and Tush by Patricia Polacco (Bantam, 1992). A young African-American boy gives a lonely Jewish widow a kitten named Tush. The cultural and age differences between the boy and the older woman only add to their special friendship, which grows and lasts throughout their lives.

Remember Me? Alzheimer's Through the Eyes of a Child/¿Te acuerdas de mí? Pensamientos de la enfermedad, Alzheimers a travez de los ojos de un niño by Sue Glass (Raven Tree Press, 2003). A young girl is perplexed. She cannot understand why Grandfather no longer remembers her. Did she do something wrong or make him angry or hurt his feelings? When she tells her mother about this problem, her mother explains about Alzheimer's disease. They both learn that sharing the knowledge about what is happening to a family member is better for everyone involved. In English and Spanish.

Sachiko Means Happiness by Kimiko Sakai (Children's Book Press, 1990). Sachiko is upset when her grandmother, who has Alzheimer's disease, no longer recognizes her. Slowly she grows to understand how patience and love help maintain a caring relationship.

Singing with Momma Lou by Linda Jacobs Altman (Lee & Low, 2002). Tamika is frustrated with visiting her grandmother at the nursing home each week, especially now that Alzheimer's disease has robbed Momma Lou of so much memory. When nine-year-old Tamika begins to bring and show her grandmother old photos and yearbooks, and newspaper clippings related to her grandmother's arrest during a civil rights demonstration in her visits, the sparks of memory and relationship are rekindled.

Somebody Loves You, Mr. Hatch by Eileen Spinelli (Aladdin, 1996). An anonymous valentine turns unsociable Mr. Hatch into a friend of everyone in the neighborhood. When he learns the valentine was meant for someone else, Mr. Hatch reverts to his old ways until his true friends come to the rescue. A wonderful book to dramatize with children!

Stranger in the Mirror by Allen Say (Houghton Mifflin, 1995). Sam, an Asian-American boy, does not want to get old like his grandpa, but one morning he awakens with the face of an old man. His family, teacher, and friends treat him as if he is not the same person on the inside. "Who cares what I look like. I am Sam. Nobody can change that." A subtle and perceptive look at societal views on aging.

Sunshine Home by Eve Bunting (Clarion, 1994). Timothy visits his grandmother, who has broken her hip. Timothy and his parents have a hard time leaving Gram at the nursing home. They know that an aging person with physical difficulties still needs love.

Too Young for Yiddish by Richard Michelson (Charlesbridge, 2002). Aaron loves his *zayde* (grandfather), though he is embarrassed by his funny accent and arm-waving gestures. Aaron longs to read Zayde's treasured books, which are written in Yiddish, but Zayde says, "You are too young . . . speak English like everyone else." As the years pass, Aaron and his grandfather realize the importance of preserving family history and culture, agreeing that you are never too young—or old—for Yiddish. Includes a glossary and author's notes.

Wilfred Gordon McDonald Partridge by Mem Fox (Kane/Miller, 1985). A young boy tries to discover the meaning of "memory" so he can help an elder friend.

A Window of Time by Audrey O. Leighton (NADJA, 1995). Grandpa's time machine is "on the fritz." Sometimes he confuses the present with the past—imagining himself riding horses on his farm rather than remembering his current life in the city. His grandson, Shawn, recognizes that Grandpa may forget what he did earlier today but remembers an event from 65 years ago. A sensitive account of the effects of Alzheimer's disease.

Fiction: *Elders*

Recommendation from the Field
by Gail M. Kong, President,
Asian Pacific Fund

The Bonesetter's Daughter by Amy Tan (Ballantine Books, 2001). Ruth Luyi Young is a busy writer and stepmom, and she tries to be a good daughter by visiting regularly with her mother, LuLing. Lately, LuLing seems more confused and disoriented. Ruth cannot tell if her mother is sick or if they just cannot communicate because Ruth has become Americanized, losing her ability to speak Chinese. As LuLing recalls many vivid details of her childhood in China, Ruth begins to know her mother in a new way even as she accepts that her mother has early-stage Alzheimer's disease.

Students can use the story to discuss how families feel about elder parents or how all elder immigrants might relive the disorientation of coming to America as they age. They can discuss helpful ways to visit with elders. Written against the backdrop of Amy Tan's struggle with her own mother's illness, we see that Alzheimer's disease and dementia are frightening for elders, their families, and other people who care for them. Still, these elders often have important—and accurate—stories to share with us. Writing those stories can be an important service to the families and the elder person. 403pp., young adult

---

The Cay by Theodore Taylor (Avon, 1969). Phillip, separated from his mother when their ship was torpedoed in 1942, is stranded on a remote cay with an old black man who worked on the ship's deck. Blinded by a blow to his head, Phillip becomes reliant on his elder companion and must confront the racist beliefs he learned from his parents. A story of survival, friendship, and trust. 144pp., grades 4–8

Doing Time Online by Jan Siebold (Albert Whitman, 2002). A "practical joke" that led to an elder woman's injury leaves twelve-year-old Mitchell remorseful. As a consequence of his actions, he is required to participate in a police program involving twice-a-week online chats with a nursing home resident, Wootie Hayes. Despite initial misgivings, Mitchell grows to depend on Wootie for advice, and a valued relationship grows. 90pp., grades 4–7

The Graduation of Jake Moon by Barbara Park (Aladdin, 2000). Fourteen-year-old Jake Moon treasures his relationship with his grandfather, Skelly. The past four years have been difficult, though, because Alzheimer's disease has changed everything. Now roles are reversed, and Jake is a caregiver. Although Jake rebels, his love for his grandfather remains. And when the elder man wanders off, Jake is determined to find him. 115pp., grades 4–7

Handbook for Boys by Walter Dean Myers (HarperCollins, 2002). The wisdom of age becomes apparent to reluctant Jimmy as he meets three elder men. After school, sixteen-year-old Jimmy must spend his afternoons at a barbershop, Duke's Place, in a "community mentorship" program as an alternative to a juvenile facility. As these "old guys" talk about their lives, Jimmy begins to think for himself about staying out of trouble, about making better choices, and about true success. 179pp., grades 6–12

> "It's not that you're wrong Jimmy, it's just that your approach needs a lot of work.... Too many young people think that because somebody down the road has said you deserve this or deserve that, then all you have to do is wait around until it comes your way. Believe me, it won't."
> FROM *HANDBOOK FOR BOYS*

Recommendation from the Field
by Denise Dowell, Program Assistant,
Louisiana Learn and Serve America

The Hundred Penny Box by Shannon Bell Mathis (Viking, 1986). One-hundred-year-old

continued ⟶

Aunt Dew has come to live with her nephew John, his wife Ruth, and their young son, Michael. John feels responsible for Aunt Dew, since she raised him after his parents drowned when he was a young boy. Ruth, who feels the older lady does not like her, treats Aunt Dew as though she were a child. Michael loves Aunt Dew and promises that even though his mother has burned Aunt Dew's belongings in the furnace, he will keep her hundred penny box safe. This may be a well-used box with a broken lid, but to Aunt Dew it is her life. When she was thirty years old, her husband gave her thirty pennies, each one dated for a year of her life. The tradition of collecting a dated penny continued. For each penny, Aunt Dew remembers important events. Michael and Aunt Dew open the box and talk about the times of life.

Several threads can be discussed after the class reads this book. Students can look at their own families to identify traditions and how they were started. Will those traditions be carried on by their generation? Are they old or new traditions? Also, a discussion of the importance of intergenerational relationships and the care of older people would be appropriate. Although John and Michael love Aunt Dew, Ruth has the role of caregiver. The book can lead students to gather oral histories from elders in their community; the historians could include the topic of family traditions. 47pp., grades 1–4

Petey by Ben Mikaelson (Hyperion, 2000). In 1922, at the age of two, Petey is placed by his parents in the state's insane asylum when he was actually suffering with severe cerebral palsy. His life in institutions continues to age seventy, with brief moments when his caretakers recognize his ability to communicate and his passion for learning and living. In his advancing years, while living at a nursing home, Petey meets Trevor, an eighth grader who is frustrated by a lack of friends and minimal parental attention. The depth of their relationship offers both companionship and much joy. Based on a true story, this book delves into the tragedy of misdiagnosis and inappropriate care. 256pp., grades 5–9

Tiger, Tiger, Burning Bright by Ron Koertge (Orchard, 1994). In a modern-day western setting, Jesse takes the role of protector of his grandfather, Pappy, who loves to ride in the desert and play poker. Pappy's Alzheimer's disease has Jesse's mom looking into a nursing home. Jesse follows a path of deceit to keep his mom from knowing a secret: Pappy sees tiger tracks in the California hills! 179pp., young adult

Recommendation from the Field
by Devora Kaye, high school student

Tuck Everlasting by Natalie Babbitt (Farrar, Straus and Giroux, 1985). After drinking water from the spring of eternal life, the Tuck family wanders from place to place living as inconspicuously as possible. Winnie Foster, a young girl, learns of their secret. The Tucks attempt to explain to her the importance of living life naturally and of regarding age as a gift to be valued. At the same time, though, Winnie is being followed by a man who yearns to sell her this special water!

Tuck Everlasting could be used as an introduction to service learning related to elders. It clearly shows the importance of living life day by day and valuing each stage. It can also be used to emphasize the importance of learning from older people and appreciating their knowledge. For a project, students could collaborate on making a book, telling about people of every age from one to a hundred. Each student could find someone of a certain age and write about that person or could write about what he or she knows about that age and what is special about it. Another variation is creating a "decades" book that includes historical information and personal memories about a series of decades. 139pp., grades 5–8

The War with Grandpa by Robert Kimmel Smith (Dell, 1984). Peter likes the idea of Grandpa moving in but he is furious about having to give up his room to relocate to the stuffy third floor. Peter declares war! As a consequence, Grandpa teaches Peter lessons about war, friendship, and family relationships. 140pp., grades 3–6

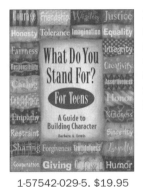

free spirit
PUBLiSHiNG®

www.freespirit.com

Helping kids
help themselves™
since 1983

Hundreds of
service project
ideas right at
your fingertips!

Free Spirit Publishing
Celebrating 20 years
of reaching and teaching
children and teens.

Interviews with Authors:
The Story Behind the Story

In the following interviews, we find out the "story behind the story" from Eve Bunting (*Sunshine Home, Gleam and Glow, Smoky Nights, Summer Wheels, Your Move, Someday a Tree, Fly Away Home, A Train to Somewhere, A Day's Work, The Wednesday Surprise*), Richard Michelson (*Too Young for Yiddish*), and Eileen Spinelli (*Somebody Loves You, Mr. Hatch*).

Three authors, three different reasons for their selection. I was familiar with many of Eve Bunting's books, and I wanted to learn why she continuously writes stories on such important social themes. In the case of *Too Young for Yiddish*, Richard Michelson's story of a language nearly lost along with its tradition and history captivated me. And after years of referring to the heartwarming story *Somebody Loves You, Mr. Hatch* in teacher workshops, interviewing Eileen Spinelli, the book's author, was simply a must—and a treat. After the interview, Eileen mailed me the recipe for Mr. Hatch's brownies!

Eve Bunting, author of Sunshine Home, Smoky Nights, A Day's Work, The Wednesday Surprise

I grew up in Northern Ireland, where there was tremendous discrimination. As a Protestant, I was fortunate in that the prejudice was not aimed toward me; Catholics were the targets. Growing up in a small town, I thought all Catholics were poor and begged and had no bathrooms in their homes. I knew no Catholics personally until I was older and attending university. For the first time, I knew Catholics and began to see the intolerance in Ireland.

When my husband and I immigrated to the United States, one important reason was to bring our children away from prejudice and discrimination. However, in this country, we found prejudice of a different kind, and just as much unfairness. At the beginning, I did not understand. We lived next door to a Catholic family. Our children played together, and I was delighted. Then, as months and years passed, I became acutely aware of unfairness against other ethnic groups, people who are homeless, gender inequities.

As an author, I never intended to write about social issues. These stories came out of me; this is in my heart, what interests me and is important to me. Early in my writing career, when reviewers began to talk about my "social issues books," I did not know what they were talking about. Now I fully understand this description

I select a theme for a book from what is going on in my life. Once I identify a subject, I think more deeply, and then a catharsis occurs. Here is an example. My husband's mother came here from Ireland and, at age 86, lived independently in a little apartment near our home. I called her every day, and she often came for meals. One day I called and she did not answer. I rushed over and found her on the rug, where she had fallen and stayed all night with a broken back. We soon learned she would not walk again. Since I could not lift her or provide the care she required, having her live in our home was not an option. We decided to find a place nearby where she would be comfortable, and that was difficult. We did find a place. My book *Sunshine Home* was written out of a need to show her and tell ourselves that sometimes you don't have an option for a beloved family member. As long as the person knows you love them and always will care for them and not abandon them, it will be all right. We all have pangs of guilt when we do this, even though we know it is necessary.

When I am writing a picture book, I think about the story for a very long time. I subconsciously examine the situations from all directions and from all the characters' viewpoints—not thinking in order or logically. Every character has a problem, big or small. I come up with different endings; perhaps this is somewhat deliberate to have an element of surprise. This occurs in *Sunshine Home* when, after saying good-bye to Gram, seven-year old Timmy returns to give her his school picture and finds her in tears. The family gathers to share their true feelings about her living situation and their hopes.

I have had wonderful letters (and I answer each one) about this book. It seems like my words and the illustrations by Diane de Groat capture what most nursing homes look like. Sunshine Home is the generic place. Many letters are from adults (they read picture books, too) saying, "This is just like the nursing home my mother is in. How did you describe this place so accurately?" A man wrote a letter that his wife was living in a similar facility. "Such a comfort," he wrote, "for me to read this book." Children also write me of their visits with grandparents.

For children who want to be writers, I recommend that you read. I was a voracious reader. There was lots of rain in Ireland and no television, and I would stay in and read and read. With the first break in the rainy weather, my mother would say, "Take your nose out of that book and go outside and play!" Also keep a journal. Think of things in your own life that you care about, and write for fun. Remember that words rarely come out right the first time. We all rewrite. Sometimes I bring stacks of different revisions into classrooms, each on a different color paper. The students are in awe over the piles of blue papers, then pink, then yellow—all to show the different stages.

Even though I write young adult novels also, I love to write picture books. They are my favorites. When I get stuck on a novel, I rejoice and go write a picture book and come back to finish the novel. The picture book is the truth being distilled through the economy of words and the economy of thought. When holding one of my newly published picture books, I know that in this tiny little book, I have the essence of truth as I see it.

To be a writer, or a learner of any kind, be open to all experiences and all people. My book that says that best is *Smoky Nights*. This book reminds us to get to *know* other people. You might find out you like them a lot and they may not be so different from you. When we stick with our own kind, we miss a lot.

Sometimes we avoid knowing people because of fear. Being an elder myself, I think that some children are a little bit afraid of older people. We don't have the same kinds of hands as their mothers. Our hair is gray. We can be intimidating to them or appear cranky or bossy. Many children are brought up by grandparents, and that can soften the feelings people have about us. We were young once, and now we, in part, live our lives through the young. I know this from having five grandchildren, whom I adore. When children communicate with older people, there is a mutual advantage. We can give them so much, and they can give to us also. These interactions spark the older people and teach the younger people that they have so much to give to other generations. Examples of this reciprocity can be found in two of my books. In *The Wednesday Surprise*, a child teaches her grandmother to read. In *A Day's Work*, a grandfather teaches his grandson a lesson about honesty. Stories make these wonderful relations apparent. We humanize people by removing the clichés and showing people in all situations and by helping and caring for each other.

Richard Michelson, *author of* Too Young for Yiddish

I happened to know Aaron Lansky, who started the National Yiddish Book Center. During visits there with my own kids, I began to realize how little they and their friends knew of even recent ancestors' life stories. With both parents often busy and overworked, our society doesn't value the free time when family history is traditionally passed down from generation to generation. Swapping stories nightly around the dinner table is rarely part of the day-to-day routine in our fast-food culture. Even growing up in the fifties, I knew little about my own grandparents' lives. I was too absorbed in the American way of life to care, and they were too busy making a living to share.

When a young person does eventually become curious about his or her family history, there are often only a few relatives with firsthand knowledge still alive. With Eastern and Central European Jews, the situation is especially distressing, because the native Yiddish-speaking world was virtually wiped out by the Nazis during World

War II. A whole link in the chain that reaches backward to teach us where we're coming from is cut off, gone. How can we know the direction in which we are heading? So there is an added immediacy to this situation. The few native speakers of Yiddish who survived the war by escaping to the United States tried hard to fit into the American way of life, abandoning their own language and customs for those of their adopted country. Even that generation is dying off, and we are in danger of an entire culture being lost.

I wanted to write about this, and my first inclination is always to create a story as an avenue for parents and children to start discussing their heritage. In this book, I make reference to the fact that in school we learn about "wars and kings and knights in shining armor." We don't think of history as what happens to real people. Our grandparents lived through history. The record of our own families is as valid as the events we study in school. My children learned French and Spanish, and they know many things—for example, about how the British aristocracy lived—but they've learned almost nothing about Polish *shtetl* life, and it never occurred to them to study Yiddish.

The final spark for the book occurred when my son was doing a school report on the sixties. Reading over what he'd written, I remarked on a section I thought was incorrect. "This is not the way it happened," I insisted, "and I know because I was there!" His response was, "I don't have time to listen to you right now; my assignment is due tomorrow!" In his class, they were already studying an era I'd lived through, but with the pressure-filled high school schedule, our teenagers don't have time to pay attention to our stories when we do offer them. I am hopeful *Too Young for Yiddish* will help inspire a conversation between generations.

Usually, the local community is filled with people eager to tell their stories. Schools should encourage grandparents or other family members to share experiences. In our local area, there is an organization that brings Vietnam veterans into the classroom. This is fascinating for kids and helps to make history come alive. War is something that can tear families apart, affecting our lives and those of our next-door neighbors.

I know that *Too Young for Yiddish* isn't going to change the world, but I hope it plants seeds in the minds of young people. Down the road, they might read another book that interests them on a similar subject. After a while, I hope they develop the curiosity to ask simple questions like, "Did you grow up speaking a different language? What was your neighborhood like?" Recently, I read my book at a reception held at the National Yiddish Book Center. Afterwards, Aaron Lansky's young daughter asked her father, "When are you going to teach me Yiddish?" That is the response I hope for from this book.

Eileen Spinelli, *author of* Somebody Loves You, Mr. Hatch

When I was six years old, I wanted to be a writer. My father gave me his manual typewriter, and I began my career typing with two fingers. I first wrote poetry. After having kids, I began to write picture books. I find picture books to be a form of poetry; they come from the same place. Children's books move on a thread with a sense of focus toward a clear culmination, a lyrical ending, like the punch line of a joke or the last line of a poem.

The story of *Somebody Loves You, Mr. Hatch* began with the idea of kindness being important in life. I have known several people who were standoffish or who seemed stern or not so friendly. I discovered they were either very shy—which can appear unfriendly—or were dealing with a lot of sadness in their lives. This became "Mr. Hatch," who is a little shy and a little different and lonely. He may seem unfriendly, but his heart is friendly. He needs the little spark of love to bloom, which is the way we all are.

Once I had the main character, the idea came to me that he gets a message that someone loves him. How would this happen? I thought of the valentine. Stories arrive in different ways. Some come fast; some come in little pieces that swish inside of you for years and do not come together as easily. I am tickled when the end comes first.

While developing a story I draw on memories of my own. For example, I was trying to think of a humorous place where he could work. I liked shoelaces when I was little. They always fascinated me! So Mr. Hatch works in a shoelace factory. That he eats prunes for dessert just seemed like a funny image.

Like many other writers, I wanted to make a statement that kindness is important, even underrated, and can make a big difference in the world. I was able to say this in a humorous way. Mr. Hatch is endearing, and the art makes him even more so. Artist Paul Yalowitz brings another layer of richness. I would never have thought to change the color of the book from dreary colors to bright cheerful colors so that the pictures and the text work together. The art is inspiring.

How have people responded to *Mr. Hatch?* A businessman in New York read *Mr. Hatch* and began to send flowers anonymously to his employees. He uses *Mr. Hatch* when making presentations and encourages management to honor employees in an anonymous way to create more kindness in the workplace.

One teacher told me that on Valentine's Day she placed a bag of candy at the door of a neighbor who had been giving her a hard time. She told the kids, and they made valentines for classmates they were having a hard time with. I have heard of kids taking brownies and lemonade to the fire department; others have visited nursing homes. They have done things for people who work at school.

Without kindness and love, life is pretty dreary. We have learned that on September 11, 2001, people in danger were not concerned about their bank accounts or revenge. They left phone messages saying, "I love you." This is what life is about.

We can also show kindness even to people we don't know very well. We underestimate what can come from going that extra inch to be nice to the person waiting on the table, to be thoughtful to a new kid at school, or to give a smile to a person you don't know in the cafeteria line. Mr. Hatch is a sweet character who, with just a bit of kindness from others, returns the kindness many times over.

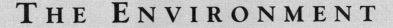

CHAPTER 8

THE ENVIRONMENT

> When one tugs at a single thing in nature, one
> finds it attached to the rest of the world.
>
> JOHN MUIR, AUTHOR

Majestic redwood trees, waves cresting near tidal pools, deserts with cacti and coyotes—these are a few images from the diverse landscapes that make up our environment. To define this all-encompassing term, we need only look at the word. At the center of "environment" is the Latin root *viron*, meaning "circle." This simple yet profound image reveals the interconnectedness of air, water, plants, animals, and all of our ecosystems.

At all ages, young people can develop understanding of and respect for our environment. They can acquire a vocabulary that will allow them to participate in conversation and intelligent debate about such topics as acid rain, ozone depletion, alternative energy sources, watersheds, erosion, and composting. They can learn to carefully examine multiple sides of issues and develop informed ideas. Knowing that the earth is dynamic and constantly changing, they can consider which of our human actions protect and preserve and which cause irreparable harm. Knowledge and the ability to respond can join to create a citizenry prepared to ensure a healthy environment for generations to come.

> The frog does not drink up
> the pond in which he lives.
>
> SIOUX PROVERB

Preparation: Getting Ready for Service Learning Involving the Environment

The following activities can be used in the preparation stage to promote learning and skill development related to the environment. These activities can be used with different age ranges during preparation to help your students examine key issues through research, analyze community needs, and gain the knowledge they need to effectively contribute to the design of their service plan. Since literature is often an important part of preparation, you can find recommended titles on this theme in the Environment Bookshelf later in this chapter.

Activity: Litter by Litter. Young people have been the best advocates for eliminating litter and promoting recycling. How can your school or class join in? Investigating and addressing the issue of litter at school can lead to more complex projects that tackle recycling or even how trash is processed in the community or region. The following suggestions have successfully helped elementary, middle, and high school classes start exploring environmental issues in the world at large by getting them to look at the environment right around them—school.

- Create a school survey to identify litter "hot spots" (usually near the lunch area). Students can walk around the school campus at different times of the day—at breaks or lunch or just after passing periods in middle or high schools—to find out where the trash accumulates. Students can make posters to designate these places as "hot spots" to be cleaned up.

- Establish a litter-free zone in one specific area of the school. Add to the beauty of this area—for example, plant flowers. Students can make signs and promote this campaign through public-address announcements at school. One litter-free zone can be the start of a litter-free school.

- Use books such as *The Great Trash Bash, The Wartville Wizard* and *I Want to Be an Environmentalist* as resources to develop campaign ideas for cleaning up litter. From these and other books, develop plays or choral readings to educate other students and school community members.

- In a math class, maintain records about the quantities of trash produced by the school—a good way to teach about graphs, statistics, and percentages. Guide students into thinking about how much trash is produced by their community, their city, even their country and what can be done to reduce it. Successful waste reduction at school can lead students into the community to help.

Once the school is on its way to being litter-free, initiate recycling or expand existing efforts using a similar process of education, awareness, promotion, and feedback. Then students can take their expertise into the community, helping other schools and even businesses and government offices to reduce, reuse, and recycle.

Activity: Take the Challenge. What environmental challenges face your community? Are they related to energy conservation? Fire safety? Land use? Using newspapers and the Internet, find a topic that is currently affecting your locale. Learn about all sides of the issue. Plan a debate with invited guests to increase community awareness and understanding of the topics.

> First I thought I was fighting
> for the rubber tappers, then I thought
> I was fighting for the Amazon, then I realized
> I was fighting for humanity.
>
> CHICO MENDEZ, RAIN FOREST ACTIVIST

Find Out More About the Environment

To learn more about these issues and to get ideas for service and action, visit these Web sites and organizations online:

www.earthday.net The Earth Day Network includes environmental education curriculum and resources for K–12 teachers and promotes the April 22nd annual Earth Day event that began in 1970.

www.adopt-a-watershed.org Adopt-A-Watershed is a school-community learning experience that uses local watersheds as living laboratories to develop collaborative partnerships and reinforce learning through community service.

www.earthforce.org Earth Force is a youth-driven organization, engaging young people in problem solving to discover and implement lasting solutions to environmental issues in their communities.

www.arborday.org/kids/kidsdif.cfm At the National Arbor Day "Kids Make a Difference" Web site, you can find many activities, plenty of resources, and programs and projects all across the country that encourage tree planting.

www.nrdc.org The National Resources Defense Council has easy-to-read information and photographs on a variety of environmental topics, including wildlife and fish, global warming, energy use, and clean air, water, and oceans.

Making Connections Across the Curriculum

Some service learning activities naturally lend themselves to interdisciplinary work and making connections across the curriculum. These connections strengthen and broaden student learning, helping them meet academic standards. More than likely, you'll be looking for these connections and ways to encourage them well before the students ever start working on service learning activities. As with the entire service learning process, it helps to remain flexible, because some connections can be spontaneously generated by the questions raised throughout and by the needs of the project. To help you think about cross-curricular connections and where you can look for them, the Curricular Web for this chapter (page 125) gives examples of many different ways this theme can be used in different academic areas. (The

The Environment Across the Curriculum

English/Language Arts
- Write stories or a collaborative book about a special natural setting in your community
- Read biographies of environmentalists then create a living "wax museum" where students take on the identities of these people and tell their life stories
- Study how classical haiku capture a moment in nature

Social Studies/History
- Study different Native American tribes' relationships with the land they lived on, how they interacted with the environment, and their concepts of "owning" land
- Learn about how Earth Day began as a grassroots event in 1970 and has spread internationally
- Research government policy on an environmentally sensitive area in your region; discuss and debate the issue

Languages
- Find out the words for "reduce, reuse, and recycle" in many languages and create a poster
- Compare the political positions of different countries with U.S. policies on environmental issues
- Compile a book of original poetry in different languages about the environment

Theater, Music, & Visual Arts
- Prepare a skit or play about the environment to be performed in a natural setting
- Create and perform jingles or raps to promote clean schools and playgrounds
- Decorate trash bins at school to make them attractive receptacles

The Environment

Math
- Present environmental statistics on the public-address system at school each morning
- Analyze the pattern of waste disposal at school
- Review the water or electrical bills at school and develop a conservation program to reduce costs

Physical Education
- Study the effect of pollution on the lungs and overall health
- Create a public service announcement on outdoor activities
- Plan a field trip to a nature reserve or park and hike!

Computer
- Design and make flyers of recycling tips for the community
- Find out what happens to discarded computers in your community and research options for re-use
- Research and discuss: Does computer use result in less paper consumption?

Science
- Learn about and then make recycled paper
- Study science careers in environmental testing and protection
- Compare the effects of composting and recycling with landfills and incinerated waste

service learning scenarios in the next section of the chapter also demonstrate various ways this theme can be used across the curriculum.)

Service Learning Scenarios:
Ideas for Action

Ready to take action? What follows are projects that have been successfully carried out by elementary, middle, or high school students. Most of these scenarios and examples explicitly include some aspects of preparation, action, reflection, and demonstration. These scenarios can be a rich source of project, resource, and curriculum ideas for you to draw upon. While the grade levels are given as a reference, most project ideas can be adapted to suit younger or older students, and many are suitable for cross-age partnerships.

Caring for Earth: Grades K–8. At a rural school in Briggs, Oklahoma, students at many grade levels learned the history of Earth Day and decorated 390 grocery bags with environmental slogans such as "Don't Litter!" and "Reduce, Reuse, Recycle." The bags were distributed to the public at the local supermarket on Earth Day.

From Frogs to Petroglyphs: Grades K and 2. Four classes of kindergartners and second graders in El Cerrito, California, set out to learn more about their neighborhood creek and park. Naturalists took the students on nature walks to teach observation skills. They listened to Pacific Chorus frogs singing at dusk, found tiny hummingbird nests, and raised buckeyes, oaks, and willows for creek restoration projects. After discovering a "plucking tree" where Cooper hawks deposit tiny feathers of the birds they hunt and catch, students gathered samples of the feathers and sent them to the Golden Gate Raptor Observatory, where scientists conduct research about what the hawks eat. They studied the petroglyphs etched into the boulder next to the pond and learned some of the history of the area and the people who once lived along the creek. They published an illustrated guidebook— "From the Tops of the Trees to the Bottom of the Pond"—and delivered copies to all the homes in the neighborhood to encourage others to make wonderful discoveries at the creek.

Oak Forest Sprouts: Grades 2–12. Students and other members of one central California community are working together to protect and restore forests of valley oaks, the largest of all oak trees in North America. A local river preserve has the best remaining examples of these oak forests, which once flourished in California's Central Valley. Most of the preserve is left to natural regeneration; however, active restoration efforts are needed in some areas. During one school year, more than a thousand students from four elementary schools and a high school participated in oak forest restoration field trips. Second and third graders gathered over 14,000 acorns. Fifth and sixth graders washed, sorted, counted, and bagged the acorns. Students from all four elementary schools and the high school helped to plant nearly five acres of land that one day will return to oak forest. This project was successful because of the cooperative efforts of the Nature Conservancy, Bureau of Land Management, California Department of Fish and Game, and many parent and community volunteers. In-class lessons that related to the project crossed all curriculum areas, including math, language arts, science, social studies, and fine arts. Several schools also hosted their own tree-planting activities.

> Plant trees. They give us two of the most crucial elements for our survival: oxygen and books.
> A. WHITNEY BROWN, WRITER

Give It to the Worms: Grade 3. A composting project that began in one Palo Alto classroom grew over four years to involve many teachers and students and resulted in promoting the benefits of composting to the entire school and its surrounding community. As part of the science curriculum students learned about ecosystems, and after hearing a guest speaker from the Integrative Waste Management Board, students wanted to get involved in a project. They created a chart to record waste at school and brainstormed ideas for waste reduction. They prepared a video presentation and spoke to other classes about ecology, especially how to reduce food waste through composting. The kids became composting and worm bin experts. They collected school food waste and watched as it was transformed into deep, rich soil that they used in their school garden and donated to gardeners who lived in a nearby senior residential facility. The students' next step was community outreach. They hosted a parent information night with a site tour and composting lessons. They distributed monthly copies of their newsletter, "Warm Ways," in the neighborhood and participated in the local Chinese New Year parade, where—costumed as a giant worm—they handed out informational pamphlets on worm bins and composting called "Give It to the Worms!"

The Mystery of Crabby Kathy: Grades 3 and 6.

Every year a class of third-grade students at an elementary school in Chico, California, partners with a class of older students on a project where they make a book telling a story about something they've learned. One year the students noticed that a teacher at school was often crabby and wondered why. Through their environmental studies, the children began to look for possibilities in their surroundings to solve this mystery and wrote an entertaining and informative book on their findings. Their story identifies many possible culprits: mold, stinky pens, chemicals used for cleaning, and poor ventilation. With funding from the National Institute of Environmental Health Sciences, copies were made and distributed. The story can be downloaded from the NIEHS Web site at *www.niehs.nih.gov.*

Lessons from Trash: Grade 4.

Fourth graders in New Jersey analyzed school trash during a recycling project that included practice computing with fractions and percentages. They determined that 85 percent of the trash could have been recycled. As part of a campaign for awareness and school change, the students put up posters and created PowerPoint presentations to teach others in their school. Learning continued in math as the students tracked and charted their household garbage for a week. In science class, they learned about renewable versus nonrenewable resources. The next step was to compost lunch leftovers, adding earthworms to help. This resulted in newly enriched soil for the vegetable gardens planted by the kindergarten classes.

Too Much Water, Water Everywhere: Grade 5.

"How much water do you use?" This question led a class of fifth-grade students to a formidable task: evaluating school and home water usage. In school the students learned to read water bills, and they took a walking tour of the school to identify, with assistance from maintenance staff, ways to conserve water. At home, the students developed a survey to record how much water each family member used per week; they compared the results with the average use (in the United States) of between 80 and 100 gallons of water each day. After hearing a guest speaker describe "water use reduction in the home" and conducting research through literature and the Internet, students created and distributed a family-friendly guide, "Save Water—We Need Every Drop." Their next project? Cutting back on electricity.

Ancient Egypt and Water Conservation: Grade 6.

"I'm teaching about ancient Egypt. How can I tie this to service learning?" The response came from another teacher: "I just was in Egypt. Water use and conservation have been huge issues from early times to the present." Students compared methods employed in the past with water use and conservation methods used now. Next, they prepared and distributed literature on water conservation for homes, applied water conservation strategies in the school garden, and also planted drought-resistant plants at a nearby senior center.

The Lead-Based Paint Project: Grade 7.

Some environmental materials can make us sick right in our own homes. Middle school science classes began to investigate issues related to toxic materials in homes, such as lead-based paints, and created informative fact sheets. Copies were given to realtors, homeowner associations, and parent groups and made available through local libraries and social service agencies.

Environmental Heroes: Grades 7–8.

A middle school teacher in Baton Rouge, Louisiana, initiated a service learning program that aligns environmental education and activities with required state standards and benchmarks. Over four years 1,600 students, teachers, adult volunteers, and partners dedicated 23,000 hours to service projects. Students planted over 1,400 trees, picked up over 600 bags of trash, collected truckloads of junk, and participated in water quality monitoring programs. Over the course of this program middle school students worked alongside community experts to plant trees, perform water quality testing, identify plants, gain hands-on experience with local wildlife, test for soil quality, and learn about the many challenges facing the Louisiana wetlands. The middle school students used this knowledge to lead over 2,000 fifth and sixth graders on wetland trips. One seventh grader reflected on her experience this way: "If the plants and animals could talk, I think they would say we are their heroes. That is what I feel like when we are working in the wetlands."

Improving the Air We Breathe: Grade 8. At the beginning of a science project on air pollution, middle school students in West Palm Beach were described by their teachers as "unaware." The students went on to spend two hours a week investigating air quality issues in their community. They conducted air quality tests and identified pollutants around the school and community, as well as learning about laws, regulations, and practices that made the situation worse. After surveying their peers about transportation-related issues, the students presented a play on environmental pollutants, created posters, and distributed information on alternatives to driving to school.

Community Revitalization from the Ground Up: Grade 8. For four years, every eighth-grade class in rural Ainsworth, Nebraska, has been making improvements to a local nature area. Initially, students formed committees and helped to create a plan for short- and long-term activities. Students draw on art, math, earth science, social studies, English, and technology as they work on trails, bridges, stairs, and picnic areas, help at the information centers, and make project presentations. The teachers continually integrate the idea of community revitalization into the project to increase youth awareness of the broader region and environment.

The Fractal-Mural-Community Connection: Grades 9 and 10. Through service learning, a high school in Spokane, Washington, set out to make new community connections and enrich already established relationships, particularly with a nearby elementary school. By developing a reciprocal relationship with younger students, older students hoped to provide meaningful service to the neighborhood. One immediate need was to reduce or eliminate vandalism and graffiti at a sports field house in a local park. Since murals are proven to be a deterrent to both, planning started to create one for the field

house. Students from a high school geometry class taught upper elementary students about the geometry concepts used in fractals, which are reoccurring geometric shapes. While fractals can be extremely complex, the simple rules upon which they are based make them an approachable subject for students of all ages. This service learning activity connected the sometimes esoteric discipline of geometry with an aspect of everyday life. After learning about fractals, the elementary students used their new knowledge to design a mural to decorate the field house and one for their school gymnasium. The geometry students also helped to transfer the younger students' small-scale fractal art plans to the wall murals, then everyone painted. Parents and community volunteers also assisted with the painting or donated supplies.

To Help with Recovery: Grades 9 and 10. After a massive local wildfire destroyed more than a hundred homes, a high school biology class in Carlsbad, California, worked alongside elementary school children to plant a native garden at a local park to help demonstrate and study how nature recovers from wildfire.

A Restorative Process: Grades 9–12. During a meeting of their school's environmental club, a teacher asked students to think about issues affecting the future of their community. Students, with input from the local university and the city parks and recreation department, set up a community forum on local environmental issues. Together, they decided that cleaning and restoring the watershed of a nearby creek was crucial to frog and bird habitats. Club members researched previous restoration efforts and brought in environmentalists to discuss what makes a healthy watershed. With a work plan in hand, the students helped to clean and restore five miles on either side of the creek, learning about native and invasive plants in the process. At the conclusion of their project, they made flyers and invited local citizens to discuss how improper disposal of oil and use of pesticides on lawns can impact the watershed and the animal species that depend on it.

Energy Efficient Teens: Grades 9–12. A local energy company contracted with a high school drama class to write and perform a production on energy efficiency. The high school players read literature from the energy company and developed a program with skits, a rap, poetry, and a pop quiz for the audience. The high school players put on assemblies for elementary school audiences to rave reviews.

> This Earth is not ours; it is a treasure
> we hold in trust for future generations.
>
> AFRICAN PROVERB

Collaboration for Restoration: Grades 9–12. A science teacher in Cedarburg, Wisconsin, initiated a project that—with the help of additional teachers and students—resulted in the restoration of a park to its native woodland habitat. Students determined what had grown in the area before settlers arrived. English students developed an informative pamphlet about the history of the park, highlighting the settlers who were buried there. The art class visited the park, learned about the history of these settling families, and did the graphic design for the project pamphlets. These pamphlets were given to the local preservation committee and the chamber of commerce. A woodshop class constructed benches to replicate those used by the early settlers.

The Tar Creek Story: Grades 9–12. What if you had a toxic creek near your school? Imagine seeing mountains of toxic waste from mining wherever you looked. Students in Miami, Oklahoma, actually live in those surroundings. In fact, their community was so badly polluted it has been identified as a Superfund site. At the local high school, a school counselor and the students took the challenge of educating the community about their hazardous surroundings, including Tar Creek, the most polluted body of water in the United States. More teachers, community members, and national organizations have joined the collaboration every year. Students have become knowledgeable advocates for saving their community—the people and the land. Through their classroom and extracurricular work, students continue to conduct extensive research on a range of topics, including the history of

mining in the area, water contamination, and the results of human exposure to toxic heavy metals. Student research papers, poetry, and personal essays have been published in two books that tell the story of "Our Toxic Place." Students have traveled to state and national conferences to lead in-depth workshops. They've given "toxic tours" for students and adults to educate people from the region about this Superfund site. The students also host an annual conference that brings together state and national government officials, leaders of Native American groups, and members of the surrounding community to wrestle with the environmental and personal issues that result from the toxic pollution.

Adopt a Highway: Grades 10 and 11. For several years, high school students in Idaho have participated in the "Adopt a Highway" program. Four times a year, the students picked up litter from their adopted two-mile section of highway. The eight to ten bags of litter collected each time have sparked discussions about wasteful packaging and aesthetic damage to the environment. The students, upset with the amount of trash thrown from vehicles, have been more aware of and conscientious about their surroundings as a result.

Going Tropical? Grades 11 and 12. Students conducted research on products that originate in tropical rain forests and created tools for evaluating the trade-off between the need for the item and the environmental impact of producing it. The students composed letters to the products' manufacturers to find out about their commitment to conservation of tropical rain forests. Another class made a list of similar products that didn't use rain forest materials, and the product lists were provided during presentations to parent groups and other classes. "Make a choice," students advised, "when buying products, to protect our environment."

> The elders were wise.
> They knew that man's heart, away from nature,
> becomes hard; they knew that lack of respect
> for growing, living things, soon led
> to lack of respect for humans, too."
>
> CHIEF LUTHER STANDING BEAR
> OF THE LAKOTA SIOUX

The Environment Bookshelf

It's a big world out there. Clearly, "the environment" covers many aspects of the planet, and this breadth is reflected in the Environment Bookshelf. To help you find books relevant to your particular projects, the book chart classifies the titles into several topic areas: overview of the environment, natural resources, recycling, and appreciation.

In general, the bookshelf features:

• An annotated bibliography arranged and alphabetized by title according to the general categories of nonfiction (N), picture books (P), and fiction (F). For nonfiction and fiction, length and recommended grade levels are included. The entries in the picture book category do not include suggested grade levels, since they can be successfully used with all ages.

• A chart organized by topic and category to help you find books relevant to particular projects.

• Recommendations from service learning colleagues and experts that include a book summary and ideas for service learning connections. (The number of recommended books varies in each bookshelf.)

The Environment Bookshelf Topics

Topics	Books	Category
Overview of the Environment These "big picture" books cover a range of environmental topics. Ecosystems are highlighted in many of the titles.	ChaseR (see page 86)	F
	The Empty Lot	P
	Issues in the Environment	N
	I Want to Be an Environmentalist *	N
	Judy Moody Saves the World *	F
	A Life Like Mine: How Children Live Around the World * (see page 196)	N
	The Missing 'Gator of Gumbo Limbo	F
	One Less Fish	N
	Saving the Planet	F
	There's an Owl in the Shower	F
	What Planet Are You From, Clarice Bean? *	P
	You Are the Earth: Know the Planet So You Can Make It Better *	N
Natural Resources These books focus on life-sustaining resources that are at risk—trees, water, and food.	A Cool Drink of Water	N
	Fernando's Gift/El Regalo de Fernando	N
	The Gift of the Tree	P
	The Great Kapok Tree	P
	Island of the Blue Dolphins	F
	One Good Apple: Growing Our Food for the Sake of the Earth	N
	Our Poisoned Waters	N
	The People Who Hugged the Trees: An Environmental Folktale	P
	A River Ran Wild *	P

continued ——→

Topics	Books	Category
Natural Resources continued	*The Shape of Betts Meadow: A Wetlands Story* *	P
	Someday a Tree *	P
	Wildlife Refuge *	P
Recycling Reduce, reuse, recycle: This is the mantra of the recycling movement. These books tell of the subject from various perspectives.	*Crashed, Smashed, and Mashed: A Trip to Junkyard Heaven*	N
	The Great Trash Bash *	P
	Recycle Every Day! *	P
	The Wartville Wizard	P
Appreciation Taking time to appreciate our planet and our resources is part of the environmental story.	*Be Good to Eddie Lee* (see page 210)	P
	Dear Children of the Earth	P
	The Table Where Rich People Sit	P
	This House Is Made of Mud/Esta casa está hecha de lodo	P

Page references are given for books that do not appear in the Environment Bookshelf but that can be found in the bookshelf lists of other chapters.
* These books include examples of young people in service-providing roles.

Nonfiction: The Environment

A Cool Drink of Water by Barbara Kerley (National Geographic Society, 2002). "We live by the grace of water." This photo essay takes us on a global journey to see water stored in clay pots and a burlap bag. We see people drink from a river, a well, and a thin tin cup. We travel from Thailand to Rome to Canada. A note on water conservation gives statistics and strategies for protecting our planet's precious supply of water. 32pp., all ages

Crashed, Smashed, and Mashed: A Trip to Junkyard Heaven by Joyce Slayton Mitchell (Tricycle Press, 2001). Have you ever wondered what happens to the cars headed for the junkyard? Through photographs with text, see an engine that is pulled apart and cars that are shredded. Includes information about recycling. 32pp., grades 1–4

Fernando's Gift/El Regalo de Fernando by Douglas Keister (Sierra Club, 1995). Friends Fernando and Carmina, who live in the rain forest of Costa Rica, discover Carmina's climbing tree has been cut down. What can stop the devastation of the rain forest? Teaching people and planting trees! A bilingual book with photographs. 32pp., grades K–3

Issues in the Environment by Patricia D. Netzley (Lucent Books, 1998). Ready for a book that tackles controversies regarding the environment? Here it is. Controversies discussed include the ozone layer, garbage, endangered species, wilderness protection, and the cost of environmentalism. 94pp., grades 6–12

I Want to Be an Environmentalist by Stephanie Maze (Harcourt, 2000). Meet dedicated people who work hard to protect many different aspects of our environment—botanists, economists, organic farmers, biologists, scuba divers, and more. Includes the history of environmentalism and ways young people are involved. 48pp., all ages

Did you know . . . that tropical forest land shrinks by eighty thousand square miles due to expanding agriculture, logging, and development? . . . . that 55 percent of air pollution in the United States is caused by sources of transportation, such as cars, trucks, buses, and planes? . . . . that recycling a ton of paper saves seventeen trees?

FROM *I WANT TO BE AN ENVIRONMENTALIST*

One Good Apple: Growing Our Food for the Sake of the Earth by Catherine Paladino (Houghton Mifflin, 1999). Apples, strawberries, peaches, corn—foods we love. Yet these foods, and many others, are being sprayed with chemicals that affect living things, from the tiniest organisms to the humans who grow and eat the produce. Through sustainable agriculture, the balance of nature can be maintained, and we can nourish ourselves and the soil we rely on. 48pp., grades 5–12

One Less Fish by Kim Michelle Toft and Allan Sheather. (Charlesbridge, 1998). The informative narrative in this counting book tells how something is wrong in Australia's Great Barrier Reef. As the fish disappear one by one, we learn of the potential hazards of offshore drilling, trash in the ocean, over fishing, and more. Each tropical fish is identified, and a glossary is included. 32pp., grades K–6

Our Poisoned Waters by Edward Dolan (Cobblehill, 1997). Industry and farming waste choke our rivers. Sewage and oil spills damage our coastal waters. Rapidly growing populations deplete our fresh water supply. In this balanced presentation of water use and supply, key questions are raised: How has this occurred? What is the role of governments and private organizations? What can we do as individuals? 128pp., young adult

You Are the Earth: Know the Planet So You Can Make It Better by David Suzuki and Kathy Vanderlinden (Greystone Books, 2001). This book is about what we need to stay alive—clean air, water, soil, ecosystems, and the sun's energy. Information is plentiful in this blend of facts, Native American stories, colorful illustrations, and cartoons. The author also talks about the interdependence of people and animals, plus tells of actions taken by young people to change the world, now! 24pp., grades 4–7

Picture Books: The Environment

Dear Children of the Earth by Schim Schimmel (NorthWord Press, 1994). Mother Earth sends a letter to her children telling of the need to protect the planet and her many wondrous creatures.

The Empty Lot by Dale Fife (Sierra Club Books, 1991). Harry sets out to sell his "empty" lot. "What good is an empty lot?" he wonders while driving to put up a "For Sale" sign. While eating lunch on the lot, he hears a woodpecker tapping and sees baby sparrows in a nest, dragonflies hovering over a stream, and children playing. Harry has a change of heart.

> The earth beneath Harry's feet was alive. Pulsing. Harry watched a line of ants crawl in and out of their ant-mountain home. He thought about beetles and fungi and molds, earthworms and minute bacteria deep in the soil. He wondered how many wild things were watching him, mice and owls and hawks, from the jungle of the nearby blackberry thicket.
>
> And then Harry heard the voices of children.
>
> FROM *THE EMPTY LOT*

The Gift of the Tree by Alvin Tresselt (HarperCollins, 1992). By following a tree's life cycle, we find out about animals that depend on it for shelter and food.

The Great Kapok Tree by Lynne Cherry (Harcourt, 1990). Many different animals living in a great Brazilian kapok tree convince a man with an ax of the importance of the rain forest.

The Great Trash Bash by Loreen Leedy (Holiday House, 1991). When Mayor Hippo has a feeling that "something is wrong in Beaston," he discovers trash on the highway, a polluted swimming hole, and an overloaded landfill. The resident animals decide to make less trash and clean up their town now and for the future.

The People Who Hugged the Trees: An Environmental Folktale by Deborah Lee Rose (Robert Rinehart, 1990). This folktale from India tells of Amtra Devi, who inspired her community to protect the trees because the trees protect the community from the winds.

Recycle Every Day! by Nancy Elizabeth Wallace (Cavendish, 2003). A young bunny named Minna ponders the best way to make a poster about recycling, hoping her art will be selected for a Community Recycling Calendar. Her rabbit family spends the week doing various kinds of recycling as Minna considers many options for her poster. The student calendar is designed to teach lessons about recycling throughout the entire community. Great ideas for service learning!

A River Ran Wild by Lynne Cherry (Harcourt, 1991). The Nashua River, which once provided food to the indigenous people in New England, is polluted by industry and cities. Can a determined local citizen restore the river?

The Shape of Betts Meadow: A Wetlands Story by Meghan Nuttall Sayres (Millbrook Press, 2002). Follow Gunnar Holmquist, a medical doctor who became a "wetland doctor." His efforts restore Betts Meadow, a 140-acre dry pasture, to its original state: a wetland bursting with wildflowers, elk, and tree frogs. Includes a glossary of wetland terms and resources.

Someday a Tree by Eve Bunting (Clarion, 1993). A special oak tree grows near Alice's home—a perfect setting for picnics and gazing through the leaves at the clouds. When the surrounding grass turns yellow, a tree doctor determines that someone has dumped chemicals by the roots. The community unites in trying to save the tree.

The Table Where Rich People Sit by Byrd Baylor (Aladdin, 1998). Young Mountain Girl knows her family doesn't have enough money. Why don't her parents get real "indoor" jobs? As her family sits around their scratched kitchen table, her mother and father say they are "rich." As they determine the value of all they have—being able to see the sky all day, sleeping under stars, viewing the majestic mountains—the girl begins to understand they may be rich after all.

This House Is Made of Mud/Esta casa está hecha de lodo by Ken Buchanan (Northland, 1991). A family's life is interwoven with the natural environment in the Sonoran Desert. Watercolors of azure skies, mountains, giant cacti, and howling coyotes capture the harmony possible when the earth is treasured.

The Wartville Wizard by Don Madden (Aladdin, 1993). A man turns "wizard" to fight a town of litterbugs by making litter stick to the person who dropped it! A memorable and colorful tale of how people learn about the consequences of their actions. Easily adapted to an amusing play with an important message.

What Planet Are You From, Clarice Bean? by Lauren Child (Candlewick Press, 2001). Clarice is wild about her environmental studies at school but not enthusiastic about a project on snails she has to do with her neighbor, Robert. When her brother, granddad, and parents camp beside (and in) a tree scheduled to be chopped down, Clarice and her friends set out to "Free the Tree!"

Wildlife Refuge by Lorraine Ward (Charlesbridge, 1993). Join a classroom of children on a visit to a wildlife refuge, where animals hunt for food, build homes, and defend their territories.

Fiction: The Environment

Recommendation from the Field
by Antoinette C. Rockwell, teacher

Island of the Blue Dolphins by Scott O'Dell (Scott Foresman, 1987/1960). Based on a true story, *Island of the Blue Dolphins* tells of Karana, a Native American, whose tribe escapes by ship after losing a battle with a Russian hunting group. Karana jumps off the ship and swims back to the island to care for her young brother, who missed the boat. When her brother is killed by wild dogs, she blames herself. For eighteen years, Karana lives alone on Saint Nicholas Island off the coast of California, struggling to meet basic needs and facing many difficult choices, such as whether to go against her tribe's rules by making a weapon or killing wildlife for food.

This book can lead to a variety of service learning projects. Students can discuss such questions as: Why are cultural traditions important in our society? Which natural resources should be sustained, how, and to what degree? What survival issues face people who struggle to meet basic needs in our area, and what resources are available?

As one example of a service project, students can study the local natural resources, their use, and any issues surrounding these resources. They can interview community members and resource professionals for some solutions and perform a field study or restoration project that monitors or restores a natural resource on school grounds or in the community. Building bat boxes and planting native plants are restoration project examples. 184pp., grades 4–7

Judy Moody Saves the World by Megan McDonald (Candlewick Press, 2002). When her teacher informs the class about the destruction of the rain forest, endangered species, and recycling, Judy is determined to save the world single-handed. Only after she gets her third-grade class involved does Judy realize that "she no longer had to do it by herself," and the results take root. 145pp., grades 3–6

The Missing 'Gator of Gumbo Limbo by Jean Craighead George (HarperTrophy, 1992). Liza and her mother live in one of the last natural ecosystems, the Florida Everglades. There, with a small community of "woods people" who live on the land, Liza searches for Dajun, the glorious alligator that protects this fragile environment. When a state official arrives to kill Dajun, Liza discovers that the danger extends far beyond the threat to the alligator. Called an "eco mystery," this book provides a wealth of information about the animal and plant world of the Everglades. 144pp., grades 4–6

A group of children in Iowa planted the original prairie grasses in their yards to restore a strand of the prairie ecosystem.... A family in Connecticut sowed wild lupine to save an endangered butterfly.... And there are millions of young people who know that recycling, planting, protecting, and controlling pollution is the silk that mends the web—and they are enthusiastically reconnecting the strands.

FROM THE FOREWORD,
THE MISSING 'GATOR OF GUMBO LIMBO

Saving the Planet by Gail Gauthier (Putnam, 2003). After losing his summer job, sixteen-year-old Michael ends up living and working in Vermont on an environmentalist magazine with Walt and Nora, his grandparents' elder friends. While Michael is trying to become accustomed to vegetarian cuisine, a room filled with recycled Styrofoam, paper and plastic bags, and bicycling to work, he stumbles upon an ecological intrigue and a surprising romance. What a summer! 232pp., grades 6–10

There's an Owl in the Shower by Jean Craighead George (HarperTrophy, 1995). Spotted owls have cost Borden's father, Leon, his job as a logger in the old growth forest of northern California. Intending to kill a spotted owl for revenge, Borden finds an owlet and brings it home. Surprisingly, Leon cares for and about this growing owl. As he learns about the ecological impact of "the ravaging of old growth forests," Leon and his family change their views. 134pp., grades 4–6

Interviews with Authors:
The Story Behind the Story

In the following interview, we find out the "story behind the story" from Don Madden (*The Wartville Wizard*). While there are many important and well-written books on the environment, there is one that captures a common desire: to completely rid the planet of litter. Author Don Madden's ingenious book combines art and words to create a hilarious story that jumps off the page and sticks to your memory. Including an interview with the "real" Wartville wizard was simply a must.

Don Madden, author of
The Wartville Wizard

I am actually "the Wartville Wizard." My home is situated on a road halfway between two fast-food restaurants. When I wrote the book in the early 1980s, people would eat and drive, and they would arrive in front of my driveway as they were finishing their meal. I got really fed up with their trash coming right out the window, landing on my front yard, and cluttering up the roadway. How dare they throw their trash! That really lit my fuse. So I had the idea that all the trash should go back and stick to them. That's what happens in the book. Kids like the illustrations; their favorite seems to

be the one with the woman who has a filled trash bag stuck to her backside.

After I wrote the book, I felt better. I got the frustration out of my system. I've received a lot of mail from teachers and kids about *The Wartville Wizard*, as well as from recycling groups who don't seem to mind that I don't tackle recycling in this book. They enjoy the story and get the message.

I would like kids to come away with a feeling of taking care of the environment. I always enjoy hearing about kids getting involved and doing something to help out. I am actually a humanist and that's the message of humanism—to look out for each other. That will make things better for everyone.

I don't notice so much trash on the road anymore. I think some of the laws about bottle returns and so forth have done well in New York state. And I think kids are very aware, and that helps a great deal. Whether our young people will continue to be advocates for our environment, we will have to see. Once you start along those lines, you must continue the work to maintain the improvements.

The Wartville Wizard would definitely advocate taking care of the world we live in. It's the only one we've got! So do your part to make this world a better place.

CHAPTER 9

GARDENING

> You can complain because roses have thorns,
> or you can rejoice because thorns have roses.
>
> ZIGGY, COMIC STRIP CHARACTER

Sweet peas and cucumbers, tomatoes and daffodils, strawberries and corn. A garden is a place to watch—and help—things grow, where nature's cycles become apparent, and the impact of care and neglect are dramatic lessons in cause and effect. *Planting, growing,* and *transformation* are just a few of the words in a common language used to describe gardening as well as human development and relationships. It's no coincidence that gardens are such an effective way to bring people together and help them grow.

School and community gardens are springing up in many regions, with many hands tending the plants. All ages can work cooperatively to make a garden grow. Even reluctant students or urban youth who have never planted a seed can usually find a connection in the garden with the other gardeners, as well as with the soil, plants, flowers, and produce.

Learning possibilities abound in gardening. Science comes literally alive as students identify the parts of plants in real life and diligently watch as the stages of their garden's life cycle unfold. Students have used computers to design a garden and math skills to measure their plot and estimate the cost of materials. They have serenaded their plants with music and painted murals to keep their garden in bloom year-round. A book such as *The Ugly Vegetables* can lead students to writing their own stories. Harvested food is often shared with shelters and food banks, so the garden can also be used to raise awareness around issues of hunger and poverty in the community and the region. Students come to appreciate and understand how agriculture, farm workers, and environmental issues interconnect through the process of planting and maintaining a garden. Planting, growing, transformation: How will your garden grow?

Preparation: Getting Ready for Service Learning Involving Gardening

The following activities can be used in the preparation stage to promote learning and skill development related to gardening. These activities can be used with different age ranges during preparation to help your students examine key issues through research, analyze community needs, and gain the knowledge they need to effectively contribute to the design of their service plan. Since literature is often an important part of preparation, you can find recommended titles on this theme in the Gardening Bookshelf later in this chapter.

Activity: An Old Fashioned Almanac. Beginning in 1792, farmers turned to printed almanacs for a variety of information concerning agriculture, including sunrise and sunset tables, planting charts, weather patterns and predictions, and recipes. Students can learn a great deal by reviewing the almanacs available in most libraries. The students can identify topics to research in preparation for creating their own gardens and their own version of an almanac, which can be distributed to community members. The students' almanac could include a planting schedule, tips from gardeners, strategies for dealing with pests, recipes tested by the students, and a problem-solving section. Students could even create short scenes based on their almanac to perform for younger students or community members in (where else?) the garden! *The Green Truck Garden Giveaway: A Neighborhood Story and Almanac*, a picture book in almanac format, and *A Harvest of Color: Growing a Vegetable Garden*, written by very young gardeners, can serve as prototypes for student publications.

135

Activity: Community Gardens. Community gardens are lovely to look at, and they also provide a valuable resource: fresh produce. Community gardens, like the Victory Gardens of World War II, provide affordable vegetables and fruits to many families, and the surplus is often given to local food shelves or shelters. These are just some of the benefits of a community garden.

Your students can research and learn about local community gardens and their benefits before they start their own garden. There are many different questions that can come up. Does our community already have any community gardens? If so, what are the land use policies in the gardens? How do people reserve or share garden plots? What help is needed to maintain the gardens or to expand the opportunities for participation? Who in the community could benefit from the garden's produce? If there are no community gardens in the area, how could one be started? National and local organizations that support the development of community gardens with funds and expertise are good sources of information for students doing research on many of these questions. In addition to planning their own garden, students can become advocates for garden programs, collaborating with local government agencies and schools. Gardens are not only about seeds, compost, plants, and harvesting, they are also about people and building community.

Find Out More About Gardening

To learn more about these issues and to get ideas for service and action, visit these Web sites and organizations online:

www.kidsgardening.com KidsGardening!, a program of the National Gardening Association, offers a host of gardening resources including books, curriculum, more Web connections, and grant opportunities.

www.nwf.org/backyard The National Wildlife Federation's Backyard Wildlife Habitat program teaches students about the wildlife right in their own backyard or schoolyard and includes resources to create gardens that are habitat-based learning sites in schoolyards.

www.abcdbooks.org/curriculum/garden.html Visit "How Does Our Garden Grow?" at ABCD Books for gardening curriculum connections you can use in grades 1–5.

Making Connections Across the Curriculum

Some service learning activities naturally lend themselves to interdisciplinary work and making connections across the curriculum. These connections strengthen and broaden student learning, helping them meet academic standards. More than likely, you'll be looking for these connections and ways to encourage them well before the students ever start working on service learning activities. As with the entire service learning process, it helps to remain flexible, because some connections can be spontaneously generated by the questions raised throughout and by the needs of the project. To help you think about cross-curricular connections and where you can look for them, the Curricular Web for this chapter (page 137) gives examples of many different ways this theme can be used in different academic areas. (The service learning scenarios in the next section of the chapter also demonstrate various ways this theme can be used across the curriculum.)

Service Learning Scenarios: Ideas for Action

Ready to take action? What follows are projects that have been successfully carried out by elementary, middle, or high school students. Most of these scenarios and examples explicitly include some aspects of preparation, action, reflection, and demonstration. These scenarios can be a rich source of project, resource, and curriculum ideas for you to draw upon. While the grade levels are given as a reference, most project ideas can be adapted to suit younger or older students, and many are suitable for cross-age partnerships.

Gardening Takes Root in an Entire District: Grades K–12. In one school district, gardens became an important part of student life at several schools. Students found many different ways to contribute to their gardens and to use the produce that was the result of their efforts. Students at one elementary school began to eat plenty of leafy greens after harvesting certified organic produce from their on-site garden, adding the tastes of bok choy and arugula to the cafeteria food. At another elementary school in the district, students took surplus produce to a

Gardening Across the Curriculum

English/Language Arts

- Research and write about gardens and herbs
- Write letters soliciting donations for community gardens
- Write poetry about the flowers, fruits, or vegetables (or aspects of the garden) to "plant" or display in the school garden

Social Studies/History

- Research the indigenous plants in your area and Native American gardening methods
- Learn about local gardening organizations
- Study World War II Victory Gardens

Languages

- Learn the vocabulary of gardening in the language of study
- Research fruits and vegetables grown in the country where the language is spoken
- Make multilingual signs for the garden identifying the plants; or translate community gardening materials and distribute them

Theater, Music, & Visual Arts

- Create and perform a dramatization to teach about gardening
- Perform songs about plants and growing
- Design and paint a mural to create a year-round garden

Gardening

Math

- Create a budget and price list for plants and materials to purchase
- Measure space for planting
- Chart observations of plant growth and change; calculate expected yields and compare to actual harvest

Physical Education

- Prepare a warm-up exercise routine to do before working in the garden
- Research the impact on the body of bending and lifting and other gardening movements, then find the healthiest ways to do these activities
- Plan a garden tour for very young children that includes pretending that they are seeds that grow and grow into a plant

Computer

- Read and research software and literature on garden design
- Create a computer slide show on garden development
- Use the Internet to learn about careers in landscape architecture, horticulture, topiary design, and agriculture

Science

- Identify and compare seeds and plants, then observe and record life cycle of plants
- Examine and test soil
- Study invasive exotic plants

homeless shelter each week. At yet another elementary school with extensive gardens, students progressed through various gardening tasks by grade level, moving from raising berries and vegetables to building ponds and garden structures. Greenhouses at the district middle schools allowed students to start seedlings for the elementary students, and high school students planned nutrition classes and a health fair to teach students across the district about gardening, cooking, and nutrition. The younger students contributed ideas about what to plant, while high school students planned and organized all aspects of the health fair from fund-raising to publicity. Benefits extended in all directions. One school, for example, included a large population of Hmong and Hispanic students, who sometimes had a difficult time sharing expertise at school. The garden provided a way for Hmong and Hispanic families who worked in the agricultural industry to participate. Local businesses (such as nurseries and excavation companies, which provided topsoil) and local nonprofit organizations became collaborators and assisted with the building of garden beds.

A Giving Garden: Grades 1–3 (with middle and high school helpers).

Three first- through third-grade classrooms in West Salem, Wisconsin, designed, constructed, planted, maintained, and harvested a garden on school grounds, with help from middle and high school students and community members. After hearing a speaker from the food pantry talk about the pantry and the needs it addressed, the students came up with the idea of planting a garden to help serve their community. The garden was intended to produce vegetables for fifty families per month who used the local food pantry. The project was designed to teach students about community participation by providing opportunities to work with teachers, parents, and other community members. In addition to learning gardening skills, the students learned about the relationships between people, plants, and wildlife and practiced leadership skills in work crews. Students from the junior high constructed benches for the garden, and high school students helped with planting. Classroom reflection included discussion of the concept of community and the reasons a community might need a food pantry, such as job loss and poverty. Students wrote journals throughout the project. And

to keep the garden healthy year-round, the students created a weekly schedule for families to work in the garden during the summer.

> It is not enough to be busy; so are the ants. The question is: What are we busy about?
>
> HENRY DAVID THOREAU, PHILOSOPHER

A Poetic Garden Adds a Mural: Grades 2–4.

An elementary school garden added beauty to a Los Angeles neighborhood. Students who were planting, tending seedlings, or harvesting would strike up conversations with neighbors passing by. The neighbors commented on the poetry "planted" among the vegetables. Students explained how they had read books about gardening and had been inspired to write poems by the curly pea vines and the large zucchini leaves. Their poems, mounted on boards and laminated, were interspersed with the greenery. During the off-season, however, the area looked pretty dull. The students gathered in their garden to think about what could be done. They designed and received approval to make a garden mural so the beauty of things growing would be present all year long.

Planting a Butterfly Garden: Grades 2 and 7.

After elementary students read *Butterfly Boy*, they wanted to create a butterfly garden alongside a local senior center, which was located in a park. The teacher thought the job seemed too large for her class alone, so when she contacted the city parks and recreation department for permission to plant the garden, she also asked for assistance. She was referred to the middle school, and a seventh-grade class at the school offered to help. Their teacher wove the experience into literature by selecting *Butterflies and Lizards, Beryl and Me* for her students to read. Many groups assisted, including the senior citizens, a community college life-sciences class, and a local conservation group. Students conducted research to identify the appropriate plants. The teacher also asked the students for ideas to begin a relationship with members of the senior center. As a result, the students hosted a "butterfly" party at the center and with assistance from the center's art director and the elders who used the center made three-dimensional butterflies to display in the local library.

To Learn, to Share, to Experience Peace: Grades 3–5. Sometimes a garden has many purposes. In Dulles, Oregon, an elementary garden serves three needs. First, the garden offers numerous hands-on learning experiences for children. The students manage the greenhouse, weather station, worm garden, and composting, and grow flowers and vegetables. Second, the produce and flowers are given to people in need within the community. And third, the garden is a place for reflection and peace where students can sit quietly and write in journals or simply enjoy the beauty and peace around them.

Singing for Plants: Grade 4. Students at one Illinois elementary school were interested in planting some native species around their school. To raise money to help them buy the necessary supplies, they decided to do what youngsters do well—sing loudly! They planned a concert and chose songs that pertained to plants and their importance to people, animals, and the earth. The students sold tickets to the concert and used the money they raised to help them buy several varieties of native flowers, vegetables, and herbs. Students not only planted a beautiful garden around their school but also learned how to care for the plants by weeding and watering the garden.

History That's for the Birds: Grade 5. Fifth-grade students in Galt, California, put hammer to nail as they worked on rebuilding a chicken house. While  helping the local historical society to develop a living history ranch, they learned construction methods of the past and present. They also planted several acres of pumpkins that were enjoyed by kindergarten classes during fall harvest activities.

From Worm Bins to Radishes: Grade 5. Fifth graders in West Hollywood, California, who began the school year with little, if any, knowledge of gardening had green thumbs by year's end. During science lessons, they planted and cared for seedlings, charting growth and changes. That was just the beginning, then they: read books about gardens, such as *Jack's Garden* and *Wanda's Roses*, to younger students; built compost bins at school and collected appropriate food waste during lunch time; tasted their first radishes;

displayed worm bins at the local farmers' market; lead tours for visitors and had them write comments in the guest journal; and published a booklet, "How to Start a Container Garden," for distribution throughout the community. What was left? The next year, the gardeners created a coloring book called "From Apples to Zucchinis: The ABCs of Gardening" to share their expertise and inspire other young gardeners.

Recipes and Remedies: Grades 5–8. Good food grown in gardens may taste even better when used in recipes that teach about culture and tradition. After students in Oklahoma researched traditional plants used by Native Americans for cooking and for herbal remedies, they cooked up a cookbook with art and detailed information to share their new knowledge and recipes for the community.

Language Skills and Gardens Grow: Grades 6–8. Student and adult volunteers in Houston, Texas, created an urban garden with dual objectives: to grow fresh produce for a local food pantry and to learn Spanish related to gardening. In this "speak Spanish" garden, students learned Spanish words for various tools and vegetables and even the vitamins in the produce. The students also learned how to talk to community members in Spanish about why a garden is important and how to get a garden started.

A Victory Garden: Grade 7. As middle school students were preparing to plant a garden, their teacher read aloud essays to them from *Down to Earth: Garden Secrets! Garden Stories! Garden Projects You Can Do!* An essay by Gloria Rand about her father's "Victory Garden" planted during World War II led students to conduct research to learn more about these gardens. Students used history books and conversations with community members who had firsthand experience with Victory gardens to learn more. The students then considered what kind of garden they would like to plant to commemorate an event from their own era. They decided to plant a garden to honor the people who died in the terrorist attacks on September 11. To recognize the fact that people of many different ethnic groups lost their lives, the students included plants from different parts of the world in their peace garden.

A Neighborly Garden: Grade 8. As part of a community cleanup around the school, eighth-grade students in Texas spruced up an elder neighbor's front yard. The invitation to "come back again" began a relationship that grew. Students received permission to create a garden in this new friend's backyard and walked over several times each week to do the necessary work. The students found that their older friend greatly enjoyed their companionship—as well as the produce from the garden, which was also shared with the local food bank. Students helped to deliver and return library books for their neighbor as well.

> All plants are our brothers and sisters. They talk to us and if we listen, we can hear them.
> ARAPAHO SAYING

Two Cultures Growing: Grade 8. In partnership with a historical society, an eighth-grade class in Wisconsin created Native American and European gardens to show the difference between the two cultures. Activities expanded with student input to include making Native American tools, writing brochures about the gardens, and creating a display case. During the summer, the gardens were maintained by young students from Somalia who had come to the community as refugees. One outcome of this project was that the Somalis planted their own community garden. For this group, the garden helped in the transition from an agricultural society. (See *Native American Gardening: Stories, Projects and Recipes for Families* in the bookshelf for more about planting a Native American garden.)

Gardening Partnerships: Grades 9 and 10. Environmental biology students stopped building virtual gardens and created a greenhouse on their Santa Monica, California, school campus to try out their ideas and to grow produce for a local shelter. Once the greenhouse was operational, the students addressed the larger challenge of taking what they had practiced into the community. A nearby residential facility for active seniors contacted the high school asking for help in creating an on-site garden. When students visited the facility with their plans, they found a huge flaw: the residents would be unable to bend down to work in a garden. With assistance from shop classes, the students found a solution: raised-bed gardens. This solution led to another dilemma. The elder gardeners

wanted to invite elementary classes to visit and receive gardening tips, but the raised-bed gardens where too high for the children! The shop class constructed easy-to-move platforms that would bring the children up to dirt level.

A Touch Garden: Grades 9–12. As part of a dropout prevention program, high school students in Fort Myers, Florida, were given responsibilities and the necessary skills and knowledge to create a "children's touching garden." This required a comprehensive education about planting and plant care, the construction of pathways, and building benches. Students were mentored by master gardeners and other community volunteers. They also created a children's brochure. Once open, thousands of young children had visual and tactile experiences in this colorful and well-planned garden.

Profits Keep Growing: Grades 9–12. Inner-city high school students in Los Angeles transformed themselves into entrepreneurs as they transformed their garden into a business by growing most of the ingredients for a salad dressing. Local business people contributed time and expertise to guide the students in many necessary tasks, from recipe development to promotion. Profits were divided: half goes back into the business and the rest goes to a college scholarship fund. The students have visited many schools to share their knowledge and inspire others.

> A book is like a garden carried in the pocket.
> CHINESE PROVERB

The Gardening Bookshelf

Books from the Gardening Bookshelf can teach us the fundamentals of gardening and frequently show how gardens illuminate many aspects of life and community. Seedlings, like infants, need careful nurturing. By harvest time mature plants can seem like old friends. Bonds can form with the garden and among the people who tend it. The garden can be a source of beauty that grows the soul as well as the produce that feeds the body. To help you find books relevant to your particular projects, the book chart classifies the books into two topic areas: planting and growing, and transformation.

In general, the bookshelf features:

- An annotated bibliography arranged and alphabetized by title according to the general categories of nonfiction (N), picture books (P), and fiction (F). For nonfiction and fiction, length and recommended grade levels are included.

The entries in the picture book category do not include suggested grade levels, since they can be successfully used with all ages.

- A chart organized by topic and category to help you find books relevant to particular projects.

- Recommendations from service learning colleagues and experts that include a book summary and ideas for service learning connections. (The number of recommended books varies in each bookshelf.)

Gardening Bookshelf Topics

Topics	Books	Category
Planting and Growing Methods for planting and providing care are featured in these selections, along with the strong, hardworking people who work the fields.	Compost! Growing Gardens from Your Garbage	P
	Compost Critters	N
	Down to Earth: Garden Secrets! Garden Stories! Garden Projects You Can Do! ‡	N
	Gathering the Sun: An Alphabet in Spanish and English	P
	A Harvest of Color: Growing a Vegetable Garden	N
	Jack's Garden	P
	My First Garden	P
	Native American Gardening: Stories, Projects and Recipes for Families	N
	The Ugly Vegetables	P
Transformation In a garden, change happens; a small seed becomes a huge green watermelon or a juicy red tomato. People can change along with the plants. These are their stories.	Bud	P
	Butterflies and Lizards, Beryl and Me	F
	Carlos and the Cornfield/Carlos y la milpa de maíz	P
	The Chalk Box Kid	F
	City Green *	P
	The Gardener	P
	The Garden of Happiness *	P
	The Green Truck Garden Giveaway: A Neighborhood Story and Almanac *	P
	A Place to Grow (see page 168)	P
	Seedfolks *	F
	The Summer My Father Was Ten	P
	The Victory Garden *	F
	Wanda's Roses	P
	Xóchitl and the Flowers/Xóchitl, la niña de las flores	P

Page references are given for books that do not appear in the Gardening Bookshelf but that can be found in the bookshelf lists of other chapters.
* These books include examples of young people in service-providing roles.
‡ These books are out of print but still worth finding.

> Books are the bees which carry the quickening pollen from one to another mind.
>
> JAMES RUSSELL LOWELL, AUTHOR

Nonfiction: *Gardening*

Compost Critters by Bianca Lavies (Dutton, 1993). Text and close-up photography give an inside picture of a compost heap and how creatures, from bacteria and mites to millipedes and earthworms, aid in turning compost into humus. 32pp., grades K–8

Down to Earth: Garden Secrets! Garden Stories! Garden Projects You Can Do! edited by Michael J Rosen (Harcourt, 1998). "A garden plot is more than just a piece of land. It's a story." So begins this extraordinary compilation of poetry, stories, artwork, and recipes for successful and creative gardens. Forty-one children's book authors and illustrators contributed their work, with proceeds supporting Share Our Strength, an anti-hunger organization. Out of print but worth finding. 64pp., all ages

A Harvest of Color: Growing a Vegetable Garden by Melanie Eclare (Ragged Bears, 2002). Six young children celebrate the experience of growing five different vegetables. We learn how they measure the plot, thin the seedlings, and come to appreciate worms. Along with the brilliant photographs is a recipe for a vegetable salad. 32pp., grades K–3

> I love carrots because they are sweet and crunchy. And I can share them with my pet rabbit.
>
> I sprinkled seeds into rows as deep as my thumbnail. We planted three rows of carrots, each one as far apart as the distance from my middle finger to my elbow. To be sure the rows were straight, we attached string to two sticks and put them in the soil at each end of the garden bed. . . . In about ten days little plants that looked like ferns showed through the soil.
>
> FROM *A HARVEST OF COLOR: GROWING A VEGETABLE GARDEN*

Native American Gardening: Stories, Projects and Recipes for Families by Michael Caduto and Joseph Bruchac (Fulcrum, 1996). Combining gardening and storytelling, the authors provide information needed to pursue "Three Sisters" gardening: growing the traditional Native garden of corn, beans, and squash. Includes information about the relationships between people and the gardens of Earth, seed preservation, Native diets and meals, natural pest control, and the importance of the Circle of Life. 176pp., all grades

Picture Books: *Gardening*

Bud by Kevin O'Malley (Walker and Co., 2000). Bud Sweet-William, a young rhinoceros, has a passion for gardening that mystifies his parents. To their surprise, his grandfather also likes to garden. Soon, all are knee deep in dirt and celebration.

Carlos and the Cornfield/Carlos y la milpa de maíz by Jan Romero Stevens (Rising Moon, 1995). Young Carlos tries to rush the planting process when he cares more about the money he will earn than the corn he will grow. His conscience causes him to set things right. *Cosechas lo que siembras*—you reap what you sow. English and Spanish text.

City Green by DyAnne DiSalvo-Ryan (Morrow, 1994). Marcy's plan to turn a vacant lot into a city garden inspires everyone to pitch in, except grouchy, elder Mr. Hammer. Then a few surprises bloom!

Compost! Growing Gardens from Your Garbage by Linda Glaser (Millbrook Press, 1996). A simple story about composting, from adding garbage to using the soil in a garden.

The Gardener by Sarah Stewart (Farrar, Straus and Giroux, 1997). The hard times of the Depression force Lydia to move to an unfamiliar city to stay with her Uncle Jim, a baker with a frown. With determination, she brightens her corner of the world and her uncle's life with flowers.

The Garden of Happiness by Erika Tamar (Harcourt, 1996). Marisol, a young girl, and her diverse neighbors turn a vacant New York City lot into a lush, multicultural garden with a sunflower mural.

Gathering the Sun: An Alphabet in Spanish and English by Alma Flor Ada (HarperCollins, 2001). Twenty-seven poems pay tribute to farm workers and to nature's delicious gifts. Using the Spanish alphabet as a guide, the book takes us into the fields and orchards to learn about people and the pride they carry for their culture. Includes an historical reference to César Chavez. Illustrator Simón Silva grew up in a farm worker's family.

The Green Truck Garden Giveaway: A Neighborhood Story and Almanac by Jacqueline B. Martin (Simon & Schuster, 1997). When two people pass out seeds and gardening supplies, neighbors who claim to have no interest in gardening or their community are transformed. Along with the engaging story, the author offers historical information about plants, recipes, and advice for up-and-coming gardeners. Out of print but worth finding.

Jack's Garden by Henry Cole (Greenwillow, 1995). Text and illustrations show what happens to Jack's garden after he plants his seeds.

My First Garden by Tomek Bogacki (Farrar, Straus and Giroux, 2000). When a young boy hears that a garden used to grow in a courtyard, he sets out to do all the work to make the garden bloom anew. The illustrations in impressionistic pastels return us to the author's small town in Poland and show incisive details of his work and his community.

The Summer My Father Was Ten by Pat Brisson (Boyds Mills Press, 1998). Every year, as the narrator and her father plant their garden, she hears the story "about Mr. Bellavista and the summer my father was ten." What starts as a joke—using a tomato as a baseball—becomes a careless act of vandalism in a neighbor's garden. The elder immigrant neighbor simply asks, "Why?" The next year, to make amends, her father asks to help replant the garden. An act of forgiveness begins a lifelong friendship and a family tradition.

> "Mr. Bellavista?" my father began. "Are you going to plant a garden this year?"
>
> Mr. Bellavista's eyes looked straight into my father's. "So you can destroy again?" he asked.
>
> "No," my father stammered. "... I'm sorry about last year, and I thought maybe I could help."
>
> Mr. Bellavista didn't say anything at first. He studied my father for a few minutes, then rubbed his jaw with the back of his hand.
>
> "Tomorrow," he said at last. "Tomorrow we'll make a garden."
>
> FROM *THE SUMMER MY FATHER WAS TEN*

The Ugly Vegetables by Grace Lin (Charlesbridge, 1999). A young girl notices the differences between her mother's garden and the ones planted by her neighbor. The neighbor's flowers are "beautiful" while her mother's Chinese vegetables are "ugly." At harvest, the aroma of the "ugly vegetable soup" attracts everyone to join in the feast. Recipe included.

Wanda's Roses by Pat Brisson (Boyds Mills Press, 1994). When Wanda discovers a thorn bush in an empty lot, she is sure it is a rosebush ready to bloom. She clears away trash and waters her "bush." When no roses appear, her neighbors and friends have a surprising solution.

Xóchitl and the Flowers/Xóchitl, la niña de las flores by Jorge Argueta (Children's Book Press, 2003). Young Xóchitl and her parents, immigrants from El Salvador, work hard to transform a garbage filled backyard into a blooming nursery to provide income for their family. When their landlord tries to stop them, Xóchitl discovers the value of community in her new home in the United States. Based on a true story, this book is written in English and Spanish.

Fiction: Gardening

Butterflies and Lizards, Beryl and Me by Ruth Lercher Bornstein (Marshall Cavendish, 2002). During the Great Depression in 1936, Charley moves with her mom to a rural town. While her mother works in "the smell cannery," eleven-year-old Charley is drawn to Beryl, an optimistic elder woman, called "crazy" by other children. Together, Charley and Beryl plant a garden. Beryl provides the friendship and encouragement Charley desperately needs. Within this caring relationship, Charley grows like the plants she cherishes. In spite of conflict with her mother, a near tragedy, and a deep loss, Charley finds her heart, her home, and a way to give. 144pp., grades 5–9

The Chalk Box Kid by Clyde Robert Bulla (Random House, 1987). A new neighborhood, a new school, and an unhappy birthday make life hard for nine-year-old Gregory. After he discovers an abandoned chalk factory behind his house, his school assignment of planting a garden develops in a most unusual and creative way. 59pp., grades 2–4

Seedfolks by Paul Fleishman (HarperCollins, 1997). These well-written short stories introduce the people in a diverse urban Cleveland neighborhood. One by one, people of varying ages and backgrounds transform a city lot that is filled with garbage into a productive, beautiful garden. In the process, they are also transformed. 69pp., grades 5–10

The Victory Garden by Lee Kochenderfer. (Delacorte, 2002). Teresa Marks and her entire Kansas town await news that World War II will end soon. Many serve, like her older brother Jess, a fighter pilot. To keep busy, Teresa and her dad, like people all over the United States, plant a victory garden to provide fresh produce so other foods can be sent to troops overseas. In spring, when her neighbor is hospitalized, Teresa rallies her friends to tend his garden. As she tries to raise prize-winning tomatoes, Teresa questions the purpose of gardens and of war. She also finds that her garden grows new friendships. 166pp., grades 6–8

> "Do you ever think about why we were born in this country instead of where the war is?" I asked Maria.
>
> She gave me a strange look, but it was a question I had asked myself over and over.
>
> FROM *THE VICTORY GARDEN*

Interviews with Authors:
The Story Behind the Story

In the following interviews, we find out the "story behind the story" from Ruth Lercher Bornstein (*Butterflies and Lizards, Beryl and Me*) and Pat Brisson (*The Summer My Father Was Ten* and *Wanda's Roses*).

Ruth Bornstein's book *Butterflies and Lizards, Beryl and Me* captivated me initially with its title and then with its story. I conducted the interview in Ruth's home and found her to be an accomplished artist as well as a thoughtful writer. I called Pat Brisson to learn more about her protagonist Wanda, a girl with perseverance and creativity. Pat later introduced me to the story of *The Summer My Father Was Ten*, which moved me to tears. Both of her books are included on this bookshelf.

Ruth Lercher Bornstein, author of
Butterflies and Lizards, Beryl and Me

Being a dedicated painter, I thought this visual art form would allow me to say what I needed to in this lifetime. But then, in 1970, I found myself drawing little green elephants talking to flowers and rabbits peeking out of the ground. I was creating funny little drawings instead of big serious paintings. I was having fun, so I just let it happen. Then, in 1971, I grew my first vegetable garden and spent more time holding hands with the cucumber vines than I did doing anything in my studio.

By some mysterious, organic process, in November, when the plants began to die and sink into the ground, and feeling that I had experienced the whole span of birth and death in one summer, I began to write. Simple words like *green* and *grow* and *flower* became as real and solid to me as paint. I filled up sketchbook after sketchbook with words and pictures of everything I imagined or loved. My first picture book was published in 1973, and interspersed with periods of painting, I haven't stopped writing since.

In 1987, on a trip to New Zealand, I visited my friend, Beryl, who was dying of cancer. Inspired by her courage—even her humor—in the face of death, I began to write about her on the flight home. I sent the few pages to my editor, Charlotte Zolotow, who wrote back, "Ruth, this is not a picture book. This is a novel."

A novel! How do you write a novel? But somehow I knew she was right, and I continued to jot down feelings, thoughts, memories, ideas. Slowly, through the years and through many, many revisions and rejections, a shape emerged. The story is not autobiographical. A bitter, careworn mother appeared and an absent father, but there are also my own feelings about making art and growing a garden. And, as I worked, I realized that I was telling a story of forgiveness, of being loved, and of learning to give back.

The story takes place during the Great Depression because I needed trains that ran between small towns and a hobo one didn't have to be afraid of. I wanted a "crazy" old woman named Beryl who "grows" butterflies and gives names to lizards and who gives eleven-year-old Charley the gift of the wonder of being alive, the wonder of "all of us poor, beautiful creatures being here together."

Writing this story has given me the chance to be both the child, Charley, and her old woman soul mate, Beryl. It's given me a second chance to grow up, a chance to be able to say with Charley at the end, "the space inside of me is big enough to hold it all."

Pat Brisson, author of The Summer
My Father Was Ten and Wanda's Roses

I wrote *Wanda's Roses* when winter was almost over but spring hadn't yet arrived. Wanda's longing for something beautiful was mine, too. Of course, this longing is not entirely for roses—it is for something beautiful beyond ourselves, something worth striving for, something we can give our hearts to. I wanted to show a girl who was willing to work hard to make her dream come true. When you share your dream with others, I believe they will do what they can to help you achieve your dream. I often ask students, "What is your dream? What are you willing to work hard at?"

Typically, when I begin writing a book, I don't know how a story will end. With *Wanda's Roses*, I wanted to have a little girl who had a rosebush. As the story developed, I thought, "Oh yes, she will turn this into a blooming bush with paper roses." Wanda's neighbors watch her work hard for a month cleaning the lot and caring for her plant. Wanda's dedication touches the people around her; they sincerely want to help. I've been honored, too, that some students have helped to create beauty by planting rosebushes after reading *Wanda's Roses*.

In *The Summer My Father Was Ten*, a group of boys vandalize a neighbor's garden. When I first read the story to my son, he exclaimed, "Mom, those kids are really bad!" But kids who are not "bad" do "bad" things. The boy who threw one tomato did not intend to destroy a garden. The kids got carried away. While ravaging the garden, they were not considering their actions, only their "fun." How did this happen? Kids can identify with this mistake.

Librarians tell me they can hear a pin drop when reading *The Summer My Father Was Ten* aloud. Sometimes at the end, children express relief saying, "Phew, he got through it." The book is not just about the boy. This would have been a different story if Mr. Bellavista had denied the boy the opportunity to make amends. In the crucial moment when the boy asks to replant the garden, the man thinks, "Do I forgive? Do I give him a chance?" And the boy's life is changed. A true friendship develops. When the boy becomes a father, he is compelled to relate this story every spring to his daughter. Mr. Bellavista's moment of forgiveness affects future generations. The girl now tells us the story. We do not know how one moment of forgiveness will reach distant shores.

Does writing stories come easily to me? I wish I were brimming with ideas for stories that would flow forth as soon as pencil met paper. But for me, writing is work: occasionally frustrating, generally satisfying, but always worth striving for. It is something I believe in, something I have given my heart to, just as Wanda believed in her roses.

My approach is character driven. My interest is in what the characters are thinking and doing and feeling. Keep in mind that people approach the writing process in different ways. Writing requires a kind of problem solving—you figure out what words fit best, how much tension to establish, and the number of characters to include and consider if each character adds to the story or should be eliminated.

People often ask, "Did the book look like you expected?" I am not very visual when writing. I know the tone and feeling of the story. I know who the people are from the inside; sometimes I even hear the character's voice in my head. I may not know what she looks like but I know what she is going through. I am happy if the illustrations match the tone of the story, as they do in these two books.

Do all people respond to my books in the same way? A book exists in relationship to the specific reader or the person listening to the story. Every person brings ideas, experiences, and personality. The reader may see what the author intended and may also find additional meaning. This has happened with a number of my books. For example, I did not write *Wanda's Roses* as a book on ecology or gardening. Only when a teacher described it as "a great ecology book" did I think, "Oh yes, I can see this is also about ecology!"

Literature enables the reader to think, "that could be me" or "that might be me someday." Books allow us to know the reality that exists for others and broadens our limited perspective. A book can also lead the reader to have a change of heart. That is how social action begins, with a change of heart, with the ability to empathize. You don't have to change the whole world. One kind action can change someone's day or someone's life and can in turn help that someone to see people in a fresh way. By tutoring one person or befriending a child who is ignored or teased, you can make a world of difference.

CHAPTER 10

HUNGER AND HOMELESSNESS

> If you don't like the way the world is,
> you change it. You have an obligation
> to change it. You just do it one step at a time.
>
> MARIAN WRIGHT EDELMAN,
> FOUNDER, CHILDREN'S DEFENSE FUND

Hunger and homelessness are global problems. They are sometimes considered urban ills, but the reality is they are found in every country and in every community, rural and urban. Hunger and homelessness have many different causes. People throughout history have been uprooted and left without homes because of war or famine. Indigenous groups such as the Native Americans in the United States have been driven from their ancestral lands. Natural disasters also take a toll: floods, droughts, tornados, hurricanes, earthquakes, and fires can all devastate a community or destroy crops. Sometimes, events that do not affect entire communities create havoc in individual lives: People may face poverty and homelessness after losing their jobs or because of unexpected medical expenses.

Children are frequently those most affected by poverty in modern society. Many children live at or below the poverty level. In the United States, almost 12 million children live in poverty.[1] Children account for between 25 percent[2] and 39 percent of the homeless population.[3] (Worldwide nearly 650 million children live in extreme poverty.)[4] Other children may see people living on the streets, in cars, and in shelters and wonder why. During their first years of school, children learn about people's basic needs: food, clothing, shelter. Yet some of the same children lack these basic

necessities, and most are cognizant that many people live and struggle without them.

> Peace, in the sense of absence of war, is of little value to someone who is dying of hunger or cold. Peace can only last where human rights are respected, where people are fed, and where individuals and nations are free.
>
> TENZIN GYATSO, THE FOURTEENTH DALAI LAMA

Through service learning, students can examine conditions that cause poverty and lead to hunger and homelessness. They can become familiar with local needs and the services that address them. Studying history through the lenses of hunger, homelessness, and poverty can make it come alive by making it more human and real. Literature, both fiction and nonfiction, can vividly bring these events and the people who were affected by them into students' lives today. Although affecting policy concerning people who are homeless is very challenging, students can work to help shape sustainable programs, can participate in new and existing programs, and can help in many other ways to meet immediate needs.

Preparation: Getting Ready for Service Learning Involving Hunger and Homelessness

The following activities can be used in the preparation stage to promote learning and skill development related to hunger and homelessness. These activities

---

[1] *Low Income Children in the United States*, Lu Hsien-Hen (New York: National Center for Children in Poverty, 2003).
[2] *A Status Report on Hunger and Homelessness in America's Cities* (Washington, DC: U.S. Conference of Mayors, 2001).
[3] *A New Look at Homelessness in America* (Washington, DC: The Urban Institute, 2000).
[4] *The Progress of Nations 1999* (New York: UNICEF, 1999).

can be used with different age ranges during preparation to help your students examine key issues through research, analyze community needs, and gain the knowledge they need to effectively contribute to the design of their service plan. Since literature is often an important part of preparation, you can find recommended titles on this theme in the Hunger and Homelessness Bookshelf later in this chapter.

Activity: *What Shape Is Your Pyramid?* From the four food groups to the food pyramid, is there really one shape for all of us? Ask students to share their families' particular relationship to eating and nutrition. In diverse communities, students will have the opportunity to learn about a range of foods, from bok choy and dal to grits and falafel, and to find out how different cultures and communities address their dietary requirements. This can help students develop appreciation for the diversity in their communities and better analyze and understand the needs of those communities.

Activity: *Learning About the Issues*. How do we put a face on hunger and homelessness? How do we separate fact from fiction, myth from knowledge? You can try one or all of the following activities to start your students thinking.

- Give each student a piece of drawing paper and a crayon or marker (keep this simple). Ask students to draw a picture of somebody who is hungry. Let them know they can make a simple drawing and that they will have five minutes to finish. Encourage them to work individually and quietly. When everyone is done, ask students to place their drawings where others can see them. Ask the students to describe the person they drew—young, old, single, part of a family, man, woman, child—and how this person portrays hunger.

- Have students work in small groups. Assign each group one population: senior citizens, veterans, immigrants, families with children, unemployed people, people who are homeless. The students will spend five minutes thinking why this particular population might be hungry and might need assistance with food. They will then share their thoughts with classmates, who can ask questions. As a follow up, you or a guest speaker can

present facts on these populations (provided by local, state, or national agencies), *and/or* each small group can research its assigned population to gather information about hunger and poverty to be presented to the class.

- Invite a representative from a local agency who works with people who are in need of assistance with food to help answer questions and brainstorm ways the class can provide meaningful assistance.

> The outrage of hunger amidst plenty will never be solved by "experts" somewhere. It will only be solved when people like you and me decide to act.
> FRANCES MOORE LAPPE, AUTHOR

Find Out More About Hunger and Homelessness

To learn more about these issues and to get ideas for service and action, visit these Web sites and organizations online:

www.strength.org Share Our Strength mobilizes individuals and industries to lend their talents to raise funds and awareness for the fight against hunger and poverty, addressing immediate and long-term solutions. Their Great American Bake Sale program offers educational curriculum and opportunities to work toward eliminating childhood hunger in America.

www.oxfamamerica.org and *www.oxfam.org* Both Oxfam America and Oxfam International are dedicated to finding long-term solutions to poverty, hunger, and social injustice around the world. Visit their pages for youth to find ways to become involved.

www.nationalhomeless.org The National Coalition for the Homeless (NCH) engages in public education, policy advocacy, and grassroots organizing. Become educated about homelessness and learn the many ways students can become knowledgeable and involved.

Making Connections Across the Curriculum

Some service learning activities naturally lend themselves to interdisciplinary work and making connections across the curriculum. These connections strengthen and broaden student learning, helping them meet academic standards. More than likely, you'll be looking for these connections and ways to encourage them well before the students ever start working on service learning activities. As with the entire service learning process, it helps to remain flexible, because some connections can be spontaneously generated by the questions raised throughout and by the needs of the project. To help you think about cross-curricular connections and where you can look for them, the Curricular Web for this chapter (page 149) gives examples of many different ways this theme can be used in different academic areas. (The service learning scenarios in the next section of the chapter also demonstrate various ways this theme can be used across the curriculum.)

Service Learning Scenarios: Ideas for Action

Ready to take action? What follows are projects that have been successfully carried out by elementary, middle, or high school students. Most of these scenarios and examples explicitly include some aspects of preparation, action, reflection, and demonstration. These scenarios can be a rich source of project, resource, and curriculum ideas for you to draw upon. While the grade levels are given as a reference, most project ideas can be adapted to suit younger or older students, and many are suitable for cross-age partnerships.

A Community Collaboration: Grades K–12. Eight hundred public school students in Rhode Island have worked together in a cross-age service learning project to produce food that will feed people who are hungry in their community. The local food bank has received five tons of produce from the students' gardening efforts over four years. While older students teach younger ones about civic involvement, the environment, and how everyone can have a role in ending hunger, both groups enjoy working in the gardens and greenhouse—the latter built through the support of local businesses and volunteers. The broad scale of this project has encouraged the whole community to explore how food, agriculture, abundance, hunger, and society interconnect.

Quilting: Grade 2. In a second-grade class, a teacher read *The Teddy Bear* to initiate conversation about people who are homeless. Students eagerly discussed people they had observed in their semi-rural Washington state community who seemed to have no residence. The children expressed concern and wanted to know who helped people who were homeless in their community. A speaker from a local shelter was invited to answer prepared questions and listen to students' ideas for helping. The class decided to make two quilts that could be used at the shelter. Students applied math and art skills and learned to sew. With parental assistance, they delivered two quilts for permanent use at the shelter.

Children's Hunger Network: Grades 4 and 5. Elementary students in a fourth/fifth-grade combined classroom created a Children's Hunger Network to study national geography, to explore issues of hunger and poverty around the United States, and finally to work on these issues in their own Los Angeles community. To start their geography unit, they identified a school in each of six regions in the United States. Through letters, faxes, and email, they challenged participating classrooms to learn about hunger and homelessness in their communities, find out what organizations were already helping, find a way to make a difference, and report back what they had learned. A local college student helped document the results, and copies were sent to all participating classrooms. For the initiating classroom, U.S. geography came alive as students connected with peers across the country who also wanted to help others. A variety of methods—speakers, field trips, books, and journals— were part of the learning process. The students' direct service included conducting an art exchange with children who lived in a shelter and donating art supplies for their use.

Hunger and Homelessness Across the Curriculum

English/Language Arts
- Define "home" and its attributes; contrast with "homelessness"
- Research myths and facts about homelessness and use them in a persuasive writing piece to share information
- Find examples of how people who are homeless or living in poverty are depicted in literature

Social Studies/History
- Study historical events that led to hunger or homelessness such as the Irish famine
- Interview a city council member or deputy about the government's role in providing services for people in need
- Conduct a demographic and economic study of people who are hungry or homeless in your community

Languages
- Look at and compare the statistics for poverty and hunger in different countries
- Discuss issues of poverty and government programs in a country where this language is spoken
- Study the different kinds of structures used for homes in different countries and learn the associated vocabulary

Theater, Music, & Visual Arts
- Adapt literature that features a person who is homeless into a performance piece with opportunities for discussion with the audience
- Compose simple songs that teach basic concepts like numbers or colors; record and distribute them to a family shelter
- Research what art supplies are needed at a local shelter and prepare art kits

Hunger and Homelessness

Math
- Read food labels to find out serving quantities and nutritional values
- Create a statistical chart to compare national and local statistics on hunger; discuss how statistics can be used in a food drive campaign
- Chart how many cans or pounds of food are needed and received by the local food bank in order to serve their target population

Physical Education
- Discuss the effects of malnutrition on physical health and well-being
- Create a child-friendly exercise video for a family shelter
- Visit a food bank and "get physical" while sorting cans and stocking shelves

Computer
- Develop a brochure for a local food shelter
- Type résumés for people who are looking for work and have no computer access
- On the Internet, find slogans and quotes to use in a marketing campaign for a food drive

Science
- Learn about the food pyramid and nutritional needs of children and adults
- Study the effect of hunger on student achievement in school and on adults trying to enter the workforce
- Compare the nutritional value of different foods and the associated costs

An Art-Full Environment: Grade 6. After a food bank relocated, its coordinator visited a class and  described how "sterile and unwelcoming" the new waiting area appeared with its rows of chairs and bare white walls. The middle school students made posters and art work to decorate the area and created a child-care area stocked with donated art supplies.

A Garden That Serves: Grades 6–8. What began as a garden for a class science project expanded when students wanted to continue planting, weeding, and harvesting. After five years of year-round participation at school, the students continue to tend an organic garden in a community lot to provide fresh produce for families in need and hundreds of residents of local shelters. A partner agency assists with food distribution.

What Is Hunger? Grade 7. Everyone says it: "I'm hungry!" Is "hungry" a growling stomach before the lunch bell or a longing for an after-school snack? Students in social studies classes discussed hunger and came to understand how the word is experienced by people in poverty. They found out that people who don't eat, or who don't eat regular, nutritionally balanced meals, have impaired immune systems and may get sick more often. Their ability to study or work is reduced, too. These effects can lead to a downward economic spiral unless intervention and assistance are provided. Students partnered with local agencies to prepare written materials for distribution at schools, libraries, youth clubs, and other organizations. The materials provided facts about local hunger, ways in which people can help, and tips for running food and clothing drives.

Kids Sew for Kids: Grade 8. In an eighth-grade home economics class, students working in pairs selected an outfit to make for a child at a homeless shelter. The outfits were color coordinated, and each partner sewed one piece. Outfits ranged from sweat suits to shorts sets. Some students also made backpacks for school. To fund the project, community partnerships were established with local fabric stores.

Functional Math: Grade 8. Middle school students combined math lessons with studies of homelessness to provide community assistance. The students learned about the business math concepts of profit, loss, gross, net, discounts, taxes, and so forth and then applied these skills in a fund-raiser aimed at buying food to make bag lunches for a local soup kitchen. Partnerships were created among the students, the school, community food wholesalers, potential donors, and the soup kitchen itself.

Monthly Dinners: Grades 8–12. In addition to advocating for service learning in schools, a youth service learning advisory board in Maryland plans, buys ingredients for, and prepares dinners for the women and children at a shelter twice each month.

Shelter Help: Grades 9–11. After helping a shelter for women and children with room decorations, students in Maryland asked what else they could do to be helpful. The agency and student representatives met to discuss needs and ideas. Students acted on several ideas, including making journals to give to the young people when they arrive and constructing doll houses for use in play therapy.

From Activity Center to Family Album: Grades 9–11. At a "drop in" agency in San Pedro, California, that helps to find temporary housing, food, and other services for families in need, young children often waited for hours with nothing to do. High school students created an activity center with shelves of games and books. On the day they set up the center, the students played games with and read to the children on-site. One student took photographs, careful not to take pictures of the children because of issues concerning confidentiality. However, one parent approached the photographer, asking, "Can you take a picture of my child? I have no pictures of my children." Students then took the initiative to address this situation. They secured donations of an instant camera and film and returned on a regular basis to keep the games and books in good shape and to take photos of the children to give to their parents.

"Gotta Feed Them All": Grades 9–12. The "Gotta Feed Them All" citywide canned food drive was designed by alternative high school students in southern California and coordinated through their partnerships with city government, schools, and the local food bank. After helping to sort and stock food supplies at a local food bank, the students learned that the food bank is always low on supplies during spring and summer months. The students' campaign, held in April, has become an annual event. It is publicized through street banners and with specially marked containers placed by markets, in schools, and at city hall. This event has been a welcome windfall for the food bank.

> As a result of their homelessness, children are struggling in school, their health is hindered, and they are not getting enough to eat.
>
> HOMES FOR THE HOMELESS, A PROGRAM OF THE INSTITUTE FOR CHILDREN AND POVERTY

Donated Eggs: Grades 9–12. Students raising chickens for an agricultural project found that the local food pantry was an appreciative recipient of their eggs. After learning more about the needs of the community, the students helped to organize and promote the collection of other needed resources.

A Video Donation: Grade 10. Following a tour of a food bank, several students expressed interest in doing more than just "donating food." They worked to develop a video for the agency that featured a video tour of the facility and an interview with a woman who had experienced poverty. The students, with help from their teacher and agency staff, wrote a four-page curriculum with suggestions on how to use the video with upper elementary, middle, and high school classes. This video is now used to educate the local community on poverty and hunger.

Teaching at a Shelter: Grades 11–12. Through research, high school students in Chicago learned that children who live in extreme poverty or are homeless often are ill-prepared for kindergarten. The students contacted a shelter for women and children and prepared educational activities such as workbooks and game boxes for preschoolers. With support from teachers and agency personnel, the high school students led educational lessons with the children while learning valuable skills themselves.

A Book Club: Grades 11–12. Students in a class on contemporary issues read fiction and nonfiction literature about poverty and homelessness. After hearing the director of a shelter for men speak about the facility and the programs available for the residents, the students discussed unmet needs. One student commented on the speaker's remarks about how many of the men spend their evenings reading. The class submitted a proposal to the shelter to start a book group in which the male teens and the men in the facility would read the same fiction and would meet two evenings per month for discussion. The reflective writings of the students showed the respect they developed for the men and their knowledge, courage, and resilience.

> What do we live for, if it is not to make life less difficult for each other.
>
> GEORGE ELIOT, AUTHOR

The Hunger and Homelessness Bookshelf

Whether describing the past or examining the present, the works in the Hunger and Homelessness Bookshelf show us that these conditions have touched many lives in many places. To help you find books relevant to your particular projects, the book chart classifies the titles into several topic areas: learning from history, communities today, national perspective, and international needs.

In general, the bookshelf features:

- An annotated bibliography arranged and alphabetized by title according to the general categories of nonfiction (N), picture books (P), and fiction (F). For nonfiction and fiction, length and recommended grade levels are included. The entries in the picture book category do not include suggested grade levels, since they can be successfully used with all ages.

- A chart organized by topic and category to help you find books relevant to particular projects.

- Recommendations from service learning colleagues and experts that include a book summary and ideas for service learning connections. (The number of recommended books varies in each bookshelf.)

Hunger and Homelessness Bookshelf Topics

Topics	Books	Category
Learning from History Is hunger new? Or homelessness? Through the lens of history, find out what occurred in the past and what lessons we can learn.	The Adventurous Chef: Alexis Soyer	P
	Black Potatoes: The Story of the Great Irish Famine, 1845–1850	N
	Feed the Children First: Irish Memories of the Great Hunger	N
	Grapes of Wrath	F
	The Long March: The Choctaw's Gift to Irish Famine Relief *	P
	Orphan Train Rider: One Boy's True Story	N
	Potato: A Tale from the Great Depression	P
	Rodzina	F
	A Train to Somewhere	P
Communities Today In our own modern times and our own communities, social problems lead too many people into lives of homelessness or hunger. The stories in this category show a variety of situations and needs.	The Can-Do Thanksgiving *	P
	A Castle on Viola Street *	P
	Changing Places: A Kid's View of Shelter Living	N
	Darnell Rock Reporting	F
	Drop Dead Inn	F
	Fly Away Home	P
	The Greatest Table: A Banquet to Fight Against Hunger ‡	P
	Home Is Where We Live: Life at a Shelter through a Young Girl's Eyes	N
	The House on Mango Street (see page 199)	F
	The Hundred Dresses	F
	The King of Dragons	F
	Money Hungry	F
	Saily's Journey	P
	Sam and the Lucky Money *	P
	Soul Moon Soup	F
	The Teddy Bear	P
	Uncle Willie and the Soup Kitchen *	P
	Where I'd Like to Be	F
National Perspective How does a nation respond to the needs of people who are homeless? What are the underlying issues, controversies, and possible solutions? As public debate and planning continue, how do people who live on the streets survive?	Homeless Children	N
	Homelessness *	N
	Homelessness: Can We Solve the Problem?	N
	Homelessness: Whose Problem Is It?	N
	Nickel and Dimed: On (Not) Getting By in America	N
	The Other America: Homeless Teens	N

continued ⟶

Topics	Books	Category
International Needs	*Asphalt Angels*	F
Hunger and homelessness have no boundaries. These stories take place across the globe.	*Dream Freedom* * (see page 199)	F
	A Life Like Mine: How Children Live Around the World * (see page 196)	N
	The Lost Boys of Natinga: A School for Sudan's Young Refugees	N

Page references are given for books that do not appear in the Hunger and Homelessness Bookshelf but that can be found in the bookshelf lists of other chapters.

* These books include examples of young people in service-providing roles.

‡ These books are out of print but still worth finding.

Nonfiction: *Hunger and Homelessness*

Black Potatoes: The Story of the Great Irish Famine, 1845–1850 by Susan Campbell Bartoletti (Houghton Mifflin, 2001). The Irish potato famine of 1845–1850 had international repercussions. The Irish people were starving to death. Approximately one million died and two million fled Ireland, with many of those immigrants coming to the United States. The history of this disaster unfolds in vivid text that draws from news reports and first-person narratives. 160pp., grades 6–10

Changing Places: A Kid's View of Shelter Living by Margie Chalofsky, Glen Finland, and Judy Wallace (Gryphon House, 1992). Eight children arrive at a shelter, each with a different story. The first-person narratives help the reader understand the complex situations that arise in families and affect these young people. A preface and an afterword provide a helpful context and include ways to assist at local shelters. 61pp., grades 4–8

Feed the Children First: Irish Memories of the Great Hunger by Mary E. Lyons (Simon & Schuster, 2002). The great Irish potato famine, caused by a fungus that wiped out the staple potato crop, was one of the worst disasters of the nineteenth century. More than a quarter of Ireland's country's eight million people died or emigrated. First-person accounts evoke the time and place, the suffering, and the survival. The introduction includes an overview and examples of the aid received. *The Long March*, also listed in this bookshelf, describes the contribution made by the Choctaw to Irish famine relief. 48pp., grades 4–12

Home Is Where We Live: Life at a Shelter through a Young Girl's Eyes by Bonnie Lee Groth (Cornerstone Press, 1995). "We moved to a shelter this year—Mamma, me, William, and our baby sister, LaTasha." So begins this photo essay about how a young girl acclimates to shelter life and comes to accept the people who help her. 30pp., grades 4–8

Homeless Children by Eleanor H. Ayer (Lucent Books, 1997). What is being done for children who are homeless? Topics include resources provided by agencies and youth-led programs, educational issues, health concerns, and various aspects of daily life. Includes a glossary of terms. 95pp., grades 4–8

Homelessness by Sara Dixon Criswell (Lucent, 1998). Homelessness, a national problem, requires attention from all sectors. This useful book discusses the role of government, charities, nonprofit organizations, and everyday citizens, including youth. In the chapter "Life on the Streets," the subculture of homelessness is described, along with issues of mobility, health care, and self-identity. Education, service providers, and the struggle to turn lives around are candidly presented. 112pp., grades 7–12

Homelessness: Can We Solve the Problem? by Laurie Rozakis (Henry Holt, 1995). The issue of homelessness is presented in a straightforward manner, with chapters on "The Face of Homelessness," "How Do People Become Homeless?" "What Problems Do the Homeless Face?" and "What Can Be Done?" Stereotypes are refuted, and issues such as mental illness, the effects on children, and failures in the social services systems are explored. 64pp., grades 4–6

> All across the United States, citizens are banding together to run soup kitchens, shelters, and neighborhood associations for the homeless. Some fix up abandoned buildings and build new homes for the poor. They pressure local leaders to protect tenants from being unfairly evicted from their apartments.
>
> FROM *HOMELESSNESS: CAN WE SOLVE THE PROBLEM?*

Homelessness: Whose Problem Is It? by Ted Gottfried (Millbrook Press, 1999). Beginning with the history of homelessness in the United States, the author presents a broad and balanced range of issues. Policies, welfare reform, illness, substance abuse, and education, among other topics, are examined. Readers are invited to formulate their own opinions. Organizational resources are included. 128pp., young adult

The Lost Boys of Natinga: A School for Sudan's Young Refugees by Judy Walgren (Houghton Mifflin, 1998). This photo essay takes the reader inside a refugee camp and school for boys, established in 1993 in southern Sudan. Because of the country's civil war, the boys have been forced from their homes. Many came to the camp when they were orphaned or otherwise separated from their families. "Every day these boys struggle to get food, to stay healthy, and to go to school." 44pp., grades 5–8

Recommendation from the Field

by Susan Vermeer, Project Manager, Education Commission of the States

Nickel and Dimed: On (Not) Getting By in America by Barbara Ehrenreich (Metropolitan Books, 2001). *Nickel and Dimed* is an easy and enjoyable yet somewhat painful read about what it takes to survive in modern America on poverty-level wages. In the style of an undercover reporter, Ehrenreich provides an inside view of what it's really like to wait tables, work at Wal-Mart, serve meals in a nursing home, and work at least two jobs simultaneously to survive. Welfare reform, a livable wage, and affordable housing are a few of the societal issues that come to life for the reader.

By reading *Nickel and Dimed*, students can develop empathy and knowledge from this up-close look at what the people they meet might be experiencing. Their perception of low-wage workers will change as they gain a new respect for and understanding of the working poor. This book could prompt significant classroom discussion. It will be powerful when combined with a service learning experience that addresses some of the issues that the working poor must struggle with every day. 221pp., young adult

---

Orphan Train Rider: One Boy's True Story by Andrea Warren (Houghton Mifflin, 1996). "Children without Homes"—so read the signs announcing the arrival of the Orphan Trains that left New York City heading west. Children on board were orphans or had been abandoned by families who could no longer care for them. Over 200,000 children made such journeys to the Midwest from 1854 to 1929. This book tells the story of one boy, providing an important historical account of societal conditions that predated foster homes and homeless shelters. 80pp., grades 4–8

The Other America: Homeless Teens by Gail B. Stewart (Lucent Books, 1998). "This ruins everything." "We're a close-knit street family." "Sometimes you just feel you're wasting your whole life." "I don't think too many people care." Words from young people, the stories of their plight, and the people who reach out to help turn their lives around are presented. 112pp., young adult

Picture Books: *Hunger and Homelessness*

The Adventurous Chef: Alexis Soyer by Ann Arnold (Farrar, Straus and Giroux, 2002). In this unique biography, meet Alexis Soyer, flamboyant chef and inventor of kitchen tools, who defied tradition, improved cooking methods, and helped people in need. His philanthropic work led him to create the soup kitchen model in Dublin during the Irish potato famine and to work alongside Florence Nightingale to reform and improve military cooking methods during the Crimean War.

The Can-Do Thanksgiving by Marion Hess Pomeranc (Albert Whitman, 1998). When Dee brings a can of peas to school for the canned food drive, she keeps asking, "Where do my peas go?" Her persistent questioning results in a class project to prepare and serve food for people in need at Thanksgiving. An excellent resource for transforming the traditional canned food drive into a service learning project.

A Castle on Viola Street by DyAnne DiSalvo-Ryan (HarperCollins, 2001). On Viola Street, a family joins Habitat for Humanity volunteers as they restore a home. In time, they learn that another home will be restored for them. As the father says, "Big dreams are built little by little," and many generous hands have helped in the dream building.

Fly Away Home by Eve Bunting (Clarion, 1991). A boy lives in an airport terminal with his father, who continually tries to earn enough money to rent an apartment. The boy wonders when his life will change and gains hope when he watches a bird trapped inside the building find an open window to freedom.

The Greatest Table: A Banquet to Fight Against Hunger edited by Michael J. Rosen (Harcourt, 1994). This is a twelve-foot-long accordion book with artwork contributed by sixteen illustrators. At this great table, there is room for all people who come and plenty of food to share. Out of print but worth finding.

The Long March: The Choctaw's Gift to Irish Famine Relief by Marie-Louise Fitzpatrick (Tricycle Press, 1998). The year is 1847, and Choona, a young Choctaw, has learned of a famine in Ireland. From what precious little they have, the Choctaw collect $170 to help the starving Irish. As Choona learns the terrible truth about his own tribe's long march, he must decide whether to answer another people's faraway cry for help. Based on actual events.

> We have walked the trail of tears.
> The Irish people walk it now. We can help them
> as we could not help ourselves. Our help will be
> like an arrow shot through time. It will land
> many winters from now to wait as a blessing
> for our unborn generations.
>
> FROM *THE LONG MARCH:*
> *THE CHOCTAW'S GIFT TO IRISH FAMINE RELIEF*

Potato: A Tale from the Great Depression by Kate Lied (National Geographic Society, 1997). "This is a story about my grandfather and my grandmother. It is also a story about the Great Depression and how hard things were." A family that has lost their jobs and home turns to farm work. The family members pick potatoes—many, many potatoes—which they eat and also use to barter for other goods, "even a pig." The author wrote this book at age eight to pass on a true family story and to explain why she likes potatoes.

Saily's Journey by Ralph da Costa Nunez (White Tiger Press, 2002). When Saily the Snail loses his shell in a storm, he goes on a journey to find a new home. Along the way, he experiences a range of emotions , including despair, fear, and hope, until he finds the generosity of others that help him find a home once again.

Sam and the Lucky Money by Karen Chinn (Lee & Low Books, 1995). For Chinese New Year, Sam receives lucky money in traditional *leisees*—decorated red envelopes. Sam can buy either sweets or a toy. Near the open market, before the festival lion dances through the street, Sam sees a man who is homeless and barefoot. On this wintry day, Sam considers the best use for his money.

The Teddy Bear by David McPhail (Henry Holt, 2002). A special teddy bear, lost by his little boy, is found and loved by an elder man who lives on the street. Months later, the boy is amazed to find his bear sitting on a park bench. Reunited with his bear at last, the boy hears the cries of a bearded man, "My bear! Where is my bear?" The boy's actions show understanding and compassion.

A Train to Somewhere by Eve Bunting (Clarion, 1996). In 1878, a young girl rides the Orphan Train out west hoping somehow to find her mother, who has abandoned her. With each stop she watches other children being adopted. At the last stop, in the town of Somewhere, she finds a home.

Uncle Willie and the Soup Kitchen by DyAnne DiSalvo-Ryan (Morrow, 1991). When Willie's nephew works at the neighborhood soup kitchen preparing and serving food, he gains admiration for people who lend a hand.

Fiction: *Hunger and Homelessness*

Asphalt Angels by Ineke Holtwijk (Front Street, 1995). In Rio de Janeiro, Alex lives among street kids, alone and scared. Thrown out of his house by his stepfather, Alex lives by his wits among "the Asphalt Angels." Although he intends to avoid crime, Alex reluctantly falls into a life of theft and panhandling for survival. 184pp., grades 10–12 (mature themes)

Darnell Rock Reporting by Walter Dean Myers (Delacorte, 1994). Darnell fails his middle school classes and spends too much time in the principal's office for behavior problems. His last opportunity to get his act together is the school newspaper. Encouraged by the librarian and his sudden interest in Sweeby Jones, a veteran who is homeless, Darnell demonstrates initiative and an understanding that everyone needs a second chance. 135pp., grades 4–7

Dew Drop Dead by James Howe (Simon & Schuster, 2000). When Sebastian Barth and his friends decide to sneak into an abandoned inn, the last thing they expect to find is a dead body. The mystery spills over into the new homeless shelter at the church, as evidence suggests a person using the facility might be the murderer. Against this backdrop, the challenges and turmoil of being homeless are revealed, along with the thoughtful response of a caring community. 156pp., grades 4–7

Recommendation from the Field

Nelda Brown, Executive Director, State Education Agency K–12 Service Learning Network

The Grapes of Wrath by John Steinbeck (Penguin, 1939/1992). Service learning can make this classic American novel come alive, particularly in the areas of immigration and hunger and homelessness. After reading about the Joad family's arrival in California and the "Welcome Committee" at the government camp, students can create a "Newcomer's Welcome Guide and Orientation" for families new to this country. Preparing written materials, such as guides, public service announcements,

continued ⟶

and role-play scenarios, gives students an opportunity to apply writing skills in a variety of formats. Students can explore immigration issues by researching local trends in new student arrivals. At the same time, they can gain an understanding of and respect for different cultures and experiences. A newcomer orientation project can also welcome students new to the school community and may be especially effective for groups of students transitioning from elementary to middle school or middle to high school. This project also offers a context in which to explore issues of teasing and bullying.

Steinbeck poignantly describes how unpicked fruit rotted and livestock was destroyed while the Oklahoma immigrants starved. After assessing the community's needs, students can research and identify opportunities for "salvaging" food from local restaurants and grocery stores and giving it to food banks or meal assistance programs. Using lessons in persuasive essay- and letter-writing skills and oral presentations, students can work with local grocers, restaurateurs, and human service providers to make unused resources (for example, bread, canned foods, fruits, vegetables, excess meals) available to their neighbors in need. 619pp., young adult

The Hundred Dresses by Eleanor Estes (Harcourt, 1944). Wanda Petronski is teased by classmates for living in a poor part of town and wearing the same dress every day. One girl, Maddie, is confused by the taunting and by Wanda's insistence that she has "one hundred dresses at home." When Wanda's dad moves the family to escape the relentless teasing, Maddie and her friends face up to their behavior and see Wanda's dresses. 80pp., grades 3–7

The King of Dragons by Carol Fenner (McElderry, 1998). Eleven-year-old Ian and his father, a Vietnam veteran, live in a deserted courthouse. Homeless for several years, Ian knows how to stay out of sight and manage on few resources. When his dad does not return to the courthouse and renovations begin to transform the musty halls into a kite museum, Ian finds a unique role as a kite expert to handle his precarious situation. 216pp., grades 4–8

Money Hungry by Sharon G. Flake (Hyperion, 2001). Raspberry Hill is thirteen and knows what it's like to be homeless, and she swears she won't live on the streets again. Her endless schemes at earning money may get her some cash, but not enough to prevent her mother from packing their belongings in plastic bags, leaving the projects, and facing the fears and frustrations of life without a home once again. 188pp., grades 5–8

Rodzina by Karen Cushman (Clarion, 2003). The year is 1881, and Rodzina Clara Jadwiga Anastazya Brodski would rather be anywhere than on an orphan train heading west to an unknown future. Since she is a big girl and already twelve, she is placed in charge of the little children, which only makes her yearn more for her deceased family. What family would want a scruffy orphan from the streets of Chicago? As each child finds a new home, Rodzina's future seems truly unknown. 215pp., grades 4–7

Soul Moon Soup by Lindsay Lee Johnson (Front Street, 2002). In this prose-poem, Phoebe Rose, age eleven, describes life "in the hard poor middle of the city," where she and her mother sleep in shelters or doorways. When her dream of being an artist is torn away, no one notices; she becomes invisible. Only when she is sent to live in the country with her Gram does Phoebe learn, "When things come apart it's your chance to rearrange the pieces." 134pp., grades 7–10

> But lucky days are running out
> in the mean dirty city,
> where the hungry eyes of strangers watch,
> where the quick hands of strangers wait
> to take their chance,
> my chance, my shoes,
> my soul.
>
> FROM *SOUL MOON SOUP*

Where I'd Like to Be by Frances O'Roark Dowell (Simon & Schuster, 2003). After living in her share of foster homes, Maddie, age twelve, moves into the East Tennessee Children's Home. She finds an eclectic group of kids who join together to build a fort, a home of their own. As they fill this structure with their stories and dreams, Maddie wonders whether she will find a place to really call her home—or at least find people who feel like home. 232pp., grades 4–7

Interviews with Authors:
The Story Behind the Story

In the following interviews, we find out the "story behind the story" from Lindsay Lee Johnson (*Soul Moon Soup*) and Marion Hess Pomeranc (*The Can-Do Thanksgiving*). As soon as I read *Soul Moon Soup*, I wanted to call Lindsay Lee Johnson and find out how she could capture so accurately the voice of her protagonist—a young girl grappling with her challenging life. *The Can-Do Thanksgiving* deals with a canned food drive—perhaps the most common community service project. How perfect to find a book on the subject! I had to find out what in particular had inspired author Marion Hess Pomeranc to write the book.

Lindsay Lee Johnson, author of
Soul Moon Soup

We often talk about a person having a particular "mind-set" to accomplish something. But I credit my desire to write about homelessness and other social justice issues with having a "heart-set" for service. I grew up in a helping family. Whether that meant taking in stray, injured animals or bringing a meal to needy neighbors, it's simply what we did. My father was a doctor and my mother a nurse. Their professional values of caring and helping became our family values.

Later I married a man with similar values, and not surprisingly, our children always seemed to befriend the outsiders and speak up for the "underdogs." However, I don't believe you have to come from a family like this to be drawn to service; this "heart-set" can be contagious and inspired by others. This happens friend to friend, teacher to student, author to reader. Adults and older teens can model behavior that encourages children to seek ways to live that give their lives meaning. The values of compassion and service are not derived from thinking "I ought to help" but from thinking "What can I do to help?"

When I began writing *Soul Moon Soup*, I did not think about "homelessness." I began with a character who has a story to tell. She lived in my mind first, and it's her story, but I believe the story is fed by my personal experience. I focused on words that have emotional currency beyond face value, radioactive words that jump off the page. For instance, the word *home* means much more than a place of residence. In the same way, each word in the book's title resonates with personal as well as universal meaning.

This story began to percolate during my experience as a volunteer baby rocker for a social service agency. These babies had been damaged by abuse or neglect. The moms were in desperate situations, either in jail or facing jail for various reasons. They had to prove their ability to be good caregivers in order to regain custody of their children. These were ordinary women who, for one reason or another, had experienced some catastrophe, and their lives had gone wrong. They were human beings who responded to love and friendship and wanted something better.

As a volunteer at various shelters, again I saw individuals in difficult circumstances, people experiencing homelessness rather than "homeless people" as a group. Labels can stop us from wanting to get involved and take action. People having difficulties certainly don't choose their circumstances. When people experience homelessness, they lose a sense of identity gained by having a place to be themselves, a home. A person can feel lost and have difficulty moving forward. Growing up is hard under the best circumstances, but for children without that "home" in their lives, it is nearly impossible.

Homelessness is a huge and growing problem, especially for children. According to my research, about 40 percent of people who are homeless are children with an average age of six. The best way for me to contribute to people's awareness of this situation is to tell a story, the story of one girl, Phoebe Rose, who lives on the "stoop-sitting, gutter-spitting streets." Her voice spoke to me so clearly and powerfully. I had to pass on what she was telling me, heart to heart and soul to soul.

Phoebe Rose's story is sad in a way, but it also contains hope. Phoebe learns to feed her imagination with art to keep her soul alive. When a child, or anyone, loses imagination and the ability to picture what might come next in life, this is true hopelessness. When Phoebe reclaims her ability to envision her future in the world of art, it is a turning point for her and indicates that she can survive. In writing *Soul Moon Soup* I learned of a nonprofit organization that provides art supplies to children in homeless shelters, along with volunteers to help them explore and express the often unspeakable things in their hearts. It is this sort of service project that inspires me.

As I wrote *Soul Moon Soup*, Phoebe's voice naturally took the form of free verse, with a lyrical poetic quality. I wanted the book to have beautiful language in spite of the harsh realities of the story. Also, I wanted the book to be accessible. For reluctant readers, a book with a lot of text can be off-putting; short lines and sections appear more manageable, like little bites. A more accomplished reader is drawn in to the rhythm and music of the language, the pace of the story. I hope readers of all ages and abilities find their own hearts in these pages and the courage to make connections with people around them who may need something they can give.

While group service projects can be valuable, remember that one-to-one outreach is also important. In one early scene in the book, Phoebe discards a pretty package of soap and shampoo from a girl at school when the girl says, "It's from my mother, I don't care." A true gift, like the gifts Phoebe receives later in the story from Ruby, can only be given with a genuine heart.

I would like to see readers become less fearful of making these honest connections. People want to be treated respectfully, not as projects or special cases. An episode of a lost job or mental illness can suddenly cause people who think they are very secure to end up in trouble.

Phoebe's character demonstrates a strength that will enable her to survive. I imagine her going to art school and becoming a teacher. In the future, I would like to write more about Phoebe. I think she has a lot more to say.

For me, *Soul Moon Soup* is the most meaningful story I have ever written. I hope this is conveyed and that Phoebe's voice is passed along. Then I know I will have accomplished something worthwhile.

Marion Hess Pomeranc, author of The Can-Do Thanksgiving

How did I choose the topic of a canned food drive for my book? I was bringing a can of food into my synagogue's food drive when I thought to myself, "Where do these cans really go?" I realized that kids across the country collect cans of food, and they too want to know where the cans go.

My question turned into action. I began calling different food banks and ended up at a soup kitchen in my neighborhood. It was a cold day, with people lined up outside. When the doors opened, volunteers handed out coffee and breakfast, while men and women sat inside eating their meal. From bringing in a can of food and visiting this kitchen, my story grew.

I want kids to know that whatever you bring to the food banks and kitchens is really going to help. Knowing where the food goes does matter because we need to connect with the places where people get some assistance and with the people who are in need. This helps us remember that whatever we do can make a difference. In my story, Dee saved her own money to buy the can, and her can of peas made a difference.

I would like to see my book inspire canned food drives all year long, because urban children are faced with seeing people in need on the street all the time. When my son was young, he wanted to help the people who were asking for food and money on the streets of New York City. We gave out bagels. I wanted him to view all people, regardless of their need or situation, as part of our human family.

As you read the book, remember we are all like Dee and we are all like Tyler. We will sometimes be in the position to help others, and we will sometimes need help ourselves. The most important thing is to be there for each other.

CHAPTER 11

IMMIGRANTS

> When we escaped from Cuba,
> all we could carry was our education.
> ALICIA CORO, EDUCATOR

What causes a person to uproot and move to a new country, where language and cultural differences may seem insurmountable? History offers up many reasons: famine, political differences, financial hardships, war, forced relocation, and slavery. Of course, people have immigrated for positive reasons, too, such as a sense of adventure, a hope for better employment or a better education, a promise of streets paved in gold, or simply the expectation of a better life waiting. In today's world, are the reasons for immigration so different?

Immigration means moving somewhere to settle—not a vacation, not passing through. This new place becomes home. Sometimes families who make such moves are separated from loved ones. They face isolation and the challenges of learning a new language while unraveling the mysteries of a foreign culture. Young people in particular may struggle with whether to identify with their culture of origin or to abandon it, even temporarily, in order to fit in with their peers.

Service learning offers opportunities for reaching across differences of language, experience, and culture to learn about these new neighbors and to create an inclusive, diverse community. Kids are naturally curious and want to learn. The challenge is to ensure that their inquisitive minds develop in ways that make them open and thoughtful about others' experiences.

Preparation: Getting Ready for Service Learning Involving Immigrants

The following activities can be used in the preparation stage to promote learning and skill development related to immigrants. These activities can be used with different age ranges during preparation to help your students examine key issues through research, analyze community needs, and gain the knowledge they need to effectively contribute to the design of their service plan. Since literature is often an important part of preparation, you can find recommended titles on this theme in the Immigrants Bookshelf later in this chapter.

Activity: Bringing the World Home. Where in the world are people coming from? This information is the foundation of any immigrant-based service learning project. You can't help until you know who to help. Conducting a survey is a good way to find out where people lived before coming to your city or town. The survey's target population could be other students, school faculty, or a specific group in the community, such as members of an adult education class. Decide how far back to research. For example, the class could agree to find out the last three places a family responding to the survey has lived. Students may also want to find out the year of each move and the reasons for moving. Remind students that responding to all of the survey questions should be optional for the person completing the survey.

Next, using both world and national maps, track the survey responses using pins or stickers and string to depict the immigration and any other moves visually. Help students to understand the difference between moving within a country and moving between countries. Discuss what immigrants bring to their new home, including language, values, information, skills, ideas, culture, and resources. Identify any stereotypes students may have about immigrant groups in their community, then have speakers from those groups or from agencies that serve immigrant populations address and discuss misinformation and prejudices. Once your students have identified the immigrant groups in the community and have learned more about their cultures, it is much easier to identify ways to reach out and address genuine needs.

Activity: Who Helps? Community agencies that assist immigrant populations can help students learn more about the recent immigrants in the region, find out who helps them become acclimated, bridge potential language or cultural confusion, and identify needs that can be addressed by youth. The following activities are easily tailored to students' abilities, the timeframe for the project, and the course curriculum.

- To encourage students to start thinking about immigration issues, they can read one of the bookshelf titles in this category or have a book read aloud to them. In *My Name Is Yoon*, for example, a young girl changes her name to try to fit in to this new country. *Any Small Goodness* describes an immigrant boy in East Los Angeles, where daily life combines blessings and risk. *Behind the Mountains* tells of a girl moving from Haiti to New York and experiencing an uneasy adjustment. These books can generate conversation regarding the challenges facing young people and their families and what the young people could have done in these stories to mitigate the problems.

- Continuing education is often very important for adult immigrants, so they can learn a new language or other information that will help them adapt to and thrive in their new home. Resources for continued learning can include local and state government offices and the school district, as well as nonprofit agencies. Adult schools may have information about enrollment in classes teaching English as a second language. Students can find out from the school program coordinators what services are offered and if there are needs that can be met through youth involvement. Based on the needs, students can then identify worthwhile projects and collaborate with agencies to carry them out.

- Students can interview other students or adults who are immigrants to learn about their experiences and needs. Preparation for the interview process is important, and professionals who work with immigrant populations can provide extremely useful assistance. Some students who

are immigrants themselves or who have relatives who are immigrants may also come forward to volunteer knowledge and guidance.

Interacting with people who are immigrants always offers a multitude of opportunities for exchange and reciprocity that leave everyone richer in knowledge and understanding. Working with people from another culture is not a one-way street with help flowing in a single direction. Again, just as when working with elders, make sure to look for or create activities that make these mutual benefits explicit for everyone involved.

Find Out More About Immigrants

To learn more about these issues and to get ideas for service and action, visit these Web sites and organizations online:

www.uscis.gov The Bureau of Citizenship and Immigration Services includes information on naturalization eligibility, the process, forms, news, frequently asked questions, citizenship quizzes, and the *Guide to Naturalization* publication.

www.theirc.org International Rescue Committee is a voluntary agency providing assistance to refugees around the world, including the United States. Many United States cities have local offices and information about the program's involvement.

www.studycircles.org The Study Circles Resource Center is dedicated to finding ways all kinds of people can engage in dialogue and problem solving on critical social and political issues. Their free resource materials for middle and high school grades include a unit on immigration, called "Changing Faces, Changing Communities," that can lead to social action projects.

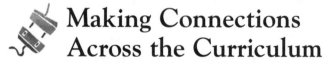 # Making Connections Across the Curriculum

Some service learning activities naturally lend themselves to interdisciplinary work and making connections across the curriculum. These connections strengthen and broaden student learning, helping them meet academic standards. More than likely, you'll be looking for these connections and ways to encourage them well before the students ever start working on service learning activities. As with the entire service learning process, it helps to remain flexible, because some connections can be spontaneously generated by the questions raised throughout and by the needs of the project. To help you think about cross-curricular connections and where you can look for them, the Curricular Web for this chapter (page 162) gives examples of many different ways this theme can be used in different academic areas. (The service learning scenarios in the next section of the chapter also demonstrate various ways this theme can be used across the curriculum.)

Service Learning Scenarios:
Ideas for Action

Ready to take action? What follows are projects that have been successfully carried out by elementary, middle, or high school students. Most of these scenarios and examples explicitly include some aspects of preparation, action, reflection, and demonstration. These scenarios can be a rich source of project, resource, and curriculum ideas for you to draw upon. While the grade levels are given as a reference, most project ideas can be adapted to suit younger or older students, and many are suitable for cross-age partnerships.

A Good Trade: Grade 2. When a teacher in Washington state began to teach origami to her class, she quickly realized that she needed help in guiding all of her students in this hands-on task. A colleague knew of Japanese exchange students attending a local community college through an exchange program. After a few phone calls, six exchange students had volunteered to help the teacher. The volunteers ended up helping nearly every day over a two-week period. They also brought in recent immigrants from Japan who worked with the students on the craft project and told stories about their experiences in Japan and moving to this country. To reciprocate, the children invited the college students and recent immigrants for a special program and presentation. The children taught about important Americans, including men and women of diverse cultures and ethnic groups, who had made contributions to United States society. Each

guest received a compilation of these student-written stories as a gift. The exchange students let the children know how much the interaction had helped them learn and practice their English skills.

A Music Fest: Grade 3. Third-grade students in a Spanish immersion elementary school in Los Angeles enjoyed learning the rhythms and songs of Latin American music. They performed at a senior center that drew primarily Spanish-speaking elder community members. The elders so appreciated the students' joy in music that they invited the students to come again, this time to be taught dancing by the older people. The younger students returned several times during the school year for singing, dancing, and, of course, cookies.

Refugee Youth Project: Grades 3–12. In Pennsylvania, a service learning collaboration that included the International Rescue Committee and the American Red Cross was formed to meet the needs of young refugees resettled from Africa and the former Yugoslavia. College students tutored refugee students from elementary, middle, and high schools after school. The refugee students then extended their own learning and experience by doing service projects on weekends. These opportunities had multiple benefits for all involved. By helping with community cleanups, working in food shelters, and creating murals depicting their international experience, the students came to know and build community. They learned about community resources, gained skills through volunteering, and became engaged in the civic life of their new country.

The Story Cloth Museum: Grade 4. Fourth-grade classes in central California read *The Whispering Cloth* as a way to become more familiar with Hmong culture and the growing Hmong population in their community. Two parents from Cambodia visited the class and brought Hmong story cloths. Students were fascinated with the artistry and story telling on the fabric. They developed a project to teach the community about Hmong culture by making their own story cloths. After engaging in research, students told some of their family stories through a combination of drawing on fabrics and sewing to give the pictures more depth. The students invited the community to see their museum of story cloths, including Hmong cloths

Immigrants Across the Curriculum

English/Language Arts

- Read stories about the personal experiences of immigrating to a new country
- Study interview techniques and practice listening and note taking
- Create English vocabulary books for English as a second language programs

Social Studies/History

- Conduct interviews with immigrants of different ages from the same population and compare their experiences
- Research reasons people leave specific countries and compare how this has changed over recent decades
- Learn about and document the contributions of immigrants in your community in a range of areas—social, political, cultural, and artistic

Languages

- Find words in English that have their roots in the language being studied
- Prepare lessons to tutor immigrants in English language skills
- Translate the school handbook for immigrant populations

Theater, Music, & Visual Arts

- Create collaborative theater events with people from many countries sharing talents
- Listen to world music and invite musicians from other countries into the classroom
- Explore the influence of many cultures on styles of art and architecture

Immigrants

Math

- Compare the decimal system with the metric system used in many parts of the world
- Study and chart statistics reflecting the number of immigrants in your region, where they are coming from, and their reasons for moving
- Make easy-to-use guides to money conversion for new immigrants

Physical Education

- Learn about games and approaches to exercise from different cultures
- Research athletes who are immigrants or children of immigrants who have made and continue to make contributions to sports
- Create a multilingual guide to places in your region for outdoor exercise

Computer

- Create computer-generated lessons on colloquial expressions for teen immigrants
- Research ways the Internet is used for genealogy and country of origin research
- Study language translation programs that can assist students who are learning English

Science

- Research how indigenous gardening techniques have been influenced by immigrants who bring their methods and plants
- Discuss whether or not the food pyramid is an accurate shape to depict the eating and nutrition practices of people from different countries
- Learn about folk traditions and remedies for health concerns used by immigrants from their country of origin

on loan from local families. Serving as docents, the students explained their cultural studies and shared family histories. Much to the students' delight, a local library, bank, and city government offices asked to display the museum pieces.

Oral History—Across the Decades: Grade 6. Using a U.S. Library of Congress collection of interviews and oral histories from the 1930s, students learned about the everyday life of ordinary people who were immigrants. With guidance from teachers, the students then began collecting oral histories from recent immigrants in their own communities. The steps included doing background research, identifying interview subjects, developing interview questions, scheduling and conducting the interviews, and supplementing them with selections of primary source material, including photographs from magazines and from some of the immigrants. Students then wrote papers to compare the experiences of immigrants across the decades. Copies of these comprehensive portfolios were given to the immigrants involved, to support agencies, and to school and local libraries.

Let's Talk: Grades 6–8. Learning English requires practice, practice, and more practice. At one middle school, students learning English are paired with English-speaking students for conversational practice during physical education classes. Both student groups received orientation on the project. The English-speakers worked with counselors and a language specialist to develop skills, such as listening, speaking more slowly, repeating phrases, and answering questions. The English-learners prepared by working with a counselor and developing a document that addressed stereotypes or possible put-downs that could come up in these relationships. Together, both groups of students created a written agreement of how they would work together to be mutually respectful. Then they participated in a getting acquainted activity to identify common interests and topics to talk about, though much of the talking centered on the P.E. class work. As an unexpected benefit, some of the English-learners coached their partners in sports skills!

Neighborhood Resource Project: Grades 7–8. A middle school in New York has students from Cuba, Jamaica, Puerto Rico, Honduras, Mexico, Nicaragua, and Haiti. Many of them have been identified as being at risk, and often their families aren't familiar with the services available through government agencies and other providers. To remedy this, the students collaborated with a local agency to provide the neighborhood population with information regarding available services, including health care, after-school activities, drug prevention programs, adult literacy classes, and language and career training. Based on information acquired from field trips to local government meetings, civic organizations, and guest speakers, the students published a directory of services. The students met several educational objectives: basic awareness of social problems and their solutions, an in-depth study of government, computer literacy, knowledge of the immigrant experience, work skills, and cultural awareness.

¡Sí se puede!
Yes, it can be done!
CÉSAR E. CHÁVEZ, SOCIAL ACTIVIST

In Honor of New Citizens: Grades 7–8. After participating in a two-week simulation about immigrants entering this country through Ellis Island, a middle school social studies class in Portland, Maine, wanted to do more. They knew their community was a resettlement area for refugees from around the world. To learn more, they met with staff from Immigration and Naturalization Services (INS), and an idea emerged. The students made a proposal to the INS asking to host a swearing-in ceremony for new citizens at their school. Students found out the countries of origin of the 32 people being sworn in and researched the culture, foods, art, and social and political histories of those countries. They reached out to the community for food donations (including many ethnic treats) and made room decorations. They also arranged for the educational television channel to record and air the event. On the day of the ceremony, they greeted the guests and interviewed the new citizens, compiling their stories (with permission) into books with smiling family photographs. Many of the families wrote letters thanking the students for a most meaningful and memorable event. Still, the students were not finished—they had found another need to fill. They created "welcome kits" for the children of the immigrant families that included cartoon-style maps of the area, places to go for entertainment and sports, lists of after-school and weekend activities, a guide to youth expressions, and a small journal and pen.

ESL Tutors: Grade 9. In Minnesota, several ninth-grade social studies classes spent one class period every two weeks throughout the academic year tutoring new immigrants in English and other basic skills. These freshman linked their experiences to what they were learning about different cultures and current events. Unexpectedly, the teacher noticed that the students' writing skills improved as they began to pay more attention to sentence structure and communicating clearly.

Beginning with Earthquakes: Grades 9 and 10. A high school English-as-a-second-language class in Los Angeles completed an in-depth study of earthquakes. Where to take their knowledge? To a traditional science class. The ESL students developed interactive lessons; each agreed to lead a small-group discussion. The lessons were successful on many levels: The ESL students became more confident in their English skills, students who often kept to their own cultural group became acquainted with others, and the science students agreed to continue the exchange by leading an interactive lesson in return. Although the project was led by a student teacher who was only with the class for a limited time, this reciprocal arrangement continued for the remainder of the school year.

A Cup of Knowledge: Grades 9–11. Enterprising high school students from around the world cooked up language skills as they served coffee. A nonprofit organization north of Los Angeles created a coffee shop, "A Cup of Knowledge/*Taza de Conocimiento*," to connect ESL students with their community. Students in ESL classes plus additional students identified by school counselors worked with representatives from the nonprofit on planning the coffee house including design and marketing. The students suggested ways to make the coffee house more enticing for a teen crowd and along the way learned entrepreneurial and food service skills. The students improved language skills through free classes and workshops they offered for younger students. The older teens also offered bilingual story hours, quilt-making classes, and art classes in the coffee shop to attract families and their children as regular customers. To promote these offerings, students created flyers for community bulletin boards and to send to neighborhood newspapers.

Welcome Buddies: Grades 9–12. New kid in school? Welcome Buddies are there to greet you. Young people designed, improved, and continue to implement this ongoing project at their Los Angeles high school, which registers many immigrant students each semester. Pairs of students drawn from world history and language classes meet, greet, and assist young people coming into their school. Orientation programs are held every few months; special mixers and other activities help students become acclimated and stay involved with positive social and academic activities. "Welcome Buddy" programs can also help students to find their way around campus, supply a buddy to have lunch with, and provide homework helpers.

Helping to Address Challenges: Grades 10–11. A high school in Hawaii with a large number of immigrants recognized the challenges that many students faced attending a new school and living in a new country. High school classes partnered with a local immigration center and became knowledgeable about the services offered and the potential difficulties immigrants in the community could encounter. Students combined this new information with skills learned at school to assist the center in updating the brochures given to new immigrants. This project met the writing, civic, and diversity standards.

Oral History—An Exchange in Spanish: Grade 11. To foster improved community relations and to emphasize the value of being literate in a second language, students in an advanced Spanish class adopted an adult literacy class for recent immigrants. During four visits to the class, held at the local community center, students interviewed the immigrants in Spanish to create written histories of their immigration and life experiences. Using computers at school, students wrote the histories in Spanish, adding photographs and other graphics to produce a book. Copies were presented to the adults at a final gathering. The book was meaningful reading material for the new immigrants and provided a way for students to improve their language skills while acquiring knowledge found outside of their textbooks.

A World View: Grades 11–12. As part of a World Studies class, students in Chicago examined immigration issues. To further students' understanding of the problems facing immigrants, the teacher collaborated with a community organization to work toward a service learning project. The first step was to lead students through team-building activities. Next, guest speakers discussed local issues related to immigration: the problem of work conditions for day laborers and immigrant documentation, specifically referencing a federal initiative that enabled documented immigrants to help family members who were not documented. The students discussed their options and ideas, and decided to work on the documentation issue. With training from lawyers specializing in immigration issues, the students hosted a day to begin the documentation process of immigrants. Two hundred local residents attended on that day and received assistance from students and legal experts. The teacher continually linked the experiences with classroom learning and guided the students in reflection.

Language in Action: Grades 11 and 12. High school advanced language students put their skills to use as "cultural aids." After developing lists of project ideas, students individually or in pairs selected a project that would assist community members. Projects included helping prepare a bilingual brochure for families on how to access local resources, acting as a guide for back-to-school night, helping with health aid programs, translating materials for local agencies, maintaining bilingual information on the school's Web site, and translating school correspondence sent home to parents. Once this program was in place, language teachers saw skill levels rise and classroom discussion became enriched as students brought real-life problems to solve into the classroom.

Civics with a Purpose: Grade 12. A high school civics class established a valuable partnership with a local refugee center, resulting in benefits for all involved. The students applied their classroom knowledge to coach new immigrants who were studying for their citizenship tests. Students came to value their own citizenship as they learned that people sometimes put their lives at risk to move to their new country. Students also provided child care during classes and study groups.

> Reading makes immigrants of us all. It takes us away from home, but more important, it finds homes for us everywhere.
>
> HAZEL ROCHMAN, AUTHOR

The Immigrants Bookshelf

The books on the Immigrants Bookshelf give us the opportunity to walk, if only for a while, in the shoes of another person. For young people who are immigrants, the books may ease the telling of their own life stories. For others, understanding may encourage empathy and comradeship. To help you find books relevant to your particular projects, the book chart classifies the titles into several topic areas: learning from the past, the story of many, focus on one story, and fitting in.

In general, the bookshelf features:

- An annotated bibliography arranged and alphabetized by title according to the general categories of nonfiction (N), picture books (P), and fiction (F). For nonfiction and fiction, length and recommended grade levels are included. The entries in the picture book category do not include suggested grade levels, since they can be successfully used with all ages.

- A chart organized by topic and category to help you find books relevant to particular projects.

- Recommendations from service learning colleagues and experts that include a book summary and ideas for service learning connections. (The number of recommended books varies in each bookshelf.)

Immigrants Bookshelf Topics

Topics	Books	Category
Learning from the Past These stories, drawn from the not-so-distant past, shed light on the experience of immigrants and reveal their similarities to today's immigrants.	The Clay Marble	F
	A Different Kind of Hero	F
	Dragonwings	F
	Esperanza Rising	F
	Oranges on Golden Mountain	P
	The Whispering Cloth: A Refugee's Story	P
The Story of Many These books offer an overview of the issue of immigration, with all of its political, economic, and personal implications.	Immigration: How Should It Be Controlled?	N
	The Middle of Everywhere: The World's Refugees Come to Our Town	N
	A Very Important Day	P
Focus on One Story From the perspective of one cultural group, what is the story that moves people from one place to another to find a new home?	The Bonesetter's Daughter (see page 117)	F
	Breaking Through: Sequel to The Circuit	N
	The Circuit: Stories from the Life of a Migrant Child	N
	Dancing with Dziadziu (see page 115)	P
	A Day's Work	P
	Dear Whiskers (see page 182)	F
	The Grapes of Wrath (see page 155)	F
	Harvest	N
	Journey of the Sparrows	F
	Lupita Mañana	F
	A Movie in My Pillow/Una película en mi almohada	P
	My Diary from Here to There/Mi diario de aquí hasta allá	P
	My Name Is Yoon	P
	A Place to Grow	P
	The Revealers (see page 101)	F
	The Skirt	F
	The Summer My Father Was Ten (see page 143)	P
	Tangled Threads: A Hmong Girl's Story	F
	Tomás and the Library Lady (see page 182)	P
	Too Young for Yiddish (see page 116)	P
	To Seek a Better World: The Haitian Minority in America ‡	N
	Xóchitl and the Flowers/Xóchitl, la Niña de las Flores (see page 143)	P
Fitting In Books in this category show the challenges experienced by immigrants—coping with a new culture that may clash with family traditions; experiencing loneliness; and struggling for acceptance.	América Is Her Name	P
	Any Small Goodness	F
	Behind the Mountains	F
	Born Confused	F
	Children of the River	F

continued ⟶

Topics	Books	Category
Fitting In continued	*The Gold-Threaded Dress*	F
	Happy Birthday Mr. Kang	P
	Miss Happiness and Miss Flower	F
	Shadow of the Dragon (see page 102)	F
	Stella: On the Edge of Popularity	F
	A Step from Heaven	F
	The Ugly Vegetables (see page 143)	P
	Uncle Rain Cloud	P

Page references are given for books that do not appear in the Immigrants Bookshelf but that can be found in the bookshelf lists of other chapters.
‡ These books are out of print but still worth finding.

Nonfiction: Immigrants

Breaking Through: Sequel to The Circuit by Francisco Jiménez (Houghton Mifflin, 2001). These stories continue the struggles of the Jiménez family through separation, poverty, prejudice, and hope. Each episode reveals the tenacity and fortitude brought by hard work and "the generous people who commit themselves to making a difference in the lives of children and young adults." The family members come alive in Francisco's recounting of his journey toward adulthood. 200pp., young adult

The Circuit: Stories from the Life of a Migrant Child by Francisco Jiménez (University of New Mexico Press, 1997). This autobiography starts with the author as a young boy living in a Mexican village in the late 1940s, who then travels with his family as they enter California illegally to find work. The family moves continuously from picking cotton to topping carrots, from one labor camp to the next, from one school to another. They remain close despite backbreaking work and poverty. These compelling short stories intertwine and paint an intricate picture of the life of migrant *campesinos*. 134pp., young adult

Harvest by George Ancona (Marshall Cavendish, 2001). Photographs, text, and interviews depict the lives of *campesinos*, migrant farm workers who come to the United States from Mexico in search of a better life. In the backbreaking fields, working twelve-hour days, six days a week, they labor under the hot sun, inhaling dust and pesticides. A vivid description of lives that are based on hard work and hope for a better future for their children. 48pp., grades 4–7

Immigration: How Should It Be Controlled? by Meish Goldish (Henry Holt, 1997). This informative survey of issues looks at immigration, primarily into the United States. Stories of people entering legally and illegally and coming as refugees are all included. 64pp., grades 4–6

The Middle of Everywhere: The World's Refugees Come to Our Town by Mary Pipher (Harcourt, 2002). Liem's dad had been a prisoner of war in Vietnam. Two teens lived in northern Bosnia during the war. Two sisters, Shireen and Meena, arrived with their family from Pakistan. From Sierra Leone, Kosovo, Macedonia, from across the globe, refugees arrive in Lincoln, Nebraska, their new home. Their stories enlighten us about the world and about how Americans are perceived by others. 390pp., grades 9 and up

> Most of the refugees who arrive in Lincoln [Nebraska] didn't choose to come to our city. They were handed a plane ticket by INS officials when they got off a plane in New York or Los Angeles. They may know nothing about the Midwest, and they may have been separated from their closest friends. . . . They may have bodies adapted to tropical climates or skills such as deep-sea fishing that they cannot use in the Midwest. They may be moving in to a town where no one speaks their language or even knows where their country is. Most newcomers arrive broke. . . . They have been warned not to trust strangers, yet everyone is a stranger.
>
> FROM *THE MIDDLE OF EVERYWHERE: THE WORLD'S REFUGEES COME TO OUR TOWN*

To Seek a Better World: The Haitian Minority in America by Brent Ashabranner (Cobblehill, 1997). Half a million people from Haiti live in the United States. Where do they live? What do they do? What are their contributions to America? What is happening to those who arrive illegally?

Learn about Haiti's troubled history and its effect on immigrants. Out of print but worth finding. 96pp., grades 5–10

Picture Books: *Immigrants*

América Is Her Name by Luis J. Rodríguez (Curbstone Press, 1997). América, a Mixteca Indian girl from Oaxaca, Mexico, suffers because of people who insult her background and her life of poverty in a Chicago ghetto. Her love of writing keeps her spirit alive and gives her family hope.

A Day's Work by Eve Bunting (Clarion, 1994). Young Francisco acts as translator for his *abuelo* (grandfather), who recently arrived from Mexico and wants to find a job. Eager to help, Francisco lies to an employer and says that his grandfather, a carpenter by trade, is an able gardener. After ruining the gardening project and learning of Francisco's dishonesty, Abuelo teaches his grandson about integrity and earns the respect of the employer.

Happy Birthday Mr. Kang by Susan L. Roth (National Geographic Society, 2001). Mr. Kang paints poems, reads the *New York Times*, and cares for his hua mei bird as his grandfather did in China. On Sunday, Mr. Kang carries his bird in a bamboo cage to Sara Delano Roosevelt Park in Manhattan, joining other Chinese immigrants with their birds. When his seven-year-old grandson questions whether "a free man should keep a caged bird," Mr. Kang opens the bamboo door. Will the hua mei fly away?

A Movie in My Pillow/Una película en mi almohada by Jorge Argueta (Children's Book Press, 2001). Young Jorge moves to San Francisco from his beloved El Salvador, bringing with him sights, sounds, and smells of his native rural home. He also carries the sorrow of war and of leaving loved ones. To this is added the confusion and joy of reuniting with family in his new urban home. Through Jorge Argueta's poetry and accompanying artwork by Elizabeth Gomez, each story comes alive. In English and Spanish.

> Here in the city
> there are wonders everywhere
> Here mangoes
> come in cans
> In El Salvador
> they grew on trees
> Here chickens come
> in plastic bags
> Over there
> they slept beside me
>
> FROM A MOVIE IN MY PILLOW/
> UNA PELÍCULA EN MI ALMOHADA

My Diary from Here to There/Mi diario de aquí hasta allá by Amada Irma Pérez (Children's Book Press, 2002). Amada writes in her diary, "I overheard Mamá and Papá whispering . . . about leaving our little house in Juárez, Mexico, where we've lived our whole lives, and moving to Los Angeles. . . . Am I the only one scared to leave? What if we're not allowed to speak Spanish? What if I can't learn English?" Young Amada learns she has the strength to survive the exciting and painful move. Through her family and her diary, Amada finds a new home. In English and Spanish, based on the author's experience.

My Name Is Yoon by Helen Recorvits (Farrar, Straus and Giroux, 2003). Yoon's name means "Shining Wisdom." When written in Korean, her name looks happy, but the shapes seem lonely when written in English. Yoon tries out different names—*cat, bird,* even *cupcake.* Only as she finds her place in her new country does she become Yoon again.

Oranges on Golden Mountain by Elizabeth Partridge (Puffin, 2001). During the California gold rush, many Chinese sailed across the Pacific to work and live. When hard times hit Jo Lee's family, he, too, is sent to stay with his uncle in this foreign land called "Gold Mountain." He saves every coin earned by hard work—fishing and growing orange trees—in hopes that his mother and young sister will soon join him.

A Place to Grow by Soyung Pak (Scholastic, 2002). A family, like a seed, needs a safe place to grow. A father uses a blooming garden to tell his daughter why he immigrated to a safe place to raise a family. The story has depth and can provoke discussion of the reasons that people immigrate.

Uncle Rain Cloud by Tony Johnston (Charlesbridge, 2001). Carlos delights in the stories his uncle Tio Tomás tells him of Mexico and the tongue-twister gods, *los dioses trabalenguas.* Sometimes, though, Tomás is stormy, having difficulty adjusting to his life in Los Angeles and his frustration with English. Carlos has his own struggles in third grade. As they forge a partnership, each teaching the other, change comes more easily.

A Very Important Day by Maggie Rugg Herold (Morrow, 1995). All over New York City, families from many countries prepare for the memorable day when they will become citizens. The Patel family from India share breakfast with their neighbors, the Stousos family close their Greek restaurant, and Yujin Zeng's friend gives him a special gift. The event in the courthouse brings all the families together.

The Whispering Cloth: A Refugee's Story by Pegi Deitz Shea (Boyds Mills Press, 1995). Little Mai watches the Hmong women in the refugee camp in Thailand as they stitch stories onto cloth. Traders buy the brightly colored *pa'ndau.* Mai's grandmother shows her how to stitch the border, but only Mai can find the story for her cloth. Mai's cloth whispers the story of her escape, life in the camp, and dreams for a bright future—her cloth is not for sale!

Fiction: *Immigrants*

Any Small Goodness by Tony Johnston (Scholastic, 2001). Moving from Mexico to Los Angeles with a little English in his pocket, eleven-year-old Arturo Rodriguez struggles to make sense of his world. As his father says, "In life there is *bueno* and *malo*. If you do not find enough good, you must yourself create it." Arturo's journey includes reclaiming his heritage, valuing his teachers and mentors, rescuing the family cat, and living where "what you love is always at risk." His "retaliation" is heartwarming. A glossary translates the Spanish vocabulary used. 128pp., grades 4–8

Behind the Mountains by Edwidge Danticat (Scholastic, 2002). Young Celiane records her life in Haiti in a "sweet little book" given to her by her teacher. We follow her through the fall of 2000, when bombing during the Haitian elections nearly kills her and her mother. Celiane writes of leaving her treasured home in the mountains to join her father in the harsh streets of Brooklyn. This first-person story is marked by love of family and proverbs from the Haitian tradition. 153pp., grades 6–10

Born Confused by Tanuk Desai Hidier (Scholastic, 2002). The art of balancing two cultures is carefully dissected by Dimple Lala, deep in the throes of adolescent self-discovery. While she has great respect for her immigrant parents, Dimple is challenged by how to integrate her language and culture from India with the New York hip scene. After meeting Karsh, a son of Indian friends, Dimple's idea of who is a "suitable" match unravels, and complications arise. 500pp., grades 9–12

Children of the River by Linda Crew (Dell, 1989). Sundara escaped the Khmer Rouge army in Cambodia with her aunt's family and lives in Oregon. Now in high school, she finds that her Cambodian traditions clash with being an American teenager. How will she live up to family expectations if she is drawn to Jonathan, the blonde high school football player? And what of the memories that continue to haunt her? 213pp., young adult

The Clay Marble by Minfong Ho (Farrar, Straus and Giroux, 1991). After fleeing their war-torn Cambodian village, twelve-year-old Dara and her family create makeshift dwellings in refugee camps on the Thai-Cambodian border. The terror is inescapable, as are calamities and tragedies they face in daily life. Separated from her loved ones, Dara discovers the courage and confidence to find her family. 163pp., grades 5–8

A Different Kind of Hero by Ann R. Blakeslee (Cavendish, 1997). Twelve-year-old Renny is not tough enough to please his Irish father, Lon. When Renny befriends and promises to protect a Chinese boy attending school—most unusual in the 1880s—his dad is infuriated. Lon and others are enraged by the presence of Chinese people in this Colorado mining town; they fear that more Chinese families will follow and work for less pay. Renny holds to his commitment to keep his friendship and demonstrates courage even his father comes to admire. 143pp., grades 4–7

Recommendation from the Field
by Carolina Goodman, Curriculum Coordinator
P.S. #1 Elementary School

Dragonwings by Lawrence Yep (HarperTrophy, 1975). *Dragonwings* is written from the perspective of a young boy named Moon Shadow, who, in the early 1900s, grows up on a farm in China with his mother and grandmother. At age seven, he journeys across the Pacific to meet his father. Windrider, along with many other Chinese men, had immigrated to the United States to earn money for their families in China. In the course of the novel, we learn about Chinese culture, the Wright brothers' first flight, the San Francisco earthquake, and the prejudice faced by the Chinese in their new country.

There are many curricular connections to be made: comparing Chinese picture writing with the English alphabet; reading and writing poetry; honoring ancestors; comparing lunar and solar calendars; learning the use of an abacus; finding out about the stereopticon, an early 3-D slide projector; learning about aeronautics; and studying earthquakes. Any of these can lead to service activities. For example, after studying earthquakes, students could make safety posters or preparedness brochures and assemble earthquake kits for low-income families. 336pp., grades 5–9

Esperanza Rising by Pan Muñoz Ryan (Scholastic, 2000). Esperanza lives in luxury on her father's ranch in Mexico and assumes that her lifestyle of fancy dresses and servants will last forever. A tragedy on the eve of her birthday in 1930 shatters all she knows. She and her mother escape to California to become migrant farm workers. Esperanza is ill prepared for hard labor and the financial struggles of the Great Depression, but her mother's illness causes her to rise above oppressive circumstances. 262pp., young adult

The Gold-Threaded Dress by Carolyn Marsden (Candlewick Press, 2002). In America, Oy's teacher renames her "Olivia." Having just arrived from Thailand, Oy is unaccustomed to many of the behaviors she encounters in school, from being left out of games to being teased. When the other children learn about her traditional silk dress, they taunt her by promising to be her friend if only she will bring it to school. Will Oy betray her family to fit in? 73pp., grades 3–5

Journey of the Sparrows by Fran Leeper Buss and Daisy Cubias (Lodestar, 1991). Maria, a sixteen-year-old Salvadoran refugee, cares for her siblings during their difficult journey to Chicago. Together, they start a new life with help from their community. 165pp., young adult

Lupita Mañana by Patricia Beatty (Beech Tree, 1981). When her father dies, thirteen-year-old Lupita and her brother leave their Mexican village and head to the United States to earn money. Her struggle is eased by the help of others. 186pp., young adult

Miss Happiness and Miss Flower by Rumer Godden (HarperTrophy, 1960). Eight-year-old Nona longs for her home in sunny India, but instead she lives in a cold English village with her aunt, uncle, and three very British cousins, including Belinda, who hates her. When two Japanese dolls arrive as gifts, Nona wants to build them a proper Japanese house. Over time, and with help from her cousins and new friends, Nona creates a home for the dolls and herself. Includes plans for a Japanese dollhouse. 199pp., grades 3–6

Recommendation from the Field
by Jill Addison-Jacobson, Youth Service California

The Skirt by Gary Soto (Delacorte Press, 1992). On Friday afternoon, Miata leaves her mother's skirt on the bus. She needs that skirt. Her troupe is to dance the *folklorico* on Sunday. If she is the only girl without a costume, her parents, Mexican immigrants living in central California, will "wear sunglasses out of embarrassment." Miata and her friend Ana work together to recover the skirt before her parents discover its absence. The effort leads them to break rules and cooperate with their nemesis—and may end up being unnecessary.

This charming tale raises challenging questions that can lead to service extensions for young readers, especially regarding immigration and conflict resolution. Through discussion, students can generate ideas.

Immigration: Miata and her family are relatively new to central California. Are there ways to help new students at school or new families in your neighborhood? What services in our community help immigrant families? Are there ways you can help these agencies? What services are there for children your age? What do you think is needed?

Conflict Resolution/Peer Counseling: Miata and Ana have trouble on the bus. Ana also seems uncomfortable with their adventure, but goes along. Miata makes choices that would be unacceptable to her parents in order to please her parents. Does your school have or need a conflict resolution program to facilitate problem solving and effective decision making? Where can students go for help with disputes? What activities could students develop to encourage peer interaction or provide ideas to improve parent-child communication? 74pp., grades 4–5

Stella: On the Edge of Popularity by Lauren Lee (Polychrome Publishing, 1994). Seeking acceptance in a seventh-grade clique, Stella follows the direction of the "popular girls" despite their biased attitudes. Her Korean grandmother nags Stella to follow her own cultural traditions, causing her embarrassment. Stella's confusion is intensified when her father is one of a group of men victimized in a racial incident. Will she learn a lesson from her old-fashioned grandmother: "Be who you are"? 178pp., grades 4–8

A Step from Heaven by An Na (Front Street, 2001). Moving from Korea to California is supposed to bring Young Park's family closer to heaven. Instead, learning English, financial hardships, and her father's rage and abuse cause painful difficulties. Each chapter adds to a poignant portrait of a young girl from age four to eighteen striving to turn her dream of finding heaven on earth into a reality. 156pp., young adult

Tangled Threads: A Hmong Girl's Story by Pegi Deitz Shea (Clarion, 2003). After spending ten years in a refugee camp in Thailand, Mai Yang travels to Rhode Island with her grandmother to join the only living relatives—aunts, uncles, and cousins who had gone five years before. The cultural differences are exacerbated by her rebellious cousins, while Mai uses the threads of the traditional *pa'ndau* cloth to help her stay connected to her Hmong heritage. 236pp., grades 4–8

Interviews with Authors:
The Story Behind the Story

In the following interview, we find out the "story behind the story" from Francisco Jiménez (*The Circuit*, *Breaking Through*, and *La Mariposa*). In *The Circuit* and then *Breaking Through*, Francisco Jiménez created vivid, honest descriptions of life as a migrant farm worker and hope found through love of family and education. He graciously agreed to an interview but needed to postpone it for a week, since he was going to Washington, D.C., to receive an award for these books. Fortuitously, I was also going to be in D.C., so I attended his award ceremony, where I met his brother and sister-in-law, both of whom are important figures in his stories.

Francisco Jiménez, author of
The Circuit, Breaking Through,
and La Mariposa

The inspiration for these books comes from the community of my childhood and my teachers. The migrant families that I grew up with worked and carried courage, tenacity, and hope amidst adversity. These values have been a constant to me in my personal and professional life.

It is important for children and young adults to appreciate farm labor work, the means by which fruits, vegetables, and other foods they have at every meal arrive at their table. We seldom think of the people responsible. I want readers to have a better insight into the hard life that farm workers experience.

Another reason for writing these books is to document the experiences of many migrant families—from the past and the present. For the most part, this sector of society has been ignored. This experience, as painful as it might be, is part of the American experience. To understand the essence of our country, we must learn about different groups that have contributed. Within the Mexican-American community, the farm worker is one of the groups that sustains our agricultural economy.

I wrote *The Circuit* and *Breaking Through* to pay tribute to my teachers. In *The Circuit*, Mr. Lema, my sixth-grade teacher, encouraged me to learn English though I was having difficulty caused by moving from place to place. He valued my Mexican cultural background. During a unit on California geography, he asked me to read aloud the names of the towns and cities on the map because, as he said, "I know you will pronounce them correctly." My native language was being valued. That one small effort on his part made a world of difference in developing my self-concept.

In *Breaking Through,* I mention my sophomore English teacher, Mrs. Bell, who had the class write short essays describing childhood experiences. I began to write of my migrant experiences. She then had me read *The Grapes of Wrath*. For the first time I was able to see the importance of literature in making a connection with one's life. I learned about the power of literature to move hearts and minds. Later, as I thought of writing my own books, I reflected on the importance of children seeing themselves reflected in literature. When growing up, there was hardly any material in school I could relate to regarding my cultural background. I hope to contribute literature that many children can relate to, especially those from similar backgrounds.

In writing the children's book *La Mariposa*, I retold the story "Inside Out" found in *The Circuit*. I realized that not knowing a word of English and the frustration and alienation I felt might be common to many children who enter our school system. The responses I receive from teachers and children indicate I was right.

If you compare the two versions, you will see one significant difference. In *La Mariposa*, the child is prohibited from speaking Spanish. When the teacher has Francisco open the jar and the butterfly emerges, Francisco says, "Hermosa," in a low voice. The teacher translates, saying, "How beautiful." In that moment I used my imagination so the teacher would value the child's language to "break through." Using the metaphor of the butterfly, both are transformed: The child becomes the teacher and the teacher becomes the student.

One of the greatest rewards is hearing how my books affected young people. Letters from teachers point out that after reading the memoirs, students who normally were quiet begin to open up and talk about their experiences. This is one of my intents.

A North Carolina teacher describes using *The Circuit* so students will learn about migrant workers and their difficulties. The teacher had the class connect with a community of migrant workers in their state. The class decided to bring in clothing, food, and books to give to people in the migrant camps. They also made a quilt with squares based on each of the stories in my book and contributed this to the migrant community. The teacher uses the book to help students become more compassionate toward other children who don't have the same socioeconomic background. These actions are meaningful. We must be aware that it is one thing to extend a hand and try to be helpful, to give to others in need. Another is to feel solidarity with them. There is a difference.

My use of Spanish in the books has helped students form a stronger community. Some teachers say that when English-only students come across the Spanish words, they ask the Spanish-speaking students to explain the meaning. This is usually an exchange that has not taken place before and gives value to having a second language.

Overall, these books demonstrate the value of obtaining an education, an important means by which we can improve our lives. Children or young adults are usually told that, "With education you will get a better job." This is true, but equally important is how education enriches our lives in other ways. We enjoy the things that surround us when we have learned about biology or music or art. We can appreciate all that life gives us and makes available to us.

I also want to impart the importance of hard work, respect, and faith in your own talents. Develop these with the help of parents, teachers, and community. People say, "You were able to break through without bilingual education." I respond by saying, "Any success attributed to me is really the success of many people who helped along the way. I made it thanks to many teachers and my family and I will do everything within my power to help others make it as well." In our society we have an overemphasis on individualism that can be a drawback to a commitment to helping others help themselves. In coming from a culture that emphasizes community over individualism, this is what I find more helpful in building a better society.

On a personal level, writing an autobiography is a catharsis; we learn more about ourselves. There is self-discovery as I reflect on my childhood from an adult point of view. I have gained a deeper sense of purpose for the things I do now as a teacher.

CHAPTER 12

LITERACY

> When I look back, I am so impressed again with the life-giving power of literature. If I were a young person today, trying to gain a sense of myself in the world, I would do that again by reading, just as I did when I was young.
>
> MAYA ANGELOU, AUTHOR

Reading unlocks the door to new worlds. It can provide knowledge and opportunity, excitement and adventure, humor and tragedy. For many, learning to read comes easily, but for others, and for many reasons, reading is a struggle fraught with frustration and embarrassment.

Service learning provides many opportunities to help people who are having difficulty with reading. Tutoring and mentoring activities are the most common; but young people can also help by making books, performing to create enthusiasm for reading, and helping with general language development when the reader's first language is not English.

Preparing for literacy service learning opportunities, especially for tutoring, involves understanding struggling readers' emotions and recognizing how hard reading can be for them. Works listed in the Literacy Bookshelf such as *Thank You, Mr. Falker* and *La Mariposa* can provide insight.

The bookshelf also includes works such as *Richard Wright and the Library Card* and *The Year of Miss Agnes* that are about people whose reading difficulties arose from social and cultural disadvantages rather than reading disabilities or language differences. These books remind us that the opportunity—as well as the ability—to read is closely linked to the rights to life, liberty, and the pursuit of happiness in modern society.

Preparation: Getting Ready for Service Learning Involving Literacy

The following activities can be used in the preparation stage to promote learning and skill development related to literacy. These activities can be used with different age ranges during preparation to help your students examine key issues through research, analyze community needs, and gain the knowledge they need to effectively contribute to the design of their service plan. Since literature is often an important part of preparation, you can find recommended titles on this theme in the Literacy Bookshelf later in this chapter.

Activity: Cross-Age Tutoring in Reading Skills. Elevate tutoring programs from a casual experience to high-level service learning. Here are some tips to prepare student tutors before they begin and to support continued preparation and skill review for ongoing tutoring relationships.

- Discuss the challenges some students have in learning. Ask students to think of their own challenges. This can be discussed in small groups or written in journals with feedback from the teacher.

- Use fiction and nonfiction from the Literacy Bookshelf to build knowledge and empathy.

- Invite a reading specialist to talk with the class to review the specific needs of the children who will be tutored.

- Ask students to bring in some of their favorite children's books from home or from the library. Discuss what makes a story engaging. Practice reading aloud to each other in pairs or small groups.

- Have tutors get to know their tutees by using the Personal Inventory form (see page 33). The tutors can pair up and practice using the form and the interview process. Discuss ways this can be helpful in getting to know the tutee and identifying high-interest books.

- In pairs or small groups, ask the tutors to design kinesthetic experiences that could help students learn the alphabet, punctuation, or any other writing skill. For example, making letters out of tactile materials or magnets, having students trace over letters with their fingers, or use their bodies to make the shapes of letters. (Simple stretches before a tutoring session can help by removing the "squirmy" factor in learning.)

- Ask students to consider all the reasons why listening skills are essential for the reader and learner. Have students think of ways to reinforce listening—for example, by reading a passage to the tutee and having the child summarize.

- Brainstorm with the tutors ways that quotes might be used with their tutees. Useful quotes are brief, convey an important message, and call for analyzing the meaning of a very short piece of writing or interpreting a metaphor. Some quotes relate directly to the tutoring experience: "No matter what accomplishments you make, somebody helps you" (Wilma Rudolph, athlete). Another metaphorical quote extols the value of reading: "A book is like a garden carried in the pocket" (Chinese proverb). Another removes the pressure of always "getting it right": "If you can't make a mistake, you can't make anything" (Marva N. Collins, educator). Find more quotes throughout this book.

- Since reflection is an important part of the service learning process, suggest that students use reflection with their tutees. For example, the tutor can have the tutee reflect on such ideas as "Today I learned . . ." and "What I want to remember is . . . " Responses can be written down by the tutor and reviewed in the next session to reinforce lessons and skills learned.

- Tutors can involve their tutees in *doing* service learning. Tutees can make alphabet books to demonstrate their skills, write stories or poetry, or create other compilations. Copies can be given to the class or library or exchanged with other students for continued skill development. Many other service learning possibilities exist that often can be linked back to the students' original inventory of interests, skills, and talents.

Activity: A Right or a Privilege? Students generally attend school without considering this question: Is education a right or a privilege? Students can develop research questions to investigate both the history of education and the current struggles to learn for people in many parts of the world. What historical events have made education accessible to the masses? Slavery, women's rights, and child labor laws are part of this story. Where in the world are students now deprived of education because of war, famine, forced child labor, or other factors? In Malawi, for example, as well as other African nations, students can only attend classes if they can afford classroom supplies. In times of war schools close and in refugee camps there may be no schools.

The next step is using this new knowledge and awareness to determine ways to take action. Immigrants locally may need support in order to take full advantage of available opportunities. For example, students could provide free child care during language classes. Advocacy for children in other nations can be accomplished through international organizations such as Oxfam (*www.oxfamamerica.org*), Amnesty International Kids (*www.amnestyusa.org/aikids*), and Peace Corps Kids World (*www.peacecorps.gov/kids*). Collections of school supplies or books may also help.

Find Out More About Literacy

To learn more about these issues and to get ideas for service and action, visit these Web sites and organizations online:

www.nationalservice.org The National Service Resource Center, a service of the Corporation for National Service, offers information and many publications, including "Reading Helpers" and "Tutoring Manuals."

www.ilo.org The International Labour Organization has a virtual classroom on child labor—with resources for

continued ——→

elementary and high school students and teachers; includes information on what kids are doing to end child labor and enable all kids to attend schools.

www.iamfoundation.org Million Books for Kids, a project of the I AM Foundation, encourages kids and adults to provide books for children who have none in their homes. Click on "Million Books for Kids Campaign" for more information.

Making Connections Across the Curriculum

Some service learning activities naturally lend themselves to interdisciplinary work and making connections across the curriculum. These connections strengthen and broaden student learning, helping them meet academic standards. More than likely, you'll be looking for these connections and ways to encourage them well before the students ever start working on service learning activities. As with the entire service learning process, it helps to remain flexible, because some connections can be spontaneously generated by the questions raised throughout and by the needs of the project. To help you think about cross-curricular connections and where you can look for them, the Curricular Web for this chapter (page 176) gives examples of many different ways this theme can be used in different academic areas. (The service learning scenarios in the next section of the chapter also demonstrate various ways this theme can be used across the curriculum.)

Service Learning Scenarios: Ideas for Action

Ready to take action? What follows are projects that have been successfully carried out by elementary, middle, or high school students. Most of these scenarios and examples explicitly include some aspects of preparation, action, reflection, and demonstration. These scenarios can be a rich source of project, resource, and curriculum ideas for you to draw upon. While the grade levels are given as a reference, most project ideas can be adapted to suit younger or older students, and many are suitable for cross-age partnerships.

Everything You Need to Know About Kindergarten: Kindergarten. Think of the big difference between kindergartners on their very first day of school and on the last day of the school year. Kindergarten teachers in Los Angeles have harnessed that growth and transformation into a creative and valued service learning activity. In early spring, the soon-to-be first graders identify what they have learned: how to sit in a circle, where to put their lunches, how to take care of library books, where to recycle paper, and so on. They use their knowledge to produce a booklet, "All About Kindergarten." Students work individually or in pairs to create one page of the book on a selected theme. After drawing illustrations, the students dictate the words to an adult. All work is done in black ink for easy duplication. As parents register their children for the next year's kindergarten, the family receives a copy of "All About Kindergarten." On the first day of school, one parent reported, "My daughter slept with her kindergarten book all summer, it was her security for the transition."

Collections: Grade 1 (with Grade-6 Helpers). First graders focus on literacy as they sponsor an all-school new and "gently used" book drive to support libraries. Counting skills come in to play, as well as writing, since each student writes a book review of one book he or she is donating. With the help of middle school students, the children sort the books into groups according to reading level. The books are personally delivered by the children.

Original Books for the Community: Grades 1–5. So many original books are written by students, but where do they go? Usually home, and that's it. Students at a school in Washington state make two copies of each book (or more if the book is a class collaboration), so one copy can be contributed to a place that needs more books: a library, children's center, after-school program, homeless shelter, hospital, emergency room, or free health clinic. Students learn about the community as they select a place for their books to go and often deliver the books themselves and read them aloud to younger children. Some children have added multiple languages to produce bi- and even tri-lingual books that have a broader community reach.

Books on Tape: Grade 2. Books on tape are welcome in many places. Second graders in a Chicago suburb

Literacy Across the Curriculum

English/Language Arts

- Discuss: What is your favorite book and why?
- Study stories and practice storytelling techniques, including those from other cultures
- Prepare annotated bibliographies of recommended books for peers

Social Studies/History

- Create and "attend" a classroom environment from the past, e.g., the early 1900s
- Study the Indian Schools established in 1879 by the federal government and its impact on tribal culture then and now
- Learn about pending current legislation that would impact your school and education

Languages

- Learn about education in the countries of the language being studied, and compare to your own
- Create lessons to familiarize younger children with this language and culture
- Identify idioms and slang expressions that would be hard to translate into the language being studied, and find similar kinds of expressions in the language being studied

Theater, Music, & Visual Arts

- Write skits that promote reading as an adventure
- Find and learn contemporary or popular songs that promote learning and education
- Find quotes in books, online, or elsewhere about the wonders of books and reading, then create posters

Literacy

Math

- Research literacy rates for your state and compare with national statistics
- Prepare "math in a box" kits of basic math concepts with directions and games
- Discuss: What does it mean to be "math literate?" How has this changed with calculators and computers?

Physical Education

- Discuss: How does physical activity help children learn?
- Design an activity to teach the alphabet by having students forms the letters with their bodies either individually on in groups
- Create an annotated list of books about sports or athletes to share with younger children

Computer

- Access the Internet for illiteracy data and local resources and programs
- Make a list of computer terms and meanings in a picture book format
- Research places in the community that need computers for kids, like shelters or community centers, and seek donations from businesses

Science

- Study about learning differences, variations of learning styles, and learning disabilities
- Prepare science lessons for young children that incorporate various learning styles
- Help younger students record science experiments

discovered this fact after taping a choral reading for the Junior Blind organization. Next, they made tapes to donate to emergency waiting rooms, hospitals, and a ward for premature infants, who seemed to do better when listening to the lovely voices of children. Recording original stories also gave students an incentive to improve their writing skills.

Idioms in Pairs: Grade 2. Two schools, two different socioeconomic groups, two languages, and grade-two children: a perfect partnership. Students in West Hollywood, California, met for cultural, recreational, and academic interaction that led to a service learning activity. The project began when one of the schools hosted a Russian storytelling troupe. A second-grade class invited the predominantly Russian-born second-grade students from a nearby school to participate. After social interaction (and lunch), teachers from both schools led activities on idioms, which are very difficult for students learning English as a second language to grasp. Working in pairs, students took an idiom, such as "Don't let the cat out of the bag," and discussed its interpretation and meaning. The students also drew two pictures to illustrate; for example, for "Don't let the cat out of the bag," one picture showed a cat peeking out of a sack, and one showed a child saying "Shh!" The pictures were compiled into a workbook for use in these and other neighboring schools.

Turn Off the TV! Grades 3–5. In a multiage classroom that included grades three through five, the children used a chart to keep track of how much television they each watched in one week's time. For two TV programs, they counted any violent images they saw during the shows or commercials. The next week they recorded how much time they played or read books outside of school. A huge class chart consolidated the data and students compared the amounts. Using information from the TV-Turnoff Network (*www.tvturnoff.org*), the teacher presented information about how violent images impact children and about the "couch potato" syndrome—how inactivity effects children's weight and health. Students decided to educate the rest of the school. They made presentations to other classrooms along with posters and signs announcing "Turn Off the TV Week." Many students in the school pledged to exchange television for books for an entire week, culminating in a read

aloud and book exchange project to keep the pages turning, and the television turned off. For more on television versus literature, read *Aunt Chip and the Great Triple Creek Dam Affair* (see page 181).

> I must say that I find television very educational.
> The minute somebody turns it on,
> I go to the library and read a book.
> GROUCHO MARX, ACTOR

Especially for New Parents: Grade 4. An elementary teacher in Maine asked her students, "Do you enjoy having your parent or a teacher read you a story?" The response was an overwhelming "Yes!" Students eagerly described what they liked about story times. Later, teachers discussed in a staff meeting the finding that parents in their community didn't spend much time reading to their children. They decided to invite students to address this issue. Children began gift-wrapping original books and writing letters explaining "why it's important to read to your child—and why I like someone to read to me." With assistance from a local community organization, the wrapped books were donated to the local county hospital and given to each new parent as a "welcome baby" gift.

Tutor Buddies Build Community: Grade 4. Entering fourth grade brings a special privilege at one elementary school in Mount Vernon, Washington. Every fourth grader, regardless of skill level, is partnered with a younger student. These "tutor buddies" meet four times a week, twenty minutes each time, and work on the younger children's reading skills. On the fifth day of the week, the tutors continue their training and work on development of their own skills. The school atmosphere has been transformed by these relationships. Every student is valued as having something to offer. Older children have greater empathy for the role of teacher. Younger children look up to their mentors as role models. Service learning is woven into the fabric of this school.

Math Support: Grade 6. Literacy extends to math as well. In one school, sixth graders willingly gave up their usual lunchtime activities to eat with and then tutor their peers in math. The tutors took extra time to learn how to break down a skill into manageable steps and to teach it effectively. Lunch buddy math tutoring became a much sought-after program.

Kids for Computer Literacy: Grades 6–8. The rural community of Kansas, Oklahoma, had no public library to provide access to computers, and many families did not have computers at home. What could middle school kids do to help? They decided to open their school's computer lab on Tuesday evenings and Saturday mornings for instruction and assistance. To prepare, the students practiced creating and leading  computer lessons, and learned how to use the résumé templates on the computer. After surveying parents and community members to find out their interests, they also located Web sites that would provide information the community was interested in.

Giving a Head Start with Reading: Grades 6–8. Middle school students in the rural community of London, Kentucky, wanted to write books. They immersed themselves in children's literature, exploring the nuances and writing styles of their favorite books. In further preparation, a communication specialist visited the students and talked about writing short stories. Students took their creative ideas and applied them for a specific audience—preschool children. They used computers and other forms of technology to organize and produce their books. Finally, children from a local Head Start program visited the middle school library, and met the "big kids," who read to them and presented them with a classroom full of original picture books.

Knowing the Triggers: Grades 7 and 8. Confidence, stress reduction, and homework completion are interwoven topics covered by middle school students in Hialeah, Florida. First semester, seventh and eighth graders study stress reduction methods and anger management to overcome tension and anger that can interfere with learning. After learning the triggers for emotional conflict, they apply their knowledge to meet a community need. School counselors had identified third graders as the age where learning good homework habits was most essential in the transition to the upper elementary grades. The middle school students reinforce their own learning by discussing these issues with the counselors, and then writing lessons for mentoring third graders at a nearby elementary school on successful homework strategies. Second semester, the tutoring continues every week.

A Broad Approach: Grades K–8. An independent school in Minnesota takes a broad approach to promote literacy and service learning. All students read books about service to inspire discussions, ideas, and class projects. For example, some fifth-grade students are tutoring beginning readers once a month at a nearby public school while others are sharing book selections with elder friends at a residential facility. At the middle school, students select and read to second graders poetry that can stimulate conversations about making wise choices. Story analysis, discussion and reflection are well-integrated into this school-wide effort.

Dependable Tutors: Grades 9–11. As part of a high school community service class, students went to a local elementary school for one period daily as tutors for younger students. The high school students had been taught tutoring techniques by a local community college instructor to prepare for the experience. At the end of the semester, they produced a unique reflection piece to present to others—teachers, parents, community members, and peers. Teachers at the elementary school provided regular feedback on the high school students' performance, and skill development was ongoing. Students also learned about dependability. One student wrote: "When I didn't show up on Tuesday, I thought it wouldn't be a big deal. On Thursday, I came in as if everything was normal, and Sara, a little girl I always read to, wouldn't talk to me. Finally, after about twenty minutes, she climbed on my lap with tears in her eyes. 'Where were you? I missed you!' I was speechless. I didn't know she was counting on me."

Romeo, Romeo! Grade 10. In love with Shakespeare? Tenth-grade English students in Alabama discovered an unexpected passion for the great bard, so they decided to share their excitement with younger students. The tenth graders used several strategies. One group performed short versions of the play *A Midsummer Night's Dream* in modern language. Another group made "Shakespeare's Tales" story books. The upper elementary students were delighted with their introduction to Shakespeare.

A Hero's Journey: Grades 11 and 12. For a British literature course, students in South Carolina went on their own "hero's journey" while reading *Beowulf*. Each student found a way to be heroic in the community by providing a service to an individual or organization. The students documented their experiences in language comparable to that used in the epic poem. The culmination of the semester was a video presentation made by several students set to music. Recipients of the service were invited to the presentation and learned how much the students had gained from the experience.

> When I got [my] library card,
> that was when my life began.
>
> RITA MAE BROWN, AUTHOR

The Literacy Bookshelf

The ability to read is one part of literacy, and some of the books on the Literacy Bookshelf deal with issues related to this ability. Other stories tell of people yearning for an education, and others describe appreciation of books. To help you find books relevant to your particular projects, the book chart classifies the titles into several topic areas: seeking an education, learning to read, and appreciation of books and reading.

In general, the bookshelf features:

- An annotated bibliography arranged and alphabetized by title according to the general categories of nonfiction (N), picture books (P), and fiction (F). For nonfiction and fiction, length and recommended grade levels are included. The entries in the picture book category do not include suggested grade levels, since they can be successfully used with all ages.

- A chart organized by topic and category to help you find books relevant to particular projects.

- Recommendations from service learning colleagues and experts that include a book summary and ideas for service learning connections. (The number of recommended books varies in each bookshelf.)

Literacy Bookshelf Topics

Topics	Books	Category
Seeking an Education When social inequities exist, education is usually withheld from some part of the population. These books contain stories of people's struggles simply to be in a place where they can learn, to get to a school, to create a school to be in.	*Breaking Through* (see page 167)	N
	A Bus of Our Own *	P
	The Circuit (see page 167)	N
	Indian School: Teaching the White Man's Way	N
	A Life Like Mine: How Children Live Around the World (see page 196)	N
	Linda Brown, You Are Not Alone: The Brown v. Board of Education Decision (see page 196)	N
	The Lost Boys of Natinga: A School for Sudan's Young Refugees (see page 154)	N
	We Need to Go to School: Voices of the Rugmark Children (see page 197)	N

continued ⟶

Topics	Books	Category
Seeking an Education continued	Richard Wright and the Library Card	P
	A School for Pompey Walker	F
	The Strength of Saints *	F
	The Year of Miss Agnes	F
Learning to Read Learning to read is not a "one size fits all" proposition. It can be a challenging process for some young people and adults. Language barriers, embarrassment, and lack of resources can be stumbling blocks; community support can make all the difference.	All Joseph Wanted	F
	Dear Whiskers *	F
	The Hard Times Jar	P
	Illiteracy	N
	Just Call Me Stupid	F
	Just Juice	F
	La Mariposa	P
	Learning Disabilities	N
	Once Upon a Time	P
	Prairie School	F
	Read for Me, Mama	P
	Sahara Special	F
	Thank You, Mr. Falker	P
	The Wednesday Surprise *	P
Appreciation of Books and Reading Some people go to great lengths to have books in hand. Appreciation, joy, pleasure, excitement—all to be found within the covers of books and in the libraries where books live.	Across a Dark and Wild Sea	P
	Aunt Chip and the Great Triple Creek Dam Affair	P
	The Bookstore Mouse	F
	Fahrenheit 451	F
	Goin' Someplace Special	P
	The Library Card	F
	A Series of Unfortunate Events: The Bad Beginning	F
	Stella Louella's Runaway Book	P
	Tomás and the Library Lady	P
	Too Young for Yiddish (see page 116)	P

Page references are given for books that do not appear in the Literacy Bookshelf but that can be found in the bookshelf lists of other chapters.
* These books include examples of young people in service-providing roles.

Nonfiction: Literacy

Illiteracy by Sean M. Grady (Lucent Books, 1994). "Literacy is a skill, a technique of using patterns of letters to preserve ideas." Literacy is highly valued in most societies, but the challenge of learning to read can seem almost insurmountable. Illiteracy in the United States and other nations is profiled in this comprehensive overview, which also discusses how literacy extends beyond "reading and writing." A valuable resource for literacy and tutoring programs. 96pp., grades 6–12

Indian School: Teaching the White Man's Way by Michael L. Cooper (Clarion, 1999). In 1879, eighty-four Sioux boys and girls were forced to leave their tribal homes to attend the Carlisle Indian School. This was the first institution opened by the federal government for the education of Native American children, intending to "civilize" the Indian children and teach them the "white man's way." While a few children succeeded in this setting, for the majority it was an isolating and painful experience in acculturation. 103pp., grades 5–10

Learning Disabilities by Christina M. Girod (Lucent Books, 2001). This book provides a substantial overview of learning disabilities that is useful for a young person engaged in tutoring or other service learning activities with youth or adults with learning disabilities. The many challenges faced both by the struggling reader and by educators are noted. Topics include the history and types of learning disabilities, coping with learning disabilities, and current controversies. 96pp., young adult

Picture Books: *Literacy*

Across a Dark and Wild Sea by Don Brown (Millbrook Press, 2002). Columcille lived in a remote part of Ireland in the year 521. As this mixture of legend and history begins to unfold, Columcille develops a love for writing. (Did he really eat a cake filled with alphabet letters?) As a monk and scribe, his fervor grows until he is caught in a dispute over a manuscript he has copied. The resulting battle and loss of life cause him to move abroad. In Scotland, Columcille leaves a legacy that illuminates a corner of the Dark Ages. Includes the uncial alphabet of his time.

Aunt Chip and the Great Triple Creek Dam Affair by Patricia Polacco (Philomel, 1996). In Triple Creek, everyone watches television except Eli's Aunt Chip, who went to bed fifty years ago to protest the library being replaced by a television tower. Yearning for stories, Eli tells his aunt, "Teach me to read!" Soon all the children want to learn to read fables, fairy tales, adventures, and more. In this contemporary fantasy, children restore reading and a librarian to their town.

A Bus of Our Own by Freddi Williams Evans (Albert Whitman, 2001). Mabel Jean wants to attend school, a five-mile walk from home. She tries to find a way for the black children to have a school bus like the white children have. With support from family and friends, she succeeds. Based on real events in 1949.

> "Last week, Lil' Mable Jean asked if I could get a school bus," Cousin Smith told her parents. "I've been figuring on it and decided to buy a bus if enough parents support me. They will have to pay for the children to ride. Now I know we're already paying taxes, and rightly, we should have a bus. It looks like we have to pay twice for our children to get a good learning."
>
> FROM A BUS OF OUR OWN

Goin' Someplace Special by Patricia McKissack (Simon & Schuster, 2001). Tricia Ann is on her way to someplace special in the segregated Nashville, Tennessee, of the 1950s. After riding in the "colored section" of the bus, nearly sitting on a "for whites only" park bench, and suffering hurtful words of discrimination, she arrives at the public library where the sign says, "All Are Welcome."

The Hard Times Jar by Ethel Footman Smothers (Farrar, Straus and Giroux, 2003). Although young Emma Turner loves books, she has none at home. The money earned by her family of migrant workers goes strictly for necessities. So Emma works and saves her money until her plans are interrupted: she must attend school! There she finds books, but these cannot be taken home. Will Emma be able to follow the rules?

La Mariposa by Francisco Jiménez (Houghton Mifflin, 1998). Francisco sits in first grade without understanding a word in this English-only school. His desire to learn begins to center on the caterpillar in the jar next to his desk: How does it turn into a butterfly? How long will it take? Through determination and imagination, Francisco overcomes his confusion and isolation and teaches others about tolerance and the love of learning.

Once Upon a Time by Niki Daly (Farrar, Straus and Giroux, 2003). Sarie struggles to read aloud in her South African school. Letters run together and "trip on her tongue," bringing giggles from her classmates. Auntie Anna, Sarie's elder friend, reads Cinderella over and over to the young girl, unlocking the mystery of reading during imaginary trips in a wheel-less car, until the words "pour out [of Sarie] as clear as spring water."

Read for Me, Mama by Vashanti Rahaman (Boyds Mills Press, 1997). Young Joseph loves reading. Each Thursday, he takes home two books from school, one to read himself and "one harder book someone else can read to you." While Mama is "the best storyteller in the world," she asks neighbors to read the "hard books" to Joseph. One evening, Mama admits to Joseph and then to her community, "I have to learn to read." With community support and Joseph's admiration, Mama does learn.

Richard Wright and the Library Card by William Miller (Lee & Low, 1997). Based on a scene from Richard Wright's autobiography, this story tells how seventeen-year-old African American Richard craves books he cannot take from the library because of his race. When a white man at work loans him a library card, Richard can finally read the books he has dreamed about for so long.

Stella Louella's Runaway Book by Lisa Campbell Ernst (Simon & Schuster, 1998). Oh no! Stella cannot find her library book, and it is due at five o'clock today! In her search, she finds that her book has been read and enjoyed by everyone: her brother, the postal carrier, Officer Tim,

Sal who mends chairs, and more. Each person has a different favorite part of the story. Soon the entire town is following Stella to the library to talk to the librarian. A surprising and pleasing ending.

Thank You, Mr. Falker by Patricia Polacco (Philomel, 1998). At first, Trisha loves school, but her difficulty reading makes her feel stupid. Finally, in fifth grade, a teacher helps her overcome her problem. The rest of her odyssey is a learning adventure, and she grows up to write books for children. This semi-autobiographical tale inspires learners, teachers, and tutors!

> But at the new school it was the same. When she tried to read, she stumbled over words: "the cah, cah. . . cat . . . rrrr, rrr. . . . ran." She was reading like a baby in the third grade!
>
> And when her teacher read along with them, and called on Trisha for an answer, she gave the wrong answer every time.
>
> "Hey dummy!" A boy called out to her on the playground, "How come you are so dumb?"
>
> FROM THANK YOU, MR. FALKER

Tomás and the Library Lady by Pat Mora (Knopf, 1997). Tomás and his family of migrant workers gather under a tree to hear grandfather's stories. "There are many more in the library," Grande Papa tells young Tomás. Soon Tomás becomes an avid reader and teller of wondrous stories. Based on the real-life story of Tomás Rivera, who became chancellor of the University of California, Riverside.

The Wednesday Surprise by Eve Bunting (Clarion, 1989). A child and her grandmother prepare a special birthday gift, one that involves a commitment to each other and to the joy of being able to read. In this book, the child is the tutor!

Fiction: Literacy

All Joseph Wanted by Ruth Yaffe Radin (Macmillan, 1991). More than anything, Joseph wants his mother to be able to read. Finally, Joseph reaches for help. 80pp., grades 3–5

The Bookstore Mouse by Peggy Christian (Harcourt, 1995). He lives in a bookstore behind a wall of words. He snacks on letters from cookbooks. He throws sharp words at his enemy. And then one day, this bookstore mouse literally lands right inside one of the books, headed for a great adventure with an unprepared knight as they set out to confront a dragon and free the storytellers. 134pp., grades 4–7

Dear Whiskers by Ann Whitehead Nagda (Holiday House, 2000). During a cross-age school project, fourth-grader Jenny is discouraged because her second-grade pen pal Sameera, a new student from Saudi Arabia, does not speak English. Despite her initial frustrations, Jenny sees the challenges Sameera faces and becomes determined to break the silence. 76pp., grades 2–4

Recommendation from the Field
by Christopher Galyean, high school student

Fahrenheit 451 by Ray Bradbury (Simon & Schuster, 1953/1993). Guy Montag was a fireman—not a fireman who put out fires but one who started them. Guy and the other firemen were paid to burn books. He never questioned this occupation until one day he met Clarisse, a girl who changed his outlook. The questioning attitude he adopted wasn't favored by his peers, however. One day he saved a book from the fires, hoping to find answers within the book. Instead, he was taken on a journey of self-discovery.

Students can debate whether books are necessary to preserve information now that we have the technology to store everything electronically. Issues of social and political control are also prevalent in the novel, and students can discuss the fairness and effectiveness of the political systems of the world. Finally, they can decide for themselves what would happen if there were no more challenges in the world.

In terms of service, students can select their favorite books from middle or elementary school. They can then arrange for classroom visits to discuss the value of reading in general and these books specifically with the appropriate students. In honor of *Fahrenheit 451*, students could memorize a passage and create a performance piece to encourage appreciation of literature. 190pp., young adult

Just Call Me Stupid by Tom Birdseye (Puffin, 1993). When fifth-grader Patrick tries to read, he remembers his dad calling him stupid, and he freezes. Even his time in the resource room makes him feel as if he is suffocating. Only drawing and medieval fantasies nurture his creative talents. When Celina moves next door, Patrick, for the first time, has a reason to read. 181pp., grades 4–7

Just Juice by Karen Hesse (Scholastic, 1998). Fourth-grader Juice just does not like school. Reading and math are too hard, and she would rather be with her unemployed Pa in his makeshift metal shop. When the family has one last chance to pay back taxes or lose their home, Juice realizes that knowing how to read is more than important—it will help them survive. 138pp., grades 3–6

Recommendation from the Field
by Nan Peterson, The Blake School

The Library Card by Jerry Spinelli (Scholastic, 1996). Join the four teenagers featured in this action-packed short story collection of serious, humorous, and exciting adolescent adventures. All the teens are profoundly changed by discoveries found in library books. These adventures feature many themes—literacy, love of learning, poverty, homelessness, parent loss, teenage crime, media addiction, and friendship. Many of the themes can lead to worthwhile activities. Students can investigate issues of hunger and homelessness and the income needed to meet basic needs and pay for transportation, medical costs, and child care. (The book *Nickle and Dimed: On (Not) Getting By in America* can add to this research.) They can study the impact of media on children or teens and promote a "Trade Your TV for a Book" week.

Since *The Library Card* explores, among its themes, the riches found within books, students can consider these questions and add their own: Why do some people not learn to read? Why do some people not enjoy reading? What is the value of reading? What is the value of education? This can lead to a "pay it forward" approach (as described in the book *Pay It Forward* on the Social Change Bookshelf) to instill the love of reading in others. Students can encourage a younger student by reading with the younger child and coauthoring a book that meets that child's particular need. In collaboration with a

---

program for English as a second language, students can read with recent immigrants on a regular basis. Also, many shelters, hospitals, and community centers may appreciate the donation of used books. 148pp., grades 5–8

Prairie School by Avi (Harper, 2001). In 1880, Noah likes working the family farm and roaming the Colorado prairie. He certainly doesn't want to learn to read from his Aunt Dora. What use does he have for reading? Nine-year-old Noah doesn't expect his feisty aunt to have him push her wheelchair so she can explore the prairie and reveal the wealth of book knowledge available for a young boy who can "learn to read and you'll read the prairie." 48pp., grades 2–4

Sahara Special by Esmé Raji Codell (Hyperion, 2003). Sahara intends to be a writer. At home she is a prolific reader, yet at school her hand never seems to raise to answer a question, and doing homework? Never! Is Sahara's obstinacy a reaction to her father leaving, or does she have a learning problem? When Sahara repeats fifth grade, her new teacher, Miss Pointy, uses unusual methods and quiet support to unlock the joy of learning. 175pp., grades 4–7

A School for Pompey Walker by Michael J. Rosen (Harcourt Brace, 1995). "Who would have thought anybody'd applaud a man who spent much of his life a slave, and so much more of it a criminal—at least to some eyes." Pompey Walker stands before children at a school named in his honor, which was on the site of the Sweet Freedom School he had established earlier for black children. Pompey tells of brutalities of slave life and his friendship with Jeremiah Walker, a white abolitionist. Pompey and Jeremiah devised a dangerous plan to gain money from slave owners needed to build the school. As described in the author's note, the incidents are based on recollections of elder freed slaves. 42pp., grades 4–6

You are so blessed, each and every one of you.
Learning and books are yours every day.
First book my eyes knew what to do with,
I was twenty-two years of age.
FROM *A SCHOOL FOR POMPEY WALKER*

Recommendation from the Field

*by Terry Pickeral, Executive Director,
National Center for Learning and Citizenship*

A Series of Unfortunate Events: The Bad Beginning by Lemony Snicket (HarperCollins, 1999). This is the first in a series about three recently orphaned siblings: Violet, Klaus, and Sunny Baudelaire. The book introduces the children and their recent bad luck: their house burned down and their parents perished. The series follows the children as they are introduced to distant relatives, who become responsible for them. Violet is an inventor and Klaus, a reader. Sunny uses her teeth and creates her own language. As the children move from relative to relative, they encounter the strangest streak of bad luck and unfortunate events.

Students put themselves in the place of the Baudelaire orphans and identify how they would handle adversity. In addition, they can identify individuals they consider family and consider why. With regard to service learning activities, students can discuss "worst-case" scenarios and develop problem-solving skills by creating contingency plans. Also, Klaus is always examining language and the meanings of words. Students could create books for younger children to creatively teach about language, words, and meaning. 176pp., grades 4–7

The Strength of Saints by Alexandria LaFaye (Simon & Schuster, 2002). Harper, Louisiana, 1936. Fourteen-year-old Nissa Bergen has a mind and will of her own. As the librarian in a small town with narrow ideas about integration, she has created "separate-but-equal" libraries. Still, she is plagued with a conscience that wants to unite the community. Doing what is right may not be easy, but Nissa's independent spirit and convictions triumph. This third book about Nissa easily stands on its own. 183pp., grades 6–10

The Year of Miss Agnes by Kirkpatrick Hill (Aladdin, 2000). A new teacher arrives in a remote Alaskan town. Frederika, "Fred" for short, age ten, doubts that Miss Agnes will last in this community that smells of fish. But the one-room schoolhouse comes alive as never before with the creative spirit of a dynamic teacher, who reaches out and values every child, including Bokko, Fred's twelve-year-old deaf sister. 113pp., grades 4–8

> Miss Agnes used the big map to teach us geography. She pointed out the continents with a yardstick, and then she showed us how to find Alaska every time.... Miss Agnes said she was going to teach us every one of the countries on the big map, so we'd know everything about the world. There were places where it was hot all the time and where they had never seen snow.... I could hardly wait.
>
> FROM *THE YEAR OF MISS AGNES*

Interviews with Authors: The Story Behind the Story

In the following interview, we find out the "story behind the story" from Alexandria LaFaye (*The Strength of Saints*). The strong character of Nissa caused me to call this author. I wanted to know more about Nissa and found out from her that this book is the third in a series. During the interview, I learned about the author's motivation and her passion for writing. Afterward, I satisfied my desire for more of Nissa by reading *The Year of the Sawdust Man* and *Nissa's Place*.

Alexandria LaFaye, author of The Strength of Saints

In *The Year of the Sawdust Man*, we first meet Nissa and follow the story of her mother leaving the family. In the second book, *Nissa's Place*, Nissa has to step out of her mother's shadow to have a life of her own. *The Strength of Saints* is the third book about Nissa. In it, she must discover if she has the strength to do the right thing in a racially divided town.

In my writing process, I don't plan the book ahead of time. I see where the character leads me.

I began writing novels at age twelve. Back then, I started writing with a definite idea of what I wanted people to learn as a result of the book. The books were more like infomercials than literature! One of my college professors said, "You have to get rid of your agenda. You must let the message come out of the story."

Since I wanted to be an actor and a writer, my approach to writing evolved to combine both: I become the characters. I have a strong affinity to my characters. When I think of the story, it all comes out of the character I am following. As a result, I am as surprised as Nissa when she realizes she could not build just one library in this town. She did the best she could in the situation.

While the first two novels come out of Nissa's development as a person and her relationship with her family, *The Strength of Saints* is as much about the society she lives in as it is about her. This was a different experience for me. Nissa's life, before this point, was so insular. She had frequently taken on the role of caretaker for her family. Now she has taken on the role of caretaker for her community. Nissa thinks the two libraries will be appreciated, but there are diverse opinions, especially within the African-American community. There is not one opinion. This, like real life, evolves through story.

One component of creating a character that is fascinating to me as a writer is how multifaceted each character is. The knowledge Nissa gains by creating the library is complex: She learns about herself, her family, her town, and ultimately her country.

In addition to writing, I teach children's literature at the university level. I challenge my students to stop looking at books as teaching tools. A book can't teach a person anything. Reading is a reciprocal process, a relationship between what the book and the teacher have to offer and what the child brings and takes away. What the child takes away will be different for each child and for each time they read the book. A reader once complimented one of my novels, saying, "I didn't realize the book was so funny until I read it a second time." This shows the multilayered nature of a book. The second time, the book is new, yet familiar.

I hope readers carry new things away when they look at or think about any book I've written. I love watching a movie a second time and reading a book a second time. I am glad my books have complexities to review again and again. I hope, too, that reading about Nissa suggests a lot of questions to children about navigating their way in a family, about standing up for what they believe is the right thing to do, and about differences in perspective. Nissa figures out the danger of making assumptions about what is best for others. She begins to look at situations from different angles. Through this act, she gains more respect and understanding for people.

CHAPTER 13

SOCIAL CHANGE: ISSUES AND ACTION

> If we have learned one thing from our past,
> it is that to live through dramatic events
> is not enough; one has to share them
> and transform them into acts of conscience.
>
> ELIE WIESEL, AUTHOR

Social change by its very nature brings with it a call to action. Change can't happen without awareness, movement, and momentum. The need for social change is frequently rooted in intolerance. This intolerance can be focused on issues of race or ethnicity, religion, sex, poverty, sexual orientation, physical ability, or immigration status among others. It can be rooted in simple ignorance or stereotypes and bloom into prejudice, discrimination, or even hate crimes. In all of its many facets, intolerance is something to recognize, discuss, and finally, address. Sometimes classroom discussion can work wonders at opening minds and eyes alike, but that can be just the beginning.

Social and political action are often the direct result of the need for change. The action can take many forms: raising community awareness through letters to the editor, making public service announcements that air on local cable, and participating in the actual democratic process by speaking at city council meetings or writing letters to Congress. Students have been involved in establishing a much-needed community youth center, working for inclusion in government advisory committees, and even working against unjust actions such as slavery in the Sudan. Social change can be local *and* global in its scope and ambition.

Social change can also be the key to achieving real depth in service learning by driving students to investigate public policy, question the world around them, extend their practice into new areas, and encourage their peers to become active in the civic process. However, there can be some challenges that

come with this particular kind of service learning. Results can take time to achieve, and curriculum requirements may push you to move on to the next lesson or activity, leaving opportunities behind.

You may also find yourself working with students who are unaware or disengaged. They may be apathetic or even angry because they feel powerless: "We're just kids. What can we do?" Some students are reluctant. They're told "You need to give back to the community," but they don't believe that they've received much from it yet and think that whatever they have to offer the community doesn't want. Civic engagement and democratic processes also may not seem real to students whose only opportunity to participate in "government" are school elections that are frequently more about popularity than ideas.

You may not face these issues, but they are real challenges for some young people and the educators who work with them. Integrating service learning into your curriculum, extending projects through multiple grades or classes so they are built upon year after year, and making project results visible to the community are all ways to mitigate these challenges.

Your students will find themselves questioning a variety of assumptions as they learn about social change issues. Do people have equal access to vote? Is life in a new country always better for immigrants than the one they left behind? How does economic status impact recreational, educational, and employment opportunities? These questions show that your students are beginning to look at familiar issues in new ways.

More good news is that as students learn about their world—the issues, the problems, the people and programs helping to create social change—they begin to find their own place as social activists. This is as true for reluctant students as it is for enthusiastic ones. Young people of all ages want their beliefs and actions to have value and relevance, and they will respond when offered a challenge, even when it comes with hard work and struggle. Often they are

186

surprised at what they can accomplish when they set their minds and hearts on it.

> Until the great mass of the people shall be filled with the sense of responsibility for each other's welfare, social justice can never be attained.
>
> HELEN KELLER, AUTHOR

Preparation: Getting Ready for Service Learning Involving Social Change

The following activities can be used in the preparation stage to promote learning and skill development related to social change issues. These activities can be used with different age ranges during preparation to help your students examine key issues through research, analyze community needs, and gain the knowledge they need to effectively contribute to the design of their service plan. Since literature is often an important part of preparation, you can find recommended titles on this theme in the Social Change: Issues and Action Bookshelf later in this chapter.

Activity: Vocabulary That Matters. Prejudice, stereotype, discrimination, tolerance—these are influences that shape our ideas and actions. What do they mean? Even young children can learn these words and concepts, and recognize the behaviors that promote positive ways of interacting with others or stop the negative ways. The following activities can get students thinking about their beliefs and local social issues, so they are better able to design projects that promote communication and tolerance both within the school and the larger community.

- *A Look at Prejudice.* Students can examine and discuss the roots of the word, *pre* and *judge*. How does prejudice happen? How do we learn attitudes about others? Students can discuss the quote, "You can't judge a book by its cover," and then identify the various "covers" or categories they use to judge people. Examples of these "covers" can include: size, race, language ability, athleticism, religion, wealth.

- *Recognizing Stereotypes.* Examine the term beginning with the roots of the word. A stereotype can be defined as an oversimplified generalization about a particular group, race, or sex, which usually carries derogatory implications. Using different forms of media, including television programs, print advertisements, and children's books, students can learn to recognize stereotypes. Create a simple checklist for students to identify tokenism, inaccurate information, favoritism, or ridicule.

- *Discrimination Happens.* Students can look at historical examples of discrimination, particularly with youth. Have students write a list of words or short phrases that describe a time they felt discriminated against as a young person. Then turn these into either collaborative class poetry, short paragraphs, creative nonfiction stories, or essays. Beginning with their own experiences can lead into next examining discrimination against others—ethnic groups, elders, people in poverty, and so on.

- *Teaching Tolerance.* Ask each student to think of a time he or she felt "different." Students often think of wearing glasses, speaking a different language from others, being unable to hit a baseball, or feeling left out of a social gathering. Younger children can share these stories and talk about ways to increase respect and understanding for the experiences of others. Older students can draw an image that represents their experience at the top of a page. Underneath, students can make two columns placing "respecting others" and "knowledge and understanding" at the top of each. In each column, students articulate their thoughts and feelings that emanate under that heading. From these activities, ask students to consider, "What is tolerance?" How can we respect, learn about, and appreciate others who are both similar and different from ourselves?

  Tolerance.org, a Web project of the Southern Poverty Law Center, has interactive pages for kids and teens about issues of tolerance, as well as many teacher resources to assist with and expand these activities. (See Web site resources listed on page 188.)

Activity: Social Commentary. Where do we find social commentary in today's media? And how do people get their ideas and opinions into the public arena? These are important questions for students to address and think about as they start preparing to work for social change. There are many different kinds of media that students can explore and learn to use. Consider these options:

- *Fact or Opinion*. Compare two newspaper articles on a similar topic—one that is a standard news story and one that is an editorial. Have students find as many similarities and differences as possible, and then create a chart of do's and don'ts for each category. They can continue their research by reading books that clarify the differences, or having a speaker visit the class. A high school newspaper editor can be an ideal visitor for an elementary or middle school class, or contact your local newspaper.

- *Dear Editor*. Select several letters to the editor for your students to review. Have the students form small groups and give one letter to each group. What is different about this form of writing in comparison to a news article or editorial? Ask each group to write their own sample letter to the editor that conveys an idea, an emotion, or both.

- *Political Cartoons*. Find several political cartoons on different subjects. Depending on the age of the students, have them identify how this medium uses humor or satire to tell a point of view. Are there consistent themes or symbols that appear? (For example, donkeys represent the Democratic Party and elephants represent the Republican Party.) Why are the cartoonists choosing those symbols? Show several to convey the variety of approaches used by these artists.

- *PSAs*. Public service announcements (PSAs) inform people about a variety of issues, including voter registration, eliminating discrimination, gun safety, and the hazards of cigarette smoking. Students can view examples of PSAs on the Internet at Web sites like *www.rockthevote.org*. (Rock the Vote is an organization that mobilizes young people to create positive social and political change and uses media campaigns to increase young voter turnout.) Students can research

how PSAs are used on radio, on television, on the Internet, and even in movie theaters to educate and inform. If media facilities are available through the school or community (often through cable access), students can apply what they've learned to create social marketing campaigns that can make a considerable impact. Children as young as second graders have used PSAs as a vehicle to educate the community about important issues, to raise awareness around social action projects, and to invite participation from the community at large.

Find Out More About Social Change

To learn more about these issues and to get ideas for service and action, visit these Web sites and organizations online:

www.freethechildren.org Free the Children, an organization founded by then teenager Craig Kielburger, works internationally on many issues related to children's rights, including education, health, and youth leadership.

www.iabolish.com The American Anti-Slavery Group includes the S.T.O.P. (Slavery that Oppresses People) Program that educates and empowers students from fourth grade through high school by involving them in abolitionist activities. The site features free curricula and activism guides for teachers.

www.tolerance.org Tolerance.org, a Web project of the Southern Poverty Law Center, promotes and supports anti-bias activism in every venue of American life and includes information and resources for teachers, parents, and children on fighting hate and promoting tolerance. Be sure to check out "Mix It Up at Lunch Day."

pbskids.org/zoom/action Zoom Into Action, a Web site of PBS's Zoom television program, has service learning project examples and resources for kids, teachers, and parents. Young people up to age 12 are invited to share their service learning stories.

www.kidsvotingusa.org Kids Voting USA supplies educational kits and encourages kids to vote with their parents at the polls by casting ballots (similar in content to the official ballot) at Kids Voting USA locations.

www.amnestyusa.org and *www.amnestyusa.org/aikids* At Amnesty International and Amnesty International Kids students can learn about and participate in human rights advocacy efforts.

www.dosomething.org Do Something is an organization that helps young people get involved in their communities by identifying the issues they care about and creating projects that turn ideas into action.

Making Connections Across the Curriculum

Some service learning activities naturally lend themselves to interdisciplinary work and making connections across the curriculum. These connections strengthen and broaden student learning, helping them meet academic standards. More than likely, you'll be looking for these connections and ways to encourage them well before the students ever start working on service learning activities. As with the entire service learning process, it helps to remain flexible, because some connections can be spontaneously generated by the questions raised throughout and by the needs of the project. To help you think about cross-curricular connections and where you can look for them, the Curricular Web for this chapter (page 190) gives examples of many different ways this theme can be used in different academic areas. (The service learning scenarios in the next section of the chapter also demonstrate various ways this theme can be used across the curriculum.)

Service Learning Scenarios: Ideas for Action

Ready to take action? What follows are projects that have been successfully carried out by elementary, middle, or high school students. Most of these scenarios and examples explicitly include some aspects of preparation, action, reflection, and demonstration. These scenarios can be a rich source of project, resource, and curriculum ideas for you to draw upon. While the grade levels are given as a reference, most project ideas can be adapted to suit younger or older students, and many are suitable for cross-age partnerships.

Young Advocates: Preschool. In one Pasadena, California, preschool, a student remarked, "That's not the color of *my* skin!" when he was handed a "flesh-colored" adhesive bandage for a cut. This comment led to an impromptu classroom survey. Each child took a turn to see if the bandage matched her or his skin color. Within this classroom's diverse population, 10 percent more or less matched, 40 percent of the children came close, but 50 percent definitely didn't match. After discussing how melanin contributed to the color of their skin and reading books that featured children of all skin colors, the kids decided to write the bandage company and report their results. They also suggested that the company find a new term to describe the product. The company responded with a thank-you letter and another box of "flesh-colored" bandages! Still, the seeds of activism had been planted.

> Pick battles big enough to matter, small enough to win.
>
> JONATHAN KOZOL, AUTHOR

Kids that Type: Grade 1. After hearing the book *Click, Clack, Moo: Cows That Type* read aloud by their teacher, first-grade students decided they wanted to be "Kids That Type." They decided to look for improvements needed in their surroundings and to write letters to start things changing for the better. First they walked around their school and found several areas on the playground that were in disrepair. They met with the principal to learn more about getting the playground fixed and found out that three requests had already been submitted to the district office. The children composed a letter and visited other first-grade classes, read their letter aloud, and asked for signatures from their peers. The mailed letter was signed by over 100 children. The repair was made within three weeks. For the "Kids That Type," this would be the first of many letters.

Youth Helping Youth: Grade 3. An elementary student saw a television newscast about children living in shelters because they had been victims of domestic violence. The student initiated a discussion of the issue in class, and fellow students wanted to learn more and find ways to help. A social service worker identified by a parent showed the class an age-appropriate video and answered questions. The class generated a range of options for helping and presented their ideas to other classrooms at various grade levels. The students collected needed materials for children living in shelters, including backpacks with school supplies, journals and pens, and current magazines. Letter writing to local businesses assisted in skill development and yielded a substantial quantity of donated goods. Students also discussed showing respect to peers living in a variety of settings, including shelters.

Social Change Across the Curriculum

English/Language Arts

- Read a biography or autobiography about a person who has worked for social change
- Compare newspaper editorials to learn about methods and styles used to persuade public opinion
- Discuss and write an essay on how young people experience stereotyping and prejudice

Social Studies/History

- Study how each branch of state and federal government directly impacts the life of your community
- Read about Cesar Chavez and the migrant farm worker movement; research current migrant worker issues in your area
- Learn how voting rights were won by suffragettes, during the Civil Rights movement, and in the aftermath of South Africa's apartheid era

Languages

- Create public service videos in different languages about the school, local government, or helpful organizations; distribute through local agencies and cable access
- Learn about opportunities to serve in other countries, including the Peace Corps
- Study the needs and challenges of refugees being resettled in the United States, including language and prejudice

Theater, Music, & Visual Arts

- Adapt a piece of literature about social change for a reader's theater performance
- Find out how folk music has been used as social and political messages, inspiring people to learn and to take action
- Examine murals as expressions of public opinion; include graffiti art in the research

Social Change

Math

- Create a public opinion poll regarding an issue in the community; survey, tabulate, and report student responses
- Write biographies of famous mathematicians and the impact of their work for society
- Examine the cost and benefits of fund-raising events that aid the community; develop ideas to cut costs and keep records

Physical Education

- Study Title IX of the Educational Amendments of 1972, which bans sex discrimination in schools and especially impacts school athletics
- Research playground safety information and then visit a local public playground; document any needed changes and make recommendations for improvement to the appropriate local government agencies
- Research how physical challenges such as walk-a-thons are designed to engage the community and also benefit social causes

Computer

- Ask local community agencies, such as shelters, meals-on-wheels, or immigrant centers how students can help with computer technology needs
- Create a database of agencies that need student assistance through service learning projects or as volunteers and a database of project ideas and student skills that community agencies can access
- Through the Internet, research careers in public service; create a Web page with links to service agencies and organizations in your community

Science

- Find out how economics impact decisions on environmental issues such as waste disposal, incinerator placement, and toxic site cleanups
- Research community needs of people in low-income housing for safety equipment such as smoke alarms or earthquake emergency kits
- Learn about the connection between science and public relations by researching how social marketing campaigns are used to educate communities about health issues

Identifying a Female State Hero: Grades 4 and 5. While preparing for a visit to their state capitol, fourth graders in Connecticut learned about the state flowers, state song, and state flag. When the time came to tour the capitol building, they found a huge statue of a male "state hero" in the rotunda. The students wondered, "Is there a female state hero?" This observation redirected their course of study. Step by step, the students demonstrated their capabilities as they defined what heroes are and what actions are heroic, researched appropriate female role models from their state, and debated their selection. After learning how a bill becomes a law, they found a state legislator willing to introduce a bill that named their designee, Prudence Crandall, as the Connecticut state heroine because of her stand against prejudice. In spite of the students' informed presentation to the legislature, their bill failed. The kids regrouped. As fifth graders, they created a play about their hero's life and toured the state to gather signatures from the populace in support of their new bill. The second time around, the bill passed; and again, kids made history.

Creating a Web of Opportunity: Grade 6. Middle school students in computer classes found their talents valued. Local nonprofit organizations were in dire straits. Some were being bombarded with more requests than they could handle for youth volunteer opportunities; others were not contacted at all. The need: building kid-friendly, information-rich Web pages for the organizations so young people could learn about specific issues and base their involvement on social concern. At first, students thought they could create dozens of Web pages in a flash, but instead they discovered they had to slow down to learn enough about the issues to create meaningful connections. In the process, the students shared knowledge about the agencies in their English and social studies classes, which led to other service learning activities. Several students began to volunteer their computer skills after school to help with agency needs. The students also made presentations to high school humanities classes, where service learning was part of the curriculum. Feedback from the agencies was extremely positive, and many other agencies wanted to "sign on."

Turning Dreams into Reality: Grades 5–8. Middle school students in Baltimore, Maryland, realized that kids need a place to go after school to keep them off the streets. They decided to accomplish an ambitious plan: raise enough funds to open a youth center. With teacher support and a written agreement to see the project to completion, they went into action. Through a comprehensive letter-writing and phone-calling campaign, students have raised over $250,000 from government, nonprofit, and corporate grants. This money will help buy and renovate a house into a youth center for their neighborhood. Experience and determination have enriched these students with confidence achieved from learning to write grants, make spread sheets, develop budgets, establish community partnerships, and present their ideas to their city council, and most importantly, to work as a team. In the words of one "Youth Dreamer," this is "life-changing for the better."

Unity and Diversity Week: Grades 6–8. "We had been studying about the Civil Rights movement in social studies, and we decided to create a day of school unity. But once we began listing our ideas, the day grew into a week's worth of activities, and we needed more help. Every social studies class in the entire school took part!" The eighth-grade students in this social studies class did not imagine their idea would have such an impact on students, teachers, parents, and the community, but everyone helped turn "possibilities" into "plans." The students wanted to create events that would stimulate ongoing conversation and a veritable buzz of excitement. What occurred? English classes assigned students to read either *If You Come Softly* or *The Circuit* for discussions and writings on social inequalities and racism in society. In social studies, sixth-grade classes used *Through My Eyes*, while seventh- and eighth-grade classes read and discussed selections from *Linda Brown, You Are Not Alone: The Brown v. Board of Education Decision*. Students delivered famous speeches, and choirs sang about peace and harmony at lunch rallies. Every social studies class had guest speakers from community agencies who led workshops on local issues of tolerance related to immigrants, people with special needs, and racial issues. During "Unity Tonight," students and teachers performed music and slam poetry for the invited community. On the last day of the week, the students who had initiated the Unity Week project led reflection sessions in every social studies class. In addition to finding out what was learned, they asked, "What ongoing activities can we establish at school to continue building unity and community?"

Student Planners: Grades 6–10. Students in a university course on facility planning and management worked with the local school district to identify a school in need of remodeling, additions, or new facilities. They surveyed the buildings and grounds; interviewed students, faculty, and administrators; and researched the history of the school and buildings. Then they worked to redesign existing areas they considered to be misused, as well as to design additional space for present or future needs. Middle and high school students became actively engaged in the process, attending university classes, offering feedback and ideas, and preparing drawings and presenting them to the college students, school administrators, and parents. The process allowed students, who are often neglected in the creation of schools and other public places, to become involved, learn community organizing methods, and make decisions.

A Mural to Honor Social Change: Grade 7. A California middle school humanities class wanted to make a mural on an outside school wall. They had been reading biographies and at first wanted to represent their favorite people in the books they had read. A student suggested finding *real* people in the community to honor and the other students decided this was perfect. To find their subjects, they created a public service announcement for the local radio station and wrote a story for the neighborhood newspaper asking for nominations. They selected eight people who represented the community's diversity and had made a variety of different community contributions. Students conducted interviews, made sketches of their honorees, and, with the help of a local artist, completed a ten-foot mural. The students also wrote a booklet of stories about how they selected their mural subjects and what their accomplishments were. The cover of the booklet is the mural.

Voter Education Project: Grades 7–8. To make an impact on voters in the 2000 elections, students in Chicago planned two approaches. First, they developed a voter education guide highlighting the presidential candidates. Then the students researched the candidates and the issues to develop the informational guide, which was distributed to students, parents, and community residents. The second approach was helping register new voters at their school by advertising to parents and unregistered voters in their community. The students teamed up with community organizations to make the registration drive a success. Teachers reported that students followed the election closely and had a true investment in the process. For follow-up, students worked with the high school to make sure each eighteen-year-old received a birthday card with a voter registration form inside. Next step? Students hope to examine school government election procedures and transform "popularity" elections into elections involving substance and issues.

Taking a Preventive Approach: Grades 7–10. A nonprofit organization in Delaware helps teens take a preventive approach to teen pregnancy and drug use. Students complete a series of classes to become mentors for others; to have this responsibility, students must demonstrate the ability to model and communicate ideas and behaviors. Then they form two committees: an action committee that develops programs for local schools and a newsletter committee that creates a quarterly publication to be handed out at schools and low-income housing developments. To make sure the skills being learned are connected to the classroom curriculum, partnerships are maintained between the agency and the schools. Schools are invited to be part of the process by helping to recruit mentors, identifying students who are at-risk academically, advertising school credit for service, integrating the appropriate learning skills into the curriculum, and encouraging students to participate in the Student Action Committee and submit work for newsletter publications.

Emergency Preparation: Grade 8. When earthquakes, tornadoes, or hurricanes occur in their community, students usually learn first-hand the meaning of "being prepared." They may also learn that people of lower socioeconomic groups lack the resources for preparation. In partnership with a social service agency, students in California took part in a county-wide survey to find out what natural emergency resources were available for low-income families and elders and what was missing. Their campaign included collecting donated merchandise, preparing emergency kits, and notifying the public of the kits' availability. In language classes, students assisted with translation of promotional flyers and instructions for use of the kits. Presentations were made in adult education programs. Displays were set up at high school sports events. The community response was most favorable.

A Site to Behold: Grades 9–11. Was there really a sacred Native American site on the school campus? The rumor had been floating around for years, but finally an American history class in Los Angeles decided to study the history of the school site and find out whether the story was myth or reality. Students discovered that in fact a stream on the school's site had been important to the indigenous people in the area. In collaboration with local Native American groups, the students set out to restore the area. Overcoming hurdles with the school board and the city took time and skill. The project was eventually handed to the next year's class, so more students became invested in the process. The day the area was permanently restored and opened to the public was a festive community celebration bringing together people of diverse cultures and ages.

Acting Out: Grades 9–12. Community education is a major focus for drama students at a magnet high school for the arts. Students devote several hours per week to developing plays to perform for children. The plays have a variety of themes related to important community topics identified through surveys and community feedback: diversity and tolerance, fire safety, and school violence. Students are sharing their methods through a documentary describing the "how-tos" of using theater as a vehicle for service learning.

Advocates for Elders: Grades 11–12. High school students completely absorbed in reading the state

regulations for convalescent homes? While this may not sound "normal," it did occur. After making several visits to a residential care and convalescent facility to conduct interviews, students in Minnesota became upset by what they perceived as poor care. Upon reviewing state regulations and debating interpretations, students composed a letter outlining their concerns and suggesting ways in which they could provide assistance to the facility. They added that they were prepared to send a copy of the letter to the state licensing agency. The response was favorable. The residential care director took the recommendations seriously, outlined a course of action, and even thanked the students, inviting them to return. Two students were hired for summer jobs.

A School Out of Balance: Grade 12. High school seniors wanted to draw attention to what they believed to be educational inequities in their Santa Monica, California, school. After investigating issues of racial discrimination on their campus, they made a proposal to the school administration to plan and lead a one-day summit to address these issues and begin a plan to make significant changes. The event brought together students, parents, faculty, administration, the district superintendent, and community members. The program began with testimonials from African-American and Latino students regarding bias on the part of counselors and teachers. Next, a local education policy expert presented a study of inequities within the school district based on race and socioeconomic background. Finally, in small groups, participants discussed the findings and proposed recommendations and follow-up plans, to be compiled, summarized, and published by the student leadership group. Additional meetings were scheduled to factor this information into the plans for restructuring the high school into smaller learning communities.

> As young people, we have learned that knowledge is power. Child labor is a very complex issue but that is no excuse to ignore the problem. Who better than children to feel and understand the needs of other children?
>
> CRAIG KIELBURGER, AUTHOR

The Social Change: Issues and Action Bookshelf

The Social Change: Issues and Action Bookshelf is an annotated bibliography of works covering a broad spectrum of topics. To help you find books relevant to your particular projects, the book chart classifies the titles into several topic areas: historical perspectives, planning for action, prejudice and discrimination, and working for change.

In general, the bookshelf features:

- An annotated bibliography arranged and alphabetized by title according to the general categories of nonfiction (N), picture books (P), and fiction (F). For nonfiction and fiction, length and recommended grade levels are included. The entries in the picture book category do not include suggested grade levels, since they can be successfully used with all ages.

- A chart organized by topic and category to help you find books relevant to particular projects.

- Recommendations from service learning colleagues and experts that include a book summary and ideas for service learning connections. (The number of recommended books varies in each bookshelf.)

Social Change: Issues and Action Bookshelf Topics

Topics	Books	Category
Historical Perspectives The past is a rich source of information and examples of action undertaken by individuals and groups working for the benefit of many. Their stories influence our own.	Before We Were Free	F
	Out of Bounds: Seven Stories of Conflict and Hope	F
	Passage to Freedom: The Sugihara Story *	P
	Pink and Say	P
	Sisters in Strength: American Women Who Made a Difference *	N
	Slap Your Sides	F
	Spitting Image	F
	This Land Is My Land	P
	Through My Eyes	N
	We Are the Many: A Picture Book of American Indians *	N
	We Were There, Too! Young People in U.S. History *	N
	You Forgot Your Skirt, Amelia Bloomer!	P
Planning for Action Are you ready for action? These books can help with the key stage of preparation. Information, planning tools, ideas, and *The Little Engine That Could* are waiting.	The Kid's Guide to Service Projects: Over 500 Service Ideas for Young People Who Want to Make a Difference *	N
	The Kid's Guide to Social Action: How to Solve the Social Problems You Choose—and Turn Creative Thinking into Positive Action *	N
	The Little Engine That Could	P
	Stand Up for Your Rights *	N
	Teen Power Politics: Make Yourself Heard *	N

continued ⟶

Topics	Books	Category
Prejudice and Discrimination These books delve into such topics as prejudice, stereotypes, discrimination, and racial intolerance. (Many books in other theme bookshelves, especially the Immigrants Bookshelf, address these topics.) The stories also tell us about strength of spirit, character, and resolve to overcome injustice.	*Animal Farm*	F
	Bat 6	F
	Eagle Song	F
	The House on Mango Street	F
	If You Come Softly	F
	Issues in Racism	N
	Jemma's Journey	P
	Linda Brown, You Are Not Alone: The Brown v. Board of Education Decision	N
	My Name is María Isabel	F
	Smoky Nights (see page 99)	P
	To Kill a Mockingbird	F
	Walk Two Moons	F
	White Lilacs	F
	Also see titles on the Immigrants Bookshelf	
Working for Change In *Something Beautiful*, a girl removes one word of graffiti from her front door. A beginning. The path of social change is a long, well-traveled road, and these examples guide us and remind us of what we can accomplish.	*Big Mouth and Ugly Girl* (see page 99)	F
	Click, Clack, Moo: Cows That Type	P
	Dream Freedom *	F
	Edwina Victorious *	F
	Free the Children: A Young Man's Personal Crusade Against Child Labor *	N
	Generation Fix: Young Ideas for a Better World *	N
	Hoot * (see page 86)	F
	Hope Was Here *	F
	In the Time of the Butterflies *	F
	It's Our World, Too! Young People Who Are Making a Difference: How They Do It—How You Can Too *	N
	Kids with Courage: True Stories About Young People Making a Difference *	N
	A Life Like Mine: How Children Live Around the World *	N
	Listen to Us: The World's Working Children *	N
	Pay It Forward *	F
	Rabble Rousers: 20 Women Who Made a Difference	N
	¡Sí, Se Puede! Yes, We Can! Janitor Strike in L.A. *	P
	Something Beautiful *	P
	Summer Wheels * (see page 99)	P
	Vote! *	N
	We Need to Go to School: Voices of the Rugmark Children *	N

Page references are given for books that do not appear in the Social Change: Issues and Action Bookshelf but that can be found in the bookshelf lists of other chapters.

* These books include examples of young people in service-providing roles.

> I recognize no rights but human rights—I know
> nothing of men's rights and women's rights.
>
> ANGELINA E. GRIMKÉ, SUFFRAGETTE

Nonfiction: Social Change

Free the Children: A Young Man's Personal Crusade Against Child Labor by Craig Kielburger (HarperCollins, 1998). In 1995, at the age of twelve, Craig read a newspaper article about a Pakistani four-year-old who was sold into slavery. Outraged by this child's account of degradation and forced labor, Craig and his friends sought information and later founded Free the Children, a human rights organization. This book chronicles Craig's trips to South Asia to save children forced into labor. 316pp., grades 7–12

Generation Fix: Young Ideas for a Better World by Elizabeth Rusch (Beyond Words Publishing, 2002). As Sol Kelley-Jones, age fourteen, says, "Youth are totally on the front lines of every single movement in history." The stories of twenty young activists who have committed themselves to social action give credibility to this statement. The author provides an informative introduction to each of the book's seven themes, including peace, hunger, and health concerns. A comprehensive list of organizations is included. 176pp., grades 4–12

Issues in Racism by Mary E. Williams (Lucent Books, 2000). Beginning with the torture and murder of James Byrd Jr. in June 1998, this book examines the dynamics of racism. How serious a problem is racism? How does society respond to racial diversity? Is there hope for race relations? This survey presents information and that can stimulate debate and inspire social action. 112pp., young adult

It's Our World, Too! Young People Who Are Making a Difference: How They Do It—How You Can Too by Phillip Hoose (Farrar, Straus and Giroux, 1993). A collection of stories about young people who have made significant contributions, some with the help of a school or organization. Includes "A Handbook for Young Activists." 166pp., all ages

The Kid's Guide to Service Projects: Over 500 Service Ideas for Young People Who Want to Make a Difference by Barbara Lewis (Free Spirit Publishing, 1995). Ideas for both simple and large-scale service projects for young people. 192pp., grades 4–12

The Kid's Guide to Social Action: How to Solve the Social Problems You Choose—and Turn Creative Thinking into Positive Action by Barbara Lewis (Free Spirit Publishing, 1998). What began as a way to help sixth graders address a toxic waste problem became a resource guide for students and teachers to learn social action skills and solve problems on a local, state, and national level. Loaded with ideas and reproducible documents. 224pp., grades 4–12

Kids with Courage: True Stories About Young People Making a Difference by Barbara Lewis (Free Spirit Publishing, 1992). These stories tell how young people are helping our communities and our world by improving the environment, fighting crime, and taking risks. 192pp., grades 4 & up

A Life Like Mine: How Children Live Around the World (DK Publishing and UNICEF, 2002). In this book filled with vivid photographs, we meet eighteen children from around the globe and visit 180 countries. Are the basic needs of water, food, and somewhere to live being met for children? Do children have the right to be safe from war? Does every child deserve the right to play and to know his or her rights? By examining the themes of survival, development, protection, and participation, we see how children pursue a good life for themselves and their communities often amidst seemingly insurmountable challenges. 127pp., grades 4–7

Linda Brown, You Are Not Alone: The Brown v. Board of Education Decision edited by Joyce Carol Thomas (Hyperion, 2003). The Brown v. Board of Education decision affected the life of every child in the United States and provoked a range of reactions. This book includes personal reflections from ten accomplished authors of children and young adult literature. Their essays, stories, and poems capture the many viewpoints from 1954 and encourage us to consider the impact of social change resulting from this historic event. Contributors include Jerry Spinelli, Katherine Paterson, and Leona Nicholas Welch. 114pp., grades 5–8

Listen to Us: The World's Working Children by Jane Springer (Groundwood Books, 1997). "Who says childhood is golden?" The photographs, profiles, and statistics presented in this comprehensive survey of child labor practices expose horrors experienced by young people around the world. Includes "Kids Helping Kids," resources, and glossary. 96pp., grades 5–12

Rabble Rousers: 20 Women Who Made a Difference by Cheryl Harness (Dutton, 2003). Twenty women dared to defy the status quo and pursue their vision for "Life, Liberty, and the Pursuit of Happiness." To others of their time, they appeared "unladylike, dangerous, crazy, and radical" yet they understood that our republic is truly founded on the power that lies in three words: "We the people." 64pp., grades 3–6

Sisters in Strength: American Women Who Made a Difference by Yona Zeldis McDonough (Henry Holt, 2000). Learn about eleven women who shaped history as they triumphed over adversity, made huge sacrifices, and held fast to their beliefs. 48pp., grades 4–8

Stand Up for Your Rights by Peace Child International (World Books, 1998). This book about human rights, written by and for the young people of the world, presents a global vision of needs and activism. It includes a review of the Universal Declaration of Human Rights and poses the question, "What are we doing about it?" Packed with information, resources, and ideas. 96pp., grades 4–8

Teen Power Politics: Make Yourself Heard by Sara Jane Boyers (Millbrook Press, 2000). Wait until adulthood to become involved in politics and make a difference? Not with this book in hand! From the initial list of government decisions that affect youth, through a history of voting rights, to examples of and strategies for youth activism, the ideas and resources are inspiring and motivating. "It's your world. There is no longer any excuse not to be in it." 120pp., young adult

Through My Eyes by Ruby Bridges (Scholastic, 1999). An act of courage by her family led Ruby Bridges to be the first black child to attend an all-white school in New Orleans in the early days of social activism for school integration. Through the eyes of a six-year-old, return to this critical time in American history. 64pp., grades 4–12

Vote! by Eileen Christelow (Clarion, 2003). It's time for a mayoral election, but what does it mean to vote? Does voting matter? How does a person register to vote or campaign for a candidate? What happens if the results are too close to announce a winner? In this mixture of cartoon-style art and text, questions about voting are answered. Also included is a historical timeline of voting rights and a list of resources for additional information. 48pp., grades 1–4

We Are the Many: A Picture Book of American Indians by Doreen Rappaport (HarperCollins, 2002). For thousands of years before Europeans arrived, groups of people now called Indians lived in what is now the United States. "In 1492 more than five hundred languages were spoken." Sixteen men and women, selected from the many American Indians who have made exemplary contributions and achievements, are profiled here, including Tusquantum, Sacajawea, and Maria Tallchief. Each story re-creates a significant moment in the person's life. Includes a pronunciation guide and additional resources. 32pp., grades K–4

We Need to Go to School: Voices of the Rugmark Children by Tanya Roberts-Davis (Groundwood Books, 2001). At age sixteen, the author traveled to Nepal to live with children who had spent years in forced labor in carpet factories. Now in Rugmark rehabilitation centers attending school, these children tell their stories through oral accounts, poetry, and pictures. Opportunities to become active in working to end child labor are included, along with other resources, a glossary, and an overview of Nepal. 48pp., grades 5–12

We Were There, Too! Young People in U.S. History by Phillip Hoose (Farrar, Straus and Giroux, 2001). What role have young people played in American history? How have they made their mark, their contribution? In this comprehensive collection of stories and photographs, we see that young people, from the boys who sailed with Columbus to the young activists of today, have been a significant force in history. An indispensable reference and an inspiring book to read. 264pp., all ages

> In the 1830s, the mill women and girls began to stand up for themselves, organizing strikes for more pay and shorter hours. Eleven-year-old Harriet Hanson, also the daughter of a rooming-house keeper, was one of the fifteen hundred girls who walked out of the Lowell mill in 1836.... Harriet never regretted what she did. Many years later she said that leading that walk-out was one of the best moments of her life.
>
> FROM *WE WERE THERE, TOO! YOUNG PEOPLE IN U.S. HISTORY*

Picture Books: *Social Change*

Click, Clack, Moo: Cows That Type by Doreen Cronin (Simon & Schuster, 2000). When Farmer Brown's cows find a typewriter in the barn, they start making demands and go "on strike" when the farmer refuses to give them what they want. As the other animals join in, what will the farmer do?

> Dear Farmer Brown,
>
> The barn is very cold at night. We'd like some electric blankets.
>
> Sincerely,
>
> The Cows.
>
> FROM *CLICK, CLACK, MOO: COWS THAT TYPE*

Jemma's Journey by Trevor Romain (Boyds Mills Press, 2002). Grandma kept telling about the "old days" in Ocoee. Ocoee was a town where "peaceful black folk . . . jawed about the lives of people who lived there." Then, on November 2, 1920, two black men tried to vote on election day; riots followed, resulting in many deaths and one lynching. When Jemma hears how the lynching tree was cut down, this young girl sets out to honor her grandmother's memory and reminds us to "always remember to never forget."

Recommendation from the Field
by Don Hill, Youth Service California

The Little Engine That Could by Watty Piper (Grosset and Dunlap, 1930/1978). This is a delightful picture story about a train laden with toys and food for children who live on the other side of a mountain. When the train engine breaks down, the toys, dolls, and clowns become sad because they know how disappointed all the children will be in the morning.

Three times, the toys, dolls, and clowns plead with strong engines that come by to pull their train over the mountain, but the engines are too proud or selfish to waste their time. When hope has almost gone, a small blue engine stops and listens sympathetically to their pleas. Although the blue engine has never gone over the mountain and does not know if it has enough power, it agrees to try. Slowly the little blue engine makes its way up the mountain, saying to itself, "I think I can, I think I can, I think I can" until it reaches the crest and says, "I thought I could, I thought I could, I thought I could."

This simple story offers much for reflection. Why do powerful engines in this story and in life refuse to help others in need? What helped the little blue engine get to the top of the mountain? When you are trying to do things that are difficult, does it make a difference if you say to yourself "I think I can" rather than "I know I can't"? Can people get extra energy when they are doing something to help others?

To identify service possibilities, discuss the following with students: Is there an unmet need in our school or community where we could be like the little blue engine and try to help—even if we are not sure that we can do what is needed?

Passage to Freedom: The Sugihara Story by Ken Mochizuki (Lee & Low, 1997). In 1940, five-year-old Hiroki Sugihara, the son of the Japanese consul in Lithuania, saw hundreds of Jewish refugees from Poland ask in desperation if Consul Sugihara would write visas for them to escape the Nazi threat. When the Japanese government denied Sugihara's request to issue visas, the Sugihara family decided to do what they could to save thousands of lives, even if it placed their own lives at risk.

Pink and Say by Patricia Polacco (Philomel, 1994). The author's great-grandfather Sheldon "Say" Curtis meets Pinkus "Pink" Aylee during the Civil War. Pink, a black Union soldier, brings Say, a wounded white Union soldier, to his mother. Once Say is healed, the boys must return to their units, only to be confronted by Confederate troops. A tribute to telling stories about the people we meet who touch our lives.

¡Sí, Se Puede!/Yes, We Can! Janitor Strike in L.A. by Diana Cohn (Cinco Puentas Press, 2003). Carlitos, a young boy, is proud of his mother who works long hours for low pay as a janitor. In April of 2000, when 8,000 janitors in Los Angeles put down their mops and brooms and went on strike, his mother is among the leaders. Carlitos wants to help and he does: he joins with other children to make posters and join the marchers. The book includes an essay by author Luis J. Rodriguez, whose father was also a janitor. The inside of the dust jacket is an informative poster that explains the role of labor unions and strikes. In English and Spanish.

Something Beautiful by Sharon Dennis Wyeth (Doubleday, 1998). When a little girl searches in her neighborhood for "something beautiful," she finds that through her actions and sense of community, "something beautiful" can happen.

This Land Is My Land by George Littlechild (Children's Book Press, 1993). Through paintings and words, the author shares the history and experiences of native peoples of the Americas to promote cultural understanding.

You Forgot Your Skirt, Amelia Bloomer! by Shana Corey (Scholastic, 2000). Amelia Bloomer was never one to keep quiet about wrongdoing. No surprise she stood up for women's rights and popularized the wearing of a new style of women's wear—bloomers!

Fiction: *Social Change*

Animal Farm by George Orwell (Prentice Hall, 1946). The animals on Manor Farm rebel and chase off Farmer Jones and his men. Subsequently, the animals rule themselves, led by the pigs. Eventually, all the revolution's lofty goals are subverted. This classic allegory contains universal themes that can prompt meaningful discussions about power and privilege, propaganda and journalistic integrity, the class system, and real education/learning. 140pp., young adult

Bat 6 by Virginia Euwer Wolff (Scholastic, 1998). The sixth-grade girls of Barlow and Bear Creek Ridge eagerly await their chance to play in the annual softball game, Bat

6. Something is different this year, 1949. World War II is over. Aki and her family return after living in Japanese internment camps. Shazaam, whose father was killed at Pearl Harbor, lives here now. Twenty-one girls tell this story of two communities facing prejudice. 230pp., grades 5–9

Before We Were Free by Julia Alvarez (Knopf, 2003). Anita de la Torre never expected her life to be completely turned upside down by the politics in the Dominican Republic. But by her twelfth birthday, most of her relatives had immigrated to the United States, her uncle is in hiding, her father receives mysterious phone calls, and the secret police regularly search her house. Under the dictatorship of General Trujillo no one is safe. 167pp., young adult

Dream Freedom by Sonia Levitin (Harcourt, 2000). Marcus and his fifth-grade classmates learn of tens of thousands of men, women, and children captured and forced into slavery. Even with his own family problems, Marcus joins in raising money to redeem the slaves. Alternate chapters tell the story of the slaves, the people who enslave them, and the people working for their freedom. Based on a true story and contemporary events. Includes historical background, a bibliography, and ways to help. 178pp., young adult

> Peace is no harder to make than war.
> Both need effort and skill.
>
> FROM DREAM FREEDOM

Eagle Song by Joseph Bruchac (Dial, 1997). Danny Bigtree's family moves from the Mohawk reservation to New York City, and Danny cannot fit in. He refuses to sacrifice his cultural identity to make friends. His father provides a lesson in courage for Danny and helps Danny's classmates to feel pride in themselves and move toward peace. 80pp., grades 4–7

Edwina Victorious by Susan Bonners (Farrar, Straus and Giroux, 2000). Mayor Granger has been repairing a playground, transforming a vacant lot, and planning a long needed makeover of the zoo, all inspired by letters received from ninety-year-old community activist Edwina Osgood. However, the letters are actually written by young Edwina Osgood posing as her namesake great-aunt! What happens when the truth is revealed? 131pp., grades 3–6

Hope Was Here by Joan Bauer (Puffin, 2000). When sixteen-year-old Hope moves with her aunt from Brooklyn to Mulroney, Wisconsin, to work in a diner, she finds more cooking than expected. To the town's surprise, diner owner G.T. announces his candidacy to oust the corrupt mayor. Hope and other young people rally together, adding the vital ingredient of youth action to the campaign. Recommended for "City Reads" programs. 186pp., young adult

The House on Mango Street by Sandra Cisneros (Vintage Books, 1991). A series of short vignettes tells the story of Esperanza Cordero, her family, her neighborhood, and her aspirations. While they do not follow a linear plot, the novel's vignettes present a compelling narrative that raises important themes of gender, race, and poverty. For example, the chapter "Those Who Don't" describes the fear felt by strangers who stumble into Esperanza's neighborhood, as well as Esperanza's own anxiety about crossing neighborhood boundaries into areas where she is not surrounded by people of her own race. 110pp., young adult

If You Come Softly by Jacqueline Woodson (Putnam, 1998). Teenagers Jeremiah and Ellie, an interracial couple, confront prejudice from family, strangers, and society. In chapters that alternate between first and third person, we get to know these smart and sensitive characters and experience the shocking conclusion. 198pp., young adult

Recommendation from the Field
by David M. Donahue, Assistant Professor of Education, Mills College

In the Time of the Butterflies by Julia Alvarez (Plume Books, 1994). Inspired by a true story, Alvarez blends fact and fiction to tell the story of three Mirabal sisters, known as "the butterflies," who became involved in an underground resistance movement to overthrow Rafael Trujillo, dictator of the Dominican Republic. As a consequence of their work against tyranny, they were murdered in 1960 by government security forces. Dede, the fourth and surviving sister, had refused to join her sisters' efforts for fear of losing her husband and her life. The others, headstrong Minerva, religious Patria, and sensitive Maria Teresa, suffered hardship and torture to fight for justice and human rights.

The novel raises provocative questions about the sacrifice required for justice. Service learning projects, such as petitions and letter-writing campaigns to support victims of human rights abuses, can be found through Amnesty International. Check out information about the Urgent Action program and starting a student group. 325pp., grades 9–12

My Name Is María Isabel by Alma Flor Ada (Atheneum, 1993). Third grader María Isabel starts a new school two months after the year begins. All is going well until her teacher begins to call her by the name "Mary." María Isabel's pride in her name and heritage teaches the teacher and the class a lesson about fitting in and respect. Available in English and Spanish. 57pp., grades 3–6

Out of Bounds: Seven Stories of Conflict and Hope by Beverly Naidoo (HarperCollins, 2003). These seven stories, set in South Africa, span the years of apartheid, from 1948 to 2000. Each chronicles the lives of young people as they face restrictions and political upheaval, and the struggle for justice. A timeline provides a social and political context. 175pp., grades 6–10

Pay It Forward by Catherine Ryan Hyde (Simon & Schuster, 1999). Twelve-year-old Trevor takes his social studies assignment to heart: change the world. His inspiring "pay it forward" scheme has far-reaching impact even though his personal attempts seem to fail. Can this young person heal his broken family and create a contagious spirit of community and caring? 311pp., young adult

Slap Your Sides by M. E. Kerr (HarperCollins, 2001). Jubal Shoemaker, fourteen, knows that his family is no longer liked in his town. As friends shun him and sales are cut in half at his father's store, Jubal wonders if he too will follow his brother's choice to be a conscientious objector in World War II. Will the messages of hate painted on the store walls cause him to give up his Quaker beliefs or befriend the teenage perpetrator? 198pp., young adult

Spitting Image by Shutta Crum (Clarion, 2003). During the late 1960s, as part of President Johnson's War on Poverty, a Vista volunteer arrives in Beulah County, Kentucky. Twelve-year-old Jessie sees this as an opportunity to help her best friend get the new eyeglasses he desperately needs. But during this turbulent summer, Jessie's problems keep piling up, caused in part by her out-of-control temper, her desire to find out how her daddy is, and her money-earning plan that completely backfires. 218pp., grades 5–8

To Kill a Mockingbird by Harper Lee (Warner, 1961/1988). Narrated by a six-year-old girl named Scout, Lee's novel portrays small town Southern life in the 1930s, revealing all its prejudices, especially those based on race. Central to the novel's action is the decision by Scout's father, Atticus, to defend an African-American man, Tom Robinson, wrongfully accused of a crime. Knowing the case is hopeless, Atticus defends Robinson because his conscience allows him no alternative. 288pp., young adult

---

Recommendation from the Field
by Ellen Brahe, Elementary Student, and Kate McPherson, Project Service Leadership

Walk Two Moons by Sharon Creech (HarperTrophy, 1994). Thirteen-year-old Salamanca travels across the country telling her grandparents about her adventures with her best friend, Phoebe Winterbottom. She explains how she has learned not to judge people but has discovered the need to "walk" for two months in someone's moccasins to get to know who the person really is.

Children can use this novel to consider finding what people have in common or experiencing joy in people's differences, all to move toward friendship. After reading this book, upper elementary students could write and illustrate a story about learning to value someone who is different. Then students could share these stories and provide a lesson for second or third graders. The story could also stimulate discussion about stereotypes and assumptions. If read in preparation for service experiences with elders, younger children, or people who are homeless, the book may inspire students to be more open to discovering another person's gifts, concerns, and interests. 280pp., grades 4–5

White Lilacs by Carolyn Meyer (Harcourt, 1993). In 1921, Freedom was a bustling community of black residents surrounded by the white folks in Dillon, Texas. Young Rose Lee expects life to just go on as usual when she overhears a plan to forcibly relocate Freedom's residents to build a park. Can the white community, through city government and intimidation, make this happen? The presence of the Ku Klux Klan and the tarring and feathering of Rose Lee's brother ring all too true. Based on true events in Denton, Texas. 242pp., young adult

Interviews with Authors:
The Story Behind the Story

In the following interviews, we find out the "story behind the story" from Sara Jane Boyers (*Teen Power Politics: Make Yourself Heard*) and Sonia Levitin (*Dream Freedom*).

Happenstance played a part in finding the author of *Teen Power Politics: Make Yourself Heard*. A casual conversation with a parent at my daughter's high school became more intriguing when I learned that the woman I was talking with, Sara Jane Boyers, had written a book about teens taking social action. After reading *Dream Freedom,* I was compelled to speak with Sonia Levitin, an author who writes on many issues of social importance—and, in this book, explicitly shows service learning in action.

Sara Jane Boyers, author of
Teen Power Politics: Make Yourself Heard

Two key moments inspired me to write this book. First, poor voter turnout (less than 50 percent overall and abysmal for the 18-to-29-year-olds) in the 1994 United States congressional election indicated a lack of participation in the election process and other aspects of our democracy. Second, my preteen son's cogent questions about the election results made it clear that young people are more politically aware and attentive to the issues of our country than most adults realize.

I decided to focus my next book on teens, a large, powerful, questioning, and persuasive group, and write about approaches to social, political, and electoral activism that would address their concerns and help return democracy to the common citizen.

I asked young people their concerns directly. Responses varied from skateboard parks, to juvenile justice, to racial profiling. I learned what teens and youth advocates were doing to promote civic engagement, including stories of people who work toward social change even before they can vote. I looked at creative approaches to engagement used by effective organizations such as Rock the Vote.

How could I put all of this into a book that teens would want to pick up? I wanted to spark youth creativity while making a direct connection between their interests and those of their community and nation. *Teen Power Politics: Make Yourself Heard* is the result. It's a book about civic engagement, using real teen issues and solutions. We often stop short regarding citizen involvement and activism. Yet even if the process takes years, we can make positive social change by using what I call the "toolkit of democracy": service, advocacy, electoral knowledge, and political activism.

Service requires taking from your own time and doing for others. Advocacy involves finding a concern, educating yourself about it, and working toward social change. Electoral knowledge means understanding how we elect others to represent us, elect them wisely, and ensure they work for us. Through political activism we learn how to make change, even on a small, local level, giving people greater options and making societal improvements.

Teen Power Politics is a starting point for social activism and a tool to help teens discover their activist voice. In the process, teens can let adults both show them by example and follow them through inspiration to return all of us to active, involved roles in society. I have great faith in our youth in this process. "In chorus with others, you can reshape our world."

Sonia Levitin, author of Dream Freedom

My story begins in February of 1999. I had finished writing *The Cure*, a demanding work because it dealt with the persecution of Jews in the Middle Ages, when they were accused of poisoning the wells. This situation was parallel to what occurred during the Holocaust. I received a notice from the Simon Wiesenthal Center about a symposium on issues of present-day slavery. Normally, I don't have time to attend such events. This day, however, made a significant impact on my life and work. I was overwhelmed with what I heard. The abolitionists who spoke described the genocide that is going on right now in the Sudan. I saw pictures of Sudanese people being brutalized. I met former slaves. I listened to activists dedicated to stopping this horror. I even learned of school children in Colorado who raised funds to free some of the slaves.

I came home depressed. There seemed to be nothing I could do. In the morning I told my husband what I had learned, and of course he agreed that this situation is horrible. On my morning walk, still caught up in the tragedy and frustration, I suddenly realized, of course there is something I can do: I have to write about this subject.

First, I made a phone call to my contact at the Wiesenthal Center to let them know of my intentions. Next, I called my editor and gave her a thumbnail sketch of what I had learned about the Sudan and my idea for a book. I emphasized that this must be published right away, no delay! She agreed. Of course, I hadn't written one word yet.

I decided to write a novel, to use my strength in creating fictional characters out of all I have heard and what I would continue to learn. I wove in the story of the elementary class in Colorado. I included an American child, Marcus, a fifth grader, who is not wealthy and has problems of his own, and had him reach out across the world to a situation more profound and tragic. This was not to compare these sets of problems. We each live with our own concerns. When my family immigrated to this country from Europe, we were desperately poor. Still, my mother was shipping boxes to families in need in her home country. All of us, even those who are seen as underprivileged, have something to give.

For this novel, I wanted to create a feeling of truth and reality for the reader. I did not want to tell a linear story of one enslaved child. I wanted to show that slavery affects everybody, so there are many points of view. I intended to tie the stories together by repeating characters in a subtle way. One of my favorite chapters tells of a boy who goes to work with his father for the first time, his initiation to follow in his father's footsteps. He discovers that his father is a slaveholder and trades in human flesh. We know at the chapter's end that this boy will never inflict pain. He doesn't want to ride with his father. This boy begins a shift. I believe each person can make a change, starting with him or herself.

I did not travel to the Sudan; but I learned about this rich culture and met people who greatly influenced my work and life. I went to Washington, D.C., to meet Dr. Francis Mading Dang, an author and scholar with the Brookings Institute. At one time he was the Sudanese ambassador to Scandinavia. The son of a chief, he has studied all over the world and has written eight books on Sudan's politics and society, and I've read them all.

When traveling to Switzerland, I met John Eibner, Director of Advocacy for the Christian Solidarity International. He goes to the Sudan two or three times annually to bring currency to free slaves at great hazard to himself. The way I described him in the chapter called "Mercy" shows him as he truly is, a most humble person.

Of course I contacted the Colorado teacher, Barbara Vogel, and flew to Denver to meet her class. I also accompanied her fourth- and fifth-grade class to Washington, D.C. The students spoke to members of Congress to ask them to act. On another trip to D.C., the students spoke to the Foreign Relations Committee and read a passage of *Dream Freedom* into the Congressional Record. This is the first time ever that children in our country have lobbied on behalf of children in Africa.

A writer has the opportunity to be a bridge, to reach the reader on an emotional level. Our stories can show how people are the same, with the same needs, the same soul. Our words can fascinate by the differences revealed, including cultural differences. Through fiction, I want to sensitize the reader and show them much more than they would see with a cursory glance. I want to open the reader to understanding other people and caring about them. What they do with that caring is up to them.

In classrooms, the teacher can be the vehicle for the experience: to be sure the story is told, and to have children express their thoughts and feelings and put themselves in someone else's place. Then the action will come from them. When we plant the seed and keep encouraging, children can find what they care about, whether it is the Sudanese slavery issue, local hunger, or abandoned animals. While it is easy to address a problem in a superficial way, we can learn and make the idea of change part of who we are. We can only change ourselves, yet this creates the possibility for others to change as well. Our lives are so much richer when we are involved.

CHAPTER 14

SPECIAL NEEDS AND DISABILITIES

> We do have to use labels sometimes
> to give information, but in general, they are silly
> and sometimes just plain rude.
>
> Kids in this book have disabilities that you
> cannot easily see—they are hidden in their bodies
> within the brain and nervous system.
>
> ELLEN SENISI, FROM *JUST KIDS: VISITING A CLASS
> FOR CHILDREN WITH SPECIAL NEEDS*

The population of children with special needs and disabilities is growing, and chances are you have at least one young person with special needs—or perhaps several—in your classroom or group. Increasingly, that's a fact of life for most people who work with kids and teens. This chapter looks both at how to design service learning projects that address the actual needs of people with disabilities or special needs and at how *everyone* in your classroom or group can participate in and benefit from service learning. Young people with special needs or challenges can take part in service learning and make valuable contributions, regardless of whether you are teaching an inclusive class or one specifically for students with special needs. This is true for theme-based projects of all kinds, including the ones in this chapter. Projects around special needs and disabilities can take a number of different forms: students can lobby for better access for the disabled in the community, donate time and resources to agencies that work with populations with special needs, or work directly with peers with special needs.

A "special need" can be defined as anything that requires care or intervention outside of the norm; it can take the form of a disability, but it doesn't always. Some special needs are fairly visible—using a wheelchair or communicating with sign language. Others are much less obvious—attention deficit disorder or a condition such as lupus, cancer, or asthma. Often the latter are harder to identify for teachers and peers and can be more challenging for young people to understand. Information is available in many forms to teach both educators and students about special needs issues and to help them cultivate mutually respectful relationships with students and people in the community with special needs. As all students learn more about each other, differences become less significant and similarities become more important. Supportive adults can foster increased understanding by providing accurate information, raising awareness, and encouraging open day-to-day interactions.

> Be not afraid of growing slowly;
> be afraid only of standing still.
>
> CHINESE PROVERB

Preparation: Getting Ready for Service Learning Involving Special Needs and Disabilities

The following activities can be used in the preparation stage to promote learning and skill development related to special needs and disabilities. These activities can be used with different age ranges during preparation to help your students examine key issues through research, analyze community needs, and gain the knowledge they need to effectively contribute to the design of their service plan. Since literature is often an important part of preparation, you can find recommended titles on this theme in the Special Needs and Disabilities Bookshelf later in this chapter.

Activity: Understanding Dis-Ability. This activity explores the idea of differences, challenges, and disability. Start by writing the word *ability* on the board, and ask the students to share their abilities. This usually results in a broad array of different abilities, from playing football to drawing to "I can stand on my head." When students are asked, "What does the word *ability* mean?" the answer usually is "something that a person does well." Ask students to think about the talents of people they know well: "Are they all the same?"

Now add the prefix *dis* to the front of *ability*, and ask your students for a definition. Most often, they will say "something someone cannot do well." This comes from a common societal perception and from turning the word "ability" into a negative, with *ability* meaning "can do" and *disability* meaning "cannot do." Have your students take a closer look; is this really true?

For example, a blind person can't see, so the question you can pose is, "Can a blind person learn to read?" Students usually know that blind people can learn to read using braille. So blind people can learn to read, but they may have to learn in a different way and the task may be more challenging because of the disability. *Disability,* then, means something that a person can do but may do differently or may have more difficulty doing. Can a deaf person learn to speak? Can a person in a wheelchair play basketball? Yes—but with differences.

Activity: What About a Peanut? It may seem simple, but a peanut can be a useful and delicious tool to introduce and discuss the elements of special needs and disabilities. Provide each participant with peanuts still in the shell. Pose the question: "What makes these peanuts similar, and what makes them different?" Write the answers on a two-column chart with the word *peanut* at the top of the chart, *similar* over one column, and *different* over the other. Characteristics could include:

- Similar: basic shape, all have the same thing inside, most people like them.

- Different: appearances and shapes vary, uses vary.

Now cross out the word *peanut*, leaving the letter *p* and write the word *people*. Review the chart to examine how people are alike and different. Most of the characteristics listed will still apply, and new ones can be added. This chart can become quite detailed and cover a wall or two. Include emotions, attitudes, likes, and dislikes in addition to physical attributes.

Find Out More About Special Needs and Disabilities

To learn more about these issues and to get ideas for service and action, visit these Web sites and organizations online:

serviceandinclusion.org The National Service Inclusion Project is a training and technical assistance project to increase the participation of people with disabilities in service.

www.specialolympics.org Special Olympics provides year-round sports training and athletic competition to one million people with "mental retardation" in more than 150 countries.

www.bestbuddies.org Best Buddies International is an organization dedicated to enhancing the lives of people with intellectual disabilities by providing opportunities for one-to-one friendships and integrated employment, with programs specifically designed for middle and high schools; also includes an "e-buddies" program accessible at *www.ebuddies.org*.

www.projectlinus.org Project Linus is a volunteer non-profit organization providing a sense of security, warmth, and comfort to children who are seriously ill, traumatized, or otherwise in need through the gifts of new, homemade, washable blankets and afghans, created by volunteer blanketeers.

Making Connections Across the Curriculum

Some service learning activities naturally lend themselves to interdisciplinary work and making connections across the curriculum. These connections strengthen and broaden student learning, helping them meet academic standards. More than likely, you'll be looking for these connections and ways to encourage them well before the students ever start working on service learning activities. As with the entire service learning process, it helps to remain flexible, because some connections can be spontaneously generated by the questions raised throughout and by the needs of the project. To help you think about cross-curricular connections and where you can look for them, the Curricular Web for this chapter (page 206) gives examples of many different ways this theme can be used in different academic areas. (The service learning scenarios in the next section of the chapter also demonstrate various ways this theme can be used across the curriculum.)

Service Learning Scenarios:
Ideas for Action

Ready to take action? What follows are projects that have been successfully carried out by elementary, middle, or high school students. Most of these scenarios and examples explicitly include some aspects of preparation, action, reflection, and demonstration. These scenarios can be a rich source of project, resource, and curriculum ideas for you to draw upon. While the grade levels are given as a reference, most project ideas can be adapted to suit younger or older students, and many are suitable for cross-age partnerships.

A Child-Friendly Hospital: Kindergarten. A kindergarten teacher in North Adams, Massachusetts, listened to her students describe their fears of going to the hospital. They decided this was an important issue and contacted the regional hospital about how they could help children who were sick be more comfortable. The plan: to create a special place for children in one of the emergency treatment rooms. Using math skills and lots of masking tape, students measured off the amount of space they had to fill. They brainstormed a list of things that children would like to have and then began to actualize their ideas. What a wonderful day for hospital staff and the community as the children brought games, a chalkboard, safe toys, decorative murals, and self-portraits to the hospital. They even included an original book with photographs telling the story of how the room was created. A hospital administrator visited the class several months later. She brought a restraining device previously used

to strap children down in the emergency room to keep them calm. She reported that since the new child-friendly room had been in use, the restraining device had not been used at all. She also described an elder patient who was quite distraught about his health and was left alone for a while in the special emergency room. When the nurse returned, he was all smiles—busy enjoying the children's portraits and their photo album. What came next? Another year, this teacher's class created a child-friendly waiting room in the emergency registration area.

Being Good Neighbors: Grades K–8. Young students with autism in St. Louis, Missouri, created and then delivered valentines to residents at a senior residential facility next door to the school. In spring, peers from the general population of the school helped their peers with autism paint ceramic pots and plant in them. With parents and teachers, the students hand-delivered the pots to the seniors. The following weekend, parents and siblings of the students with special needs joined with some of the active seniors to plant an outdoor garden at the residence in a courtyard area in desperate need of sprucing up. The nursing staff and many residents came out to watch and compliment the children. A teacher commented, "When the parents stood back and watched their kids planting alongside the elders, some of them started to cry. This was the first time their child had done service for others. Every single parent asked when they could do this again. And the kids were delighted. Anyone who started out skeptical ended up as an advocate of service learning for all kids."

> The best and most beautiful things in the world cannot be seen or even touched. They must be felt with the heart.
> HELEN KELLER, AUTHOR

Increasing Access at School: Grades 2–10. Can students improve access for people with disabilities on their school campuses? Second graders were able to create parking for people with disabilities where there had been none at their school. Seventh-grade students worked with a shop teacher to build a portable

Special Needs and Disabilities Across the Curriculum

English/Language Arts

- Build vocabulary by learning the current and respectful terms used to describe specific disabilities

- Create child-friendly informational materials for a local organization, agency, or outreach program serving a community with special needs

- Invite someone who reads braille to talk about how they learned it; compare to the process of learning to read for sighted students. What are the similarities? Differences?

Social Studies/History

- Discuss: If money weren't a concern, how could the community be made truly accessible for everyone?

- Study about people with special needs who have been local, national, or international leaders

- Research the Americans with Disabilities Act (1990) and the impact of this and more current legislation

Languages

- Research the laws that impact people with disabilities in the countries that use the language you're learning

- Have a conversation using only picture symbols

- Compare the sign language systems of various countries

Theater, Music, & Visual Arts

- Create a theater performance about people of all abilities and needs in the community as active contributing participants

- Identify music that has repetition and easy rhythms to teach children with developmental disabilities

- Work on art projects with younger students in a special needs class and create an art display for the community

Special Needs and Disabilities

Math

- Create math activities that could be used in math centers for children who need practice identifying shapes, counting, or sorting

- Make a bulletin board of numbers or geometric shapes with each item offering a different tactile experience

- Find out and chart national statistics on disabilities

Physical Education

- Research athletes with disabilities who succeed in a range of sports, including skiing, biking, and skydiving

- Prepare dance lessons for students with special needs

- Play basketball in wheelchairs or "beep baseball" where players have assistance

Computer

- Learn how technology has been adapted to help people with special needs and disabilities be independent

- Compare Web sites that teach American Sign Language (ASL); select one and promote it within the school

- Using the Web, research health and social service careers related to working with people with disabilities

Science

- Assess an outdoor habitat or nature trail for accessibility

- Learn how the human neurological system is affected by different special needs conditions

- Select a special need and learn about recent scientific research that benefits people who have it

ramp for access to a previously inaccessible entrance. And tenth-grade students, concerned about the lack of physical accessibility in school buildings, worked with a local agency to survey the entire campus. A proposal for change was sent to the school board.

Kids and Canines: Grades 3–5. In Tampa, Florida, students who have been identified as being emotionally disturbed take part in an ongoing program by spending two sessions learning about service dogs, their handlers, and their prospective owners. The students also learn about pet care and responsibilities that come with owning a dog. Once a week, an elementary student, a service dog, and a handler visit a nearby nursing home. The interactions help the students develop social skills, empathy, and community awareness through interactions. Preparing for and carrying out basic conversations has given the students more confidence. And the elders enjoy meeting the children and being with the animals.

Swim Buddies: Grades 4–5. In an Anderson, Indiana, elementary school, every fourth- and fifth-grade student learned the skills and knowledge necessary to be an effective and responsible one-on-one swimming instructor for a special needs preschool child. The upper elementary students all received training in water safety and basic child care. Classroom integration continued as disability awareness and sensitivity training were woven into reading, health, computer skills, and civics. Youth voice and choice were evident as the swim buddies found additional ways to interact with the preschool students. They assisted during lunch and recess, and planned additional special events to enjoy their new reciprocal relationships.

Learning About Independent Living: Grades 7–8. Fifteen seventh and eighth graders in Herrin, Illinois, participated in an after-school program at a center for independent living, serving people who have special needs. Students learned about the problems and adaptations made so people with disabilities can live independently. They learned about braille and the computers adapted for this use, and studied American Sign Language. They saw firsthand how people move in wheelchairs or with canine assistance. Twice a month students provided assistance to people who are blind, deaf, and/or otherwise physically challenged. In reflection, students recognized how their ideas about people living with disabilities changed as they grew to be friends and advocates.

Family Helpers: Grades 9–11. After a series of workshops to become familiar with the role of in-home assistance for children with special needs, high school students visited homes identified by their partner agency. Students always worked in pairs. Most often, the activity involved playing with a child who is developmentally disabled whose learning benefits from additional stimulation and interaction. Students had regular meetings with the sponsoring agency for reflection, role playing, and further training.

Getting Physical: Grades 9–12. A squad of cheerleaders took their pep and enthusiasm into a class with teens who have Down syndrome. With teacher guidance and regularly scheduled visits, they taught a series of exercises that grew, over time, to be more complex. In addition to stretches and aerobics, they taught popular dance steps.

Job Coaching Mentally Challenged Peers: Grades 9–12. Leadership and Career Exploration students in a Panama City, Florida, high school provide mentoring for their mentally challenged peers as they prepare to enter the job market. Over the course of the high school years, these students volunteer together for ninety minutes a day in child-care programs, hospitals, humane societies, school and public libraries, rescue missions, teen court, and other community organizations. The mentoring students develop the work and monitor the program. The process begins in ninth grade, when special education students are placed in jobs on the high school campus to learn basic job skills and practices. With their mentors, they work the switchboard, file, make copies, and work in the library. For the next three years, at second period, 120 students on three buses leave campus for ninety minutes; on board is one job mentor for every three special education students. Tenth graders work primarily at child-care centers, and eleventh and twelfth graders are individually placed for student interests and skill levels. Once the special education students can do the jobs independently, the mainstream students take on additional tasks to help the agencies. Recruiting job mentors? Never a problem. This is a popular and well-received program.

> No act of kindness, no matter how small, is ever wasted.
>
> AESOP

Trolley Activists: Grades 9–12. The Trolley Project in Panama City, Florida, was a natural outgrowth of the job coaching program described in the preceding scenario. Through observation, class discussion, and reflection, students came to understand that some people want to work but can't because of a lack of confidence, an impairment, difficulty finding employment, or lack of knowledge about how to place themselves in the workforce. Transportation can also be a deciding factor. For example, many community members with special needs use the city's downtown trolley as a primary form of transportation for getting to work, the public library, the senior center, or the technical college. The trolley was also used by many older people who could no longer drive. When the students learned that the downtown trolley, supported by transportation disability funds, would be shut down and the money used elsewhere, they were outraged and began to speak out. In collaboration with other interested groups, they convinced city administrators to keep the trolley running. Students also spoke to groups of older people about how to use the trolley to take outings with their grandchildren. They volunteered to teach senior citizens and students with special needs how to use the trolley. A student-written coloring book that was distributed showed sights to see on the trolley and gave ideas for picnic locations. Almost every day, a school group goes out on the trolley.

School Clubs: Grades 9–12. In many New York high schools, students with and without disabilities meet weekly to share their commonalities and differences. In addition to sharing lunchtime and large group activities, they form pairs or trios and choose a school activity or service project to do together. All students receive orientation and have reflection sessions to ensure that relationships are mutually beneficial and to answer questions as they arise.

Assistance for Canine Companions: Grades 10–11. What are canine companions? They're dogs trained to assist people with disabilities and special needs, including those who are blind, use wheelchairs, or have epilepsy. When the match is ready to be made, the human and the companion dog attend two weeks of "team training," which can be costly. To help with some of the expense, high school students shopped for food, assisted in meal preparation, and served lunch for several days. They improved their skills in comparative shopping, became comfortable interacting with people who have disabilities, and learned more about the animal/human bond and the role of a service dog.

The Special Needs and Disabilities Bookshelf

The Special Needs and Disabilities Bookshelf provides information that will help students to more ably provide service or serve alongside special needs peers. To help you find books relevant to your particular projects, the book chart classifies the titles into several topic areas: learning about special needs, working with special needs populations, interaction and peer relationships, and animal therapies.

In general, the bookshelf features:

- An annotated bibliography arranged and alphabetized by title according to the general categories of nonfiction (N), picture books (P), and fiction (F). For nonfiction and fiction, length and recommended grade levels are included. The entries in the picture book category do not include suggested grade levels, since they can be successfully used with all ages.

- A chart organized by topic and category to help you find books relevant to particular projects.

- Recommendations from service learning colleagues and experts that include a book summary and ideas for service learning connections. (The number of recommended books varies in each bookshelf.)

Special Needs and Disabilities Bookshelf Topics

Topics	Books	Category
Learning About Special Needs As we learn more about special needs, we respond more appropriately and effectively. These books increase knowledge and heighten sensitivity about different kinds of special needs.	All Kinds of Friends, Even Green!	N
	Can You Hear a Rainbow? The Story of a Deaf Boy Named Chris	N
	The Cay (see page 117)	F
	Freak the Mighty	F
	Just Call Me Stupid (see page 182)	F
	My Name is Brian	F
	The Printer	P
	Seeing Things My Way	N
	Small Steps: The Year I Got Polio	N
	The Storm	P
	We Can Do It!	P
Working with Special Needs Populations Exchanges between people with differing abilities create experiences in which everyone learns.	The Acorn People	N
	Just Kids: Visiting a Class for Children with Special Needs	N
	The Year of Miss Agnes (see page 184)	F
Interaction and Peer Relationships Common interactions include: neighbors spending time together, relationships between siblings, friendships at school, and challenges being met and resolved. Reading about these dynamics can assist both in learning about specific disabilities and in recognizing the possibility of forming successful relationships.	Be Good to Eddie Lee	P
	Be Quiet, Marina!	P
	Bluish	F
	A Corner of the Universe	F
	Crazy Lady *	F
	Friends at School	P
	Ian's Walk: A Story About Autism	P
	My Brother Sammy	P
	My Sister Annie	F
	Of Mice and Men	F
	Rainbow Joe and Me	P
	Sosu's Call	P
	Stoner and Spaz	F
	The Treasure on Gold Street/El Tesoro en la calle Oro	P
	Trudi & Pia	P
Animal Therapies Animals give companionship and assistance to humans. These books show strategies to improve the lives of all community members.	Dr. White	P
	Rosie: A Visiting Dog's Story	N
	Rugby and Rosie	P

Page references are given for books that do not appear in the Special Needs and Disabilities Bookshelf but that can be found in the bookshelf lists of other chapters.
* These books include examples of young people in service-providing roles.

Nonfiction: *Special Needs and Disabilities*

The Acorn People by Ron Jones (Dell, 1976). In this true account of counselors at a summer camp for handicapped and dying youth, everyone is transformed—the counselors learn who the kids are on the inside, and the young people experience joy in their newfound freedom of expression and experience. 79pp., young adult

All Kinds of Friends, Even Green! by Ellen B. Senisi (Woodbine, 2002). "I am lucky because I have so many friends," says Moses, a seven-year-old born with spina bifida and sacral agenesis. In his full inclusion classroom, Moses ponders his assignment to write about friends. Should he write about Jimmy, who shares secrets, or Jocelyn, who also sits in a wheelchair? Moses picks a "green" friend who has "something inside her the same as me." 32pp., grades K–4

Can You Hear a Rainbow? The Story of a Deaf Boy Named Chris by Jamee Riggio Heelan (Peachtree, 2002). Chris, a deaf boy, explains how he uses American Sign Language, hearing aids, and his other senses to communicate. Through a mix of photographs and art, we see Chris playing soccer, attending school, enjoying friends, and performing in a play. 29pp., grades K–5

Just Kids: Visiting a Class for Children with Special Needs by Ellen B. Senisi (Dutton, 1998). Second-grader Cindy is assigned to spend time in a class for children with special needs. Over two weeks, she gains valuable information about autism, Down syndrome, ADHD, learning disabilities, and epilepsy and recognizes how each child learns. She also realizes that they are all "just kids." A resource for teachers and students. 40pp., all ages

Rosie: A Visiting Dog's Story by Stephanie Calmenson (Houghton Mifflin, 1994). Rosie is a dog who makes a difference. After the necessary training, Rosie visits hospitalized children and elders who live in nursing homes. Her manners and friendliness make her well loved. 48pp., grades K–4

Seeing Things My Way by Alden Carter (Albert Whitman, 1998). Second-grader Amanda, who is visually impaired, describes how she learns using different equipment. She also shows how she enjoys sports, sleepovers with friends, and dancing. 32pp., grades K–4

Small Steps: The Year I Got Polio by Peg Kehret (Albert Whitman, 1996). Peg led a normal life until the day in 1949 when she suddenly fell ill. The doctor gave the dreaded diagnosis: polio. At age twelve, Peg was isolated from her family and friends in a hospital with an unknown prognosis. In this memoir, the author chronicles the following eight months, where, aided by doctors and therapists, a supportive family, and courageous roommates, she regains the ability to walk. 179pp., grades 4–8

> I didn't want to have polio; I didn't want to leave my family and go to a hospital one hundred miles from home. . . .
>
> Later that morning, I walked into the isolation ward of the Sheltering Arms Hospital in Minneapolis and went to bed in a private room. No one was allowed in except the doctors and nurses, and they wore masks. My parents stood outside on the grass, waving bravely and blowing kisses through the window. Exhausted, feverish, and scared, I fell asleep.
>
> When I woke up, I was paralyzed.
>
> FROM *SMALL STEPS: THE YEAR I GOT POLIO*

Picture Books: *Special Needs and Disabilities*

Be Good to Eddie Lee by Virginia Fleming (Philomel, 1993). Christy has no interest in being friends with Eddie Lee, a neighbor who has Down syndrome. Eddie follows her to a pond and reminds her not to take tadpoles from their natural environment. In teaching Christy about friendship, Eddie Lee shows that "It's what's on the inside that counts."

Be Quiet, Marina! by Kirsten DeBear (Star Bright Books, 2001). Marina is four years old, likes to dress up and play on the see-saw, and screams a lot. Marina has cerebral palsy. Moira is also four; she likes to dance, see-saw, and play quietly. She has Down syndrome. At first, the girls cannot play together because of their differences. Now they are best friends. Follow this photo essay of two girls on the journey to friendship.

Dr. White by Jane Goodall (North-South Books, 1999). The pediatric ward of a hospital has a remarkable doctor—Dr. White, a fluffy white dog whose warmth and love work magic on critically ill children. This story is based on actual events at a London hospital. The author's note refers to research supporting the idea that the "love and companionship of animals can contribute to sick people's recovery and rehabilitation."

Friends at School by Rochelle Burnett (Bright Books, 1995). Enter a school where children of all abilities play together. Through photographs, we watch the children in a variety of activities—making snacks, reading books, feeding pets, and interacting with older students who are classroom helpers.

Ian's Walk: A Story About Autism by Laurie Lears (Albert Whitman, 1998). Julie wants to take a walk with her older sister, but her autistic brother Ian insists on coming along. His behaviors irritate and embarrass Julie, until he wanders off on his own and the two girls cannot find him. Once the brother and sisters are reunited, Julie realizes how much she cares for her brother. The book includes a note that addresses siblings' often mixed emotions toward their autistic brothers and sisters.

My Brother Sammy by Becky Edwards (Millbrook Press, 1999). A boy describes some of his many feelings toward his autistic brother, Sammy.

The Printer by Myron Uhlberg (Peachtree, 2003). "As a boy, my father learned to speak with his hands. As a man, he learned to turn lead-type letters into words and sentences. My father loved being a printer." The narrator tells of his deaf father's work and heroism in the printing plant where a daily newspaper was produced. Ignored by hearing coworkers, his father faced a terrible situation when a fire erupted in the noisy pressroom. How would he tell of the danger when they could not hear him? The author's note tells the story of his deaf father and why he became a printer.

Rainbow Joe and Me by Maria Diaz Strom (Lee & Low, 1999). Eloise loves everything about colors. She describes her paintings to her blind neighbor Joe, who has his own way of expressing colors—through music!

Rugby and Rosie by Nan Parson Rossiter (Dutton, 1997). Rugby the dog and his boy are joined by Rosie, a puppy being bred as a guide dog. The threesome become inseparable for a year, until Rosie's departure. Includes information about breeding and training guide dogs.

Sosu's Call by Meshack Asare (Kane/Miller, 2002). Sosu must stay in his parents' house all the time; the villagers think it is "bad luck" to have a boy who cannot walk in the village. So Sosu tends to household chores the best he can and learns to read and write from his siblings who attend school. When a great storm threatens the village, it is Sosu and his dog who risk their own lives to save many.

The Storm by Marc Harshman (Cobblehill, 1995). Ever since the car hit his bicycle, leaving Jonathan in a wheelchair, he has hated feeling different. When a storm threatens his life and his horses, Jonathan proves his abilities and hopes others will now see him more clearly.

The Treasure on Gold Street/El Tesoro en la calle Oro by Lee Merrill Byrd (Cinco Puentas Press, 2003). This is a story about a real person named Isabel, who has mental retardation, and many of the people who live in her neighborhood. Hannah, a young girl, is good friends with Isabel. Hannah likes the fact that Isabel is a grown-up who doesn't criticize and is never in a hurry. On Isabel's birthday, everyone on Gold Street recognizes the neighborhood's true treasure, Isabel. English and Spanish text.

Trudi & Pia by Ursula Hegi (Atheneum, 2003). Trudi, a girl with dwarfism, yearns to know someone "shaped like her, someone whose legs would be short, whose arms could not reach the coat hooks in her classroom." When she visits the circus, to her astonishment, Trudi meets Pia, a woman who is an animal tamer and has dwarfism. Trudi's visit reveals a secret: Feeling you belong begins with loving yourself.

We Can Do It! by Laura Dwight (Star Bright Books, 1997). This book profiles a multiracial group of boys and girls with different conditions: Down syndrome, spina bifida, cerebral palsy, and blindness. These children, all around age five, are shown in color photographs as they play with friends, interact with therapists, and describe how they can "do lots of things." An informative book to help all children learn about similarities and differences.

Fiction: *Special Needs and Disabilities*

Bluish by Virginia Hamilton (Scholastic, 1999). Natalie is different from other fifth graders in Dreenie's class. She arrives in a wheelchair wearing a wool cap, a dog on her lap, and pale skin with a bluish tint from chemotherapy. Dreenie's journal describes her fears and fascination as she develops a close friendship with a girl struggling with illness and moving toward health. And then there is Tuli, a biracial friend who so wants to be beautiful and be Latina. Most of all, this is a story of three girls who learn, laugh, and grow together. 127pp., grades 4–7

A Corner of the Universe by Ann M. Martin (Scholastic, 2002). It's the summer of 1960: Hattie relishes summer days and her upcoming twelfth birthday. But this summer turns her upside down as she meets her Uncle Adam, who no one has told her about. Hattie sees herself in this developmentally delayed young man, who opens her heart and causes her to defy her parents and grandparents. 191pp., young adult

"Miss Hagerty, what is wrong with Adam?"

Miss Hagerty puts down her teacup and looks at me for a long time. "You know, I'm not sure, Dearie. I don't think anyone has ever told me. He's just . . . funny." Miss Hagerty taps the side of her head. "I believe you would say he is mentally ill."

I sigh. Funny. Mentally ill. I decide not to ask Miss Hagerty if mental illness can run in a family.

FROM *A CORNER OF THE UNIVERSE*

Crazy Lady by Jane Leslie Conly (HarperCollins, 1993). Vernon is suffering because of his mother's death and feels lost in junior high. Then he befriends the "crazy lady," an alcoholic woman in his neighborhood, and comes to know her retarded son, Ronald. Vernon grows to understand the love between these two people. Along the way, he gains self-respect and a purpose: to raise money for Ronald to attend the Special Olympics. 180pp., grades 5–8

Freak the Mighty by Rodman Philbrick (Scholastic, 1993). An unlikely friendship between Kevin, a brilliant twelve-year-old whose birth defect prevents growth, and Max, a gigantic boy with learning disabilities, leads to adventure, risk, and ultimately, shared wisdom. 169pp., grades 4–8

My Name Is Brian by Jeanne Betancourt (Scholastic, 1993). The author draws from her experience with dyslexia to tell about Brian, a boy who forms a club with his friends called "the jokers." Brian's father criticizes his behavior, making him promise to try harder in school. He appears to be joking when he writes "Brain" instead of "Brian," but his teacher realizes he is dyslexic and provides tutoring so he can be a more successful student. 128pp., grades 4–7

My Sister Annie by Bill Dodds (Boyds Mills Press, 1997). Eleven-year-old Charles wants to join a group of tough guys at school. He wants to go to the school dance with Misty. And he wants his older sister Annie, who has Down syndrome, to disappear, at least some of the time. In this humorous and thoughtful story, Charles learns about compassion and meeting life's challenges. 94pp., grades 3–6

Recommendation from the Field
by Betty Berger, Program Director,
Giant Steps Integrative Approach to Autism,
and Omer Rosenblith, high school student

Of Mice and Men by John Steinbeck (Penguin,1937/1994). This is a story about two men who are completely different but best friends. They travel together planning to work hard, make money, and then buy some land so they can finally be independent. They need each other to make this happen. George, the smart one, tries to protect his friend, makes their plans, and knows how to get away when they get in trouble. Lenny, a very big man who can do hard work, tries to follow his friend's directions but has the mind of a child. He is very loyal to George and has a caring heart.

Unfortunately, George cannot save Lenny from tragic events.

Middle and high school students can use this book as a vehicle for understanding friendships between two people with many differences. The students will easily relate to the characters because they are timeless. Use this story to discuss these questions:

* How can differences in people become assets?

* Do you have friends who are different from you? What do you look for in friends?

* Imagine you have a friend with a disability. What would you gain? What would be enjoyable? What would be difficult?

* Could you defend a person that others were ridiculing or teasing?

* How much responsibility do we have to protect others who cannot protect themselves?

For service learning, students can partner with students with special needs on campus or in outside programs. First, the students learn about each other. Then they plan ongoing activities that they would both enjoy, such as swimming, weight lifting, attending sporting events, or acting in plays together. Students can then reflect back to the book and the main characters. What have they learned, gained, and shared? 137pp., young adult

Stoner and Spaz by Ron Koertge (Candlewick, 2002). At age sixteen, Ben, who has cerebral palsy, has no parents, no friends, and no life outside of school and the movies. An unexpected friendship with drugged-out Colleen places him in risky situations that have him making choices for the first time about relationships, engaging in an adolescent world, and letting people know what he has to offer as a thoughtful, humorous, and creative person. 169pp., young adult (mature themes)

Interviews with Authors:
The Story Behind the Story

In the following interview, we find out the "story behind the story" from Ellen Senisi (*Just Kids: Visiting a Class for Children with Special Needs* and *All Kinds of Friends, Even Green!*). When I interviewed Ellen, I got more from the conversation than I expected. Of course, I heard how she had photographed the students in *Just Kids: Visiting a Class for Children with Special Needs*, how she had studied disabilities, and how the book had evolved. But I also learned of another book just being published. *All Kinds of Friends, Even Green!* is a story of a special boy with special needs who has so many friends he can't decide which one to describe in a school assignment. I dream of this being the case for every child.

Ellen Senisi, author of Just Kids: Visiting a Class for Children with Special Needs *and* All Kinds of Friends, Even Green!

As a young person, I was drawn to writing. I received training as a teacher and then found photography. I went back to graduate school and studied educational media and technology. Through my books, I bring many aspects of my life together: my experiences as a teacher and a parent, articulating ideas as a writer, and capturing the visual image with my camera. I conceptually design my books using all these elements.

I grew up as the eldest in a family with seven children. My youngest sibling has Down syndrome. People who don't know someone with special needs, especially children, tend to tense up; they don't know how to act or what to do. Through my books, I want to communicate that people with special needs are people just like us. This is a message I particularly want to relate to kids.

I was asked to help special needs students to make books about themselves at Yates School in Schenectady, New York. As I photographed the kids, I really liked how sensitive and helpful they were to each other. The relationships between the kids, and their relationship with their teacher, were special and particularly affectionate. The emotional dynamics were alive in a way that is often missing in a traditional classroom.

I wanted to capture this classroom in a book and had to decide how to approach the story. Should it be fiction or nonfiction? Then the teacher related something that had happened a year earlier, when a girl made a derogatory remark to a special needs child. When I first visited, the girl who had provoked the incident was a volunteer helper in the class twice a week. My editor approved an approach using this scenario. After getting approvals from my publisher, parents of the students, and the school district, I returned to the classroom and began official work on *Just Kids*.

For about seven months, I spent nearly every morning, four to five days a week, in the classroom. I wanted to take time to get to know the kids so I could catch subtle behaviors and interactions. I spent the afternoons reading about autism, learning abilities, Down syndrome, and epilepsy and, in general, gaining an understanding of the basics of neurological impairments. And, of course, I wrote.

The research enriched the time spent with the kids and helped me to notice little things I would have otherwise missed. I learned it was natural for the autistic boy in the class to stare into the distance or not make eye contact, when before I had thought he was just tired, shy, or not paying attention. As a photographer, I learned to be more alert.

In *Just Kids*, special education students are shown in their own classroom, with plenty of interaction with children in traditional classrooms. Many schools now place children with special needs in regular classrooms all day. This is called inclusion, and I show that kind of classroom in *All Kinds of Friends, Even Green!* Zoller School in Schenectady is the setting for this book because the school does an excellent job with inclusion. The particular class photographed for this book, a first-grade class of twenty children, includes a teacher, a half-time special education teacher, and three full-time paraprofessionals. (However, I know of other schools where special needs students are plopped into regular classes and teachers are not given the necessary training or staff support they need to make the inclusion approach effective for all kids.)

The story photographed at Zoller School follows Moses, a child with spina bifida and sacral agenesis, who is thinking about the friends in his life as he works on a writing assignment about friendship. This book was written to help children ages four to seven to begin to understand special needs, so it shows children with easily identifiable disabilities.

I wrote *All Kinds of Friends, Even Green!* in part because once I met Moses, I knew he was exactly the right person for the story I had in mind. Sadly, Moses passed away before he saw this book in print. Still, his story is here for others to learn from.

I hope my books encourage kids to get involved with the kids with special needs who are somewhere in their school. It seems that more inclusion classes and contact between children with and without special needs can be found at the elementary level than at higher levels. In middle and high schools, kids need to be in contact with each other to prevent harmful dynamics, such as the incident I showed at the beginning of the *Just Kids* book. When kids who have special needs are only seen in the hallways of middle and high schools, and they appear "different" from other students, thoughtful interaction is highly unlikely. Yet when kids with and without special needs interact with each other on a regular basis in their environment, whether a special class or an inclusion class, they come to know and understand each other naturally.

Here is an example. In Moses's classroom, a girl with cerebral palsy couldn't hold her hand up for very long when she wanted to answer a question. I noticed how the children sitting next to her would often help her keep her hand up until she was called on. Because the children in that classroom were in daily contact, they knew what to do to help each other; and in the process, they built positive relationships. That's what all schools should be trying to bring about. Schools are a natural place to learn about people who are both similar to and different from us. If we can get kids connected during the school years, wouldn't there be a greater likelihood of this occurring afterwards? The world might then become more inclusive!

AN AUTHOR'S REFLECTION

One evening around bedtime, when my daughters were much younger, my eldest asked, "When am I going to have adventures like you?" I turned that question around in my mind for some time, realizing that, like all young people, she longed for the opportunity to extend herself into experiences unknown.

In *Identity: A Novel,* author Milos Kundera defines *adventure* as a way to embrace the world. What a beautiful image, and one I hold for our youth as they maneuver through our educational systems, weaving their own patterns of learning and understanding.

With service learning as an integral part of school life, young people have a greater likelihood of achieving a sense of self through experience. The mystery of "why am I learning this subject?" is replaced with engagement. Studies that once seemed fragmented become interconnected. Learning occurs not only in the classroom but also in the nature preserve, the senior center, the food bank. Young people interact with their community, whether by taking a short walk to read to preschoolers at a Head Start program or by extending their help across the globe as advocates for children who are forced laborers. Wait for adventure? No need. Just enter the world of service learning.

But action is not enough; reflection is essential to service learning. What does reflection look like? In the book *Something Beautiful,* a young girl seeks what is beautiful in a neighborhood filled with trash, where people sleep in doorways and the word "Die" is painted on her front door. She asks her neighbors, "What is beautiful?" and finds a variety of responses: new shoes, a baby, a ripe red apple, a rock carried in a pocket for decades. She sits on her front stoop in reflection, looking at the trash and the graffiti. In this pause, she considers her ideas and her potential for making "something beautiful." Then she stands up, gets the supplies she needs, and scrubs the word "Die" right off her front door.

In a society filled with "busy," finding time for reflection can seem "a chore." Reflection, though, actually gives us a way to sink knee-deep into an experience and find out what it reveals.

Author E. L. Konigsburg draws on an age-old adage to teach about reflection. In her book *From the Mixed-up Files of Mrs. Basil E. Frankweiler,* two children run away from home and spend several nights having an adventure hiding out in the Metropolitan Museum of Art. At the end of their escapade, they meet the eccentric Mrs. Frankweiler and have a conversation asking about the value of learning something new each day. To their surprise, Mrs. Frankweiler disagrees, stating that, ". . . you should also have days when you allow what is already in you to swell up inside of you until it touches everything. And you can feel it inside you. If you never take time out to let that happen, then you just accumulate facts, and they begin to rattle around inside you. You can make noise with them, but never really feel anything with them. It's hollow."*

In service learning lies the balance: the dynamic of combining learning and action with thoughtful integration. A sense of purpose is here to be found, along with self-discovery, knowledge, and the ability to interact and improve our planetary home.

Enjoy the journey—both the adventure and the reflection.

---

*From *From the Mixed-up Files of Mrs. Basil E. Frankweiler* (35th Anniversary Edition) by E. L. Konigsburg (Simon & Schuster, 2002), p.153.

RESOURCES

These organizations and agencies have made significant contributions to the expanding field of service learning through ongoing research and the development of outstanding materials and information.

Compass Institute
P.O. Box 270037
St. Paul, MN 55127
(651) 787-0409
A national leader in service learning, Compass Institute provides research-based professional development opportunities to K–12 educators, education departments, and nonprofit organizations. Topics include service learning, social marketing, brain-based learning, sustaining the service leader, and innovative approaches to implementing programs.

Constitutional Rights Foundation
601 South Kingsley Drive
Los Angeles, CA 90005
(213) 487-5590
www.crf-usa.org
Offering programs, curricula, and training opportunities designed to engage K–12 youth and teachers in civic participation through service learning activities, this organization also publishes a free quarterly national newsletter, *Service-Learning Network.*

Council for Service Learning Excellence
1667 Snelling Avenue North, Suite D300
St. Paul, MN 55108
1-877-572-3924
www.nslexchange.org
Under the auspices of the National Youth Leadership Council, this group offers technical assistance and professional development opportunities. It also operates the National Service-Learning Exchange, where staff answer questions about service learning or find you a peer mentor.

Florida Learn & Serve
325 John Knox Road
Building F, Suite 210
Tallahassee, FL 32303
1-888-396-6756
www.fsu.edu/~flserve
Florida Learn & Serve offers on-site visits, training, and technical assistance at the local, national, and international levels. Publications are available with program descriptions,

research on the impact of service learning, and information on linking service learning with state academic standards. The organization offers an exemplary environmental service learning model as well as expertise in youth philanthropy.

The Giraffe Project
P.O. Box 759
Langley, WA 98260
(360) 221-7989
www.giraffe.org
K–12 service learning and character education curriculum promotes compassion and active citizenship in youth. Kids learn about heroes in their communities and are inspired to make a difference through service learning projects.

KIDS Consortium
215 Lisbon Street, Suite 12
Lewiston, ME 04240
(207) 784-0956
www.kidsconsortium.org
The KIDS Consortium offers educators and community members ideas for involving students in their own neighborhoods. Trained adults help kids identify, research, and address real community challenges.

Learn and Serve America
1201 New York Avenue NW
Washington, DC 20525
(202) 606-5000
www.learnandserve.org
Learn and Serve America (a program of the Corporation for National and Community Service) provides grants and scholarships to schools, colleges, and nonprofit groups that participate in community service programs.

Maryland State Department of Education: Service Learning
200 West Baltimore Street
Baltimore, MD 21201
(410) 767-0358
www.mdservice-learning.org
The Maryland State Department of Education's Service Learning Program creates materials and develops programs designed to strengthen K–12 service learning. Find middle and high school curricula, service learning guides, evaluation rubrics, interdisciplinary service learning webs, and consultation opportunities at their Web site.

National Center for Learning and Citizenship
700 Broadway, Suite 1200
Denver, CO 80203
(303) 299-3606
www.ecs.org/nclc
This national center for service learning established by the Education Commission of the States works with state and district administrators and educators and promotes service learning opportunities in K–12 education. Publications on a range of service learning topics are available.

National Dropout Prevention Center
Clemson University
209 Martin Street
Clemson, SC 29631
(864) 656-2599
www.dropoutprevention.org
The center produces publications, videos, and other student resources, as well as organizes conferences and workshops for service learning leaders. Connecting practitioners with peer mentors, the organization also provides independent evaluations of service learning efforts.

National Service-Learning Clearinghouse
ETR Associates
4 Carbonero Way
Scotts Valley, CA 95066
1-866-245-7378
www.servicelearning.org
At their Web site, users can find materials for all grade levels, submit questions, and access documents about service learning. Funded by the Corporation for National and Community Service, the clearinghouse supports service learning in grades K–12, higher education, community-based initiatives, tribal programs, and programs for the general public.

National Service-Learning Partnership
Academy for Educational Development
1825 Connecticut Avenue NW, Suite 800
Washington, DC 20009
(202) 884-8356
www.service-learningpartnership.org
Their mission is to make service learning a core element of every K–12 student's education. Members receive news from the service learning community, ideas for strengthening service opportunities in local areas, and access to relevant publications. A free membership is available online.

National Youth Leadership Council (NYLC)
1667 Snelling Avenue North
St. Paul, MN 55108
(651) 631-3672
www.nylc.org
NYLC provides service learning training and produces publications, videos, and other resources for youth and adults involved in service projects. Contact them for information on the National Service-Learning Conference, the National Teacher Institute for Service Learning, and the National Youth Leadership Camp.

RMC Research Corporation
1512 Larimer Street, Suite 540
Denver, CO 80202
1-800-922-3636
www.rmcdenver.com
The RMC Research Corporation offers technical assistance, program evaluation, professional development opportunities, and help linking service learning to state and national academic requirements.

Vermont Community Works
P.O. Box 2251
South Burlington, VT 05407
(802) 655-5918
www.vermontcommunityworks.org
Vermont Community Works provides educators with support for service learning and community-based teaching, a wealth of resources (including curriculum options and teaching tools), technical assistance, and publications on service learning.

Youth Service America
1101 15th Street NW, Suite 200
Washington, DC 20005
(202) 296-2992
www.ysa.org
Youth Service America is an alliance of organizations committed to increasing opportunities for young Americans to serve locally, nationally, or globally. The organization sponsors National and Global Youth Service Day, which takes place each April, and hosts *SERVEnet.org*, a site with information and resources on service and volunteering.

Youth Service California
PO Box 70764
Oakland, CA 94612
(510) 302-0550
www.yscal.org
Youth Service California provides free email and phone consultation for educators implementing service learning programs. The professional staff is available for customized on-site training and consultation. Also available are curriculum development institutes and professional development workshops. Curriculum ideas, evaluation tools, and other resource materials are available for purchase.

INDEX

ABOUT THE AUTHOR

Cathryn Berger Kaye, M.A., enjoys books, nature, theater, writing, and the world of service learning. As a classroom teacher, she worked with grades K–12 in rural, suburban, and urban settings. Cathryn has worked in nonprofit organizations with national outreach developing service learning programs throughout the country. Now, as an international consultant, she is a well-respected and engaging keynote speaker and workshop leader. She assists state departments of education, university faculty and teacher education students, school districts, and classroom teachers and administrators on a variety of issues such as service learning, literacy, civic engagement, youth leadership, and improving school climate and culture.

As an author, Cathryn's publications include *A Kids' Guide to Helping Others Read & Succeed*, *A Kids' Guide to Hunger & Homelessness*, *The Service Learning Books: A Bibliography of Fiction & Nonfiction to Inspire Student Learning and Action*, *Service Learning: Raising Service Projects to the Next Level*, and *Parent Involvement in Service Learning*. She has developed a comprehensive curriculum *Strategies for Success with Literacy* integrating literacy development with character education and service learning. Cathryn's articles on improving education appear in magazines and on the Internet. She also writes fiction and nonfiction stories and books for children and adults. She is the author of *Word Works: Why the Alphabet Is a Kid's Best Friend*.

While Cathryn has lived in many places and enjoys traveling, she is glad to feel the ocean breezes at home in Los Angeles. Most of all, she adores her family—her two daughters, Ariel and Devora, and husband, Barry—who inspire her daily.

Other Great Products from Free Spirit

The Complete Guide to Service Learning CD-ROM
by Cathryn Berger Kaye, M.A.
An essential time-saving tool for integrating service learning into your curriculum and classroom. This CD-ROM includes all of the forms from the book, plus additional materials: a section on how to create a culture of service, 11 author interviews, and 45 "Bookshelf" entries. All grades.
$17.95; Macintosh and Windows compatible.

The Kid's Guide to Social Action
How to Solve the Social Problems You Choose—and Turn Creative Thinking into Positive Action
Revised, Expanded, Updated Edition
by Barbara A. Lewis
This exciting, empowering book includes everything kids need to make a difference in the world: step-by-step directions for writing letters, doing interviews, raising funds, getting media coverage, and more. For ages 10 & up.
$18.95; 224 pp.; softcover; B&W photos and illust.; 8½" x 11"

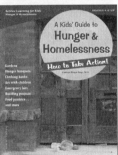

A Kids' Guide to Hunger & Homelessness
How to Take Action!
by Cathryn Berger Kaye, M.A.
Kids learn about the causes and effects of hunger and homelessness, read about what other people have done and are doing to help, explore what their community needs, and develop a service project. For grades 6 & up.
$6.95; 48 pp.; softcover; 8½" x 11"

A Kids' Guide to Helping Others Read & Succeed
How to Take Action!
by Cathryn Berger Kaye, M.A.
Kids learn about literacy—the ability to read, write, and comprehend. They explore ways to improve the literacy of others, read what others (including young people) have done and are doing to help, explore what their community needs, and develop a service project. For grades 6 & up.
$6.95; 48 pp.; softcover; 8½" x 11"

A Kids' Guide to Protecting & Caring for Animals
How to Take Action!
by Cathryn Berger Kaye, M.A., in collaboration with
The American Society for the Prevention of Cruelty to Animals
Kids learn about the welfare of domestic and wild animals around the world. They explore ways to address the needs of animals, such as cruelty prevention, emergency readiness, wildlife rehabilitation, habitat preservation, and shelter volunteering. For grades 6 & up.
$6.95; 48 pp.; softcover; 8½" x 11"

To place an order or to request a free catalog of SELF-HELP FOR KIDS® and SELF-HELP FOR TEENS® materials, please write, call, email, or visit our Web site:

Free Spirit Publishing Inc • 217 Fifth Avenue North • Suite 200 • Minneapolis, MN 55401-1299
toll-free 800.735.7323 • local 612.338.2068 • fax 612.337.5050
help4kids@freespirit.com • www.freespirit.com

Fast, Friendly, and Easy to Use
www.freespirit.com

Browse the catalog

Info & extras

Many ways to search

Quick check-out

Stop in and see!

Our Web site makes it easy to find the positive, reliable resources you need to empower teens and kids of all ages.

The Catalog.
Start browsing with just one click.

Beyond the Home Page.
Information and extras such as links and downloads.

The Search Box.
Find anything superfast.

Your Voice.
See testimonials from customers like you.

Request the Catalog.
Browse our catalog on paper, too!

The Nitty-Gritty.
Toll-free numbers, online ordering information, and more.

The 411.
News, reviews, awards, and special events.

Our Web site is a secure commerce site. All of the personal information you enter at our site—including your name, address, and credit card number—is secure. So you can order with confidence when you order online from Free Spirit!

For a fast and easy way to receive our practical tips, helpful information, and special offers, send your email address to upbeatnews@freespirit.com. View a sample letter and our privacy policy at www.freespirit.com.

1.800.735.7323 • fax 612.337.5050 • help4kids@freespirit.com